THE ESSENTIAL GUIDE TO ENTERTAINMENT LAW

INTELLECTUAL PROPERTY

Jay Shanker
Paul Supnik
Jonathan Reichman

with a foreword by Peter Dekom

EG2EL, LLC

Questions about this Publication

For assistance with shipments, billing or other customer service
matters, please call our Customer Services Department at:

1 - (323) 570-1380

To obtain a copy of EG2EL: Intellectual Property, please visit: www.EG2EL.com

See our web page about this book:

www.EG2EL.com

COPYRIGHT © 2021
by EG2EL, LLC

All rights reserved. No part of this publication may be reproduced in any form or by any electronic or mechanical means including information storage and retrieval systems without permission in writing from the publisher.

First Paperback Edition
Printed in the United States of America.
ISBN 978-1-7361695-1-3

EG2EL, LLC
2310 West Main Street
Suite 208
Richmond, VA 23220
www.EG2EL.com

— Summary Contents —

Contents vii
Foreword by Peter Dekom xxi
Preface by Jay Shanker xxv
About the Authors xxix
Disclaimer xxxiii

Chapter 1
U.S. Copyright Law

1.1. Copyright: Constitutional and Statutory Foundations 1
1.2. Subject Matter of Copyright 6
1.3. Neighboring Rights 18
1.4. Exclusive Rights in Copyrighted Works 22
1.5. Fair Use 40
1.6. Creation and Commencement of Copyright 52
1.7. Ownership, Joint Ownership, and Works Made for Hire 52
1.8. Formalities of Notice, Registration, and Deposit 57
1.9. Duration of Copyright 74
1.10. Transfers 78
1.11. Renewal and Termination Rights 85
1.12. Infringement 95
1.13. DMCA Provisions 105
1.14. Remedies 107
1.15. Manufacture and Importation 114
1.16. Copyright Royalty Distribution 118
1.17. Copyright Protection and Management Systems 119

Chapter 2
The Law of Ideas

2.1. General Principles 123
2.2. Subject Matter of Protectable Ideas 134
2.3. Exclusive Rights in Ideas 147
2.4. Fair Use 148
2.5. Creation and Commencement of Protection 148

2.6.	Ownership	149
2.7.	Formalities	149
2.8.	Duration	149
2.9.	Transfers	149
2.10.	Infringement	150
2.11.	Remedies	152

CHAPTER 3
U.S. Trademark and Unfair Competition Law

3.1.	General Principles	155
3.2.	Subject Matter of Trademark	157
3.3.	Exclusive Rights of Trademark	167
3.4.	Fair Use of Trademarks	170
3.5.	Creation and Commencement of Protection	174
3.6.	Ownership	175
3.7.	Formalities of Registration and Notice	176
3.8.	Duration	185
3.9.	Transfers	186
3.10.	Renewals and Termination	188
3.11.	Unfair Competition	189
3.12.	Infringement	193
3.13.	Remedies	195

CHAPTER 4
Publicity and Privacy

4.1.	In General	199
4.2.	Subject Matter	207
4.3.	Exclusive Rights	210
4.4.	Fair Use – Limitations to Publicity and Privacy Rights	214
4.5.	Creation and Commencement	220
4.6.	Ownership	223
4.7.	Formalities	224
4.8.	Duration	225
4.9.	Transfer	227

4.10. Infringement 230
4.11. Remedies 233

CHAPTER 5
International Copyright Treaties

5.1. The Berne Convention 235
5.2. The WIPO Copyright Treaty (Geneva 1996) 253
5.3. The Universal Copyright Convention (UCC) 261
5.4. The Buenos Aires Convention 272
5.5. The Convention for the Protection of Producers of
     Phonograms against Unauthorized Duplication of Their
     Phonograms (Geneva 1971) (the Phonogram Convention) 273
5.6. The WIPO Performances and Phonograms Treaty
     (Geneva 1996) 277

CHAPTER 6
Intellectual Property Law Principles of Entertainment Industry Practice

6.1. Copyright Matters 283
6.2. Clearing World Rights of an Underlying Source for
     Republication, Translation, and Adaptation 299
6.3. Thinking about Trademarks and Merchandising 317
6.4. Warranties and Representations 321
6.5. Indemnification Issues 328

Index 335

— CONTENTS —

Foreword by Peter Dekom xxi
Preface by Jay Shanker xxv
About the Authors xxix
Disclaimer xxxiii

CHAPTER 1
U.S. Copyright Law

1.1. Copyright: Constitutional and Statutory
     Foundations 1
     1.1.1. The Constitution 1
     1.1.2. Copyright Revision Act of 1976 2
     1.1.3. Berne Convention Implementation
            Act of 1988 3
     1.1.4. Digital Millennium Copyright Act/WIPO
            Treaties Implementation Act 5

1.2. Subject Matter of Copyright 6
     1.2.1. Section 102 Subject Matter of
            Copyright; In General 6
     1.2.2. "Originality" 7
     1.2.3. "Authorship" and "Expression" 9
     1.2.4. "Fixed in Any Tangible Medium of
            Expression" 13
            1.2.4.1. Limitation—Common
                      Law Copyright 13
            1.2.4.2. "Any Medium" 14
     1.2.5. "Works of Authorship" 15
     1.2.6. "National Origin" 15
     1.2.7. Statutory Preemption 16

1.3. Neighboring Rights 18
     1.3.1. Semiconductor Chip Products 18
     1.3.2. The Performer's Copyright? 19
     1.3.3. Protection of Original Designs 21

1.4. Exclusive Rights in Copyrighted Works 22
     1.4.1. Copyright Rights 22

		1.4.1.1. Reproduction 23
		1.4.1.2. Adaptation 25
		1.4.1.3. Publication 26
		1.4.1.4. Performance 27
		1.4.1.5. Display 29
		1.4.1.6. Digital Audio Transmission 29
		1.4.1.7. Internet Carrier Limitation 31
		1.4.1.8. Collective Works 31
	1.4.2.	Moral Rights or the Droit Moral 33
		1.4.2.1. The Right of Publication 36
		1.4.2.2. The Right of Paternity 36
		1.4.2.3. The Right of Integrity 37
	1.4.3.	Droit de Suite 38
	1.4.4.	Performer's Rights 39
1.5.	Fair Use 40
	1.5.1.	"The Purpose and Character of the Use" 41
	1.5.2.	"The Nature of the Copyrighted Work" 43
	1.5.3.	"The Amount and Substantiality of the Portion Used" 45
	1.5.4.	"The Effect of the Use upon the Potential Market for or Value of the Copyrighted Work" 47
1.6.	Creation and Commencement of Copyright 52
1.7.	Ownership, Joint Ownership, and Works Made for Hire 52
	1.7.1.	Initial Ownership 52
	1.7.2.	Joint Ownership 53
	1.7.3.	Works Made for Hire 55
1.8	Formalities of Notice, Registration, and Deposit 57
	1.8.1.	Notice 58
		1.8.1.1. Visually Perceptible Copies 60
		1.8.1.2. Form of Notice 60
		1.8.1.3. Location of Notice 60
		1.8.1.4. Collective Works 61
		1.8.1.5. Notice under the Berne Act 62
	1.8.2.	Errors in Name or Date in the Notice 62
		1.8.2.1. Under the 1909 Act 62

	1.8.2.2. Under the 1976 Act 63

- 1.8.3. Omission of Notice 64
    - 1.8.3.1. Under the 1909 Act 64
    - 1.8.3.2. Under the 1976 Act 64
- 1.8.4. Registration 66
    - 1.8.4.1. Under the 1909 Act 66
    - 1.8.4.2. Under the 1976 Act 67
    - 1.8.4.3. Incentives for Registration 67
    - 1.8.4.4. Registration under the Berne Act 69
- 1.8.5. Deposit 69
    - 1.8.5.1. Purpose of Deposit 69
    - 1.8.5.2. Exemptions from Deposit.................................. 71
- 1.8.6. Registration Procedures 72
- 1.8.7. Denial of Registration 73

1.9. Duration of Copyright 74
- 1.9.1. Works Created on or after January 1, 1978................... 75
- 1.9.2. Works Created but Not Published or
  Copyrighted before January 1, 1978 76
- 1.9.3. Works Copyrighted Prior to January 1, 1978................ 76
- 1.9.4. Works Created between 1906 and 1921 77

1.10. Transfers.. 78
- 1.10.1. In General.. 78
    - 1.10.1.1 Exceptions to the Writing Rule 79
    - 1.10.1.2. Subsequent Transfers of
      Exclusive Rights... 81
- 1.10.2. Mandatory Licenses 82
- 1.10.3. Recordation 83
- 1.10.4. Attachments of Other Interests...................................... 84

1.11. Renewal and Termination Rights 85
- 1.11.1. The Rationale behind Renewal Rights
  and Termination Rights... 85
- 1.11.2. The Renewal Right.. 87
- 1.11.3. Termination during the Extended Renewal
  Term 89
- 1.11.4. Termination of Transfers Made after
  January 1, 1978 91
- 1.11.5. Restoration of Copyright.. 93

CONTENTS

1.12. Infringement 95
    1.12.1. In General 95
    1.12.2. Essential Elements of a Cause of
        Action for Copyright Infringement 96
        1.12.2.1. Copyrightability of the Original Work 96
        1.12.2.2. Formalities of Copyright 96
        1.12.2.3. Ownership of Copyright 97
        1.12.2.4. Copying of the Protected Work 97
        1.12.2.5. Violation of Exclusive Right 100
        1.12.2.6. Permission 100
        1.12.2.7. Excuse 101
        1.12.2.8. Defense 101
    1.12.3. Actions for Infringement 104
    1.12.4. Criminal Offenses 104
1.13. DMCA Provisions 105
    1.13.1. Takedown Notices 107

1.14. Remedies 107
    1.14.1. Criminal Sanctions 107
    1.14.2. Civil Remedies 108
        1.14.2.1. Injunctions 108
        1.14.2.2. Impoundment and Disposition
            of Infringement Articles 109
        1.14.2.3. Damages and Profits 110
            a. Actual Damages and Profits 110
            b. Statutory Damages 111
        1.14.2.4. Costs and Attorney's Fees 113

1.15. Manufacture and Importation 114
    1.15.1. Manufacturing Requirement 114
    1.15.2. Importation Restrictions 115
        1.15.2.1. Piratical Copies Exclusion 116
        1.15.2.2. Territorial Exclusivity 117

1.16. Copyright Royalty Distribution 118

1.17. Copyright Protection and Management Systems 119

Chapter 2
The Law of Ideas

- 2.1. General Principles 123
  - 2.1.1. Contract Law Protections 127
    - 2.1.1.1. Express Contracts 127
    - 2.1.1.2. Implied-in-Fact Contracts 128
  - 2.1.2. Fair Practices Protections 129
    - 2.1.2.1. Quasi-Contract 130
    - 2.1.2.2. Misappropriation or Unfair Competition 131
    - 2.1.2.3. Breach of a Confidential Relationship 132
    - 2.1.2.4. Trade Secrets 133
- 2.2. Subject Matter of Protectable Ideas 134
  - 2.2.1. Requirements of Novelty, Concreteness, and Nonpublication 134
    - 2.2.1.1. Novelty 135
    - 2.2.1.2. Concreteness 139
    - 2.2.1.3. Nonpublication 139
  - 2.2.2. Ideas Protected by Contract 141
    - 2.2.2.1. Ideas Protected by Express Contract 141
    - 2.2.2.2. Ideas Protected by Implied-in-Fact Contracts 143
  - 2.2.3. Ideas Protectable under Fair Practices Standards 144
    - 2.2.3.1. Ideas Protectable under Quasi-Contract 144
    - 2.2.3.2. Ideas Protected against Misappropriation or Unfair Competition 145
    - 2.2.3.3. Ideas Protected through a Confidential Relationship 146
    - 2.2.3.4. Ideas Protectable as Trade Secrets 147
- 2.3. Exclusive Rights in Ideas 147
- 2.4. Fair Use 148
- 2.5. Creation and Commencement of Protection 148
- 2.6. Ownership 149

2.7. Formalities 149
2.8. Duration 149
2.9. Transfers 149
2.10. Infringement 150
      2.10.1. Copying 150
      2.10.2. Against Whom an Idea Creator's Rights
              May Be Enforced 151
      2.10.3. Defenses 152
2.11. Remedies 152

CHAPTER 3
U.S. Trademark and Unfair Competition Law

3.1. General Principles 155
      3.1.1. Jurisdiction 155
      3.1.2. Rationale for Protection 156
      3.1.3. Terminology 156
3.2. Subject Matter of Trademark 157
      3.2.1. In General 157
      3.2.2. Conflicting Marks 157
      3.2.3. Distinctiveness 159
      3.2.4. Secondary Meaning 160
      3.2.5. Unique Characteristics of Entertainment
             Industry Marks 161
      3.2.6. Unprotectable Marks 161
      3.2.7. Famous Marks 162
      3.2.8. The Anticybersquatting Consumer
             Protection Act 164
      3.2.9. ICANN/WIPO Arbitration of Domain Names 165
3.3. Exclusive Rights of Trademark 167
      3.3.1. In General 167
      3.3.2. Exclusive Market 168
             3.3.2.1. Territory 168
             3.3.2.2. Competing Products or Services 169
      3.3.3. Well-Known Marks 169
3.4. Fair Use of Trademarks 170

3.5.	Creation and Commencement of Protection	174
3.6.	Ownership	175
3.7.	Formalities of Registration and Notice	176
	3.7.1. Federal Registration	176
	3.7.2. State Registration	180
	3.7.3. Registration outside of the United States	180
	3.7.4. Registration of Entertainment and Creative Industry Marks	182
	3.7.5. Principal versus Supplemental Register	184
	3.7.6. Notice	185
3.8.	Duration	185
3.9.	Transfers	186
	3.9.1. In General	186
	3.9.2. Assignments	186
	3.9.3. Licenses	187
3.10.	Renewals and Termination	188
3.11.	Unfair Competition	189
	3.11.1. Common Law and State Statutory Law	189
	3.11.1.1. Vocal Performance Imitations in Commercials	189
	3.11.2. Section 43(a)	191
3.12.	Infringement	193
	3.12.1. In General	193
	3.12.2. Elements of an Action	193
	3.12.3. Defenses	194
3.13.	Remedies	195

CHAPTER 4
Publicity and Privacy

4.1.	In General	199
	4.1.1. The Right of Privacy	200
	4.1.2. The Right of Publicity	202
	4.1.3. Publicity versus Privacy	205
	4.1.4. Publicity/Privacy versus Trademark	206

		4.1.5. Publicity, Privacy, and State Jurisdiction 206
4.2.	Subject Matter 207	
	4.2.1. In General 207	
	4.2.2. Publicity/Privacy and Copyright 208	
4.3.	Exclusive Rights 210	
	4.3.1. Performance 210	
	4.3.2. Adaptation 211	
	4.3.3. Personality Products 212	
	4.3.4. Endorsement 212	
	4.3.5. Reputation 214	
4.4.	Fair Use – Limitations to Publicity and Privacy Rights 214	
	4.4.1. First Amendment 215	
	4.4.2. Mimicry and Imitation 217	
	4.4.3. Fair Use Doctrine Test 217	
	4.4.4. Fine Arts Exception 218	
	4.4.5. First Sale 219	
	4.4.6. Public Domain Limits 219	
	4.4.7. Non-Endorsement Use 220	
	4.4.8. Antitrust 220	
4.5.	Creation and Commencement 220	
	4.5.1. Privacy 220	
	4.5.2. Publicity 221	
4.6.	Ownership 223	
	4.6.1. Privacy 223	
	4.6.2. Publicity 223	
4.7.	Formalities 224	
4.8.	Duration 225	
	4.8.1. Privacy 225	
	4.8.2. Publicity 225	
4.9.	Transfer 227	
	4.9.1. Privacy 227	
	4.9.2. Publicity 228	
	4.9.3. Privacy and Defamation 229	
4.10.	Infringement 230	
	4.10.1. Privacy-Appropriation 230	

	4.10.2.	Publicity	231
	4.10.3.	Unfair Competition	231
	4.10.4.	Venue or Choice of Law	232
4.11.	Remedies		233
	4.11.1.	Privacy	233
	4.11.2.	Publicity	233

CHAPTER 5
International Copyright Treaties

- 5.1. The Berne Convention 235
  - 5.1.1. Introduction 235
    - 5.1.1.1. The Conventions and the Union 235
    - 5.1.1.2. Minimum Standards of Protection 236
  - 5.1.2. Subject Matter of Copyright 237
    - 5.1.2.1. Protectable Works 237
    - 5.1.2.2. National Eligibility 237
  - 5.1.3. Exclusive Rights in Copyrighted Works 238
    - 5.1.3.1. Basic Rights 238
    - 5.1.3.2. Limitations of the Basic Rights 239
    - 5.1.3.3. Droit Moral/Droit de Suite 239
      - a. Droit Moral or Moral Right 239
      - b. Droit de Suite 241
  - 5.1.4. Fair Use 241
  - 5.1.5. Creation and Commencement 242
  - 5.1.6. Ownership 243
  - 5.1.7. Formalities of Notice and Registration 243
  - 5.1.8. Duration of Copyright 244
  - 5.1.9. Transfers 245
  - 5.1.10. Termination and Renewal Rights 245
  - 5.1.11. Infringement 245
    - 5.1.11.1. Plaintiff 245
    - 5.1.11.2. Applicability of the Berne
      Convention 246
    - 5.1.11.3. Applicable Law 246
  - 5.1.12. Remedies 246
  - 5.1.13. Developing Nations 247
  - 5.1.14. Members of the Berne Convention 247

5.2. The WIPO Copyright Treaty (Geneva 1996) 253
    5.2.1. Key Treaty Provisions 254
        5.2.1.1. WCT and Berne 254
        5.2.1.2. Substantive Provisions 254
        5.2.1.3. Administrative Provisions 257
    5.2.2. Adopting Parties as of July 17, 2017 257
5.3. The Universal Copyright Convention (UCC) 261
    5.3.1. History 261
        5.3.1.1. Difference between the UCC and
                 Berne 262
        5.3.1.2. National Treatment 262
    5.3.2. Subject Matter 263
        5.3.2.1. Protectable Works 263
        5.3.2.2. National Eligibility 263
    5.3.3. Exclusive Rights 263
        5.3.3.1. Basic Rights 263
        5.3.3.2. Limitations on Basic Rights 264
    5.3.4. Fair Use 265
    5.3.5. Creation and Commencement 265
    5.3.6. Ownership 265
    5.3.7. Formalities 266
    5.3.8. Duration of Copyright 266
    5.3.9. Transfers 267
    5.3.10. Infringement 267
    5.3.11. Remedies 268
    5.3.12. Special Provisions 268
        5.3.12.1. Protection of the Berne Union 268
        5.3.12.2. Supremacy of Existing Multilateral
                  or Bilateral Treaties 268
        5.3.12.3. Developing Countries 269
    5.3.13. Members of the UCC as of July 2017 269
5.4. The Buenos Aires Convention 272
5.5. The Convention for the Protection of Producers of
     Phonograms against Unauthorized Duplication of
     Their Phonograms (Geneva 1971)(the Phonogram
     Convention) 273
    5.5.1. In General 273
    5.5.2. Membership Status as of July 17, 2017 274

5.6. The WIPO Performances and Phonograms Treaty
(Geneva 1996) 277
 5.6.1. In General 277
 5.6.2. Treaty Signatories 279

CHAPTER 6
Intellectual Property Law Principles of Entertainment Industry Practice

6.1. Copyright Matters.. 283
 6.1.1. Notice 284
 6.1.2. Author's Diary 285
 6.1.3. Informal Copyright 285
 6.1.4. Copyright Registration Procedures 286
 6.1.5. Registration Review 292
  6.1.5.1. Title 292
  6.1.5.2. Authorship, Creation and Publication 293
  6.1.5.3. Copyright Claimant 293
  6.1.5.4. Previous Registration and Derivative
     Work or Completion..................................... 294
  6.1.5.5. Administrative Provisions 294
 6.1.6. Deposit Account... 294
 6.1.7. Copyright Searches 294
 6.1.8. Copyright Reversions... 296
 6.1.9. Restored Copyright Review 298
 6.1.10. *La Cienaga* Review 299
6.2. Clearing World Rights of an Underlying Source for
Republication, Translation, and Adaptation........................... 299
 6.2.1. What Rights Are to Be Cleared? 299
 6.2.2. Illustration: Clearing Rights for Dramatic or
    Dramatico-Musical Adaptation 301
  6.2.2.1. Dramatic Rights 301
  6.2.2.2. Distinctions among the Dramatic Rights 302
  6.2.2.3. Similarities among the Dramatic Rights 303
  6.2.2.4. Adaptation Rights Issues.............................. 303
    a. The Right to Adapt 303
    b. Rights Flowing from the Adaptation......... 303

xviii   CONTENTS

    6.2.2.5. Territory of Rights.. 303
    6.2.2.6. Music Rights 304
    6.2.2.7. Title 304
    6.2.2.8. "Fair Use"... 305
  6.2.3. The Source Material and Places to Begin..................... 305
    6.2.3.1. Direct Clues.. 306
      a. Copyright Notice 306
      b. Acknowledgments 306
      c. Credits... 306
      d. Title and Subtitle 306
    6.2.3.2. Further Investigation 306
      a. The Writers and Authors Guilds............... 307
      b. The Library... 307
      c. Collective Administrative
        Organizations 307
      d. The Clearance Departments of the
        Broadcast Networks and Studios.............. 308
      e. Clearance Services....................................308
      f. The World Wide Web 308
    6.2.3.3. A Caveat... 308
  6.2.4. Profiling the Author 309
    6.2.4.1. Which Copyright Law Applies?...................... 309
    6.2.4.2. Duration of Copyright 309
    6.2.4.3. Rights Owners Deriving Their Authority
      through the Author 311
    6.2.4.4. Co-authors or Collaborators 311
    6.2.4.5. Authors Guild or Society Membership 312
  6.2.5. The Initial Publication.. 312
    6.2.5.1. Books and Periodicals 313
      a. Work-for-hire Authors.............................. 313
      b. Agency and Title 313
    6.2.5.2. Dramatic Productions..................................... 313
      a. The Production 313
      b. The Producer 313
      c. Music Publishers 314
    6.2.5.3. Motion Pictures and Television
      Programming.. 315
  6.2.6. Tracing the Chain of Title 315
  6.2.7. The New Work.. 316

6.3.	Thinking about Trademarks and Merchandising		317
	6.3.1.	What Is Protectable?	318
		6.3.1.1. In General	318
		6.3.1.2. Performers' Names	319
	6.3.2.	The Creation and Protection of the Mark	320
	6.3.3.	Enforcement	321
6.4.	Warranties and Representations		321
	6.4.1.	Original Work	323
	6.4.2.	Infringement	324
	6.4.3.	Publicity, Privacy, Libel, Slander, and Obscenity	325
	6.4.4.	Performance	327
6.5.	Indemnification Issues		328
	6.5.1.	Indemnity or Subrogation Grant	328
	6.5.2.	Restrictions on Indemnification	329
		6.5.2.1. Reciprocity	329
		6.5.2.2. Amount of Indemnity or "Face Value"	330
		6.5.2.3. Procedural Condition	331
	6.5.3.	Additional Protections	331
	6.5.4.	Insurance	332

Index 335

— FOREWORD —

Peter Dekom

I've been practicing entertainment law for over four decades in virtually every facet of the industry covered by these volumes (and more). I've had the good fortune of working with clients at the highest levels of the business during this period, many of whom I started working with as they graduated from film school or launched their first projects, while others came to me for representation at the height of their success – and I've seen a lot. It would have been nice to have had the benefit of access to a resource like *The Essential Guide to Entertainment Law* as I began my legal career in the industry in the 1970s. Fortunately, you now have that opportunity with the publication of this two-volume resource detailing the ins and outs of law practice and dealmaking in the entertainment industries.

Over the years I've been continually surprised by how many people think they are gifted enough to compete creatively with Hollywood (that generic "*Hollywood*" which identifies an industry and culture more than a place, and now describes a global industry with professional roots all over the United States and across the world). They are creatives, critics, marketing whizzes and others who will tell you all the things that Hollywood gets wrong or doesn't get at all. There's a tad of truth in some of this, but juxtaposed to all of these critiques and creative yearnings are the triumphs and tribulations of those who in the past took the risks... and made it. They are the professionals. God bless those risk-takers, but...

As much as creativity within film, music, books, plays, electronic gaming and television is a pinnacle for artistic expressions and reflections of our culture, it is also a rather significant part of our commercial and legal landscape. It is unquestionably big business – no, make that "huge business." And where there is that much money and power at stake, playing the game without knowing the rules, the players, and the risks of engagement is deeply unwise – even if your goal is breaking or challenging the system at some level. These books can help serious creatives, entrepreneurs, executives and legal professionals navigate these landscapes.

The legal underpinnings of these entertainment industry enterprises start with Article I, Section 8, Clause 8 of the U.S. Constitution – the so-called "copyright" clause. They extend up through the mass of legal regulations and restrictions on raising financing and trundling through piles of customs and practices in every phase of entertainment. Then there are the barriers which have been erected by insiders to keep the unaware out, establishing (and maintaining) the hurdles that have historically determined what content goes into (or is excluded from) theaters, store shelves, the airwaves and Internet. Many of these policies and practices have been established and long maintained by the industry goliaths that have succeeded, repeatedly, in turning mere ideas into gold and that still have significant sway over who gets in and who is kept out of the innermost workings of these businesses. Then there is the gatekeeping role of numerous government entities, some offering subsidies for production, others offering sticky taxing fingers, and those in many foreign territories determining what products can be distributed generally. Then there are the primary talent and labor guilds that monitor many higher-end industry productions (film, television, theater and even musical projects) through agreements with studios and producers that go on for literally thousands of pages of fine print. Navigating all of this toward success can be daunting and is not for the fainthearted. So let's just say, "It's complicated." Add into the mix globalization and the digital transformations that are reshaping our communications, entertainment, and knowledge universes, and you get "complicated on steroids."

Experienced entertainment lawyers Jay Shanker and Kirk Schroder with *The Essential Guide to Entertainment Law: Dealmaking*, and Shanker, Paul Supnik and Jonathan Reichman with *The Essential Guide to Entertainment Law: Intellectual Property*, have taken on the herculean task of explaining this complexity to those newcomers to the field who really and seriously "want in" as well as to active professionals in the field already "in" but in need of a refresher on issues they may not have encountered in a while, or perhaps at all. I know and have worked with both of these types of readers, and *The Essential Guide to Entertainment Law* delivers abundant knowledge on a broad spectrum of legal and business practices in the entertainment industries to both audiences. This book series encompasses pragmatics – from broad deal parameters to the essential little details that can kill you if neglected. The authors/editors of this project have recruited the insights of more than a dozen additional experts, many of whom I also know well and each having decades of relevant experience, to explain, teach, and warn about the intel they have accumulated in the course of their careers.

Be assured this two-volume series on the practice of entertainment industry law – comprising as it does an impressively deep survey of (i) dealmaking strategies, custom and practice and (ii) intellectual property law and other formal legal essentials, is a magnificent assemblage that can benefit anyone engaged in the industry, from neophyte to seasoned entertainment professional. Read what you care about in these volumes, in any order and level of depth you please, and you can't go wrong. Treat these books as the basis of a course in entertainment law and deal-making, or use them as a frequent reference source to get a handle on some or all of the wide range of entertainment law subjects covered here – most of which, I assure you, will arise on a recurring basis in your professional practice or careers in Entertainment.

Enjoy the read, and the ride!

***

Peter J. Dekom practices law in Los Angeles. Mr. Dekom is currently Vice-Chairman of Dick Cook Studios, partnered with former Walt Disney Studios Chairman, Richard Cook. He was formerly Of counsel with Weissmann Wolff Bergman Coleman Grodin & Evall and a partner in the firm of Bloom, Dekom, Hergott and Cook. Mr. Dekom's clients include or have included such Hollywood notables as George Lucas, Paul Haggis, Keenen Ivory Wayans, John Travolta, Ron Howard, Rob Reiner, Andy Davis, Robert Towne and Larry Gordon among many others, as well as corporate clients such as Sears, Roebuck and Co., Pacific Telesis and Japan Victor Corporation (JVC). He has been listed in *Forbes* among the top 100 lawyers in the United States and in *Premiere Magazine* as one of the 50 most powerful people in Hollywood.

Mr. Dekom has been a management/marketing consultant, and entrepreneur in the fields of entertainment, Internet, and telecommunications. As a consultant to the state of New Mexico for almost a decade, he was instrumental in creating, writing and implementing legislation to encourage film and television production in the state and supervised the film loan program portion of that incentive structure until the spring of 2011.

Mr. Dekom served on the board of directors of Imagine Films Entertainment while the company remained publicly traded and was a board member of Will Vinton Studios and Cinebase Software, among others, leaving upon change of ownership. He has also served as a member of the Academy of Television Arts and Sciences and Academy Foundation, Board of Directors, Chairman (now Emeritus) of the American Cinematheque, and on the Advisory Board of the Shanghai International Film Festival. He serves on the Governing Committee for the America Bar Association's Sports and Entertainment Law Section, where he often authored articles, delivered lectures and continues to be an active participant.

In 2012, the American Bar Association, through its Forum on Sports and Entertainment Law, honored Mr. Dekom with its highest recognition for entertainment lawyers, the Ed Rubin Service Award. The author of dozens of scholarly articles, Mr. Dekom also is the co-author of *Not on My Watch; Hollywood vs. the Future* (New Millennium Publishing, 2003) with Peter Sealey, and is the author of *Next: Reinventing Media, Marketing and Entertainment* (HekaRose Publishing Group 2014). Mr. Dekom has served as an adjunct professor at the UCLA Film School, as lecturer (entertainment marketing) at the University of California, Berkeley Haas School of Business, in addition to being a featured speaker at film festivals, corporations, universities and bar associations all over the world.

Beyond his professional pursuits, Mr. Dekom is author of the seminal public policy blog *Unshred America* (http://unshred.blogspot.com/).

—Preface—

Jay Shanker

Welcome to *The Essential Guide to Entertainment Law*.

This two-volume project has two primary objectives:

The first is to explore the basics of dealmaking in the principal entertainment industry transactional sectors (film, TV, music, theater, book publishing, electronic gaming and entertainment industry taxation), all addressed in EG2EL:Dealmaking.

The second is to similarly examine the fundamental intellectual property law principles and issues of copyright, trademark, unfair competition, rights of publicity and publicity which are the foundation for a substantial part of the industry's functioning, and which we address in EG2EL: Intellectual Property.

We encourage readers to acquire both volumes, and to also partake of the wealth of information contained in the illustrative form agreements that accompany the Dealmaking book. These are available online to those who have purchased EG2EL:Dealmaking or the two-volume set. (For more on obtaining these forms and accessing other online resources of this project, please visit www.EG2EL.com and www.jurispub.com.)

The information delivered in these volumes has been assembled by a "dream team" of nearly 20 entertainment industry legal experts who work in and with leading law firms and entertainment companies on behalf of many of the most prominent creative artists, companies and projects in the business.

With EG2EL: Dealmaking my co-editor Kirk Schroder and I recruited fourteen of these highly regarded lawyer contributors to cover the landscape of industry dealmaking. These contributors bring decades of high-level experience and insight to the many subjects addressed in this volume. Each guides you, the reader, through the fundamentals of deal structuring in their industry sectors and practices. We believe you will find their respective voices as distinctive as their approaches to their legal practices.

Likewise, in EG2EL:Intellectual Property, my co-authors Paul Supnik and Jonathan Reichman and I have sought to provide a concise yet comprehensive roadmap to the IP landscape by discussing those IP issues most relevant to entertainment industry transactions in the

United States. Understanding those issues will help establish the parameters of underlying rights – knowledge essential to securing most industry project financing and distribution. Paul and Jonathan are among the most experienced and admired practitioners in the entertainment IP fields.

These two volumes and the available E2GEL illustrative forms are intended as hands-on desk top references for both the experienced and aspiring entertainment lawyer, for industry executives and creatives, for investors in entertainment projects, and for law and business students, each of whom will be able to navigate these volumes in useful ways.

For experienced entertainment lawyers, EG2EL can offer a "checklist" on projects in which you are active, or can provide an overview of a sector or issue in which you have less experience or require a concentrated "refresher."

The volumes can also serve as a primer for lawyers for whom "entertainment" is not a primary practice focus (or perhaps is just an "aspiration"). For this audience, EG2EL may help you level the playing field in transactions with more experienced counsel, or may simply enable you to confidently recruit and effectively service new clients.

It is also our intent that EG2EL will prove equally valuable to entertainment industry business executives and professionals, "creatives," investors, MBA and entertainment industry sector pre-professional students, and others seeking a broad overview of the legal and business underpinnings of the industry. Whether as a frequent or occasional FAQ resource, EG2EL can help these readers better navigate fundamental questions which can make that initial call to a lawyer more productive (and cost-effective). Additionally, EG2EL can help readers get a fuller grasp of their lawyer's prescriptions for a transaction after the consultation has occurred or when the paperwork arrives. Packed as these volumes are with the knowledge of so many noted figures in the industry, we believe EG2EL delivers a range and quality of information that can generally only be obtained by years of active experience in the industries covered by these volumes. (If our lawyer readers recommend these books to clients to strengthen their clients' understanding of the entertainment industry's business and legal frameworks so they in turn understand the value of a competent lawyer's guidance in the service of the clients' success – we'll feel a large part of our mission with EG2EL has been fulfilled.)

Notes of gratitude are in order to those who have made this project and my involvement in it possible.

First, to David Guinn and the late Harold Orenstein, whose *Entertainment Law & Business: A Guide to the Law and Business Practices of the Entertainment Industry*, first published in 1989, informs the structure and many of the chapters in these volumes. I came on board that project as a co-author in 2004 at the request of our publisher, Juris, and nearly 15 years later EL&B guides the spirit of EG2EL.

Next, to Michael Kitzen and Cynthia Nieves at Juris, who have patiently encouraged and supported the long gestation of these two new volumes and now bring this work to new audiences.

To gifted lawyers and mentors Alan Latman, Gabriel Perle and Richard Sherwood, who live in my memory and who each were instrumental in illuminating my path to a career in entertainment law, and Peter Dekom, Tom Rowan and John Hermes who, in turn, opened doors to signature opportunities in my professional career, I am forever indebted to each of these gentlemen.

To my co-editor Kirk Schroder and co-authors Paul Supnik and Jonathan Reichman, whose exemplary work and insights on these volumes on which we collaborated have helped insure that EG2EL will provide invaluable legal and business tools for a new generation of entertainment industry readers.

To the other exceptional author-contributors whose work is embodied in the transactional volume Kirk and I have edited, you comprise a dream team I am honored to be associated with. Assembled under one roof you'd constitute one of the most formidable entertainment law firms in the industry.

Needless to say, it has been a pleasure and privilege to work with and learn from each of the distinguished professionals who have contributed to the construction of these volumes.

To Zach Oubre and Steven Cole of McAfee &Taft, and to Blake Johnson, Cullen Sweeney, Nancy Seeley and the rest of my entertainment law practice group team at Crowe & Dunlevy, my heartfelt thanks for your support and input on these volumes as this project has and will continue to evolve.

I also wish to express my gratitude to my clients and other professional colleagues of the past 35 years who have helped make my practice of law in the fields which are the subject of these volumes so stimulating and rewarding. To my parents, Ben and Shirley Shanker, who have amazed and inspired me each day in my life, and to my wife Sara Jane and our children Jorja, Rachel and Eliot, who (even more than my clients) wondrously insure that no two days in my life are alike – my love and appreciation know no bounds.

In closing, a reflection with roots in my law school years. I shopped a couple of times a year at Syms Discount Clothiers in Manhattan for the suits and ties that got me through law firm interviews and summer clerkships. As some of you may remember, Syms' ads declared, "An Educated Consumer Is Our Best Customer, ™" and this slogan, a prescription for turning quality service to customer loyalty, stuck with me. My most rewarding professional relationships over the years, whether in private practice or in-house for several dynamic entertainment companies, have been with clients who did their homework, asked good questions, and appreciated the value that knowledgeable and efficient lawyering can bring to the table in support of the strategic and dealmaking opportunities and challenges of client projects and careers.

It is my hope that these two volumes of *The Essential Guide to Entertainment Law* will support each of us (lawyers and non-lawyers alike) in our quest to provide more responsive and effective counsel to our clients and their projects in the Entertainment Industry, while at the same time enabling our clients to become better "educated consumers" of our guidance and services – and in turn our "best customers."

— ABOUT THE AUTHORS —

Jay Shanker is a veteran entertainment industry attorney whose practice encompasses a wide array of film, television, theater, music, live entertainment, new media, fine arts, publishing and sports industry transactions for individual and corporate clients, including both public and private companies, across the U.S. and abroad. His clients and their projects have over the years garnered prestigious international awards in every major creative media, including Oscar, Emmy, Grammy and Clio nominations and awards. A graduate of Yale and the NYU School of Law, Mr. Shanker has practiced law in Los Angeles since 1981, and in 2005 relocated his practice to his native Oklahoma City, where he now serves as a director at Crowe & Dunlevy, a national law firm based in Oklahoma City with additional offices in Tulsa and Dallas. He is co-author of *Entertainment Law & Business*, the third edition of which was published by Juris in 2013. He was also a contributing editor for *Entertainment Industry Contracts*, published by Matthew Bender in 1996 and co-editor of *Law and the Television of the '80s*, published by Oceana in 1982. He has taught courses on entertainment law at the University of Oklahoma and Oklahoma City University, and has lectured on entertainment industry legal matters at UCLA, USC and the American Film Institute (AFI) in Los Angeles and New York, For the Producers Guild of America, and for the American Bar Association and other leading continuing legal education forums on entertainment law topics. Mr. Shanker has served on the advisory committee of the AFI's Third Decade Council and was a founding board member of the Academy of Interactive Arts and Sciences. Jay Shanker's achievements have earned him repeated inclusion in *The Best Lawyers in America* (Entertainment Law – Motion Pictures and Television; Entertainment Law – Music). He is admitted to practice in California, Oklahoma and the District of Columbia.

For more information about Jay Shanker and his firm please visit www.crowedunlevy.com

ABOUT THE AUTHORS

Paul Supnik, based in Beverly Hills, California, practices trademark, copyright, and entertainment law. He advises businesses in the selection and use of brand identities, protects trademarks through registration strategies, enhances value through licensing, and litigates trademark and copyright disputes. Mr. Supnik has spoken on these subjects in the U.S. and internationally. Industries represented include: The Internet, apparel, cosmetic, restaurant, advertising, sporting goods, software, financial, arts, and media. As a bar association leader, Paul Supnik has served as president of the Los Angeles Copyright Society, chair of both the Entertainment/IP Law and International Law Sections of the Los Angeles County Bar, and chair of the *Los Angeles Lawyer* magazine editorial board. He has a Martindale-Hubbell Peer Review Rating of "AV" and has been selected by SuperLawyers® in the field of Intellectual Property for the years 2010 through 2013. He served as an adjunct associate professor at Southwestern Law School from 2008-2011.

For more information about Paul Supnik and his practice, please visit www.supnik.com

Jonathan D. Reichman is a partner in the New York office of Hunton Andrews Kurth LLP. He has over 30 years' experience in litigation, licensing and counseling matters in copyright, trademark, unfair competition and right of publicity law, particularly for clients in the entertainment industry. *World Trademark Review 1000* recognizes him as a leader in trademark matters and notes that he has "specific expertise in protecting rights related to fictional characters" (2016). He is ranked in New York by *Chambers & Partners USA* in the area of "Intellectual Property: Trademark & Copyright" (2014, 2016-2017). In addition, Jonathan Reichman has been recognized as a leading intellectual property lawyer by New York *Super Lawyers* (2016-2017). He is also recognized in the area of copyright law by *The US Legal 500* (2016-2017) and *U.S. News and World Report*/Best Lawyers (2015).

A major aspect of Mr. Reichman's practice involves the protection, defense, enforcement, licensing and exploitation of rights vested in fictional characters. He has handled complex issues concerning such characters and properties as Spider-Man, X-Men, Superman, Batman, Barbie, Peanuts, Strawberry Shortcake, Babar the Elephant, Teenage Mutant Ninja Turtles, Teletubbies, The Berenstain Bears, Inspector Gadget, Franklin The Turtle, Raggedy Ann and Andy, Mr. Bill and The Woodstock Festivals.

He also represents the estates of well-known entertainers, authors and artists. He has handled copyright, right of publicity, and trademark matters for such estates as that of Joseph Campbell, Mary McCarthy, Diane Arbus, Richard Avedon, Rube Goldberg, W.C. Fields and Abbott & Costello.

In 2014, he served as an advisor to the New Jersey State Senate in connection with Senate Bill No. S2212 ("The Commercial Identity Protect Act").

For many years, Mr. Reichman served as a member of the Advisory Board of Bloomberg BNA's Patent, Trademark and Copyright Journal. He is currently on the Advisory Board of *The Licensing Journal*. He has written on copyright, trademark and publicity law topics, and lectured for such organizations as The National Academy of Television Arts and Sciences, Columbia University School of Law, Columbia University School of Fine Arts, New York Film Academy, The New School for Social Research, Volunteer Lawyers for the Arts and the Institute for International Research. He has taught entertainment licensing as an adjunct professor at New York Law School, and been interviewed by such prominent media outlets as *The New York Times*, *Dateline NBC* and *New York Newsday*. He was a regular commentator on copyright and trademark law topics for the NPR radio program "Soundcheck."

For more information about Jonathan Reichman and his firm please visit www.andrewskurth.com

— DISCLAIMER —

No Legal Advice.

The materials contained herein represent the opinions of the authors and/or the editors, and should not be construed to be the views or opinions of the law firms or companies with whom such persons are in partnership, associated, or employed, nor of Juris Publishing.

Nothing contained in this book is to be considered as the rendering of legal advice for specific cases or transactions, and readers are responsible for obtaining such advice from their own legal counsel. This book and its contents are intended for educational and informational purposes only.

— CHAPTER 1 —

U.S. COPYRIGHT LAW

1.1. Copyright: Constitutional and Statutory Foundations
1.2. Subject Matter of Copyright
1.3. Neighboring Rights
1.4. Exclusive Rights in Copyrighted Works
1.5. Fair Use
1.6. Creation and Commencement of Copyright
1.7. Ownership, Joint Ownership, and Works Made for Hire
1.8. Formalities of Notice, Registration, and Deposit
1.9. Duration of Copyright
1.10. Transfers
1.11. Renewal and Termination Rights
1.12. Infringement
1.13. DMCA Provisions
1.14. Remedies
1.15. Manufacture and Importation
1.16. Copyright Royalty Distribution
1.17. Copyright Protection and Management Systems

1.1. COPYRIGHT: CONSTITUTIONAL AND STATUTORY FOUNDATIONS

1.1.1. The Constitution

The United States Constitution, in article I, section 8, clause 8, provides that Congress shall have the power

> To promote the progress of science and useful arts, by securing for limited time to authors and inventors the exclusive right to their respective writings and discoveries.

The importance of this Constitutional grounding cannot be underestimated. It provides both a rational for protecting copyright (to promote the progress),[1] criteria for protection (the creativity of authorship)[2] and the nature of protection (exclusive rights for a limited period of time).[3]

---

[1] *See, e.g., infra* §1.5.1.
[2] *See, e.g. U.S. Copyright Law, infra* §1.2.2.
[3] *See, e.g. U.S. Copyright Law, infra* §§1.4 and 1.9.

However, perhaps of equal significance, this Constitutional grounding enables copyright to withstand attacks based upon the Constitutional protection for freedom of speech in the First Amendment. Obviously, granting exclusive rights to authors to control the distribution of their works (which are all forms of speech) places copyright in tension with free speech. Without Constitutional imprimatur, it is unlikely that copyright would stand. However, because copyright is a Constitutional creation, Courts have supported it and recognized that copyright law has developed systemic means of accommodating this tension through the idea/expression dichotomy,[4] the provisions for a limited term of protection,[5] and the fail-safe of "fair use" which allows an explicit balancing between the goods of encouraging authors and encouraging free expression.[6] As summarized by one court, "there are no First Amendment rights to use the copyrighted works of others."[7]

1.1.2. Copyright Revision Act of 1976

As noted above, the Constitution empowers Congress to enact laws protecting the exclusive rights of authors for limited times. Congress has exercised this power since the founding of the Republic and passed one of the first copyright acts on May 31, 1790.[8]

There are two acts of substantive importance that must be considered: the Copyright Revision Act of 1909, codified in 1947 as Title 17 of the Copyright Act, and amendments thereto (hereinafter referred to as the 1909 Act), and the Copyright Revision Act of 1976, the current Title 17 U.S.C. §101 *et seq.* (hereinafter referred to as the 1976 Act and cited as 17 U.S.C.). Although the 1976 Act was a complete revision of the Copyright Law, those copyrights subsisting prior to January 1, 1978, the commencement date of the 1976 Act, are, with minor modifications,[9] substantially governed by the terms of the

---

[4] *See, e.g. U.S. Copyright Law, infra* §1.2.3; Harper & Row Publishers, Inc. v. Nation Enters., 471 U.S. 539, 560 (1985).
[5] *See* Eldred v. Ashcroft, 537 U.S. 186 (2003).
[6] *See, e.g. U.S. Copyright Law, infra* §1.5; Roy Export Co. v CBS, Inc., 672 F.2d 1095 (2d Cir.), *cert denied,* 459 U.S. 826 (1982).
[7] Eldred v. Reno, 239 F.3d 372 (D.C. Cir. 2001), *cert granted in part sub nom.* Eldred v. Ashcroft, 534 U.S. 1160 (2002), *aff'd,* 537 U.S. 186 (2003).
[8] May 31, 1790, ch. 15, 1 Stat. 124.
[9] *See* 17 U.S.C. §304 (2008).

1909 Act and its various judicial interpretations. For example, works copyrighted prior to 1978 operate under special rules of duration (28 years for the first term),[10] renewal (the work must be registered for renewal within one year prior to the expiration of the original term),[11] and an extended renewal term (so that the work is protected for a total of 75 years[12] but with termination provisions with respect to the extended term of 19 years that allow termination by the grantor, authors, or beneficiaries). The 75 years term was further extended an additional 20 years to 95 years and the termination period from 19 to 39 years through the Sonny Bono Copyright Term Extension Act.[13] Moreover, all transfers, assignments, infringements, and registration requirements occurring prior to 1978 are governed by the 1909 Act. Although the focus of this book is on the 1976 Act and works created thereunder, a new work may be based on a prior work protected under the law of the 1909 Act and the cases decided under that Act.

1.1.3. Berne Convention Implementation Act of 1988[14]  → optional

On October 31, 1988, President Reagan signed into law the Berne Convention Implementation Act of 1988, Pub. L. No. 100-568, 102 Stat. 2853 (1988) (hereinafter referred to as the Berne Act). This act was drafted to amend those provisions of the 1976 Act necessary to allow the United States to join the Berne Union through implementation and adherence to the Berne Convention for the Protection of Literary and Artistic Works, as revised at Paris on July 24, 1971.[15]

The Berne Act became effective on March 1, 1989.[16] Implementation of this act does not eliminate the significance of the elements in the 1976 Act amended by it. As was the case with the continuing influence of the 1909 Act after implementation of the 1976 Act, the Berne Act provides that "[a]ny cause of action arising under title 17, United States Code, before the effective date of this Act shall

---

[10] 17 U.S.C. §304(a) (2008).
[11] *Id.*
[12] 17 U.S.C. §304(a)-(b) (2008).
[13] 17 U.S.C. §304(c) (2008).
[14] Pub.L. No. 100-568, 102 Stat. 2853 (1988).
[15] *See* Berne Convention and the WIPO Copyright Treaty, *infra*. Hereinafter, this convention will be referred to as the Berne Convention unless otherwise noted.
[16] Berne Act §13(1).

be governed by the provisions of such title as [was] in effect when the cause of action arose."[17] Thus, in actions for infringement arising prior to March 1, 1989, a work created under the 1909 Act will be governed by the provisions of that act, subject to modifications imposed by the 1976 Act,[18] while works created after 1978 (the effective date of the 1976 Act) but prior to implementation of the Berne Act will be governed under the then current provisions of the 1976 Act.[19]

One significant aspect to the Berne Act is that the Congress made a specific "legislative finding" that the Berne Convention is "not self-executing under the Constitution and Laws of the United States,"[20] that no action may be "brought pursuant to the provisions of the Berne Conventions itself"[21] and that the so-called "moral rights" provisions of the Berne Convention[22] are adequately governed by Federal, State and Common Law outside of the Copyright Act itself.[23] This contradicts elements of the Berne Convention itself, which has been held to directly confer rights on copyright authors *jure conventions*.[24] Yet this is in accord with the understanding of some countries, such as the United Kingdom,[25] and may also be allowable under the provisions of the Convention which provide that at the time of ascension, a country may declare certain provisions of the convention not binding on it.[26]

---

[17] Berne Act §13(b).
[18] *See supra* §1.1.2.
[19] Berne Act §13(b).
[20] Berne Act §2(1).
[21] Berne Act §3(a)(2).
[22] *See* Berne Convention and WIPO Copyright Treaty, infra §5.3.3.
[23] Berne Act §3(b). As though to acknowledge that United States protections are, or were, inadequate, additional moral rights protections are now found in the Copyright Act based on passage of the Visual Artists Rights Act of 1990, title VI of the Judicial Improvements Act of 1990, Pub. L. No. 101-650, 104 Stat. 5089 (1990), which grants to certain types of visual artists specific protections against the mutilation, destruction, or distortion of their works and clear rights of paternity. *See infra* § 1.4.2.
[24] *See* Berne Convention and WIPO Copyright Treaty, infra §5.1.
[25] *See* Stephen M. Stewart and Hamish Sandison, INTERNATIONAL COPYRIGHT AND NEIGHBOURING RIGHTS §3.18 et seq. (1989) (hereinafter cited as Stewart).
[26] Berne Convention art. 28(1)(b).

1.1.4. Digital Millennium Copyright Act/WIPO Treaties Implementation Act

In late 1998 Congress passed the Digital Millennium Copyright Act,[27] a significant revision of the Copyright Act, including within it the WIPO ("World Intellectual Property Organization") Copyright and Performances and Phonograms Treaties Implementation Act of 1998, the Online Copyright Infringement Liability Limitation Act, the Computer Maintenance Competition Assurance Act, and the Vessel Hull Design Protection Act. Like the WIPO treaties, the primary intent of this revision is to revise copyright law to meet the challenges of new technologies, most especially copyright management technologies,[28] computer software,[29] and the Internet.[30] As was the case with the Berne Implementation Act, Congress again affirmed the position that the implementation of the WIPO Performances and Phonograms Treaty did not make either the WIPO Performances and Phonograms Treaty or the earlier Geneva Phonograms Convention (of which the U.S. was already a treaty member) self-executing. They provide no more rights than are explicitly included in the law.[31]

Implementation of the WIPO Copyright Treaty could cause problems. The treaty itself provides that the rights protected under the treaty may not be limited in ways that "unreasonably prejudice the legitimate interests of the author."[32] Indeed, this potential for conflict was confirmed by a ruling of the World Trade Organization in June 2000[33] that the broad exemption of retail and restaurant establishments from liability for the public performance of musical works under the 1998 Digital Millennium Copyright Act.[34]

---

[27] Pub. L. No. 105-304, 112 Stat 2860 (1998).
[28] 17 U.S.C. §§1201 *et seq.2008*.
[29] 17 U.S.C. §117 (2008).
[30] 17 U.S.C. §512 (2008).
[31] 17 U.S.C. §104(d) (2008).
[32] WIPO Copyright Treaty Art. Art. 16 (2).
[33] United States – Section 110(5) of the U.S. Copyright Act Report, World Trade Organization WT/DS160/R 15 June, 2000 (00-2284) accessible at: http://docsonline.wto.org/
[34] *See infra* §1.4.1.4.

1.2. SUBJECT MATTER OF COPYRIGHT

1.2.1. Section 102 Subject Matter of Copyright; In General[35]

Section 102 of the Copyright Act states, in full, as follows:

(a) Copyright protection subsists, in accordance with this title, in original works of authorship fixed in any tangible medium of expression, now known or later developed, from which they can be perceived, reproduced, or otherwise communicated, either directly or with the aid of a machine or device. Works of authorship include the following categories:
1. literary works;
2. musical works, including any accompanying words;
3. dramatic works, including any accompanying music;
4. pantomimes and choreographic works;[36]
5. pictorial, graphic, and sculptural works;[37]
6. motion pictures and other audiovisual works;
7. sound recordings; and
8. architectural works.[38]

(b) In no case does copyright protection for an original work of authorship extend to any idea, procedure, process, system, method of operation, concept, principle, or discovery,

---

[35] 17 U.S.C. §102 (2008).

[36] Although choreography is subject to copyright protection, sequences of yoga poses were held not to be subject to copyright protection. Bikram's Yoga Coll. of India v. Evolution Yoga, 803 F.3d 1032 (9th Cir. 2015).

[37] The Berne Act expands protection in this area to specifically embrace protection of "architectural plans." Berne Act §4(a)(1). Utilitarian works, however, have not been protectable under copyright unless they have copyrightable aspects either physically or conceptually separable from the utilitarian article. See Poe v. Missing Persons, 745 F.2d 1238 (9th Cir. 1984). This concept is currently being challenged in Varsity Brands, Inc. v. Star Athletica, 799 F. 3d 468 (6th Cir. 2015)(cert. granted 2016) in which copyright protection was sought for simple patterns of cheerleader outfits considered to be useful articles. Affirming, the Supreme Court held that those simple patterns could satisfy the copyright eligibility text. 137 S.Ct. 1002 (2017).

[38] The Berne Act expansion relating to architectural works was completed by the Architectural Works Copyright Protection Act, title VII of the Judicial Improvements Act of 1990, Pub. L. No. 101-650, 104 Stat. 5089 (1990) that extended for recognition to the protectability of architectural works.

regardless of the form in which it is described, explained, illustrated, or embodied in such work.

The language of this section is broadly encompassing yet precisely limiting. This is the foundation on which protection of all copyrighted work rests.

1.2.2. "Originality"

The first requirement of copyrightability is that it subsists in "*original works of authorship*" (§102(a), emphasis added). The Copyright Act fails to define this phrase, however, and the House Report explains that the phrase was "intentionally left undefined"[39] and was "intended to incorporate without change the standard of originality established by the *courts* under the present [1909] copyright statute"[40] (emphasis added). The 1909 Act neither defined *originality* nor expressly required originality for copyright protection. However, the courts uniformly inferred such a requirement under Constitutional theories that such protection is affordable only to "authors"[41] under statutory construction of the term *authors* and their successors in interest[42]. Indeed, as the Supreme Court has noted, originality is not only "the *sine qua non* of copyright,"[43] it is Constitutionally required.[44]

It has been held by the courts that for a work to be original, "the author [must have] created it by his own skill, labor and judgment,"[45] The test of originality is one with a low threshold. All that is needed is that the "author" contributed something more than "merely trivial variation"[46] or the mechanical or routine selection and arrangement of facts,[47] or the mechanical translation of a work into a tangible

---

[39] H. REP. No. 1476, 96th Cong., 2d Sess. 51 (1976) [hereafter referred to as H.R. REP.].

[40] *Id.*

[41] U.S. Const, art. I, §8, cl. 8. *See also* Emerson v. Davis, 8 F.Cas. 615 (C.C.D. Mass. 1845); Gray v. Russell, 10 F.Cas. 1035 (C.C.D. Mass. 1839).

[42] *See* 17 U.S.C. §9 (1909 Act). *See also* Remick Music Corp. v. Interstate Hotel Co. of Neb. 58 F.Supp. 523 (D. Neb. 1944), *aff'd*, 157 F.2d 744 (8th Cir. 1946), *cert. denied*, 329 U.S. 809 (1947); Goldstein v. Cal., 412 U.S. 546 (1973).

[43] Feist Publications, Inc. v. Rural Tel. Serv. Co., 499 U.S. 340, 345 (1991).

[44] *Id.* at 347. *See also* In re Trade-Mark Cases, 100 U.S. 82, 94 (1879).

[45] Dorsey v. Old Surety Life Ins. Co., 98 F.2d 872 (10th Cir. 1938).

[46] L. Batlin & Son, Inc. v. Snyder, 536 F.2d 486 (2d Cir.), *cert. denied*, 429 U.S. 857 (1976); Atari Games Corp. v. Oman, 979 F.2d 242 (D.C. Cir. 1992).

[47] Feist Publications, Inc., 499 U.S. at 362.

medium.[48] It is "little more than a prohibition of actual copying,"[49] where, for example, the integration of elements from disparate public domain works may create a new work which is itself eligible for copyright protection.[50] Originality is *not* a judgment of aesthetic merit[51] or artistic merit.[52] This is an important distinction because it assures broad protection of an author's work while preventing a court from formulating a form of censorship whereby protection could be denied simply because the courts do not like what is created.

Significantly, the term *originality* does not encompass a requirement of novelty or ingenuity[53] as is required under patent law[54] and under the Constitutional basis of patent law,[55] although such a requirement had been suggested by Justice Douglas (in a dissent from a denial of a petition for writ of certiorari).[56] The basis of this distinction is that the Constitution distinguishes between "authors" and their "writings" and "inventors" and their "discoveries" and that such a distinction provides a basis for treating the two in substantially different ways.[57] Moreover, it can be argued that such distinctions better serve the intent of the framers of the Constitution than would a conformity of requirements. Whereas "truth" may be hard to identify, practical facts are not. Once a fact is established through the existence of a practical application, it is true for all times. Whereas truth rarely exists in the abstract, it evolves and emerges from what Justice Marshall calls "the marketplace of ideas."[58] On what basis could we determine that such a truth exists, and then how could we protect it without

---

[48] Medforms, Inc. v. Healthcare Mgmt. Solutions, Inc., 290 F.3d 98 (2d Cir. 2002).

[49] Best Medium Publishing Co. v. National Insider, Inc., 385 F.2d 384 (7th Cir.1967), *cert. denied*, 390 U.S. 955 (1968).

[50] *See* Tufenkian Import/Export Ventures, Inc. v. Einstein Moomjy, Inc., 338 F.3d 127 (2d Cir. 2003).

[51] H. REP., *supra* note 39, at 51.

[52] Tenn. Fabricating Co. v. Moultrie Mfg. Co. 421 F.2d 279 (5th Cir.), *cert. denied*, 398 U.S. 928 (1970). *See also* Trifari, Krussman & Fishel, Inc. v. Charel Co., 134 F. Supp. 551 (S.D.N.Y. 1955), and Dieckhaus v. Twentieth Century-Fox Film Corp., 54 F. Supp. 425 (E.D. Mo. 1944), *rev'd*, 153 F.2d 893 (8th Cir.), *cert. denied*, 329 U.S. 716 (1946).

[53] H. REP., *supra* note 39, at 51; Feist Publ'ns, Inc., 499 U.S. at 362. 1296 (1991).

[54] *See* 35 U.S.C. § 101 et. seq.

[55] *See* Graham v. John Deere Co., 383 U.S. 1 (1966).

[56] Lee v. Runge, 404 U.S. 887 (1971).

[57] Alfred Bell & Co. v. Catalada Fine Arts, Inc., 191 F.2d 99 (2d Cir. 1951).

[58] *See* Abrams v. United States, 250 U.S. 616 (1919).

encouraging comment on that "truth"? The purpose of copyright is to encourage such contributions of thought to the common good.[59] It effectuates this purpose by protecting the *expression* of the truth (idea) – its original authorship – rather than the truth (idea) itself.[60]

The protection afforded copyrights and patents are likewise different. Whereas copyright protection is easier to obtain, it offers less protection than afforded a patent. A patent protects the idea in such a way that mere similarity, even if based on *independent* creation, may constitute infringement, whereas copyright infringement exists only where such similarity is based on copying[61] and not where similarity or even identicalness occurs through independent creation.[62] The copyright statute specifically excludes protection of ideas, concepts, and principles.[63]

1.2.3. "Authorship" and "Expression"

Related to the issue of originality is the question of authorship. The statute defines "works of authorship" by providing illustrative categories[64] that do not explain what authorship is apart from how it may be embodied.

The courts have defined authorship in the process of defining originality, and one of the most accurate definitions described the work of an author as creating "an original tangible *expression* of an idea" (emphasis added).[65] It is this *expression* of an idea that copyright law protects, and for this reason, authorship can be more accurately described and understood as the expression of an idea by a creator. This can be more clearly appreciated by comparing Picasso's "Guernica" with Ernest Hemingway's *For Whom the Bell Tolls*, both of which deal with the "idea" of the Spanish Civil War but in distinctly different ways and in different media.

---

[59] *See* Mazer v. Stein, 347 U.S. 201 (1954).
[60] *See* 17 U.S.C. §102(a-b) (2008). *See also U.S. Copyright Law, infra* §§1.2.3 and 1.2.4.
[61] *See* Alfred Bell & Co., 191 F.2d 99. *See also U.S. Copyright Law, infra* §1.13.
[62] *Id. See also* Harold Lloyd Corp. v. Witwer, 65 F.2d 1 (9th Cir.), *cert dismissed*, 296 U.S. 669 (1933), *and* N. Music Corp. v. King Record Distrib. Co., 105 F. Supp. 393 (S.D.N.Y. 1952).
[63] *See* 17 U.S.C. §102(c) (2008).
[64] *See* 17 U.S.C. §102(a) (1)-(7) (2008).
[65] Trifari, Krussman & Fishel, 134 F. Supp. 551.

The line between an "idea" and its "expression" is not necessarily clear nor easily drawn as "[e]very 'expression' ... presupposes an 'idea.'"[66] As framed by Judge Learned Hand, "[N]o principle can be stated as to when an imitator has gone beyond copying the 'idea' and has borrowed its 'expression'".[67] "[T]he right cannot be limited literally to the text, else a plagiarist would escape by immaterial variations."[68] "Decisions must therefore inevitably be '*ad hoc*'".[69] It can be stated that where an idea can only be expressed in one form, the idea and expression are said to merge, and the expression is unprotectable.[70] Where an idea can be expressed in only a limited number of ways, copyright protection is similarly limited to protection against copying that varies from the protected work to only a "trivial degree."[71] In factual works protactable expression encompasses "an author's analysis or interpretation of events, the way he or she structures material and marshals facts, the author's choice of words, and the emphasis the author gives to particular developments."[72] In creative works, protected expression would include "the 'pattern' of the work ... the sequence of events and the development of the interplay of the characters"[73] so long as that pattern is not based upon "unprotectable '*scènes à faire*,' that is, scenes that necessarily result from the choice of a setting or situation."[74] In the context of literary works, it is often difficult to find protection for characters.[75] Objects

---

[66] Gund, Inc. v. Swank, Inc., 673 F.Supp. 1233 (S.D.N.Y. 1987).

[67] Peter Pan Fabrics, Inc. v. Martin Weiner Corp., 274 F.2d 487, 489 (2d Cir. 1960).

[68] Nichols v. Universal Pictures, 45 F.2d 119, 121 (2d Cir. 1930), *cert. denied*, 282 U.S. 902 (1931).

[69] Peter Pan Fabrics, Inc., 274 F.2d at 489.

[70] Herbert Rosenthal Jewelry Corp. v. Kalpakian, 446 F.2d 738 (9th Cir. 1971).

[71] Kregos v. Associated Press, 3 F.3d 656 (2d Cir. 1993), *cert denied*, 510 U.S. 1112 (1994).

[72] Werlin v. Reader's Digest Ass'n., 528 F.Supp. 451, 461 (S.D.N.Y. 1981); Wainwright Sec., Inc. v. Wall St. Transcript Corp., 558 F.2d 91, 95-96 (2d Cir. 1977), *cert denied*, 434 U.S. 1014 (1978).

[73] Atari v. N. Am., 672 F.2d 607 (7th Cir.), *cert. denied*, 459 U.S. 880 (1982).

[74] Walker v. Time Life Films, Inc., 784 F.2d 44 (2d Cir. 1986), *cert. denied*, 476 U.S. 1159 (1986).

[75] *See* Warner Bros. Pictures v. Columbia Broadcasting System, 216 F. 2d 945 (9th Cir. 1954)(Sam Spade character in The Maltese Falcon not protectable to the extent that it is not the story being told but only the chessman in the game of telling the story). Cartoon characters tend to fair better in terms of copyright protection. Walt Disney Productions v. Air Pirates, 581 F. 2d 751 (9th Cir. 1978).

and things can take on characteristics of cartoon characters which may warrant copyright protection. Physical and non-physical qualities of the Batmobile as depicted in numerous comic books and movies were sufficiently delineated to be recognizable as the same character as it has consistent identifiable character traits and attributes to warrant copyright protection.[76] On a more limited level, expression also encompasses a sequence of expressive words,[77] or even a short (e.g., six note) musical sequence.[78]

By understanding this concept of expression we can more easily understand the "authorship" involved in "derivative works"[79] (works based on one or more pre-existing works – such as translations, adaptations, musicalizations, motion pictures, and other audiovisual adaptations of literary works), "compilations"[80] (collections of pre-existing works or facts – such as an atlas), and "collective" works[81] (separate and independent works assembled into a collective whole – such as anthologies and magazines). In these instances, the authorship will occur in the organization, layout, alterations or conversion of the existing work into another medium contributed by the new "author" in creating the new work. The new work is how that author expresses the ideas contained therein, and only that specific new expression is protectable.

At one time, it was thought that a telephone directory or other similar simple assembly of facts could be copyrighted as a compilation based on the labor and effort expended by the compiler of the work in assembling the facts contained in that work. Known as a "sweat of the brow" or "industrious collection" rule, the courts accepted the efforts

---

[76] DC Comics v. Towle, 802 F.2 1012 (9th Cir. 2015). *See also* Halicki v. Halicki Films v. Sanderson Sales and Marketing, 547 F. 3d 1213 (9th Cir. 2008)(car character ELEANOR may be protectable under copyright in *Gone in 60 Seconds* film; although not a cartoon, the car character was considered more akin to a comic book character).

[77] Salinger v. Random House, Inc., 811 F.2d 90 (2d Cir.), *opinion supplemented on denial of reh'g*, 818 F.2d 252 (2d Cir.), *cert. denied*, 484 U.S. 890 (1987).

[78] Baxter v. MCA, Inc., 812 F.2d 421 (9th Cir.), *cert. denied*, 484 U.S. 954 (1987). Recent high profile cases involving music have resulted in a jury decision supporting a claim of infringement in Williams v. Bridgeport Music, cv 13-6004-JAK (CD Cal. 2015) in the Central District of California (the Blurred Lines case) and a jury decision denying infringement in Skidmore v. Led Zeppelin (CD Cal. 2016) (involving Stairway to Heaven).

[79] 17 U.S.C. §101 (2008).
[80] *Id.*
[81] *Id.*

expended by that compiler as a substitute for the normal requirement that an author's work be "original."[82] This line of cases has been overruled. "[O]riginality is not a stringent standard; it does not require that facts be presented in an innovative or surprising way. It is equally true, however, that the selection and arrangement of facts cannot be so mechanical or routine as to require no creativity whatsoever."[83] Thus, simply collecting names, addresses, and phone numbers and arranging them alphabetically is insufficient basis for a claim of copyright.[84] In a related vein, works embodying historical facts may have a limited scope of protection to the extent that protection is sought based on theories of history, whether or not accurate.[85]

Similarly, the arrangement of public documents (e.g., court opinions) with minor alternatives such as the inclusion of parallel references and indications as to how the opinions break down by page numbers in the official source is not protectable.[86] However, an arrangement of plain beads to create jewelry can be assembled in a manner which sufficiently displays stamp of author's originality to warrant protection.[87]

The law continues to protect what is known as "hot news."[88] In these cases protection is offered to gatherers /distributors of time-sensitive, factual information against its appropriation by other distributors of this type of information where such "free riding" by the defendant will threaten the existence of the plaintiff's business or service.[89] What makes this exception interesting is the fact that while

---

[82] *See, e.g.*, Jewelers' Circular Publishing Co. v. Keystone Publishing Co., 281 F. 83 (2d Cir.), *cert denied* 259 U.S. 581 (1922).

[83] Feist Publ'ns, Inc. 499 U.S. at 362.

[84] *Id.* Interestingly, so-called "yellow pages" directories are still protectable as exhibiting sufficient originality. Key Publ'ns v. Chinatown Today Publishing Enters., Inc., 945 F.2d 509 (2d Cir. 1991); Bellsouth Adver. & Publishing v. Donelley Info. Publishing, 933 F.2d 952 (11th Cir. 1991), *vacated*, 977 F.2d 1435 (11th Cir. 1992).

[85] Hoehling v. Universal City Studios, Inc., 618 F. 2d 972 (2d Cir. 1980)(theory in book that the explosion of the Hindenburg was sabotage not copyrightable material).

[86] Matthew Bender & Co., Hyperlaw, Inc., Intervenor v. West Publishing Co., 158 F.3d 674 (2nd Cir. 1998), *cert. denied sub nom.* West Publishing Co., v. HyperLaw, Inc., 526 U.S. 1154 (1999).

[87] *See e.g.*, Jane Envy, LLC v. Infinite Classic Inc., Nos. SA:14-CV-065-DAE, SA:14-CV-081-DAE, SA:14-CV-083-DAE, 2016 WL 797612, at *8 (W.D. Tex. Feb. 26, 2016).

[88] Int'l News Serv. v. Associated Press, 248 U.S. 215 (1918).

[89] Nat'l Basketball Ass'n v. Motorola, Inc. 105 F.3d 841 (2d Cir. 1997).

"hot news" is *not* in and of itself protectable under copyright, because it is factual and does not involve original protectable authorship pursuant to the ruling in *Feist*,[90] if the criteria of "hot news" is found applicable, this protection under the tort of unfair competition or misappropriation is not preempted by copyright. By contrast, the redistribution of timely factual information that does not threaten the existence of the original gatherer/ distributor, such as rebroadcasting up-to-date scoring information taken from the live broadcast of a basketball game, is pre-empted and hence unprotectable.[91]

1.2.4. "Fixed in Any Tangible Medium of Expression"[92]

This element of §102 is both a limitation of copyright (the work must be "fixed"[93]) and an expansion of copyrightability (it eliminates prior limitations on copyrightability of new media of expression).[94] Though not litigated, fixation may in some ways be thought to be Constitutionally grounded, in that the entire copyright law is predicated upon the Constitutional mandate of protecting the "writings" of authors.

1.2.4.1. Limitation—Common Law Copyright

As a limitation, the requirement of "fixation" is the one area that preserves the former common law *copyright* and unfair-competition right previously created and regulated by the states. Under the 1909 Act and prior acts, copyright protection did not vest or become effective until "publication"[95] or until the work was registered for copyright as an unpublished work.[96] By virtue of this requirement, there existed a gap (however long or short) between the creation of the work and the point at which copyright law protected that work. From the founding of the nation up through the enactment of the 1976 Act, courts and state lawmakers have filled that gap with common law

---

[90] Feist Publications, Inc., 499 U.S. 340.
[91] Nat'l Basketball Ass'n v. Motorola, Inc. 105 F.3d 841 (2d Cir. 1997).
[92] 17 U.S.C. §102(a) (2008).
[93] *See* Letter Edged in Black Press, Inc. v. Pub. Bldg. Comm'n of Chicago, 320 F. Supp. 1303 (N.D. Ill. 1970).
[94] *See* White-Smith Music Publ'g Co. v. Apollo Co., 209 U.S. 1 (1908).
[95] Copyright Act of 1909, §6.
[96] *Id.* at §12.

copyright protection and under the terms of unfair-competition statutes.[97] The 1976 Act has preempted the vast majority of common law copyrights and related statutes[98] by vesting copyright protection rights immediately on the fixation of the work.[99] For most purposes, this coincides with its creation (such as a playwright's writing a play). About the only place that creation and fixation do not coincide are in improvisation, pantomimes, and oral sketches (whether rehearsed or extemporaneous). The protection of these nonfixed works extend under common law copyright up until the time that the work is "published" – a term of art identifying the point when the work is made available to the general public.[100] Under this Act, once the work is published or fixed, common law copyright ends, and if it does not comply with copyright law, it falls into the public domain.[101] A public performance of the work does not necessarily mean that it has been published, however.[102]

1.2.4.2. "Any Medium"

This part of §102 was drawn in broad language to anticipate future developments in the media that may warrant copyright protection and to avoid unwarranted rejection of copyright based on the medium in

---

[97] *See* Wheaton v. Peters, 33 U.S. 591 (1834).
[98] *See* 17 U.S.C. §301 (2008).
[99] 17 U.S.C. §301(a) (2008).
[100] *See* Burke v. Nat'l Broad. Co., 598 F.2d 688 (1st Cir.), *cert. denied*, 444 U.S. 869 (1979).
[101] *See* Roy Export Co., 672 F.2d 1095, *cert. denied*, 459 U.S. 826. Note that lack of compliance resulting in a work falling into the public domain has largely disappeared. Works no longer require a copyright notice on first publication or thereafter, registration or renewal, though notice is still beneficial to the copyright owner.
[102] *See* 17 U.S.C. §101 (2008). *See also* Flo & Eddie, Inc. v. Sirius XM Radio, Inc., 827 F. 3d 1016 (11th Cir. 2016)(involving claims of infringement of pre-1972 sound recordings based on state common law copyright claims of reproduction and performance); however in ABS Entertainment, Inc. v. CBS, (CD Cal. 2016), the court there stated that the versions of the old songs it played over the radio were remastered long after 1972, and thus were not actually pre-72 recordings. When that issue was referred to the New York Court of Appeals from referral of the question from the Second Circuit in Flo & Eddie, Inc. v. Sirius XM Radio, Inc. (2d Cir. 2016) the New York Court of Appeals pointed out that New York has never recognized a common law right of public performance for pre-1972 sound recordings and declined to create such a right significantly over concerns about upsetting existing expectations.

which a work is fixed.¹⁰³ It may be simpler to say that the work is protected whether it is typed, dictated into a dictating machine, videotaped, or held in a computer's digital memory. Each medium is satisfactory for fixation and hence for copyright. When a work is transferred from one medium to another (such as from the written page to an audio recording for a "talking book") and the other elements of copyrightability exist (originality, authorship/expression), then the fixation of those elements in association with the underlying work creates a derivative work.¹⁰⁴ This is an important point to consider in allowing any transfer of media of fixation because of the potential for conflict between the original author and the would-be owner of the new material in the new medium. This situation is particularly pronounced in motion pictures and television, where the contributions of numerous creative people are ultimately embodied in the film or teleplay.

1.2.5. "Works of Authorship"

For our purposes, the categories of works of authorship identified by §102(a)(1) through §102(a)(8) will satisfactorily identify works most commonly encountered in the entertainment field. However, it must be noted that these categories are illustrative only and do not preclude expansion as new forms of communication and expression are developed.¹⁰⁵ Those new forms may develop as media for entertainment education, business, or other purposes.

1.2.6. "National Origin"

An additional condition of copyrightability of subject matter is the nationality or domicile of the author as provided in §104 of the Act. Although *all* unpublished works are protected,¹⁰⁶ once the work is published the work is protected only if the author is a national or domiciliary of the United States;¹⁰⁷ a national, domiciliary, or sovereign authority of a foreign nation that is a party to a copyright treaty to which the United States is also a party, such as a country

---

[103] H. REP., *supra* note 39, at 52. *See* 17 U.S.C. §§101-103.
[104] *See* 17 U.S.C. §§101-103 (2008).
[105] H. REP., *supra* note 39, at 52. *See e.g.,* 16 Casa Duse, LLC v. Merkin, 791 F. 3d 247 (2d 2015).
[106] 17 U.S.C. §104(a) (2008).
[107] *Id.* at §104(b)(1).

adhering to the Berne or U.C.C. Conventions;[108] a stateless person;[109] the United Nations or an affiliated organization;[110] or a national, domiciliary, or sovereign authority of a foreign nation that, by presidential proclamation, is determined to provide reciprocal protection to United States copyright (for copyrightable) works.[111] By way of example, works first published in Iran are likely not protectable under copyright in the United States.[112]

Works prepared by the United States government are *not* copyrightable.[113]

1.2.7. Statutory Preemption

In order to exert greater control over copyright related rights and assure more uniformity of protections in this area, the 1976 Copyright Act included a provision preempting, with limited exception, all state common law copyright laws and other laws related to copyright subject matter. Specifically, §301(a) identifies three criteria (all of which must be met) under which state law is preempted by the Copyright Act. First, the state right in question must be a "legal or equitable right" that is "equivalent to any of the exclusive rights within the general scope of copyright as specified by section 106." Second, the right must involve a work fixed in a tangible medium of expression. Third, the work must fall within "the subject matter of copyright as specified by sections 102 and 103." As noted above, it is this second criteria which has preserved the existence of common law copyright protection.[114]

Given the liberalization of the copyright law under the terms of the 1976 Act, where, for example, protection is extended to a work immediately upon creation, the primary effect of this elimination of common law copyright was to replace the potentially perpetual term of common law protection with a fixed term of protection.[115] What is more problematic in the preemption doctrine is its impact on state law

---

[108] *Id.* at §104(b)(1)-(2).
[109] *Id.* at §104(b)(1).
[110] *Id.*
[111] *Id.* at §104(b)(4).
[112] *See* NY Chinese TV Programs, Inc. v. UE Enterprises, Inc., 954 F.2d 847, 852 (2d Cir. 1992) discussing applicability of 17 U.S.C. § 104(b)(1) to works originating in Taiwan.
[113] *Id.* at §105.
[114] *See supra* §1.2.4.1.
[115] *See infra* §1.9.

rights that are similar to, but in some ways different from, copyright or that may have grown out of common law copyright concepts.[116]

A state law which identifies as its subject works clearly falling within the defined subject matter of copyright under §102 and either attempts to expand or limit the scope of protection accorded to that work under the Copyright Act is preempted.[117] A state law that arguably touches upon copyrightable subject matter is not equivalent to copyright, and thus not preempted, where an operative element under that law is absent from a cause of action for copyright infringement.[118] Thus, for example, actions under the law of contract, unfair competition, or conversion, where the required proofs of essential elements such as "consideration,"[119] "consumer confusion,"[120] or the "unlawful retention of a physical object"[121] (respectively) must be shown, are not preempted. However, where the activity sought to be pre-empted is the rebroadcast of a motion picture performance, that is the equivalent of the assertion of a copyright claim even though the claim is styled as a right of privacy and name misappropriation.[122] This distinction is extremely important in relation to the protection of ideas.[123] Conversely, in some circumstances (e.g., the reissuance of classical recordings that have entered the public domain in their country of origin) state common law copyright may serve to protect a work not otherwise eligible for Federal copyright protection.[124] Pre-72 sound recordings are in a category of works not pre-empted by

---

[116] *See, e.g.,* Louis D. Brandeis & Samuel D. Warren, *The Right to Privacy*, 4 HARV. L. REV. 193, 195 (1890).

[117] H. Rep 130-131.

[118] Harper & Row Publishers, Inc., v. Nation Enters, 723 F.2d 195 (2d Cir. 1983), *rev'd on other grounds*, 471 U.S. 539 (1985); Del Madera Properties v. Rhodes & Gardner, Inc., 820 F.2d 973 (9th Cir. 1987).

[119] Smith v. Weinstein, 578 F. Supp. 1297 (S.D.N.Y.), *aff'd*, 738 F.2d 419 (2d Cir. 1984); Acorn Structures, Inc. v Swantz, 846 F.2d 923 (4th Cir. 1988).

[120] Nat'l Broad. Co., v. Sonneborn, 630 F. Supp. 524 (D. Conn. 1985); Ronald Litoff, Ltd. v. Am. Express Co., 621 F. Supp. 981 (S.D.N.Y. 1985).

[121] Oddo v. Ries, 743 F.2d 630 (9th Cir. 1984); Harper & Row, Publishers, Inc., 723 F.2d 195, *rev'd on other grounds*, 471 U.S. 539.

[122] Ray v. ESPN, Inc., 783 F.3d 1140 (8th Cir. 2015)(holding that telecast of wrestler's performances infringed state-law right by act of reproduction, performance, distribution or display and thus preempted by copyright).

[123] *See The Law of Ideas, infra.*

[124] Capitol Records, Inc. v. Naxos of Am., Inc., 372 F.3d 471 (2d Cir. 2004).

statutory copyright, so that protection of both the right of reproduction and the right of performance may be protectable by state law.[125]

1.3. NEIGHBORING RIGHTS

Historically, particularly in countries in Europe, advances in creative technologies have presented challenging problems in copyright. How and on what basis should works like photographs or phonograms be protected? Because these works did not immediately exhibit the level of creativity identified with the traditional arts protected by copyright, many countries hesitated to accord them the same level of protection they accorded to copyrighted works. Nonetheless, these emerging technologies were recognized as deserving of attention. One response was to develop a category of protection known as "neighboring rights" either protected under a separate statute or incorporated as a special class of works within the larger umbrella of copyrighted works. It appears that the United States is increasingly taking this approach. In recent years it has enacted special protection within the copyright statute for creative works not falling within the definition of subject matter set forth in §102. These include (i) a possible "performer's copyright" and (ii) two technical works rights: semiconductor chip products and vessel hull design.

1.3.1. Semiconductor Chip Products

The first of the neighboring rights works to receive protection under the Copyright Act are semiconductor chips and mask works (a series of images representing the layered design for a semiconductor chip).[126] This chapter is largely self-sufficient, in that it provides a complete roster of protections and terms, including a specific term (10 years after commencement) for registration, notice, and so forth.[127]

---

[125] Flo & Eddie, Inc. v. Sirius XM Radio, Inc., 827 F.3d 1016 (11th Cir. 2016)(regarding new issue of law for Florida courts certified to Florida Supreme Court; similar cases pending in other circuits; the Second Circuit certified the issue to the highest court in New York which found that there was no infringement of any common law copyright in that state, Flo & Eddie, Inc. v. Sirius XM Radio, Inc., 70 N.E.3d 936, 952 (N.Y. 2016).

[126] 17 U.S.C. §901 *et seq.*

[127] In that this subject has little application in the field of entertainment, we will not develop the details of this chapter in depth.

Normally, mechanical devices are subject to patent protection. However, presumably because these changes in semiconductor designs more closely resemble the changes in copyrighted works (i.e., finding different ways to express the same scientific facts) they are not appropriate for patent protection.

1.3.2. The Performer's Copyright?

Pursuant to agreements reached during the course of the Uruguay Round of trade negotiations and implemented in the Uruguay Round Agreements Act,[128] the United States Congress added a new and extremely ambiguous Chapter 11 to the Copyright Act (supplemented and supported by criminal sanctions pursuant to the related enactment of 18 U.S.C. §2319A). Under the provisions of this chapter, solely made up of one section (§1101), the fixation, reproduction, transmission, or distribution of copies of a live musical performance without the consent of the performer or performers involved is made "subject to the remedies provided in sections 502 through 505 to the same extent as an infringer of copyright."[129] This is in addition to the previously granted right for performers to share in the royalties earned under the DAT (Digital Audio Tape) statutory licensing provisions of Chapter 10 of the Copyright Act.[130]

The first and most obvious question this raises is does this in fact mean that performers have been given a copyright in their performances? At first glance, there appears little reason for doubt. They have been granted virtually all of the "bundle of rights" under copyright[131] and the right to enforce those rights in the same manner and to the same extent as a copyright owner could enforce in his/her copyright.[132] Yet, if that is what is intended, it is an extremely anomalous type of copyright in that it does not require "fixation" for protection,[133] there are no formalities (such as registration or notice),[134] and no durational limit upon this right.[135] Moreover, in implementing

---

[128] Pub. L. No. 103-465, 108 Stat. 4809 (1994).
[129] 17 U.S.C. §1101(a) (2008).
[130] 17 U.S.C. §1006 (2008).
[131] *See infra* §1.4.4.
[132] *See* Garcia v. Google, Inc., 786 F.3d 733 (9th Cir. 2015).
[133] *See, e.g., supra* §1.2.4.
[134] *See infra* §§1.8, 1.9.
[135] *See, e.g., infra* §1.8.

this section, Congress made no provision allowing for the continued distribution of the multitude of existing works for which the performer's consent may not have been obtained in the past, such as news footage or archival recordings.[136] If this is a form of copyright, courts may be willing to read into it durational limits and fair use standards drawn from other sections in the copyright law. However, arguing against such a finding is the fact that, unlike the rest of copyright law, the provisions of this section do not preempt, "annul or limit any rights or remedies under the common law or statutes of any State."[137] Courts have varied in their subsequent approach to this act and have left open, thus far, some questions regarding its Constitutionality.[138]

The value of the "performers copyright" has, however, been further enhanced by the passage of the Digital Performance Right in the Sound Recordings Act of 1995.[139] In creating the new exclusive right of digital audio transmission of sound recordings, Congress recognized the right of performers to participate in the royalties generated by this right. Royalties generated from statutory licenses for subscription transmission[140] are to be shared according to a formula set forth in the statute: 2½ percent to the American Federation of Musicians for distribution to non-feature musicians who have performed on sound recordings; 2½ percent to the American Federation of Television and Radio Artists for distribution to non-featured vocalists; 45 percent to the featured artist(s) on a per sound recording basis; and 50 percent to the owner of the copyright in the sound recording.[141] (Non-featured musicians and vocalists participate in a collective pool of income rather than a royalty for their work *per se.*) With respect to all other digital transmission licenses, the featured and non-featured

---

[136] Illustrative of how important this issue can be thought to be, consider the care with which Congress drafted the provisions protecting current users of works affected by the restoration of copyright provisions of 17 U.S.C. §104A (2008). *See infra* §1.11.5.

[137] 17 U.S.C. §1101(d) (2008).

[138] *See, e.g.*, U.S. v. Martignon, 492 F.3d 140 (2d Cir. 2007) (discussing prior cases addressing the issue) and Kiss Catalog v. Passport International Productions, 405 F. Supp. 1169 (CD Cal. 2005)(civil case agreeing with constitutionality decision of Martignon).

[139] Pub. L. No. 104-39, 109 Stat. 336 (1995).

[140] *See infra* §1.4.1.6.

[141] 17 U.S.C. §114(g)(2) (2008).

performers are to receive royalties according to the terms of their respective contracts.[142] For non-featured performers, this will undoubtedly be negotiated as a part of their collective bargaining agreement with producers. SoundExchange became a non-profit collecting society for sound recording copyright owners to collect and distribute performance royalties.

Since performance rights in recorded music are recognized in many countries, this legislation may lead to negotiation of reciprocal agreements between organizations administering these rights in those countries where new organizations may be established or existing organizations will add to their existing authorization to administer these rights in the United States.[143]

1.3.3. Protection of Original Designs

In 1998 Congress extended a new form of copyright protection to the creators or original designers of a useful article which makes the article attractive or distinctive in appearance to the public, and to designers of new vessel hulls, including a plug (i.e., a device or model used to create a mold) or mold (i.e., a form or matrix in which a substance for material is used.)[144] Here again, this chapter presents a comprehensive system of regulation from duration to notice to enforcement of rights. It is also a body of rights that resembles other rights including patents (particularly in relation to the hull design) and trademarks (the aspects of design relating to their appeal and recognizability by the public). The difference with respect to patent is that copyright does not require the same high degree of originality, while the difference in relation to trademark is that copyright does not require the acquisition of secondary meaning.[145]

---

[142] *Id.* at §114(g)(1).
[143] *See* David Sinacore-Guinn, COLLECTIVE ADMINISTRATION OF COPYRIGHTS AND NEIGHBORING RIGHTS: INTERNATIONAL PRACTICES, PROCEDURES AND ORGANIZATIONS, §§18.0 *et seq. (1993).*
[144] 17 U.S.C. §§ 1301 *et seq.*
[145] *See U.S. Trademark and Unfair Competition Law, infra* §3.2.3.

1.4. EXCLUSIVE RIGHTS IN COPYRIGHTED WORKS

1.4.1. Copyright Rights

A copyrighted work is an intangible intellectual or artistic property, and the fact that it must be embodied in a tangible medium to be copyrightable does not alter the characteristics of the property. The value of such a property is defined by how it may be exploited. That exploitation depends on the rights that are held by the owner, as defined in §106 of the Copyright Act (emphasis added): *Subject to §§107 through §120, the owner of copyright under this title has the exclusive rights to do and to authorize any of the following:*

1. to *reproduce* the copyrighted work in copies or phonorecords;
2. to *prepare derivative works* based upon the copyrighted work;
3. to *distribute* copies or phonorecords of the copyrighted work to the public by sale or other transfer of ownership, or by rental, lease, or lending;
4. in the case of literary, musical, dramatic, and choreographic works, pantomimes, and motion pictures and other audiovisual works, to *perform* the copyrighted work publicly;
5. in the case of literary, musical, dramatic, and choreographic works, pantomimes, and pictorial, graphic, or sculptural works, including the individual images of a motion picture or other audiovisual work, to *display* the copyrighted work publicly; and
6. in the case of sound recordings, to *perform* the copyrighted work publicly *by means of a digital audio transmission.*

These five fundamental rights – the rights of reproduction, adaptation, publication, performance, and display – are the "bundle of rights"[146] that make up a copyright. They are cumulative rights and in some cases may overlap.[147] The law equally provides specific restrictions on each of these rights in §107 through §121.[148]

---

[146] H. REP., *supra* note 39, at 61.
[147] *Id.*
[148] §§1.4.2 through 1.4.4 and §1.5 identify the sections of the copyright law drawn to restrict each "right." The actual restriction established under copyright law may involve numerous conditions and consequently the respective statutory provisions should be directly consulted with respect to any questions.

1.4.1.1. Reproduction

The right of reproduction refers to "the right to produce a material object in which the work is duplicated, transcribed, imitated or simulated."[149] Examples of this would be printing copies of a book and making multiple copies of a photograph, audio recordings, and films. It has even been held that the downloading of a computer program from a storage device (i.e., a hard disk, a floppy disk, a CD-ROM, etc.) into the active memory of a central processor creates a "copy" of the work requiring the consent of the copyright owner of the computer program, suggesting the difficulties commonly encountered when traditional notions of copyright meet new technologies.[150] Infringement of this right occurs on the reproduction – not the sale or distribution – of the copy (which is a separate infringement of the right of publication).[151]

An example of where this right is separately licensed from other rights occurs in music, where mechanical rights (the right to affix the composition in physical media containing its performance, e.g., in records, tapes, or discs) and synchronization rights (the right to record the composition in synchronization with audiovisual images, as distinguished from audio-only recordings) are frequently licensed directly to a record company or motion picture/television producer, respectively. The rights to nondramatically[152] perform those works in public over the radio or television or in *foreign* motion picture theaters[153] is separately licensed, generally by a performing rights society such as the American Society of Composers, Authors, and Publishers (ASCAP), Broadcast Music, Inc. (BMI), SESAC

---

[149] H. REP., *supra* note 39, at 61.

[150] MAI Sys. Corp. v. Peak Computer, Inc., 991 F.2d 511 (9th Cir. 1993), *cert dismissed*, 510 U.S. 1033 (1994).

[151] H. REP., *supra* note 39, at 61. *See* Capitol Records, LLC v. ReDigi Inc, 934 F. Supp. 2d 640 (S.D.N.Y. 2013)(when a new phonorecord is created on a computer, that act is a reproduction under §106(1) of the Copyright Act.

[152] ASCAP and BMI license only the nondramatic or so-called small performing rights to music. The licensing of dramatic or so-called grand rights to a musical or opera, for example, would be separately licensed by the owner thereof. See Chapters 8 (Music Publishing) and 9 (Theater Law) in THE ESSENTIAL GUIDE TO ENTERTAINMENT LAW: DEALMAKING.

[153] In the United States, under the terms of the consent decrees with the United States Justice Department ASCAP (1960) and BMI (1966) are precluded from collecting performing rights royalties for music that is a part of a motion picture being shown in that theater. Foreign societies are not so restricted. *See* §12.1.3.2.b.5.

(originally, the Society of European Stage Authors & Composers), or an affiliated society abroad to which the owner of the copyrighted composition belongs.[154]

The right of reproduction is restricted to allow limited reproduction of works by libraries and archives (§108), ephemeral records of public events by broadcast organizations (§112), compulsory licenses in nondramatic musical works for records and tapes or by means of digital phonorecord delivery (§115), copies created when a computer is turned on where the use is required to repair that computer (§117), and in connection with noncommercial broadcasting (§118). It may also be limited by the "fair use" exemption (§107). Under §121, Congress has also limited this right by authorizing nonprofit organizations or governmental agencies to make and distribute copies or phonorecords of previously published non-dramatic works in special formats for the blind or other persons with disabilities.

Finally, in order to compensate copyright owners, performers, and musicians for the potential harm caused by private home copying of digital recordings (generally in the form of CDs) by what was then the new DAT format equipment, in late 1992 Congress enacted a new Chapter 10 to the Copyright Act,[155] which authorized the incorporation of technological controls on multi-generational copying of recordings (i.e., the making of copies from copies)[156] and imposed a statutory royalty on DAT blank tapes and DAT recording equipment which is collected by the Register of Copyrights and then distributed by the Copyright Royalty Tribunal to performers, musicians, recording companies, composers, lyricists, and music publishers.[157] It is interesting to note that non-DAT recordings made from any source (i.e., analog recordings, broadcasts, or CDs) though effectively the same type of violation of a copyright owner's reproduction right as one involving DAT copying, is still essentially exempted from coverage as a "fair use." The only explanation for this anomaly is that in the case of DAT technologies, copyright owners organized to lobby Congress for protection from the harms of this technology *prior* to its becoming

---

[154] *See generally* David Sinacore-Guinn, COLLECTIVE ADMINISTRATION OF COPYRIGHTS AND NEIGHBORING RIGHTS: INTERNATIONAL PRACTICES, PROCEDURES AND ORGANIZATIONS (1993); David Sinacore-Guinn, INTERNATIONAL GUIDE TO COLLECTIVE ADMINISTRATION ORGANIZATIONS (1993-1994 Ed.) (1993).
[155] Pub .L. No. 102-563, 106 Stat. 4237 (1992).
[156] 17 U.S.C. §1002 (2008).
[157] 17 U.S.C. §§1003-1007 (2008).

widely available to the public. In the case of prior recording technologies (such as analog magnetic tapes and VCRs) copyright owners failed to organize themselves to seek political protection from the legislature and when they sought protection through the courts, the courts opted to protect the largest number of consumers.[158]

1.4.1.2. Adaptation

A "derivative work" is a work based on one or more pre-existing works.[159] This right may be infringed by actions that equally infringe the right to reproduce: where a recording of a musical work is made, the recording is a derivative work as well as a copy of the original work.[160] The right of adaptation is broader than the right to reproduce because reproduction requires fixation whereas the preparation of a derivative work, such as a ballet, pantomime, or dramatization, may or may not be fixed in a tangible form.[161]

The right of adaptation is limited by the same provisions of the act (§§107, 108, 112, 115, 118, and 121) as is the right of reproduction. With respect to architectural works that have been constructed in a publicly visible location, the architect's copyright does not include a right to prohibit others from making pictorial representations of the constructed building (i.e., photographs, drawings, paintings, etc.), though the commercial licensing of an unauthorized image may be subject to restriction.[162]

As a separate but related issue, it should be noted that to the extent the adaptor has exercised some level of original authorship[163] either in the additions to, arrangements or translations of, or the deletions from the original work,[164] that adaptor acquires copyright in the adaptor's contributions of original authorship embodied in that new adapted work. Subject to the rights retained by the author of the original work

---

[158] *See e.g.*, Sony Corp. v. Universal City Studios, Inc., 464 U.S. 417 (1984).
[159] 17 U.S.C. §101 (2008).
[160] *See* Harry Fox Agency, Inc. v. Mills Music, Inc., 543 F. Supp. 844 (S.D.N.Y. 1982), *rev'd on other grounds*, 720 F.2d 733 (2d Cir. 1983), *cert granted sub nom.* Mills Music, Inc. v. Snyder, 466 U.S. 9032 (1984), *judgment rev'd*, 469 U.S. 153 (1985).
[161] H. REP., *supra* note 39, at 62.
[162] 17 U.S.C. §120(a) (2008).
[163] *See supra* §§1.2.2, 1.2.3.
[164] 17 U.S.C. §101 (2008) (Definition of "derivative work").

and satisfaction of the condition that the adaptor must obtain the prior consent of the original author for said adaption, the new adapted work will have its own set of exclusive rights.[165]

1.4.1.3. Publication

The exclusive right of publication refers to the distribution by sale, lease, rental, or lending of physical copies of the work (or derivative works embodying the work). Infringement of this right does not depend on whether the copies were made lawfully or not. Whereas distribution of unauthorized copies would clearly be an infringement of both rights, a copy made by authority of the copyright owner for archival purposes only (and thus properly reproduced), for example, could not be distributed.

This right is specifically restricted so that the purchaser of a copy of a copyrighted work (such as a book or picture) could subsequently transfer that object (§109). Known as the "first sale doctrine," this has a long tradition in the law.[166] The first sale doctrine embodied in §109 is specifically limited to "works lawfully made under this title." As such, this doctrine does not preclude application of the copyright owner's right to prevent the importation of piratical or grey market copies of the work as embodied in §602 of the Copyright Act.[167] A special provision exists whereby buyers of phonograph records or computer software can sell their copy but may not rent, lease, or lend it (§109(b)). With respect to architectural works that have been constructed in a publicly visible location, the architect's copyright does not include a right to prohibit others from distributing pictorial representations of the constructed building (i.e., photographs, drawings, paintings, etc.).[168]

---

[165] *Id. Also see* Abend v. MCA, Inc. 863 F.2d 1465 (9th Cir. 1988), *cert. granted*, 493 U.S. 807, motion granted, 493 U.S. 990 (1989), *judgment aff'd*, 495 U.S. 207 (1990).

[166] Bobbs-Merrill Co. v. Straus, 210 U.S. 339 (1908).

[167] *See infra* §1.14.2. However, that approach has been significantly limited by the case of Kirstsaeng v. John Wiley & Sons, Inc., 133 S. Ct 1351, 1354-55 (2013). There, the U.S. Supreme Court held that the importation of textbooks lawfully purchased in Thailand could be imported into the United States without violating Section 602 of the U.S. Copyright Law.

[168] 17 U.S.C. §120(a) (2008).

1.4.1.4. Performance

The exclusive right of public performance refers to any rendition of the protected work either by live performers or by means of a reproductive device[169] in a "place open to the public ... or where a substantial number of persons outside of a normal family circle and its social acquaintances"[170] may gather. Unlike the 1909 Act,[171] there is no requirement that the performance be "for profit" in order to infringe this right. Moreover, it should be noted that the "first sale" doctrine as embodied in §109 of the Copyright Act does not affect a copyright owner's performance rights[172] (i.e., purchasing a copy of a movie or a record does not authorize the purchaser to publicly perform that movie or record). The Supreme Court has held that the making available for distribution to a single household a network television program selected and initiated by a consumer is a public performance in violation of the performance right by the company.[173]

The exclusive right of performance is subject to noncompensated use under the fair use exception (§107), the educational, religious, or charitable uses exception (§110), the use of phonograph records during promotions in a record store (§110), and the performance of video games intended for use in coin-operated equipment, purchased for the purposes of and used in a video arcade (§109(e))[174] (although this later provision expired on October 1, 1995,[175] and is inapplicable to more recent works). The law also limits the right by providing for special

---

[169] 17 U.S.C. §101 (2008).
[170] Id.
[171] Copyright Act of 1909, §1.
[172] See Red Baron-Franklin Park, Inc. v. Taito Corp., 883 F.2d 275 (4th Cir. 1989), cert. denied, 493 U.S. 1058 (1990).
[173] American Broadcasting Company v. Aereo, Inc., 134 S.Ct. 2498 (S.Ct. 2014) (not significant enough to overcome copyright infringement). See Disney Enterprises, Inc. v. VidAngel, Inc., No. 2:16-cv-04109-AB (PLAx), 2016 WL 8292206, at *7 (C.D. Cal. Dec. 12, 2016) (defendant downloaded and stripped out what it considered offensive portions of motion pictures before delivering to streaming subscribers; plaintiffs contend it circumvents technical protection measures; court considered this to be infringement at preliminary injunction stage).
[174] This provision was specifically enacted by Congress in the Computer Software Amendments Act of 1990, Pub. L. No. 101-650, 104 Stat. 5089 §803 (1990), to overrule the court decision of Red Baron-Franklin Park, Inc. v. Taito Corp., 883 F.2d 275 (4th Cir. 1989), cert. denied, 493 U.S. 1058 (1990).
[175] The Computer Software Amendments Act of 1990, Pub. L. No. 101-650, 104 Stat. 5089 §804(c) (1990).

statutory licenses for secondary transmission by cable or common carrier (§111) and use by noncommercial broadcasters (§118). Finally, the Berne Act creates a new §116A that modifies the prior §116 to provide that owners of non-dramatic musical works embodied in a phonorecord shall be entitled to negotiate a *voluntary* license for performances of their works (as opposed to the prior §116 statutory license) and only if they fail to enter into such licenses will a statutory license be imposed allowing their use.[176] The major performing rights societies (ASCAP, BMI, and SESAC)[177] and the jukebox industry entered into such a voluntary license arrangement for the period of January 1, 1990 through December 31, 1999,[178] but the decline in popularity (and consequently economic significance) of the machines as a form of public entertainment has taken the issue from the realm of priorities it once occupied for the industry.

In 1998 in the problematically named "Fairness in Music Licensing Act of 1998,"[179] Congress further limited the performance right by exempting certain small public establishments (both dining and non-dining establishments identified by limits on square footage) from coverage where those establishments were transmitting or retransmitting radio or television broadcasts by stations licensed by the Federal Communications Commission.[180] The act limits the types of retransmitting equipment allowable for use by the establishments and precludes public admission charges for viewing or listening to these broadcasts. Significantly, not only are the performing rights societies who normally license these rights precluded from seeking to license these establishments, but courts supervising the licensing of performing rights to broadcast outlets are precluded from considering this type of use in their determination of licensing rates.[181]

While this provision was ruled in violation of the WIPO TRIPS accord (The Agreement on Trade-Related Aspects of Intellectual

---

[176] 17 U.S.C. §116A (2008).
[177] *See* Chapter 8 (Music Publishing) in THE ESSENTIAL GUIDE TO ENTERTAINMENT LAW: DEALMAKING.
[178] 55 Federal Register 28196.
[179] Pub. L. No. 105-298, 112 Stat. 2827, Title II (1998).
[180] 17 U.S.C. §110(5) (2008).
[181] *Id.* at §110(10).

Property Rights) in June 2000,[182] at present adoption of corrective implementing legislation does not appear imminent.

1.4.1.5. Display

The exclusive right of public display refers to exhibition of the protected work or a copy of it (which, of course, is equally protected) in a "place open to the public ... or where a substantial number of persons outside of a normal family circle and its social acquaintances"[183] may gather. Again, unlike the 1909 Act,[184] there is no requirement that the display be "for profit" in order to infringe this right.

It should be noted that although this right would most commonly be thought of as applying to pictorial, sculptural, or graphic works, it applies equally to all other works of authorship,[185] such as displaying copies of a manuscript.

This exclusive right of display is limited by fair use (§107), public display where the copy is located (§109), educational, religious, or charitable use (§110), useful objects (§113), and noncommercial broadcasting (§118). With respect to architectural works that have been constructed in a publicly visible location, the architect's copyright does not include a right to prohibit others from exhibiting pictorial representations of the constructed building (i.e., photographs, drawings, paintings, etc.) (§120(a)). Moreover, the right of display of the building itself is limited by §109. Similarly, a sculptural work displayed in a public space as an architectural decoration may be visually recorded as an element of the landscape and the recording reproduced and displayed without infringing the rights of the creator.[186]

1.4.1.6. Digital Audio Transmission

The exclusive digital audio transmission right is a special type of performing right held by the copyright owners of audio recordings that

---

[182] United States – Section 110(5) Of The US Copyright Act Report, World Trade Organization WT/DS160/R 15 June 2000 (00-2284) accessible at: http://docsonline.wto.org/
[183] 17 U.S.C. §101 (2008).
[184] Copyright Act of 1909, §1.
[185] 17 U.S.C. § 106(5) (2008).
[186] Leicester v. Warner Brothers, 232 F. 3d 1212 (9th Cir. 2000).

is limited to the digital transmission of those works by subscription and interactive subscription services.[187] Under its remaking authority, the Copyright Office extended the protection over non-interactive digital transmission to include the "webcasting" or "streaming" of broadcast radio musical programming over the Internet.[188] The right applies to audio only transmission and does not include transmission of audio-visual works[189] nor would it apply to the performance of an audio only phonogram in front of a live audience (based upon the requirement that a "transmission" be involved).

With respect to non-interactive subscription services and non-subscription broadcast services exceeding certain performance limits, such services are entitled to claim the benefit of a special statutory license subject to certain qualifications (e.g., not publishing an advance playlist; not performing phonorecords in their entirety; limiting the number of selections from a given artist within a certain period of time; etc.), which are intended to prevent the services from becoming an alternative means for consumers to acquire copies of the music they desire without buying it in pre-recorded form or otherwise acquiring it from authorized subscription or "pay per song" services.[190] While this statutory license is subject to the voluntary negotiation of the parties in the first instance, in the event such agreements are not reached in a reasonable period of time, they may be fixed by a copyright royalty arbitration panel to be convened by the Librarian of Congress upon petition by any of the affected parties.[191]

With respect to interactive digital transmission services, in which a subscriber "selects" the music to be transmitted, licenses must be voluntarily negotiated.[192]

This performing right and the licensing of it in no way affect or alter the rights of the copyright owners of the music embodied in those sound recordings.[193] Thus, such services must still be licensed by the

---

[187] 17 U.S.C. §101 (2008).
[188] 37 CFR Part 201, 65 FR 77292 (Dec. 2000). Aff'd in Bonneville Int'l Corp. v. Peters, 347 F. 3d 485 (3rd Cir. 2003).
[189] 17 U.S.C. §114(j)(3) (2008).
[190] H. REP. (DPSR) at 21.
[191] 17 U.S.C. §114(f) (2008).
[192] *Id.* at §114(e).
[193] *Id.* at §114(j).

appropriate performing rights society[194] and, if it is found that the service involves the digital distribution of sound recordings, it will be subject to the payment of mechanical royalties.[195]

1.4.1.7. Internet Carrier Limitation

Exclusive rights in copyright can be infringed in a variety of ways on the Internet, including making copies, storing copies in memory caches, and performing works. Moreover, because the Internet is considered an important public forum for communication and free speech, Congress has been concerned about how best to protect the right of free speech for all of the people seeking to access the Internet. However, protecting the free speech of individuals presents a problem for carriers if those individuals use the Internet in a way that infringes the rights of copyright owners. In order to protect the operators, Congress in 1998 passed the Online Copyright Infringement Liability Limitation Act.[196] The essential focus of the act is to limit carrier liability for copyright infringement caused by the introduction of copyrighted material onto the Internet to actions that are the direct responsibility of the carrier (where for example, the carrier introduces the copyrighted work to the Internet by making it available on a proprietary data base),[197] where the carrier fails to prevent infringement by other users upon appropriate notice of the infringing activity,[198] or where the carrier fails (1) to take appropriate measures to notify users of the existence of policies against their use of the Internet to infringe copyright and (2) to guard against such use[199] without inappropriately intruding upon the privacy of users.[200]

1.4.1.8. Collective Works

Collective works represent something of a challenge. As noted above, they are copyrightable based upon the creative contribution

---

[194] *See* Chapter 8 (Music Publishing) in THE ESSENTIAL GUIDE TO ENTERTAINMENT LAW: DEALMAKING.
[195] *See id.*
[196] Pub. L. No. 105-304, 112 Stat. 2860 (1998).
[197] 17 U.S.C. §512(a) (2008).
[198] *Id.* at §512(c)(3).
[199] *Id.* at §512(i).
[200] *Id.* at §512(m).

made by the editors/publishers in such areas as arrangement, composition, and visual layout.[201] At the same time, most collective works (including those that are most successful) will incorporate the creative copyrighted works of others. Obviously, in order to use these underlying works in the new collective work, the publisher must acquire the rights to use these underlying works in the new collective work. While copyright owners are free to negotiate the exact terms of their licenses,[202] drafting licenses is a process fraught with difficulty and human failure. Ambiguity leads to litigation and, in the end, questions about the legal assumptions of the law. In this case, what are the assumed rights of a publisher/collective work rights owner over his/her collective work in relation to the underlying works?

The copyright statute provides that the collective work rights owner "is presumed to have acquired only the privilege of reproducing and distributing the contribution as part of that particular collective work, any revision of that collective, and any later collective work in the same series."[203] This provision is reasonably clear when we are considering traditional print publications. A publisher can "reprint a contribution from one issue in a later issue of its magazine, and [can] reprint an article from a 1980 edition of an encyclopedia in a 1990 revision of it."[204] But what about the electronic media? What happens when the publisher puts the collective work on the web or on a reference database? Is that a revision? A later collective work in the same series? Or is it a new work or use?

According to the Supreme Court in *N. Y. Times Co. v. Tasini*,[205] it is a new use. When a collective work, like the New York Times or the Wall Street Journal is made available on the web in an archive or data base like Lexis/Nexis, users are not using a collective work, they are retrieving individual works (articles, etc.) totally independent of the collective context in which they originally appeared. Moreover, according to the Court, this rule of narrow statutory interpretation accords with the provisions of §201(d)(2), which provides that each of the bundle of discrete "exclusive rights" provided by copyright[206] may

---

[201] *See supra.* §1.2.3.
[202] *See infra.* §1.10.
[203] 17 U.S.C. §201(c) (2008).
[204] H.R. Rep. 122-123.
[205] N.Y. Times Co. v. Tasini, 533 U.S. 483 (2001).
[206] 17 U.S.C. §106 (2008).

be separately owned and licensed and §404(a), which provides that the copyright notice of a collective work serves to protect *both* the copyright in the collective work and in the individual works contained therein. Given the ubiquity of electronic distribution/availability, a broader right to distribute the works contained in the collective work would make these additional copyright provisions meaningless. There would effectively be no rights to retain or separately license.

What about electronic media that is fixed and distributed in individual copies like a print publication? For example, what about a 30 CD-ROM library entitled "The Complete National Geographic"? On these CDs, the goal is literally to reproduce the exact original content, context and setting of each issue of the collective work. This clearly resembles microfilm/microfiche reproduction of a periodical tacitly approved of in *Tasini*.[207] In *Greenberg v. Nat'l Geographic*[208] the 11th Circuit initially found that the creation of such a library was not protected. This holding was later overruled and the 11th Circuit determined that certain uses were acceptable under *Tasini*.[209] However, uses of images outside the original context of the article in an introductory sequence were not similarly acceptable.[210]

1.4.2. Moral Rights or the Droit Moral

Adherence to the Berne Convention has introduced new controversies within the field of copyright law by its recognition of two types of rights for the benefit of authors not previously recognized by United States Copyright law. Those rights are referred to as *droit moral* or moral rights[211] and *droit de suite*.[212] (Both of these rights developed under French law, which is why they are frequently referred to by their French names.)[213] The most significant of these rights are moral rights.

---

[207] N.Y. Times Co., 533 U.S. 483.
[208] Greenberg v. Nat'l Geographic Soc'y, 488 F.3d 1331 (11th Cir. 2007), *reh'g en banc granted, opinion vacated*, 497 F.3d 1213 (11th Cir. 2007).
[209] Greenberg v. Nat'l Geographic Soc'y, 533 F.3d 1244 (11th Cir), *cert. denied*, 129 S. Ct. 727 (2008).
[210] *Id.*
[211] Berne Convention Art. 6bis.
[212] *Id.* Art. 141ter.
[213] *See* S. Stewart, §4.17 et seq. *Also see* infra §1.4.3 and Berne Convention and the WIPO Copyright Treaty, infra 5.3.3.

Moral rights recognize that "an author's work is a [continuing] reflection of the personality of the creator,"[214] much the way that a trademark reflects on the good will of the creator of the goods or services bearing that trademark. As interpreted by many jurisdictions, there are three basic moral rights which may be referred to as the rights of Publication, Paternity and Integrity.[215] What makes these rights particularly distinctive is that they exist independently of the author's economic rights and may be enforceable after the transfer of exploitation rights to the work.[216]

There was strong resistance to the adoption of the Berne Implementation Act based on the existence of these rights, with some parties claiming that the importation of these concepts into U.S. copyright law would wreak havoc on well-established copyright industries.[217] The adoption of the Berne Act was accomplished in part after Congress heard extensive testimony and determined that "current Federal and State laws provide adequate protections for an author's rights to constitute compliance with Berne.[218] Congress wrote this finding into law in the Berne Act,[219] but Congress was not satisfied with this finding alone. In order to make sure that "[m]oral rights will not come in, if you will [by] the back door by virtue of our adherence to Berne,"[220] several sections of the act specifically direct that laws of the United States are not altered by adherence to Berne[221] and that the Berne Convention is not self-implementing.[222]

Despite the legislative findings that current moral rights protections were adequate, Congress in 1990 enacted the Visual Artists Rights Act of 1990.[223] Under the terms of this act, which amends the Copyright Act, visual artists (i.e., painters, sculptors, photographers, etc.) who create unique or limited edition (i.e., no more than two

---

[214] *Id.* at §4.17 citing WIPO GUIDE TO BERNE 6bis.
[215] *Id.* at §4.17.
[216] Berne Convention art. 6bis.
[217] "The United State Adheres to the Berne Convention" 36 J. COPR. SOC'Y 1, 35 (excerpting the Congressional Record – Senate – October 5, 1988. Senator Hatch).
[218] *Id.* at p. 36.
[219] Berne Act §3(b).
[220] "The United States Adheres to the Berne Convention" 36 J. COPR. SOC'Y 1, 37 (Sen. Hatch).
[221] Berne Act §§3, 4(c) and 6.
[222] *Id.* at §2.
[223] Pub. L. No. 101-650, 104 Stat. 5089, Title VI (1990).

hundred signed copies) works of visual art[224] are entitled to special enhanced protections under the copyright law itself with respect to their rights of "attribution [paternity] and integrity."[225] These rights, though not subject to criminal sanction, are subject to all other remedies applicable to an action for copyright infringement.[226] These rights do not exist, however, if it can be shown that the work(s) was made as a "work made for hire."[227]

One somewhat aberrational aspect of this legislation regards the duration of these moral rights.[228] With respect to works of visual art created on or after the effective date of this act, June 1, 1991, these rights will endure for the lifetime of the author. For works created before the effective date, the titles to which have not been transferred as of the effective date, the terms shall be coextensive with the term of rights under §106 – the full term of the economic rights of copyright.[229] What makes this provision unusual is that under this provision some works created before the provision's effective date will be protected for a *longer* term (i.e., life plus 50 years PMA (abbreviated from the Latin *post mortem auctoris*, or after the author's death)[230]) than will works created *after* the provision's enactment.

This provision has resulted in a number of court actions, including one resulting in a settlement of approximately $200,000 when a new building owner whitewashed a mural on the side of its building.[231] Yahoo similarly found itself in a quandary when it trimmed grass that was part of an art installation.[232] Thus, the provision certainly provides artists with a means to protect their works although the long-term effect of the provision remains to be seen.

---

[224] *Id*. at §106A.
[225] *Id*. at §§501, 506. *See* infra §1.13.
[226] *Id*. at §§501, 506. *See* infra §1.13.
[227] Carter v. Helmsley-Spear Inc., 71 F.3d 77 (2d Cir. 1995), *cert. denied*, 517 U.S. 1208 (1996).
[228] Pub. L. No. 101-650, 1048 Stat. 5089 §106A(d).
[229] *See infra* §1.9.
[230] *Post Mortem Auctoris* or after the death of the author.
[231] Campusano v. Cort, 98-3001 (N.D. Cal, 1999).
[232] Kelly Crow, *It's Yahoo's Lawn, But This Artist Says Keep Off the Grass*, Wall Street Journal, *available at* WSJ.com (October 1, 2007).

1.4.2.1. The Right of Publication

The Right of Publication refers to the author's right to decide whether or not the work is to be made public or, in some jurisdictions (such as France,[233]) the right to withdraw the work after publication. It is not clear from the text of the Berne Convention[234] that this right is required by Berne as a moral right. Moreover, though its application in many countries resembles a moral (i.e., non-economic) right, publication is an economic right as well. As such, it is protected under §106 of the copyright law[235] granting the author the exclusive right to authorize publication (but not to withdraw it after properly authorized publication).

1.4.2.2. The Right of Paternity

The right of paternity refers to the author's right to claim authorship of a published work by (a) demanding that the author's name appear in an appropriate place, (b) preventing others from claiming authorship, or (c) preventing the use of the author's name in connection with someone else's work.[236] Most issues relating to credit for authorship, particularly with respect to the location of credit, are negotiated as elements of the contract under which the rights are to be obtained.[237] Preventing others from claiming authorship may be addressed through the law of unfair competition,[238] as may be claims brought for the use of the author's name in connection with someone else's work.[239] In instances where the publication is unauthorized, for example, the publication of an unauthorized revision or an unpublished work, use of the author's name, even if the author created the work at

---

[233] Stewart §4.18.
[234] Art. 6bis.
[235] 17 U.S.C. §106 (2008).
[236] *See* Stewart §4.19.
[237] *See infra* §8.6.
[238] Perin Film Enter. v. Two Prods., 400 PTCJ (10-19-78) A-13 (S.D.N.Y. 1978). *See infra* § 3.11. However, the ability to use the Lanham Act to do so has been severely curtailed in view of DaStar v. Twentieth Century Fox Film Corp., 539 U.S. 23, 123 S. Ct. 2041, 156 L.Ed. 2d 18 (2003).
[239] Curwood v. Affiliated Distribs., 283 F. 219 (S.D.N.Y. 1922); Geisel v. Poynter Prods., Inc., 295 F. Supp. 331 (S.D.N.Y. 1968).

issue, may constitute an invasion of that author's right of privacy[240] or a defamation.[241]

The right of paternity or attribution with respect to the creators of certain types of works of visual art, as defined in §101 of the Copyright Act, is governed by §106A of the Copyright Act. Under the terms of §106A, the author of a work of visual art "shall have the right to – (A) claim the authorship of that work, (B) prevent the use of his or her name as the author of any work of visual art which he or she did not create ... [and (C)] to prevent the use of his or her name as the author of the work of visual art in the event of a distortion, mutilation, or other modification of the work which would be prejudicial to his or her honor or reputation."[242] These rights may not be transferred, but they may be waived in a writing signed by the artist.[243]

1.4.2.3. The Right of Integrity

The right of integrity identifies the right of the author to protect his or her reputation by preventing others from altering, defacing or distorting the work without the consent of the author.[244] Under U.S. law, this right can be reserved and protected pursuant to contract.[245] However, where these rights have not been reserved, a principle means of protection arises under the law of unfair competition.[246]

Under the Visual Artists Rights Act of 1990, any visual artist may "prevent the intentional distortion, mutilation or other modification of that work which would be prejudicial to his or her honor or reputation ... and ... [may] prevent any destruction of a work *of recognized stature*, and any intentional or grossly negligent destruction of that work is a violation of that right"[247] (emphasis added). (It should be noted that the statute does not define what is a work of recognized

---

[240] Zim v. W. Publishing Co., 573 F.2d 1318 (5th Cir. 1978); *see generally Publicity and Privacy, infra* Chapter 4.

[241] Williams v. Weisser, 78 Cal. Rptr. 542 (Cal. App. 2 Dist. 1969).

[242] 17 U.S.C. §106A(a) (2008).

[243] *Id.* at §106A(e). With respect to a joint work, the signature of any co-author is binding on all other co-authors.

[244] Berne Convention art. 6bis (1).

[245] Royle v. Dillingham, 104 N.Y.S. 783 (N.Y.Sup. 1907); Manners v. Famous Players-Lasky Corp. 262 F. 811 (S.D.N.Y. 1919).

[246] Gilliam v. Am. Broad. Cos., 538 F.2d 14 (2d Cir 1976); Prouty v. Nat'l Broad. Co., 26 F.Supp. 265 (D. Mass. 1939).

[247] 17 U.S.C. §106(a)(3) (2008).

stature, and that gross negligence only refers to destruction of works of recognized stature.) These rights are limited, such that deterioration based on the passage of time, the nature of the materials used in the work of art, factors based on normal display techniques, and non-negligent conservation efforts are not an infringement of the artist's right of integrity.[248] Moreover, if a work of art is incorporated in a building, certain special rules apply. Specifically, if the work of art was incorporated in such a way that it cannot be removed without causing the destruction, distortion, or mutilation of the work, and it was incorporated with the written consent of the artist and with knowledge of this risk, then the artist's right of integrity is waived.[249] If an art work that is incorporated in a building can be removed without destruction, distortion, mutilation, or other modification, then either the author of that work can remove or pay for the removal of the work (in which case title to that work vests in the author) or the building owner can remove it without liability *if* the owner has made a good faith effort to contact the author and has failed, or the owner has contacted the author who then fails to respond within ninety days of written notice.[250] (It appears from a careful reading of the statute that a building owner cannot retain ownership of such a work of art if, for whatever reason, the work of art must be removed and the artist wants to recover title by removing it.)

1.4.3. Droit de Suite

Although applicable to writers and composers with respect to their original manuscripts,[251] the principle beneficiaries of the droit de suite are fine artists (e.g., painters and sculptors) who are given the right to share in the proceeds of the sequential sales or other exploitation of the original works as they pass through economic channels after the first sale made by the artist (*"droit de suite"* being literally translated as "the

---

[248] *Id.* at §106(c); Carter v. Helmsley-Spear, Inc., 861 F.Supp. 303 (S.D.N.Y. 1994), *aff'd in part, vacated in part, rev'd in part*, 71 F.3d 77 (2d Cir. 1995), *cert. denied*, 517 U.S. 1208 (1996).
[249] 17 U.S.C. §113(d) (2008).
[250] *Id.* at §113(d)(2).
[251] Berne Convention Art. 14ter (1).

right to follow", in this case the sales of an artist's works).[252] Recognition of this right is not required by Berne, save that no other country will accord that right to the author of a country that does not recognize the right.[253] Although the United States does not at present recognize such a right of droit de suite, California passed its California Resale Royalty Act, (California Civil Code section 986) in 1976 applicable to original works sold in that state, and the Visual Artists Rights Act of 1990 (the first U.S. law designed to protect "moral rights" of artists in with respect to their identity as authors of original artworks and control over their alteration or destruction) provides that the Register of Copyrights is to conduct a study, in consultation with the Chair of the National Endowment for the Arts, to study the feasibility of implementing such a right and to issue a report to Congress on the results of that study not later than eighteen months after enactment of that act.[254] California's Resale Royalty Act was challenged in the Ninth Circuit which partially invalidated and brought into question its validity, stating that it violated the dormant commerce clause as to out-of-state sales but leaving intact in-state sales.[255]

1.4.4. Performer's Rights

In enacting the amendment to the copyright law creating Chapter 11, Congress created an extremely ambiguous musical performer's right in relationship to their musical performance. Within the specific language of the act, one can discern the entire bundle of copyright rights identified hereinabove (i.e., adaptation, reproduction, publication, and performance), except for the right to "display" a copy of the work in public. Assuming a performer has retained all or some interest in one or more of the exclusive rights to his or her recorded performances (i.e., the performer refrained from transferring "all rights" under a

---

[252] While this is not strictly a moral right, it appears often to be classed with moral rights because it is inalienable and survives the transfer of ownership in any copyright. Berne Convention Art. 14ter (1).
[253] Berne Convention Art. 14ter (1).
[254] Pub.L. No. 101-650, 104 Stat. 5089, Title VI, §608 (1990).
[255] Sam Francis Foundation v. Christie, Inc., 784 F.3d 1320 (9th Cir. 2015)(en banc), *cert. denied* 136 S. Ct. 795 (2016). *See also* District Court decision in which the entire statute was thrown out as unconstitutional under the dormant commerce clause. Estate of Robert Graham v. Sotheby's, 860 F. Supp.2d 1117 (CD Cal. 2012).

broad grant to a producer or other party),[256] some of the problems with this act come to the fore when one considers the impact of this new bundle of performer's rights in relation to traditional rights and the numerous "exceptions" to a copyright owner's exclusive rights. For example, how does this new performer's right affect the exemptions allowing ephemeral records of public events by broadcast organizations (§108)? Does a performer's permission to record a performance in the form of a phonogram allow for the operation of the compulsory licensing provisions of non-dramatic musical works embodied in §115? If so, on what basis is the performer to receive compensation? Unfortunately, these questions remain to be answered by the courts and/or by Congress.

1.5. FAIR USE

The doctrine of fair use is perhaps one of the most misunderstood and troublesome areas in the whole of copyright law.[257] It has long been recognized by the courts that some uses of protected works are fair and justified whether permitted by the owner or not, based on the principle that the purpose of the copyright laws is to encourage creativity and contributions of knowledge to the public good and that others' use of that work may more fully develop and enhance that contribution and the public's access to it.[258] It is "an equitable rule of reason"[259] that prior to the enactment of the 1976 Act was described as "so flexible as virtually to defy definition."[260]

The 1976 Act for the first time recognized and codified this doctrine substantially in the form articulated by Judge Story in his famous 1841 decision *Folsom v. Marsh*.[261] In keeping with its equitable nature, §107 of the act is drawn in such a manner as to allow the courts broad discretion in its application. Although the House Report on the act has indicated that the statute was drafted to incorporate "without change" the doctrine as it has been developed by the courts,[262] the

---

[256] *See* Greenfield v. Philles Records, Inc., No. 1,114 slip op., 750 N.Y.S.2d 565 (N.Y. Oct. 17, 2002).
[257] Dellar v. Samuel Goldwyn, Inc., 104 F.2d 661 (2d Cir. 1939).
[258] *See* Wainwright & Co., 48 F. Supp. 620 (S.D.N.Y. 1976).
[259] H.R. REP., *supra* note 39, at 65.
[260] Time, Inc. v. Bernard Geis Assocs., 293 F. Supp. 130 (S.D.N.Y. 1968).
[261] Folsom v. Marsh, 9 F. Cas. 342 (C.C.D. Mass. 1841).
[262] H. REP., *supra* note 39, at 66.

statute does, in fact, alter the ambiguities of the doctrine by identifying a four-factor test to be considered in determining fair use,[263] as discussed in the sections which follow.

Case law for the periods prior to the enactment of the 1976 Act remains a persuasive force in identifying whether a use is fair or not. Nonetheless, as decisions being rendered on the provisions of the 1976 Act illustrate, arguments based on the four factors are increasingly persuasive. It should be noted that no one factor is determinative. Each must be considered in relation to the other "factors," along with other relevant facts in each individual case to reach an equitable result. Suffice it to say, however, that "Fair Use" is a defense against an infringement claim, and does not *per se* constitute a right under copyright.

1.5.1. "The Purpose and Character of the Use"[264]

The first factor to consider is the purpose and character of the use. The statute identifies six uses including "criticism, comment, news reporting, teaching (including multiple copies for classroom use), scholarship or research"[265] as types of use that are normally to be considered fair. Additional types of acceptable uses are for parody or burlesque,[266] mimicry,[267] and biographies.[268] The unifying concept supporting all these uses appears to be that each of these uses furthers the intent of the copyright law by assisting the public's access to and understanding of the protected works. Moreover, these uses are, in themselves, frequently copyrightable contributions of knowledge to the public good. Nonetheless, and notwithstanding the fact that these uses are generally considered fair, specific circumstances of the actual use that violate the other elements of the four-factor test could result in a finding that the use was unfair.[269]

---

[263] Pacific & S. Co. v. Duncan, 744 F.2d 1490 (11th Cir. 1984).
[264] 17 U.S.C. §107(1).
[265] *Id.* §107.
[266] *See* Loew's, Inc. v. CBS, Inc., 131 F. Supp. 165 (S.D. Cal. 1955), *aff'd sub nom. Benny v. Loew's Inc.*, 239 F.2d 532 (9th Cir. 1956), *cert. granted sub nom.* CBS, Inc., v. Loew's, Inc., 353 U.S. 946 (1957), *aff'd*, 356 U.S. 43), *reh'g denied*, 356 U.S. 934 (1958).
[267] *See* Bloom & Hamlin v. Nixon, 125 F. 977 (C.C.E.D. Pa. 1903).
[268] *See* Rosemont Enters., Inc. v. Random House, Inc., 366 F.2d 303 (2d Cir.1966), *cert. denied*, 385 U.S. 1009 (1967). *But see* Salinger, 811 F.2d 90, opinion supplemented on denial of reh'g, 818 F.2d 252, *cert. denied*, 484 U.S. 890.
[269] *See* Harper & Row Publishers, Inc., 471 U.S. 539.

The second part of this test is whether the "use is of a commercial nature or is for nonprofit educational purposes."[270] Traditionally, the fact that a use was of a commercial nature, while not determinative, is presumptively unfair, subject only to the weight of other factors.[271] Finding that a use was for a nonprofit educational purpose did not necessarily mandate a finding of fair use,[272] although in most cases it was clearly a factor in favor of such a finding. In the case *Campbell v. Acuff-Rose Music, Inc.*,[273] the Supreme Court ruled that this traditional presumption did not apply to parodies, in that virtually all parodies are intended for commercial use.

Though specifically limited to parodies, the holding in *Acuff-Rose* tends to suggest that this character of use test is really nothing more than an elaboration of the fourth factor test of whether or not the use impacts the market for the copyrighted work. In this light, the commercial use of a work evidences a market interest in the protected work. The character would impact a market analysis in the sense that a use for purposes of criticism and/or parody is not a market an owner would typically license. As argued by the Court, the central purpose is to see if the work "supersedes" the original or instead adds something new with a different purpose. To the extent that the new work is "transformative" of the original, it furthers the purpose of copyright "to promote the useful Arts" (Const., Art. I, §8, cl. 8). The more transformative its character, the less will be the significance of its commercial nature.

Applying this new analysis to the question of parody use, the Court in *Acuff-Rose* noted that the nub of parody is the use of some part of a prior work "to create a new one that, at least in part, comments on [a pre-existing] work. If, on the contrary, the commentary has no critical bearing on the substance or style of the original ... the claim to fairness in borrowing from another diminishes accordingly (if it does not vanish)." The only question is not the quality of the parody, but whether or not "a 'parodic' character may reasonably be perceived."

---

[270] 17 U.S.C. §107(1) (2008). *See also U.S. Copyright Law, supra* §1.2. A derivative work that is *not* fixed in a tangible form is protectable by common law copyright.

[271] *See* Sony Corp., 464 U.S. 417 (1984); Pacific & S. Co., 744 F.2d 1490; Triangle Publications v. Knight-Ridder Newspapers, 626 F.2d 1171 (5th Cir. 1980); Abend, 863 F.2d 1465, *aff'd sub nom.*, Stewart v. Abend, 495 U.S. 207.

[272] *See* Marcus v. Rowley, 695 F.2d 1171 (9th Cir. 1983), and Wihtol v. Crow, 309 F.2d 777 (8th Cir. 1962).

[273] Campbell v. Acuff-Rose Music, Inc., 510 U.S. 569 (1994).

The *Acuff-Rose* approach may also apply to provide greater weight to the analysis of fair use within the traditionally protected category of character of uses (e.g., news reporting, etc.). For example, use of a newsworthy video tape as news would clearly violate the fourth factor measuring the use's effect on the market for the protected video tape, whereas using an edited clip from the same video tape within a larger montage to promote the news program may be protected because of the substantial *transformation* of limited portions of the work.[274]

Probably beginning with *Campbell v. Acuff-Rose Music, Inc.*, the concept of "transformative use" began to appear in fair use decisions. Essentially, many but not all courts have found fair use to occur when a newly created work is determined to be transformative. Concern has been raised that this defense is coming close to swallowing the entire concept of copyright. Cases finding a work being fair use as transformative includes the Google Book Search case,[275] the use of 67 seconds of Abbott and Costello's "who's on first" routine in a play.[276] One court has found collages and superimposition of incongruous images on copyrighted personal photographs of Jamaican natives to be transformative and therefore not infringing .[277] A unique application of the fair use doctrine was invoked as a sword in establishing copyright protection for a stage play parody of the motion picture *Point Break*.

1.5.2. "The Nature of the Copyrighted Work"[278]

The second test is the nature of the work. Copyright does not protect facts or ideas; it protects the *expression* of those facts or ideas.[279] Therefore, works of a factual, historical, or scientific nature would provide a greater license for fair use than would the use of "a creative work"[280] because it might be argued that the authors of the

---

[274] L.A. News Serv. v. CBS Broad., Inc., 305 F.3d 924 (9th Cir.), amended & superseded, 313 F.3d 1093 (9th Cir. 2002).
[275] Authors Guild v. Google, 804 F.3d 202 (2d Cir. 2015).
[276] TCA Television Corp. v. McCollum, 117 USPQ 2d 1452 (S.D.N.Y. 2015), 839 F.3d 168, 192 (2d Cir. 2016)(reversed finding that use of 67 seconds of the Abbott and Costello "who's on first" sketch was not fair use).
[277] Carriou v. Prince, 714 F.3d 694 (2d Cir. 2013).
[278] 17 U.S.C. §107(2)(2008).
[279] *See supra* §1.2.
[280] Harper & Row Publishers, Inc., 471 U.S. 539; Abend, 863 F.2d 1465, *aff'd sub nom.*, Stewart v. Abend, 495 U.S. 207; N.Y. Times Co. v. Roxbury Data Interface, Inc., 434 F. Supp. 217 (D.N.J. 1977).

former intend that others make use of the work as prior authority.[281] Works that are created as contributions to public discourse, such as an editorial or letter to the editor, similarly invite fair use – even when the contribution takes the form of a creative work (such as a photograph).[282] The market they are being published in is one which invites comment and reaction which, again, it is assumed was intended by the author.

Embodied in this factor, a number of recent decisions have stressed the significance of whether a work is published or unpublished.[283] Although in each of the cases there were issues about how the "infringing author" obtained copies of the unpublished works (through theft[284] or breaches of confidentiality agreements[285]) that could have influenced the court, the rationale properly presented by these courts for their holdings was that an author's right of "first publication" deserves special protection. "[U]npublished, copyrighted material very rarely will be the subject of fair use ... [T]he right not to publish is a most important one ... [as is] the choices of when, where, and in what form first to publish a work ..." [citations omitted].[286] Until an owner elects to fully disclose and exploit the value or the work, no other person should be able to usurp the original owner's initial right. Moreover, this position is consistent with the terms of the Berne Convention, which specifies that the right to "make quotations from a work" (for fair use) applies only to works that have "already been lawfully available to the public."[287]

---

[281] *See* Sampson & Murdock Co. v. Seaver-Radford Co., 140 F. 539 (1st Cir. 1905).

[282] Baraban v. Time Warner Inc., No. 99 CIV. 1569 (JSM), 2000 WL 358375 (S.D.N.Y. April 6, 2000).

[283] Harper & Row Publishers, Inc., 471 U.S. 539; Salinger, 811 F.2d 90, opinion supplemented on denial of reh'g, 818 F.2d 252, *cert. denied*, 484 U.S. 890; New Era Publications Int'l ApS v. Henry Holt & Co., 873 F.2d 576 (2d Cir.), *reh'g denied*, 884 F.2d 659 (2d Cir. 1989), *cert. denied*, 493 U.S. 1094 (1990). See Monga v. Maya Magazines, Inc., 688 F.3d 1164 (9th Cir. 2012)(unpublished news photos of clandestine wedding not fair use).

[284] Harper & Row Publishers, Inc., 471 U.S. 539.

[285] Salinger, 811 F.2d 90, opinion supplemented on denial of reh'g, 818 F.2d 252, *cert. denied*, 484 U.S. 890.

[286] New Era Publ'ns Int'l v. Henry Holt & Co., Inc., 884 F.2d 659, 661 (2d Cir. 1989), *cert. denied*, 493 U.S. 1094 (1990).

[287] Berne Convention Art. 10 (1).

It must be stressed that the fact a work is unpublished does not establish a *per se* violation of copyright or a denial of fair use. This fact has been statutorily affirmed by the 1992 enactment of P.L. 102-492 amending § 107 of the Copyright Act by adding the following sentence: "The fact that a work is unpublished shall not itself bar a finding of fair use if such finding is made upon consideration of all the above factors."[288] The "fair use test remains a totality inquiry, tailored to the particular facts of each case."[289] What these decisions and the new amendment suggest is that in most instances, a plaintiff will prevail on this factor (i.e., "the nature of the work") when the work is unpublished. Yet even this idea must be considered in the context of the case. It may be that works that are unpublished but *not* held in confidence,[290] or are not commonly available to the public, where such unavailability is not by virtue of the owner restricting such access may provide greater justification for fair use.[291]

1.5.3. "The Amount and Substantiality of the Portion Used"[292]

There is a widespread misconception that there is a magic number of words or lines or bars of music that are allowable as fair use. There is no such magic number.[293] The test is "the *amount and substantiality* of the portion used in relation to the copyrighted work as a *whole*"[294] (emphasis added).

This requires a consideration of both quantitative[295] and, more importantly, qualitative substantiality. Clearly, a use that reproduces the complete original work without license or statutory privilege would

---

[288] *Cf.* H. Rep. 102-836, 102d Cong., 2d Sess. 2 (1992).
[289] Wright v. Warner Book, Inc., 953 F.2d 731 (2d Cir. 1991).
[290] *See* Diamond v. Am-Law Publishing Corp., 745 F.2d 142 (2d Cir. 1984).
[291] S. REP. No. 473, 94th Cong., 1st Sess. 64 (1975) [hereinafter cited as S. REP.].
[292] 17 U.S.C. §107(3) (2008).
[293] *See* Am. Institute of Architects v. Fenichel, 41 F. Supp. 146 (S.D.N.Y. 1941).
[294] 17 U.S.C. §107(3) (2008).
[295] Ass'n of Am. Med. Colleges v. Mikaelian, 571 F. Supp. 144 (E.D. Pa. 1983), *aff'd,* 734 F.2d 3 (3d Cir.), *aff'd,* 734 F.2d 6 (1984); New Era Publ'ns Int'l. v. Carol Publishing Group, 904 F.2d 152 (2d Cir.), *stay denied,* 497 U.S. 1054, *cert. denied,* 498 U.S. 921 (1990).

be an infringement.²⁹⁶ However, equally offensive would be the usage of a small percentage of the original work if that percentage was critical to the original work.²⁹⁷ The test is measured as to the original work and not as to the amount of substantiality in relation to the new work.²⁹⁸ Certainly the opening four notes of Beethoven's *Fifth Symphony*, if protected, could not be copied without liability. Even a close paraphrasing of an original expressive sequence can be an infringement.²⁹⁹

The Ninth Circuit has recently held that the use of a seven-second clip of Ed Sullivan introducing the musical group the Four Seasons and not containing any musical performance, when used in the musical production of the Jersey Boys to suggest the occurrence of a career milestone in a biographical context, was both sufficiently incidental and insignificant to constitute a fair use.³⁰⁰ There are rare cases in which reproduction of the whole work may be justified as a fair use where reproduction of the work is necessary to encourage the creation of transformative works that promote public discourse and the free exchange of ideas.³⁰¹ In a book critical of nuclear energy, the author reproduced a photographic ad put out by the nuclear industry and commented on its use by the nuclear industry. Elements of the work were altered (it was reduced in size and it was printed in black and white instead of color) so that it was clearly distinguishable from the original, and used for a different market. Though it did reproduce the entire work, it used no more than was necessary for the purpose of commentary and criticism. Because its use did not violate other elements of the four factor test, the court ruled this a fair use. More recently, Steven Vander Ark, a Harry Potter fan and "scholar", compiled an online "Harry Potter Lexicon" that the Harry Potter

---

²⁹⁶ *See* Benny v. Loew's, Inc., 239 F.2d 532 (9th Cir.1956), *cert. granted sub nom.* CBS, Inc. v. Loew's, Inc., 353 U.S. 946 (1957), *aff'd*, 356 U.S. 43, *reh'g denied*, 356 U.S. 934 (1958).

²⁹⁷ *See* Meredith Corp. v. Harper & Row Publishers, 378 F. Supp. 686 (S.D.N.Y.), *aff'd*, 500 F.2d 1221 (2d Cir. 1974); Harper & Row Publishers, Inc., 471 U.S. 539.

²⁹⁸ *See* Drury v. Ewing, 7 F. Cas. 1113 (C.C.S.D. Ohio 1862); Harper & Row, Publishers, Inc., 471 U.S. 539; Abend, 863 F.2d 1465, *aff'd sub nom.*, Stewart v. Abend, 495 U.S. 207.

²⁹⁹ Salinger, 811 F.2d 90, *opinion supplemented on denial of reh'g*, 818 F.2d 252, *cert. denied*, 484 U.S. 890.

³⁰⁰ SOFA Entertainment, Inc. v. Dodger Productions, Inc., 2013 WL 1004610 (9ᵗʰ Cir. 2013)

³⁰¹ Baraban, No. 99 CIV. 1569 (JSM) 2000 WL 358375.

Books' author, J.K. Rowling, actually acknowledged as a "prompt" for obscure details in her work on series novels which followed the lexicon's creation. Nonetheless, when Vander Ark sought to publish the project in book form, Rowling and Warner Bros. sued for copyright infringement. The trial court guides, in assessing Vander Ark's fair use defense, determined that the guides substantial borrowing from the Rowling novels was of itself a transformative use, but it too heavily reproduced expressive elements of the novels and other published "Potter" commentaries (rather than merely addressing elements of story or character necessary for its purpose), and that the derivative markets for Rowling licensed secondary works, if not the market for the novels themselves, could consequently be damaged. Vander Ark's publisher appealed to the Second Circuit, but dropped its appeal when Vander Ark reworked the Lexicon in a manner which appeased Rowling and Warner Bros., and the work was eventually published in a suitably revised form.[302]

This test is somewhat modified when applied to a case involving a parody. Here, the problem is that a parody *necessarily* takes the original work's most distinctive or memorable features so as to "conjure up" the original in the audience's mind.[303] The question here becomes whether or not the contributions of the parody are substantial or insubstantial when compared to the copied portions of the original. The less contributed by the parodist, the less likely one is justified in finding a fair use.

1.5.4. "The Effect of the Use upon the Potential Market for or Value of the Copyrighted Work"[304]

The fourth factor in the test goes to the economic effect of the use on the original work and has emerged as the most important consideration in fair use cases.[305] This factor goes to the heart of copyright law – namely, that an author should be granted a limited monopoly to his or her work (an economic incentive) in order to

---

[302] *See* Warner Bros. Entertainment v. RDR Books, 575 F. Supp. 2d 513 (S.D.N.Y. 2008).
[303] Campbell, 510 U.S. 569.
[304] 17 U.S.C. 107(4).
[305] *See* Harper & Row, Publishers, Inc., 471 U.S. 539; Wainwright Sec., Inc., 558 F.2d 91, *cert. denied*, 434 U.S. 1014. *See also* Ladd, *The Harm of the Concept of Harm in Copyright*, 30 J. COPR. Soc. 421 (1983).

encourage the creation of that work.[306] Allowing others to usurp the result of that incentive for themselves would clearly defeat that intent. However, this test is more than a test of *pecuniary* damages to the copyright owner.[307] It is a test that should properly discover whether or not that type of use would significantly impair the value[308] or potential value[309] of the plaintiff's work.

One recent decision has noted that "in cases where we have found the fourth factor to favor a defendant, the defendant's work filled a market niche that [it is reasonable to expect that] the plaintiff simply had no interest in occupying. [E.g., Copyright owners rarely review or parody their own works.] On the other hand, it is a safe generalization that copyright holders, as a class, wish to continue to sell the copyrighted work and may also wish to prepare or license such derivative works as book versions or films."[310] Building on this analysis, the Supreme Court has asserted that there is no protectable derivative market to be considered in relation to criticism, in that owners would not license criticism of their works, and hence, criticism is removed from the notion of a "potential market" under this factor[311] (unless, of course, it can be shown that the critical elements of the publication are so insubstantial as to fail the test of the character of the use).[312] Parody, on the other hand, while having a critical quality, is not pure criticism of the original. Thus, to evaluate potential market impact, one must consider whether or not the new work "substitutes" for the original in the relevant market, either in its original form or in a derivative form.[313]

Under this rubric, it is possible to use an entire work in a modified form without harming the market for the work. In *Kelly v. Arriba Soft Corp.*,[314] the Ninth Circuit Court of Appeal held that the creation and use of a thumbnail copy of copyrighted images used in and by a

---

[306] *See* Mazer, 347 U.S. 201.
[307] *See* Marcus, 695 F.2d 1171.
[308] *See* Harper & Row Publishers, Inc., 471 U.S. 539; Sony Corp., 464 U.S. 417.
[309] *See* Salinger, 811 F.2d 90, *opinion supplemented on denial of reh'g*, 818 F.2d 252, cert denied, 484 U.S. 890; Hustler Magazine, Inc. v. Moral Majority, Inc., 796 F.2d 1148 (9th Cir. 1986).
[310] Twin Peaks Prods, Inc. v. Publ'ns Int'l Ltd., 996 F.2d 1366 (2d. Cir. 1993).
[311] Campbell, 510 U.S. 569.
[312] *See supra* §1.5.2.
[313] Campell, 510 U.S. 569.
[314] Kelly v. Arriba Soft Corp., 280 F.3d 934 (9th Cir. 2002), *opinion withdrawn & superseded on denial of reh'g*, 336 F.3d 811 (9th Cir. 2003).

software search engine falls within the fair use doctrine. However, display of the same image full size within the same search engine violated a photographer's exclusive right to publicly display his work. While the thumbnail version could in no way affect the market of the work, the full size version clearly served the market of computer generated display. More recently, the Second Circuit found that the appearance of seven substantially reduced reproductions of Grateful Dead concert posters controlled by the Bill Graham Archives in a book on the 33-year history of the band was transformative (in the context of its biographical intent), and (noting that the reproductions in question represented "less than one fifth of one percent of the book") that this appearance of the limited and substantially reduced images did not compete with or otherwise diminish demand for the original works.[315] This issue continues to be tested both in the United States and worldwide.[316] Similarly, an artist's highly transformative parody use of a popular children's doll constitutes nominative fair use where there is no discernible impact on other derivative uses of the doll in question.[317]

In considering market effect, two final points must be noted. First, market effect is measured according to the market where the infringing work is being exploited. Thus, in the case of a derivative work, the market effect is measured according to that derivative market, not whether the use impacts the market for the original work in its original form in its originally intended market.[318] Second, the fact that the infringement promotes the value of the original work (such as a film producer taking an unknown song and making it a hit as a result of its inclusion in that producer's film, or a webcaster streaming a clip from a studio picture, ostensibly to promote video or DVD sales of that picture from the webcaster's or other online sites[319]) does *not* make an infringement into a fair use.[320]

---

[315] Bill Graham Archives v. Dorling Kindersley, Ltd., 488 F.3d 605, 614-615 (2d Cir. 2006). The book in question, The Grateful Dead, the Illustrated Trip by Robert Hunter, Stephen Peters, Chick Wills and Dennis McNally (DK Adult, 2003).

[316] *See, e.g.,* Perfect 10, Inc. v. Google, Inc., No. CV 04-9484 AHM (SHX), 2008 WL 4217837 (C.D. Cal. July 16, 2008); German Case Nos. 308 O 42/06 and 308 O 248/07 (Hamburg Regional Court 2008).

[317] Mattel, Inc. v. Walking Mountain Prods, 353 F. 3d 792 (9th Cir. 2003).

[318] *Id.*

[319] *See* Video Pipeline v. Buena Vista Home Entm't, Inc., 342 F. 3d 191 (3d Cir. 2003), *cert denied*, 540 U.S. 1178 (2004).

[320] *Id.*

Private copying for use by the consumer has been protected, where, for example, the consumer tapes copyrighted programs with his or her VCR.[321] This private use exemption is lost, however, when it is being facilitated on a large scale. This has happened on the Internet on sites set up to facilitate the copying and sharing of videograms (broadcast programs and DVD discs[322]) and music.[323] While the copying was being performed by individuals, these web sites provided the technology to facilitate that copying on a massive scale, clearly threatening the markets for owners of these works.[324] Meanwhile, for ISPs and software services whose facilitation of such file sharing is less direct (e.g., files are not directly stored on the services facilities, or the software enables peer to peer file sharing but doesn't direct the flow of content among users), liability may be avoided, although this possibility is certainly diminished where the majority of files transferred are illegal downloads.[325]

It now seems that even massive duplication of copyrighted materials for the purpose of extensive albeit transformative republication may constitute fair use. Since 2002, Google has been digitizing millions of protected and public domain books from libraries for its Google Library Project, providing access to copies from this archive to the source libraries and made this database generally search accessible in 2004. Although full copies of public domain works could be accessed, Google offered only "snippets" of copyright protected works to online search, and did not thereby provide access (even via repeat searches) to

---

[321] Sony Corp., 464 U.S. 417.

[322] *See* the actions against RecordTV.com and SCOUR. Details and the complaints in these cases can be viewed on the Motion Picture Association of America web site at: www.mpaa.org.

[323] A&M Records Inc. v. Napster Inc., 239 F. 3d 1004 (9th Cir. 2001).

[324] A study by PEW indicated that as of June 2000 there were over 13 million "Freeloaders on the Internet making over 1 billion music files available for copying!" *available at* http://www.pewinternet.org/report_display.asp?r=16 (June 8, 2000). Although many legitimate sources are now available for legal music downloads, illegal downloads still outnumber legal ones. Joseph Palenchar, NPD: Illegal Downloads Outpace Legal Downloads By 10:1 Margin, *available at* http://www.twice.com/article/CA6428045.html (March 26, 2007).

[325] *See* Metro-Goldwyn-Mayer, Inc. v. Grokster, 259 F. Supp. 2d 1029, 1039-1041 (C.D. Cal. 2003), aff'd, 380 F.3d 1154 (9th Cir.), *cert. granted*, 543 U.S. 1032 (2004), *vacated & remanded*, 545 U.S. 913 (2005).

full books. In 2005 both the Author Guild[326] and the Association of American Publishers[327] filed suit, separately, to block the continuing practice as to copyrighted works for which Google had not secured express license or waivers for digital duplication and publication. The Authors Guild sought damages on behalf of the class it intended to certify of $750 per scanned book – thus potentially billions of dollars – in damages from Google. Settlement negotiations commenced in 2006 and seemed destined for closure in 2009 when the supervising court dismissed the settlement in a Fairness Hearing primarily on anti-trust grounds, [328] and eventually dismissed the Authors Guild claim on fair use grounds, finding Google's program constituted fair use, on balance, on the basis of all four of the traditional statutory use criteria for such analysis – transformative usage (digitization for archival and research purposes), the nature of the copyrighted works exploited (primarily published, non-fiction works), the amount and substantiality of portion used (with searches not delivering full text access to scanned books, even if scanned in their entirety), and effect on potential market or value (where the books digitized were owned by and already available in collaborating libraries, and the Google Library provide access to snippets and not full access to protected texts), and that Google's purpose was to transform "expressive text into a comprehensive word index that helps readers, scholars, researchers, and others find books."[329] The Authors Guild appeal was denied review by the Supreme Court in 2016, leaving in place a Second Circuit decision which will have marked effect on the expansion of search engine "mining" of copyrighted materials to produce new forms of "transformative" online content.[330]

---

[326] Authors Guild et al. v. Google, Inc., no. 05 Civ. 8136 (S.D.N.Y. Sept. 20, 2005) (http://www.authorsguild.org/wp-content/uploads/2008/10/Authors-Guild-v-Google-09202005.pdf)

[327] The McGraw-Hill Companies, Inc. et al v. Google, Inc., no 05 Civ. 08881 (S.D.N.Y. Oct. 19, 2005) (http://thepublicindex.org/docs/complaint/publishers.pdf)

[328] Authors Guild et al. v. Google, Inc., no. 05 Civ.8136 (S.D.N.Y. March 22, 2011), order (http://www.copyright.gov/docs/massdigitization/statements/gbs_opinion.pdf)

[329] Authors Guild et al v. Google, Inc., no 05 Civ. 8136 (S.D.N.Y., Nov. 14, 2013), opinion (http://www.scribd.com/doc/184176014/Judge-Denny-Chin-Google-Books-opinion-2013-11-14-pdf)

[330] In Authors Guild v. Google., Inc., 804 F.3d 202 (2d Cir. 2015), the Second Circuit noted public access to the works is without charge, Google infringes derivative rights through the search function, and storage of these works on Google services exposes the plaintiffs to the risk of hacking and risk of lost revenues based on the

1.6. CREATION AND COMMENCEMENT OF COPYRIGHT

Unlike the 1909 Act, copyright protection currently commences on creation of the work[331] without requirements as to registration or other formalities (although registration, notice and/or other formalities may be required to preserve or exercise the protections of copyright).[332] As we have seen, creation, although undefined under the statutes, is interpreted as occurring *when the work becomes embodied in tangible form.*[333]

Under the 1909 Act, copyright did not arise until the work was "published" (a term of art) or registered for copyright in unpublished form.[334] Until those events occurred, the work was protected by common law copyright.[335] The 1976 Act preempted common law copyright[336] (with the limited exception of works not embodied in tangible form),[337] resulting in the need for §303, which established that all such unpublished works created but previously not copyrighted would be deemed created as of January 1, 1978.

1.7. OWNERSHIP, JOINT OWNERSHIP, AND WORKS MADE FOR HIRE

1.7.1. Initial Ownership

Copyright vests initially in the author or authors of the work.[338] The authors of a joint work are co-owners of the copyright in that work.[339] With respect to collective works, the copyright to the contributed piece vests initially in the contributor/author, while the owner/creator of the collective work obtains copyright in the

---

access to the libraries who permitted the copying. Despite these facts, Google's action was considered transformative fair use.

[331] 17 U.S.C. §302 (2008).
[332] *See infra* §1.8.
[333] 17 U.S.C. §102 (2008). *See supra* §1.2.4. Note: In that the requirement of fixation is fundamental to the determination of the commencement and creation of copyright under the 1976 act, where appropriate, the term "creation and fixation" is used in this book in place of the more common term "creation." As noted in the text, "creation" is a term of art.
[334] *See* Copyright Act of 1909, §23.
[335] *Id.* at §2.
[336] 17 U.S.C. §301 (2008).
[337] *See supra* §1.2.4.1.
[338] 17 U.S.C. §201(a) (2008).
[339] *Id.*

collection.³⁴⁰ In the absence of express agreement, the collective-copyright owner is presumed to have acquired only the privilege of reproducing and distributing the contribution as a part of that particular collective work and subsequently revised or expanded versions thereof.³⁴¹

Not all creative works evidence sufficient authorship to support an individual copyright claim. A significant case limiting authorship and ownership of a performance by an actor is Google v. Garcia.³⁴²

1.7.2. Joint Ownership

A joint work is defined as a "work prepared by two or more authors with the *intention* that their contributions be merged into inseparable or interdependent parts of a unitary whole" (emphasis added).³⁴³ This definition embodies two requirements: contribution and intention. As interpreted by the courts, the requirement that the work be "prepared by two or more *authors*" (emphasis added) implies that their contributions must themselves be copyrightable works of authorship within the terms of §102(a)'s definition³⁴⁴ (though it is not required that each author individually fix his or her contribution in a tangible medium prior to its incorporation in the joint work).³⁴⁵ Thus, while there is no minimum as to the share of work contributed by each

---

³⁴⁰ 17 U.S.C. §201(c) (2008).
³⁴¹ *Id.*
³⁴² 786 F.3d 733 (9th Cir. 2015)(en banc ruling holding that a weak copyright claim cannot be a subterfuge for censorship; movie producer transformed actress Garcia's 5-second performance in which she spoke two brief sentences for a film Innocence of Muslims. The producer uploaded a trailer of the film to YouTube. After receiving death threats, Garcia sought a preliminary injunction. Copyright Office did not grant copyright because her performance was not a copyrightable work for an individual actor within a motion picture which is a single integrated work. The Ninth Circuit ultimately agreed. Justice Kozinski wrote a dissenting opinion contending that her performance was a work of authorship subject to copyright protection and would not place claimed burden on Copyright Office to allow performing artists to file such claims. He contended that fixation of her work occurred at the moment it was filmed.)
³⁴³ *Id.* at §101. As Professor Nimmer points out in his treatise, this is, in fact, a definition of joint authorship. M & D Nimmer, NIMMER ON COPYRIGHT §6.01.
³⁴⁴ Childress v. Taylor, 945 F.2d 500 (2d Cir. 1991); Aitken, Hazen, Hoffman, Miller, P.C. v. Empire Constr. Co., 542 F. Supp. 252 (D.Neb. 1982); Meltzer v. Zoller, 520 F. Supp. 847 (D.N.J. 1981).
³⁴⁵ Easter Seal Soc'y. for Crippled Children & Adults of La., Inc. v. Playboy Enters., 815 F.2d 323 (5th Cir.), *reh'g denied*, 820 F.2d 1223 (5th Cir. 1987), *cert. denied*, 485 U.S. 981 (1988).

author (i.e., two co-authors need not each contribute 50% of the total work),[346] *de minimis* contributions[347] or the contribution of noncopyrightable ideas is insufficient grounds for claiming joint authorship.[348]

The second requirement is that they each *intend* that their works be merged and that they regard themselves as joint authors.[349] This does not require that the co-authors work together, know each other, or work on their part of the collaboration at the same time. It merely requires that they have the requisite intentions that the resulting combination be a joint work.[350] Nonetheless, in the absence of a clear articulated expression of intent, a plaintiff must demonstrate an objective manifestation of that intent during the creation of the work in question.[351] This would include, for example, exercising some degree of artistic control over the work.[352]

An implied intention of joint authorship has logical limits. For example, where two authors collaborate on the creation of one work and one of those authors subsequently creates a new derivative work based on that original work, the other nonparticipating author cannot claim joint authorship (or joint ownership) of the new work,[353] though, of course, that author is entitled to an equitable share of the income earned by that derivative work based on the value of the original work used by it.[354]

On creation the co-authors become co-owners of the work[355] with each co-author, unless otherwise agreed to among the co-authors in

---

[346] Maurel v. Smith, 271 F. 211 (2d Cir. 1921).

[347] Ashton-Tate Corp. v. Ross, 916 F.2d 516 (9th Cir. 1990).

[348] Whelen Assocs., Inc. v. Jaslow Dental Lab., Inc., 609 F. Supp 1307 (E.D. Pa.), *judgment amended in part*, 609 F. Supp. 1325 (E.D. Pa. 1985), *aff'd*, 797 F.2d 1222 (3d Cir. 1986), *cert. denied*, 479 U.S. 1031 (1987); Forward v. Thorogood, 985 F.2d 604 (1st Cir. 1993).

[349] Childress, 945 F.2d 500.

[350] Donna v. Dodd, Mead & Co., 374 F. Supp. 429 (S.D.N.Y.1974). *See also* Edward B. Marks Music Corp. v. Jerry Vogel Music Co., 42 F. Supp. 859 (S.D.N.Y. 1942); Cmty. for Creative Non-Violence v. Reid, 846 F.2d 1485 (D.C.Cir.), *cert. granted*, 488 U.S. 940 (1988), *aff'd*, 490 U.S. 730 (1989) .

[351] Aalmuhammed v. Lee, 202 F.3d 1227 (9th Cir. 2000).

[352] *Id.*; Thomson v. Larson, 147 F.3d 195 (2d Cir. 1998); Erickson v. Trinity Theatre, Inc., 13 F.3d 1061 (7th Cir. 1994).

[353] Weissmann v. Freeman, 868 F.2d 1313 (2d Cir.), *cert. denied*, 493 U.S. 883 (1989).

[354] *See* Ashton-Tate Corp. v. Ross, 916 F.2d 516 (9th Cir. 1990).

[355] 17 U.S.C. §201(a) (2008).

writing, receiving an equal and undivided interest in the whole without regard to the amount contributed by that co-author.[356] The relationship is described as a tenancy-in-common and thereby invokes all of the rules of such a tenancy relationship.[357] For example, in the event that one co-author registers the work in his/her individual name, the legal title thereby vested in him/her will be deemed held in trust for the benefit of his/her co-author(s).[358] Further, while each co-author is empowered to license the non-exclusive use of the whole without the necessity of consent from the other co-author, the licensing co-author will be required to account to the other co-author for any profits.[359] A single joint owner may sue third parties without joining other joint owners.[360]

Joint ownership also results from any transfer of an undivided interest in one copyright, whether voluntarily or by operation of law, to two or more parties.[361]

1.7.3. Works Made for Hire

Section 201(b) (emphasis added) states:

In the case of a work made for hire, the employer or other person for whom the work *WAS* prepared is considered the author ... and unless the parties have expressly agreed otherwise in a written instrument signed by them, owns all the rights comprised in the copyright.

The statute defines a *work made for hire* as "(1) a work prepared by an employee within the scope of his or her employment; or (2) a work specially ordered or commissioned for use [in a] collective work, ... motion picture," or other works listed in §101 "if the parties *expressly* agree in a *written* instrument signed by them that the work shall be considered a work made for hire" (emphasis added).[362]

---

[356] *See* Sweet Music, Inc. v. Melrose Music Corp., 189 F. Supp. 655 (S.D. Cal. 1960).
[357] *See* H. REP., *supra* note 39, at 121.
[358] *See* Maurel, 271 F. 211.
[359] *See* H. REP., *supra* note 39, at 121. He/she could not, of course, transfer the entire work, only his/her undivided interest in it. *Id.*
[360] Corbello v. DeVito, 777 F.3d 1058 (9th Cir. 2015).
[361] *See* Oddo, 743 F.2d 630. *See also* 17 U.S.C. §203 (2008).
[362] 17 U.S.C. §101 (2008).

On its face, §201(b) and the definition would appear to limit works made for hire to those created by "employee(s) within the scope of their employment" and independent contractors who are "commissioned" to create works enumerated in the §101 definitions, a result supported by the House Report, which acknowledges that this category was a major issue of debate and that the enumerated categories of commissions was a compromise between those that should be treated as works made for hire and those that should not.[363] Nonetheless, and subject to some dissent,[364] the courts for a period of time recognized a third category of works for hire as being by an independent contractor (1) pursuant to a lawful contract that acknowledges that the work is a work made for hire[365] and/or (2) where the work is created at the instance and expense of the employer[366] and under the supervision and direction of the employer.[367]

When the Supreme Court finally addressed this issue,[368] it rejected the existence of this so-called third category and held the works-made-for-hire doctrine limited to works created by "employees" within the scope of their employment or specially commissioned works as enumerated in the §101 definition.[369] In determining who would qualify as an "employee" the Court specifically rejected arguments that the terms should be restricted "to formal salaried employees."[370] Instead, the Court held that the term employee was to be determined according to the "general common law of agency" and would involve such relevant factors as: the "skill required; the source of the instrumentalities and tools; the location of the work; the duration of the relationship between the parties; whether the hiring party has the right to assign additional projects to the hired party; the extent of the hired

---

[363] H. REP., *supra* note 39, at 121. *See also* I.T. Hardy, "Copyright Law's Concept of Employment – What Congress Really Intended" 35 J.COPR.SOC'Y 210 (1988).

[364] *See* Meltzer, 520 F. Supp. 847.

[365] *See* Roth v. Pritikin, 710 F.2d 934 (2d Cir.), *cert. denied*, 464 U.S. 961 (1983).

[366] *See* Samet & Wells, Inc. v. Shalom Toy Co., 429 F. Supp. 895 (E.D.N.Y. 1977), *aff'd*, 578 F.2d 1369 (2d Cir. 1978).

[367] *See* Aldon Accessories v. Spiegel, Inc., 738 F.2d 548 (2d Cir.), *cert. denied*, 469 U.S. 982 (1984). See Urbont v. Sony Music Entertainment, 831 F.3d 80 (2d Cir. 2016).

[368] Cmty. for Creative Non-Violence, 846 F.2d 1485, *cert. granted*, 488 U.S. 940, *aff'd*, 490 U.S. 730.

[369] *Id.*, 490 U.S. at 742.

[370] *Id.* at 742 n. 8. This position had been adopted by the Ninth Circuit in Dumas v. Gommerman, 865 F.2d 1093 (9th Cir. 1989).

party's discretion over when and how long to work; the method of payment; the hired party's role in hiring and paying assistants; whether the work is part of the regular business of the hiring party; whether the hiring party is in business; the provision of employee benefits; and the tax treatment of the hired party."[371] These latter two factors, the provision of employee benefits and tax treatment, have been given particular weight in one recent ruling which treats them almost as a form of estopped arguing that a defendant "should not in one context be able to claim that [plaintiff] was an independent contractor [in one instance and then to] later deny him that status to avoid a copyright infringement suit."[372]

It should be noted that the work made for hire agreement must be made prior to or concurrent with the creation of the work in question. Agreements reciting that the work was made as a work made for hire entered into subsequent to creation may be enforceable as an exclusive license, but will be ineffective in preventing the author exercising his or her termination rights[373] as an "agreement to the contrary" under 17 U.S.C. §304.[374] Conversely, an incorrect attribution of authorship in a copyright registration may be subject to correction, even years after initial publication, if sufficient evidence exists that the work was in fact composed on a "work for hire" basis.[375]

1.8. FORMALITIES OF NOTICE, REGISTRATION, AND DEPOSIT

Prior to the implementation of the Berne Act, the United States was the only developed nation in the world that required its authors by law to provide notice in order to obtain copyright protection. While the implementation of the Berne Act makes the use of notice and registration voluntary rather than mandatory, it does not eliminate the significance of the use of notice on pre-implementation works,[376] nor

---

[371] *Also see* Easter Seal Soc'y for Crippled Children & Adults of La., Inc., 815 F.2d 323, *reh'g denied*, 820 F.2d 1223, *cert. denied*, 485. U.S. 981 which had earlier adopted this position.
[372] Aymes v. Bonelli, 980 F.2d 857, 862 (2d Cir. 1992).
[373] *See infra* §1.10.3 *et seq.*
[374] Marvel Characters, Inc. v. Simon, 310 F. 3d 280 (2d Cir. 2002).
[375] See Estate of Hogarth v. Edgar Rice Burroughs, Inc., 62 U.S.P.Q. 2d 1301 No. 00 CIV. 9569 (DLC), 2002 WL 398696 (S.D.N.Y. Mar. 15, 2002), *aff'd*, 342 F. 3d 149 (2d Cir. 2003), *cert. denied*, 541 U.S. 937 (2004).
[376] For example, if a work falls into the public domain based on a failure to attach notice and/or register the work, *see* §§1.8.1 et seq. *infra*, it will remain in the public

does it eliminate statutory *incentives* for the continued use of notice and registration.[377]

The purpose of the notice requirement is to indicate whether the work is protected or not – and thus, in the balance between the innocent infringer's and the author's interests, the statute required that the author exert some effort to retain his or her rights rather than impose the duty of ascertaining copyright status on the potential user. It should be noted that this same rationale supports the continued use of 'incentives' to induce copyright owners to use of copyright notice.[378]

1.8.1. Notice

U.S. copyright law no longer requires the use of a copyright notice. <u>Failure to provide a proper copyright prior to January 1, 1989 could have serious consequences to copyright owners and that still affects pre-Berne potentially eliminating Act works where actions previously resulting in distribution without proper notice, potentially still resulting in issues of validity and enforceability.</u> This has been significantly ameliorated since an amendment to the Copyright Act did away with the notice requirement. Nevertheless, in practice, use of a copyright notice is still recommended, as the failure to use a copyright notice is a basis for denying the defense of innocent infringement and in doing so potentially eliminating the ability to obtain statutory damages, profits and attorney's fees.[379] The following comments regarding notice are pertinent to works published prior to the Berne Act and may still have an impact on the protectability of those works.

Although it is a common and conservatively appropriate practice[380] to place a copyright notice on any tangible copy of a copyrighted work, such notice is not required until the work is "published ... by authority of the copyright owner."[381] Publication is defined as "the distribution of

---

domain after implementation of the Berne Act, even though the failure to attach notice would *not* cause that same work to fall into the public domain *after* implementation. *See* Berne Act §12.

[377] For example, in the event of a conflict between transfers of copyright, the one executed first *if it is recorded* prevails. 17 U.S.C. §205(e) under the 1976 Act-(d) under the act as revised by the Berne Act).

[378] *See infra* §1.8.1.5.

[379] *See* 17 U.S.C. 405(b).

[380] By providing such notice, any infringement can be argued as being willful. *See infra* §1.12.

[381] 17 U.S.C. §§401(a), 402(a), 404(a) (2008).

copies ... of the work to the public by sale or other transfer of ownership, rental lease or lending."³⁸² Therefore, there is no notice requirement with respect to public displays,³⁸³ public performance,³⁸⁴ or limited distribution (also known as limited publication)³⁸⁵ of a work. Equally, unauthorized publication that lacks notice would not impair the copyright owner's rights.³⁸⁶ However, any form of dissemination prior to the implementation of the Berne Act coupled with an intention to abandon the copyright can result in dedication of the work to the public domain.³⁸⁷ Moreover, under the 1909 Act, public display of a work of visual art without proper copyright notice in an environment in which copying is not prohibited could result in the loss of copyright,³⁸⁸ while public display combined with an offer to sell the art work may cause the same result under the 1976 Act.³⁸⁹

Traditionally, it had been understood that the distribution of phonorecords was not considered a "divestive" publication of the compositions embodied on that phonorecord and, as such, copyright owners were not required to comply with the registration and notice requirements of the 1909 Copyright Act.³⁹⁰ That changed with the ruling in *La Cienega Music Co. v. Z.Z. Top*³⁹¹ which held that such distribution did serve as publication subjecting those compositions to the requirements of notice, in the absence of which those compositions fell into the public domain.

---

[382] *Id.* at §101.
[383] *See* H. REP., *supra* note 39, at 144.
[384] *See* Heim v. Universal Pictures Co., 154 F.2d 480 (2d Cir. 1946); Georgie Porgie Co. v. Link, 332 F. Supp. 638 (S.D.N.Y. 1971).
[385] *See* Hirshon v. United Artists Corp., 243 F.2d 640 (D.C. Cir. 1957).
[386] *See* Greeff Fabrics, Inc. v. Malden Mills Indus., Inc. 412 F. Supp. 160 (S.D.N.Y. 1976), *aff'd*, 556 F.2d 556 (2d Cir. 1977).
[387] *See* Bell v. Combined Registry Co., 397 F. Supp. 1241 (N.D. Ill. 1975), *aff'd*, 536 F.2d 164 (7th Cir. 1976), *cert. denied*, 429 U.S. 1001 (1976).
[388] Am. Tobacco Co. v. Werckmeister, 207 U.S. 284 (1907); Letter Edged in Black Press, 320 F. Supp 1303; Scherr v. Universal Match Corp. 297 F. Supp. 107 (S.D.N.Y. 1967), *aff'd*, 417 F.2d 497 (2d Cir 1969), *cert. denied, 397* U.S. 936 (1970).
[389] *See* Martin Bressler. & Robert L. Seigel, "Retroactive Protection of Visual Arts Published Without a Copyright Notice: A Proposal" 7 CARDOZO ARTS & ENT L J 115 (1988).
[390] Nom Music, Inc. v. Kaslin, 227 F. Supp. 922 (S.D.N.Y. 1964) *aff'd,* 343 F.2d 198 (2d Cir. 1965); Buck v. Lester, 24 F.2d 877 (E.D.S.C. 1928).
[391] La Cienega Music Co. v. Z.Z. Top, 44 F.3d 813 (9th Cir.), *amended and superseded on denial of reh'g*, 53 F.3d 950 (9th Cir.), *cert. denied*, 516 U.S. 927 (1995).

1.8.1.1. Visually Perceptible Copies

Notice is required to be permanently affixed on all publicly distributed copies of the work as authorized by the owner prior to the Berne Act implementation.[392] For work published after implementation of the Berne Act this becomes voluntary.

1.8.1.2. Form of Notice

The notice, if it appears, is to consist of the following three elements:[393]

1. The symbol © (the letter c in a circle), the word *copyright*, the abbreviation *copr.*, or, with respect to sound recordings only, the symbol (p) (the letter p in a circle) with no other wording or abbreviation being acceptable.[394]
2. The *year* of *first* publication of the work (not the year in which that particular edition was published), except that compilations or derivative works incorporating previously published works may include only the date of publication of the compilation or derivative work. The year may be omitted from pictorial/graphic works with accompanying text reproduced on stationery or useful articles.[395]
3. The name of the owner of copyright in the work. This can include recognizable abbreviations of the name, such as initials (e.g., IBM, AT&T, etc.). With respect to sound recordings, if the producer's name is listed and no owner's name appears in the notice, the producer will be deemed to be the owner.[396]

1.8.1.3. Location of Notice

The notice is to appear "in such a manner and location as to give reasonable notice of the claim of copyright."[397] With respect to

---

[392] 17 U.S.C. §§401(a), 402(a), 404(a) (2008).
[393] *Id.* at §§401(b), 402(b).
[394] *Id.* at §402(b).
[395] *Id.* at §401(b)(2). Note: It has been argued that affixing dates would harm the market for such items by making them "dated."
[396] *Id.* at §402(b)(3). ("… if no other name appears in conjunction with the notice, the producer's name shall be considered as part of the notice.")
[397] *Id.* at §401(c).

phonorecords, the statute specifies that such notice should appear on "the surface of the phonorecord ... [and the] label or container."[398] For other types of copies the statute authorizes the Register of Copyrights to provide regulations that, although not exhaustive, illustrate acceptable locations.[399] Examples of acceptable locations are the title page of a book,[400] the first page of printed music,[401] a notice displayed at the user's computer terminal at sign-on,[402] at the beginning near the title or end of a motion picture,[403] or on the front or back of a painting.[404]

1.8.1.4. Collective Works

A single notice applicable to the collective work as a whole is sufficient to satisfy the notice requirement as to the individual contributions to the collective work.[405] However, in the event the contribution so protected (i.e., where it lacks a separate notice of its own) is infringed by a person in good faith under a purported license by the collective work owner and absent registration of the work, the innocent infringer has an absolute defense as against the true owner.[406]

The notice on a collective or derivative work does not have to identify portions of that work that are in the public domain (and thereby excluded from protection)[407] except where the collective work consists "preponderantly" of works of the United States government, which must be separately identified (either affirmatively or negatively).[408] United States government works are generally not eligible for U.S. copyright,[409] and are therefore free for use.

---

[398] *Id.* at §402(c).
[399] *See* COMPENDIUM II OF COPYRIGHT OFFICE PRACTICES §1013 (1984) [hereinafter referred to as C.C.O.P.].
[400] *Id.* at §1013.04(1).
[401] *Id.* at §1013.06.
[402] *Id.* at §1013.09(2).
[403] *Id.* at §1013.10(1).
[404] *Id.* at §1013.11(1).
[405] 17 U.S.C. §404 (2008).
[406] *Id.* at §404(b).
[407] C.C.O.P., *supra* note 400, §1004.04.
[408] 17 U.S.C. §403 (2008).
[409] *Id.* at §105.

1.8.1.5. Notice under the Berne Act

The Berne Act changes the law from a position in which the use of notice is mandatory to one in which the attachment of notice is optional.[410] Nonetheless, Congress has accepted the principle promulgated in the so-called King Report[411] that the use of notice and registration is cost beneficial to the copyright industries and should be continued. To accomplish this without violating the requirements of the Berne Convention,[412] Congress has elected to accord owners who utilize notice additional protections above those required by Berne.[413] Thus, the proper use of notice will automatically defeat a defendant's interposition of a defense based on innocent infringement in mitigation of actual or statutory damages.[414] Moreover, the affixation of notice is still required as a part of an effort to "cure" an omission of notice where copies of that copyrightable work were distributed without proper notice[415] prior to March 1, 1989, the effective date of the Berne Implementation Act.[416]

1.8.2. Errors in Name or Date in the Notice

1.8.2.1. Under the 1909 Act

Although the courts regularly recited that strict compliance with notice requirements was demanded under the 1909 Act, the failure of which would make the notice defective and invalidate the copyright,[417] the general trend was to recognize as valid those notices that *substantially* complied with the statutory requirements.[418] Substantial compliance requires, in part, that innocent persons not be misled by

---

[410] Berne Act §7.
[411] A report to the Register of Copyrights prepared by King Research, Inc. See Copyright Law Reports CCH ¶20,420.
[412] See Berne Convention and the WIPO Copyright Treaty § 4.7 *infra*.
[413] In accordance with the provisions of Berne that allow protections greater than those required by Berne. See Berne Convention art. 5.
[414] Berne Act § 7.
[415] See *infra* §1.8.3.2.
[416] See H.R. REP. No. 609, 100th Cong., 2d Sess., at 27 (1988).
[417] See Wildman v. N. Y. Times Co., 42 F. Supp. 412 (S.D.N.Y. 1941); L&L White Metal Casting Corp. v. Joseph, 387 F. Supp. 1349 (E.D.N.Y. 1975).
[418] See Mifflin v. R.H. White Co., 190 U.S. 260, *aff'd*, 190 U.S. 265 (1903).

such variation.[419] Thus, an error in the date of less than one year later than the first publication[420] or a date earlier than publication (which, it should be noted, would thus shorten the term of its protection and hasten its dedication to the public domain) are errors that have been held as not misleading to innocent persons, and the affected notices were deemed effective.[421] An error in the name of the owner, even if the person so named could direct reasonable inquiry to the true owner, was generally held as a substantial error and defective as notice.[422] A more generous view has developed that if the named owner has at least colorable claim to an interest in the copyright (e.g., was a licensee), the notice would serve to protect the copyright.[423]

1.8.2.2. Under the 1976 Act

With respect to works distributed prior to the implementation of the Berne Act,[424] the 1976 Act sought to induce the use of proper notice but attempted to ameliorate the harshness of the forfeiture of copyright for failure to comply with the requirements of notice.[425] Under the terms of §406,[426] errors in notice do not automatically result in forfeiture of copyright. An error in the name of the owner may be rectified by registration except that, prior to registration, the named "owner" has the power to grant licenses for the work to innocent infringers without notice of the true owner.[427] An error in the date where the notice date precedes the actual publication date merely reduces the term of protection[428] (which effectively applies only to anonymous works, pseudonymous works, or works made for

---

[419] *See* Freedman v. Milnag Leasing Corp., 20 F. Supp. 802 (S.D.N.Y. 1937).
[420] *See* L&L White Metal Casting Corp. v. Cornell Metal Specialties Corp., 353 F. Supp. 1170 (E.D.N.Y. 1972), *aff'd*, 177 U.S.P.Q. 673 (2d Cir. 1973).
[421] *See* Callaghan v. Myers, 128 U.S. 617 (1888).
[422] *See* Mifflin, 190 U.S. 260, *aff'd*, 190 U.S. 265. (1903).
[423] *See* Fantastic Fakes, Inc. v. Pickwick Int'l, Inc., 661 F.2d 479 (5th Cir. 1981) (licensee named); National Comics Publications, v. Fawcett Publications, 191 F.2d 594 (2d Cir. 1951), *opinion supplemented*, 198 F.2d 927 (2d Cir. 1952) (commonly owned corporations where one owned other named owner).
[424] *See* the Berne Act §7(f).
[425] H. REP., *supra* note 39, at 149.
[426] 17 U.S.C. §406 (2008).
[427] *Id.* at §406(a).
[428] *Id.* at §406(b).

hire that have set terms not determined by the life of the author),[429] and an error in the date of one year or less following publication will have no effect.[430] An error in the date that is greater than one year following publication or the omission of the name or date is treated as though the work was published without notice.[431]

1.8.3. Omission of Notice

1.8.3.1. Under the 1909 Act

The rule under the 1909 Act was that publication without notice invalidated copyright protection and dedicated the work to the public domain.[432] The statute provided a limited exception[433] only if the omission was on "a particular copy or copies."[434] The courts added an exception to §21 where the omission of notice was caused by the actions of a licensee where a requirement was made in writing that the licensee must affix proper notice to all copies,[435] the argument being that such a vital breach of contract served to negate the license, so unauthorized acts became infringements of the copyright and publication was thereby construed as being made without the proper authority of the copyright owner.

1.8.3.2. Under the 1976 Act

With respect to works distributed prior to the implementation of the Berne Act,[436] §405 of the 1976 Act codified the two exceptions created under the former §21 based on omission from a relatively small number of copies[437] (the intention being that it would be less restrictive

---

[429] *See infra* §1.9.
[430] 17 U.S.C. §406(b) (2008).
[431] *See infra* §1.8.3.2.
[432] *See* Universal Film Mfg. Co. v. Copperman, 212 F. 301 (S.D.N.Y.), *aff'd*, 218 F. 577 (2d Cir.), *cert. denied*, 235 U.S. 704 (1914).
[433] Copyright Act of 1909, §21.
[434] *See* United Thrift Plan v. Nat'l Thrift Plan, 34 F.2d 300 (E.D.N.Y. 1929).
[435] National Comic Publications v. Fawcett Publications, 93 F. Supp. 349 (S.D.N.Y. 1950) *rev'd on other grounds*, 191 F.2d 594 (2d Cir. 1951), *opinion supplemented*, 198 F.2d 927 (2d Cir. 1952).
[436] *See* the Berne Act §7(e).
[437] 17 U.S.C. §405(a)(1) (2008).

than the requirement of former §21),[438] and the omission of notice by a licensee in violation of a written license.[439] It also added a "curative" provision for omitted notice that preserves the copyright, provided that (1) registration is made before or within "five (5) years after publication without notice" and (2) that "reasonable effort is made to add notice to all [such] copies ... that are distributed to the public in the United States after the omission has been discovered."[440]

The "limited numbers" exception has been refined by the courts to eliminate the requirement that the omission be made by "error or mistake" by virtue of the analogous fact that such an omission would be curable under §405(a)(2)[441] and to establish the test of what constitutes a "limited number" (undefined by the statute) according to a formula comparing the number of copies where the notice was omitted with the total number of copies distributed.[442] Under this formula courts have allowed the omission of up to 9 percent of total copies distributed,[443] but held that omissions exceeding 22 percent of total copies exceeded the limited-numbers amount.[444] In each case, therefore, it ultimately becomes a question of fact.

The cure provision of §405(a)(2) requires registration and reasonable efforts to add notice to all copies. This provision clearly requires affixation of notice to copies held by the owner to be distributed in the United States.[445] It also arguably requires reasonable efforts to reach all copies to be distributed, which may include copies already in the hands of retailers.[446]

To balance these cure protections, the statute has added provisions under §405(b), whereby innocent infringement of a work whose notice

---

[438] H. REP. *supra* note 39, at 147.
[439] 17 U.S.C. §405(a)(3) (2008).
[440] *Id.* at §405(a)(2).
[441] *See* Hasbro Bradley, Inc. v. Sparkle Toys, Inc., 780 F.2d 189 (2d Cir. 1985). *See also* David Goldberg, *Notice of Copyright – Its Omission and "Cure,"* N.Y.L.J. 1, March 21, 1986.
[442] *See* Am. Greetings Corp. v. Kleinfab Corp., 400 F. Supp. 228 (S.D.N.Y. 1975).
[443] *See* Flora Kung, Inc. v. Items of California, Inc., 29 P.T.C.J. 515 (S.D.N.Y. Nov. 16, 1984).
[444] *See* King v. Burnett, No. 81-1792, 1982 WL 1287 (D.D.C. Sept. 29, 1982).
[445] *See* Goldberg, *Notice of Copyright, supra* note 411, at 7.
[446] *See* Shapiro & Son Bedspread Corp. v. Royal Mills Assocs., 764 F.2d 69 (2d Cir. 1985). *Contra*: M. Kramer Mfg. Co. v. Hugh Andrews, 783 F.2d 421 (4th Cir. 1986) (holding that manufacturer need only put notice on all items manufactured after discovery of omission).

was omitted is not subject to statutory or actual damages for infringements occurring prior to actual notice of registration. Moreover, the courts are granted broad equitable powers to balance the interests including establishment of a Registration reasonable license.

Keep in mind that for works first published after March 1, 1989, no notice of copyright is required under the Copyright Act.[447]

1.8.4. Registration

Under both the 1909 and 1976 acts registration is not a requirement for the creation of copyright, although such registration may be required to preserve copyright,[448] and may be a condition precedent to the right to bring an infringement suit.[449]

1.8.4.1. Under the 1909 Act

Under the 1909 Act registration of an unpublished work was completely voluntary[450] and was, in fact, restricted to the following types of works by Copyright Office practices: lectures and similar productions, dramatic compositions, motion picture photoplays, motion pictures, works of art, and plastic works and drawings.[451] The protection of all other unpublished works was relegated to common law copyright.

The 1909 Act required that, once a copyright had been obtained by publication of the work with the affixed notice, "there shall be promptly deposited" the required copies and registration claim.[452] Despite the affirmative nature of the language of this requirement, the courts have interpreted this as a voluntary requirement. It became mandatory only when, pursuant to §14 of the 1909 Act, the Register of

---

[447] 17 U.S.C. 405(a) (2015).
[448] *E.g.*, the cure for omitted notice under §405(a)(2) of the 1976 act or where demanded by the Copyright Office pursuant to §13 of the 1909 act.
[449] *See* §13 of the 1909 act and §411(a) of the 1976 act. *Contra* Berne Act §5. §411(d) now expressly refers to "infringement of the copyright in any United States work" initially added by the Berne Convention Implementation Act and broadened to this language by TRIPS.
[450] §12 of the 1909 act.
[451] *See* "Protection of Unpublished Works," Copyright Office Study No. 29, p. 6, n. 53.
[452] Copyright Act of 1909, §12.

Copyrights demanded deposit of copies.[453] Therefore, no amount of delay in filing would destroy the copyright, although, combined with other factors, it may provide the basis of an argument based on abandonment. (An abandoned copyright becomes dedicated to the public domain.) Nonetheless, deposit and registration would still be required prior to the commencement of an infringement action.[454]

1.8.4.2. Under the 1976 Act

Except for the provisions for cure of "publication without notice,"[455] under the 1976 Act there is no distinction between published and unpublished works with respect to the protection of copyright. Under the 1976 Act all copyright rights vest and become effective on creation and fixation in tangible form. All works created but unpublished prior to January 1, 1978, were effectively deemed to be protected by federal copyright as of that date and are governed by the 1976 Act.[456]

The 1976 Act has continued the voluntary nature of the registration requirements as developed under the 1909 Act subject to the §405 cure provision, (which requires registration to be effective) and registration as a prerequisite to an infringement action.[457]

1.8.4.3. Incentives for Registration

Under both the 1909 and 1976 Acts the capacity to protect the copyright (as opposed to making it a predicate to its creation) has been used as an incentive to encourage registration.[458] The protection and prosecution of copyright actions for all copyright (both those created prior to as well as subsequent to January 1, 1978) are now governed by the rules of the 1976 Act.[459] Moreover, this incentive is directed towards registration of the individual work. The registration of a

---

[453] *See* Wash. Publishing Co. v. Pearson, 306 U.S. 30 (1939).
[454] This was previously required under the 1909 act by §13 and is now governed under the 1976 act under §§411 and 412.
[455] 17 U.S.C. §405 (2008).
[456] *See id.* at §§303 (commencement) and 301 (pre-emption of prior common law copyright).
[457] *Id.* at §§411-412.
[458] *See* H. REP., *supra* note 39, at 143.
[459] 17 U.S.C. §301 (2008).

collective work (such as a magazine) does not satisfy the registration requirement for copyright works incorporated within that collective work unless the owner of the collective work owns one of the copyrightable works contained in the collective work.[460] Similarly, the owner of a derivative work must register the derivative work, even if she has registered the original work upon which the derivative work is based.[461]

Section 411 states that registration is a prerequisite to an action for infringement subject to two exceptions: (1) where application is properly made and registration is denied by the Copyright Office and (2) in claims involving sight-and-sound works first fixed on the date of transmission. In the case in which registration is denied by the Register of Copyrights (pursuant to §410(b), wherein the Register of Copyrights determines that the material is not copyrightable subject matter or the claim is invalid for other reasons), the action may be commenced with a copy of the complaint served on the Register of Copyrights, who may become a party to the action. In the case of sight-and-sound works, the owner may institute actions prior to *fixation* and registration, provided registration for the work is filed within three months after its first transmission, and the owner "serves notice upon the infringer not less than ten or more than thirty days before such fixation."[462]

Additional incentives for prompt registration are provided by § 410(c), whereby a certificate of registration before or within five years of publication constitutes prima facie evidence of the validity of the copyright and the facts stated on the certificate, and §412, precluding statutory damages (under §504) and attorneys' fees (under §505) for infringements occurring prior to registration (except for registrations occurring within three months of publication).

Finally, registration of the subject work is required to invoke the "constructive notice" of ownership provisions for recorded documents

---

[460] Morris v. Bus. Concepts Inc., 54 U.S.P.Q. 2d 1561 (S.D.N.Y. 2000), *aff'd,* 259 F. 3d 65 (2d Cir. 2001).

[461] Murray Hill Publications, Inc. v. ABC Communication, Inc., 264 F.3d 622 (6th Cir. 2001).

[462] *Id.* §411(b)(1). This rather peculiar notice requirement would suggest that this provision has very limited application. Its primary efficacy would appear as a means of obtaining injunctive relief against known and persistent infringers. For example, someone who regularly charges admission to broadcasts of live sporting events. By definition, the prerequisite only applies to "any United States work" thus excluding in general, works of foreign origin. "United States works" in Section 101 of Title 17 has a specific definition.

of transfer and assignment.[463] Such constructive notice again applies to the protection of a copyright (not its validity) and influences the determination of "willful" infringement in an infringement action.

1.8.4.4. Registration under the Berne Act

In deference to the Berne Convention,[464] the Berne Act removes the necessity of registration for all works whose country of origin under the Berne Union is not the United States[465] (i.e., a country which is a member of the Berne Union other than the U.S.),[466] as a predicate for the prosecution of an infringement action. Moreover, it has removed completely the requirement that a transfer of ownership be recorded before an infringement action by the owner of the transferred right or interest may be brought.[467] However, registration is still required[468] as a predicate for an infringement action for all works first published in the United States, or unpublished works whose authors are nationals, residents or domiciliaries, or with respect to unpublished audio-visual works whose authors are legal entities headquartered in the United States.[469] Moreover, the Berne Act continues to maintain all of the incentives for registration in the current act, such as providing that the first of two or more conflicting transfers that is recorded will prevail[470] and precluding the award of statutory damages and attorneys' fees for infringements occurring while the work was unregistered.[471]

1.8.5. Deposit

1.8.5.1. Purpose of Deposit

Under both the 1909 Act and the 1976 Act the requirements of "deposit and registration [are] separate though closely related."[472] Application for registration requires deposit of the work (or identifying

---

[463] 17 U.S.C. §205(c) (2008). *See also U.S. Copyright Law, infra* §1.10.2.
[464] Berne Convention Art. 5.
[465] Berne Act § 9(B)(1)(b).
[466] *Id.* at §4.
[467] *Id.* at §5. Prior §205(d) mandated recordation prior to suit.
[468] *Id.* at §9(b)(1)(B).
[469] *Id.* at §4.
[470] Pre-Berne Act 17 U.S.C. §205(3)-Berne Act §5.
[471] 17 U.S.C. §412 (20080).
[472] H.R. REP., *supra* note 39, at 150.

material),[473] but the obligation to deposit arises separately on publication in the United States[474] and may predate or postdate the registration of the work. This requirement is continued under the Berne Act.[475]

The primary purpose of deposit under §407 of the act, based on publication, is to provide the Library of Congress with a supplementary source of materials. On this basis, although the obligations of deposit within three months of publication are "mandatory ... exceptions can be made for material the Library neither needs nor wants."[476] Moreover, §407 requires the deposit of two copies of the "best edition"[477] with the "best edition" being defined as what "the Library of Congress determines to be most suitable for its purposes."[478] Finally, the penalty for failing to deposit the work (which, it must be noted, does not include forfeiture of copyright) is in part based on the cost of the Library of Congress to acquire copies of the work.[479]

Under §408 of the act, deposit (subject to exemption) is a required element of the process of registration. Although sharing some elements with the §407 deposit requirement (i.e., requiring two copies of the "best edition" of published works, which can be deposited concurrently to satisfy both §407 and §408,[480] and providing that the Library of Congress is entitled to add copies of unpublished works to its collection[481]), the §408 deposit requirement does serve certain additional functions: (1) to allow the Register of Copyrights to evaluate whether or not the work embodies copyrightable subject matter,[482] and (2) to establish a record, for purposes of an infringement action, that the work on which infringement is claimed is the same work for which copyright registration is based. The latter function primarily applies to unpublished works, complete copies of which must be deposited and preserved for the full term of copyright[483] as opposed to published

---

[473] 17 U.S.C. §408 (2008). See Copyright Office Circular 7(b) available at www.copyright.gov.
[474] *Id.* at §407.
[475] Berne Act §8.
[476] H. REP., *supra* note 39, at 150.
[477] *See* 17 U.S.C. §407(a) (2008).
[478] *Id.* at §101.
[479] *See id.* at §407(d)(2).
[480] *Id.* at §408(b).
[481] *Id.* at §704(b). See Copyright Circular 7(b) available on www.copyright.gov.
[482] *See id.* at §410.
[483] *Id.* at §704(d).

works, which need only be preserved for the "longest period considered practicable and desirable by the Register of Copyrights and the Librarian of Congress."[484] (It can be argued that published works do not require this preservation protection since the published edition acts as a public record of its content.)

The deposit requirement also effectively sets the start of the term of *enforceable* copyright protection for all works first published in the United States and for all unpublished copyrights, since deposit is required for registration and registration is required for the prosecution of an infringement action.[485] This is particularly important with respect to unpublished works. While it may be arguable that a work should be protected from the date of its creation, if the author registers the work at a later date, the author may be obligated to prove that the deposit copy is identical with the earlier created work – a *recreated* work (such as the new recording of a song) may not provide protection for the period prior to its creation.[486]

1.8.5.2. Exemptions from Deposit

In line with the purposes of the various requirements of deposit, there exist exceptions from those requirements.

Under §408 the Register of Copyrights has broad power to determine the nature of the deposit materials required thereunder, including the substitution of a requirement of depositing identifying materials in lieu of actual copies of the works for broad classifications of works.[487] The significant factor here is that the identifying materials be sufficient to evaluate copyrightable subject matter and preserve a record of the work.[488]

Under §407 the Register's authority is limited by the needs of the Librarian of Congress. Exception is made, however, under §407 (and incorporated by regulations under §408), where deposit would impose a practical or financial hardship on the depositor.[489] The statute automatically exempts sculptural/ pictorial/graphic works of limited

---

[484] *Id.*
[485] *See supra*, §1.8.4.3.
[486] Coles v. Wonder, 283 F.3d 798 (6th Cir. 2002).
[487] *See* 17 U.S.C. §408(c)(1) (2008).
[488] See Generally Compendium (Third), §1500 *et seq.*
[489] *Id.* at §407(c). *See also* Compendium (Third), §1511.3.

editions.[490] Other exceptions would require proper written application to the Copyright Office.[491]

1.8.6. Registration Procedures

Detailed information regarding Copyright Office practices may be found in the U.S. Copyright Office, Compendium of Copyright Office Practices (3d Edition 2014) which is available online at www.copyright. gov/comp3/comp-index.html.

Application for copyright registration must be made on a form prescribed by the Register of Copyrights (containing such facts as name and address of claimant, author's name and status, basis of ownership, statement of subject matter of copyright, etc.)[492] and must be accompanied by proper deposit and fees.[493] The effective date of application is the day on which the application, deposit, and fees acceptable for registration have all been received by the Copyright Office.[494] If the Register determines that the application, deposit, and fees are in compliance with the requirements of the law, the Register must register the claim and issue a certificate of registration under the seal of the Copyright Office.[495]

Most registrations today are accomplished online utilizing the Copyright Office website at www.copyright.gov. There are a few circumstances where a number of works might be combined into a single registration provided each was created by the same author or authors. While it may be less costly to register multiple works in one registration, there is some value to filing individual registrations. Collective registration has been a factor in limiting the scope of statutory damages.[496] The ability to file registrations for multiple works is more likely to be accomplished prior to publication of works. After publication, a single registration is likely to require that all works have been published as a unit, and submission of two copies of the best edition of the work may be required as a deposit.[497]

---

[490] 17 U.S.C.. §407(c) (2008).
[491] Compendium (Third), §1511.8
[492] 17 U.S.C. §409 (2008).
[493] *Id.* at §408. *See also U.S. Copyright Law, supra* §1.7.5.
[494] 17 U.S.C. §410(d) (2008).
[495] *Id.* at §410(a).
[496] Yellow Pages Photos, Inc. v. Ziplocal, LP, 795 F.3d 1255 (11th Cir. 2015).
[497] *See* §1.8.5.

1.8.7. Denial of Registration

Commencing with the 1909 Act[498] and continuing under the 1976 Act by virtue of §410(a) and (b), the Register of Copyrights is deemed to have broad discretion in determining the acceptance of registration. It has been suggested that such discretion includes the power, although not the obligation, to refuse registration based on illegality, public policy, sedition, obscenity, or libel,[499] although the Copyright Office will not ordinarily attempt to determine obscenity or pornography of the claimed work.[500] Such discretion clearly applies to determinations of the propriety and technical satisfaction of the submission of proper filing fees[501] and the review of applications containing mutually inconsistent claims.[502] However, where the application is "fair on its face," the courts have held that the Copyright Office must accept registration of the work.[503]

The Copyright Office has established a two level informal appeal process for works which have been denied registration. While normally informal communication with the Copyright Specialist was used in the past and still is to try to overcome minor registration hurdles. Often the Copyright Registration Specialist will contact the applicant or counsel by email with questions. Responses should be submitted within 20 days to avoid abandonment of the application.

Where this does not resolve the registration issues, a slightly greater formality exists with the appeal process. This essentially means the sending of a letter brief to the Copyright Office with payment of a $250, the current filing fee. This must be submitted within 3 months of date of refusal to register.[504] It is referred to as a First Request for Reconsideration. If still denied, a second level of informal appeal is available, a Second Request for Reconsideration, on payment of a $500 filing fee. This review is made by the Review Board consisting of the Register of Copyrights, the General Counsel of

---

[498] *See* Bailie v. Fischer, 258 F.2d 425 (D.C. Cir. 1958).
[499] Op. Att'y Gen. 121 U.S.P.Q. 329 (1958).
[500] Compendium (Third) §315 at 39.
[501] Bouve v. Twentieth Century-Fox Film Corp., 122 F.2d 51 (D.C. Cir. 1941).
[502] Op. Att'y Gen. (1974).
[503] Cadence Indus. Corp. v. Ringer, 450 F. Supp. 59 (S.D.N.Y. 1978).
[504] Compendium (Third), §1708.3.

the Copyright Office or its designees and a third individual designated by the Register.[505]

Although the existence of a valid copyright registration is prima facie evidence of originality and authorship,[506] it has been held that the determination of originality of a proposed claim is not within the domain of the Copyright Office.[507] It has been suggested that the determination of originality is better left to the courts than to an administrative agency.[508]

On refusal to accept the claim for registration, the Register must provide the claimant with written notice of the reasons for such refusal,[509] with such refusal being subject to review and correction by the courts.[510]

1.9. DURATION OF COPYRIGHT[511]

The Constitution provides that Congress shall have the power "[t]o promote the progress of science and the useful arts, by securing for *limited time* to authors and inventors the exclusive right to their respective writings and discoveries." (Emphasis added.) Since that time, Congress has exercised that power by providing limited terms copyright for creative works, generally determined according to the nature of authorship (for example by distinguishing between natural, identified individual authors, joint authors, and unidentified or corporate authors)[512] the date in which the work was created,[513] and in some cases, the type of creative work involved.[514]

---

[505] *See* Compendium (Third), §1704.02 and §§1700 et seq.
[506] Milene Music v. Gotauco, 551 F. Supp. 1288 (D.R.I. 1982).
[507] Midway Mfg. Co. v. Bandai-Am., Inc., 546 F. Supp. 125 (D.N.J. 1982).
[508] M. & D. Nimmer, NIMMER ON COPYRIGHT §7.2[A] (1998).
[509] 17 U.S.C. §410(b) (2008).
[510] Bailie, 258 F.2d 425.
[511] N.B. The Sonny Bono Copyright Term Extension Act (Pub. L. No. 105-298, 112 Stat. 2827 (1998)) extended all terms of duration by 20 years from the times then set forth to the times now identified in the text. For a particularly thorough and elegantly table (created by Peter B. Hirtle) setting forth the applicable duration of copyright based upon date of original publication and other statutory criteria, the reader is directed to www.copyright.cornell.edu/public_domain
[512] *See infra* §1.9.1.
[513] *See infra* §1.9.2.
[514] *See, e.g.* 17 U.S.C. §901 *et. seq.* (2008).

Over this time, the term of copyright has periodically been extended by Congress. It has grown from 25 years under the early copyright laws to a term that may now in some cases exceed 120 years or more (under the life of the author plus 70 year standard[515]). Congressional authority to repeatedly extend the protection for current works and the right to protect copyright for such a long term were challenged in *Eldred v. Ashcroft*,[516] decided by the Supreme Court in 2003. Plaintiffs, marketers and users of works in the public domain had argued that the continuing process of extending copyright created a virtually unlimited copyright, that extending copyright for existing works violated the purpose of the copyright clause (i.e., "to *promote* the useful arts ..."), and that such a long term was unreasonable and exceeded that contemplated within the Constitution. The Supreme Court rejected all of these arguments. The Court clearly recognized a broad right of Congressional discretion in exercising its Constitutional authority in determining the term of copyright protection.

1.9.1. Works Created on or after January 1, 1978

Copyright in a work created on or after January 1, 1978, subsists from its creation and fixation for a term equal to the life of the author plus 70 years after his or her death.[517] For joint works, the term endures for the life of the last living author plus 70 years after such last surviving author's death.[518] (Note that for "composite works," since each element is separable, each element is governed by the life of that author – not the life of the co-author.) For anonymous and pseudonymous works (unless registration is made identifying the true name of the author within the lifetime of that author plus 70 years or, in the case of a joint work, within the lifetime of the last surviving author plus 70 years) and works made for hire, copyright subsists for a term of 95 years from publication or 120 years from creation and fixation, whichever occurs first.[519]

---

[515] *Id.* at §302.
[516] Eldred, 537 U.S. 186.
[517] 17 U.S.C. §302(a) (2008).
[518] *Id.* at §302(b).
[519] *Id.* at §302(c).

Unless notice is filed with the Copyright Office that the author is still alive or providing the actual date of the author's death,[520] there is a presumption that the copyright has expired (i.e., that the author died over 70 years previously) after the earlier of 95 years after publication or 120 years following creation and fixation.[521]

1.9.2. Works Created but Not Published or Copyrighted before January 1, 1978

Copyright in those works created (and embodied in tangible form) but not yet published or registered for copyright prior to January 1, 1978, are governed by the same term as those created on or after that date,[522] except that in no event would an unpublished work's term expire prior to December 31, 2002, or, if it is published before that time, it will not expire prior to December 31, 2047.[523]

1.9.3. Works Copyrighted Prior to January 1, 1978

The term of copyright under §24 of the 1909 Act was an initial term of 28 years from the date of initial publication plus the right to renew the term on written application made within one year prior to the expiration of the original term for an additional 28 years. Failure to renew the copyright at the end of the initial term would dedicate the work to the public domain. Although §24 defines the commencement of the "date of first publication with notice," §304 of the 1976 Act has altered this language (in conformity with prior judicial interpretation of §24[524]) to define "commencement" as being from the date when copyright "was originally *secured*" (which under the prior act includes either publication with notice or registration).[525]

The most significant change that §304 of the 1976 Act made with respect to the term of copyrights created under the 1909 Act was to extend their renewal terms by 19 years, thus providing a total term of 75 years from the date in which copyright protection was initially

---

[520] *Id*. at §302(d).
[521] *Id*. at §302(e).
[522] *See supra* §1.9.1.
[523] 17 U.S.C. §303 (2008).
[524] Marx v. United States, 96 F.2d 204 (9th Cir. 1938).
[525] *See supra* §1.6.

secured. Notice that this change did not obviate the need for the owner to apply for copyright renewal at the end of the initial term (something that is not required for works created after January 1, 1978 under the 1976 Act).[526] In application this extension occurred so that for works in their initial term as of January 1, 1978, their renewal terms were extended for a period of 47 years;[527] and for works in their renewal terms (or for which renewal application was made prior to January 1, 1976), their terms were extended by 19 years (up to the total of 75 years from when copyright was secured).[528]

The Copyright Renewal Act of 1992[529] has finally and effectively ended the durational limits imposed by the renewal concept for all pre-1978 works whose initial term expires subsequent to June 1992. While maintaining incentives to encourage authors and copyright owners of these pre-1978 works to continue to file renewal registration applications,[530] the penalty of losing one's copyright upon failure to renew has been removed from the law.[531]

Finally, for all copyrights on pre-1978 works still under copyright as of October 1998, the Sonny Bono Copyright Extension Act[532] extended their term of protection for an additional 20 years up to a total term of 95 years from the date of creation.

1.9.4. Works Created between 1906 and 1921

The process of revising the copyright laws leading to the 1976 Act commenced in 1955.[533] During this time it was recognized that one element of the expected change would result in the extension of the term of copyright protection. In order to preserve the interests of those copyright owners whose protection during their renewal term would otherwise expire during this period of congressional deliberations, the Congress enacted a series of interim extensions commencing on September 19, 1962, extending the term of those affected copyrights

---

[526] *See id.* at §§1.9.1 and 1.9.2.
[527] 17 U.S.C. §304(a) (1976 – revised 1998 to 67 years).
[528] *Id.* at §304(b) (1976 – revised 1998 to total of 95 years).
[529] Pub. L. No. 102-307, 106 Stat. 264 (1992).
[530] 17 U.S.C. §102(4) (2008).
[531] *See infra* §1.11.2.
[532] Pub. L. No. 105-80, 111 Stat. 1529, Section 1 (1997).
[533] H. REP., *supra* note 39, at 47.

from time to time up through the adoption of the new act.[534] The final result was that for works whose copyright had commenced between 1906 and 1921 and had been properly renewed, their terms were ultimately extended to 75 years from commencement of copyright by the 1976 Act and again by the Sonny Bono Copyright Extension Act (1998) to a total of 95 years from commencement of copyright.[535]

1.10. TRANSFERS

1.10.1. In General

The ownership of a copyright may be transferred in whole or in part by any means of conveyance, by operation of law, by bequest, by will, or by intestate succession.[536] Moreover, any of the exclusive "bundle of rights" specified in §106 of the 1976 Act may be separately transferred and enforced.[537] To be effective such a transfer, other than by operation of law, must be in writing and signed by the owner of the copyright.[538] This requirement, while usually undertaken concurrently with the transfer, may be satisfied by later written ratification or confirmation.[539] A certificate of acknowledgment is not required for transfer but is *prima facie* evidence of the execution of the transfer subject to qualification of the issuer.[540]

The emergence of new technologies subsequent to the execution of a license agreement may present problems. Who controls these rights? While the rules of interpretation for these transfers are set by state contract law, in general it appears that the interpretation will vary according to the nature of the original grant. Where the grant is for a limited or specified right of use, such as to publication rights in a

---

[534] *See* Pub. L. No. 87-668, 76 Stat. 555 (1962); Pub. L. No. 89-142, 79 Stat. 581 (1965); Pub. L. No. 90-141, 81 Stat. 464 (1967); Pub. L. No. 90-416, 82 Stat. 397 (1968); Pub. L. No. 91-147, 83 Stat. 360 (1969); Pub. L. No. 91-555, 85 Stat. 1441 (1970); Pub. L. No. 92-170, 85 Stat. 490 (1971); Pub. L. No. 92-566, 86, Stat. 1181 (1972) and Pub. L. No. 93-573, 88 Stat. 1873 (1974).
[535] 17 U.S.C. §304(b) (2008).
[536] *Id.* at §201(d)(1). *See also* the Copyright Act of 1909, §28.
[537] 17 U.S.C. §201(d)(2) (2008).
[538] *Id.* §204(a).
[539] Arthur Rutenberg Homes, Inc. v. Drew Homes, Inc., 29 F.3d 1529 (11th Cir. 1994).
[540] 17 U.S.C. §204(b) (2008).

particular format, the courts will interpret the grant specifically and narrowly. For example, in a free-lance contract for the publication of an article in a newspaper or magazine, the courts have refused to interpret that grant to include electronic reproduction rights for the article by that publisher.[541] By contrast, where the assignment is drafted broadly as a transfer of ownership or includes a broad grant of rights, the transfer will be interpreted to include all possible means of reproduction unless the creator specifically reserves particular rights.[542]

1.10.1.1. Exceptions to the Writing Rule

There are, however, certain exceptions to the requirement of a writing. Under the 1976 Act, the definition of "transfer of ownership" includes all forms of conveyance, including exclusive licenses but excluding nonexclusive licenses.[543] Therefore, nonexclusive rights can be transferred pursuant to an oral agreement[544] (although such a transfer may fall afoul of state grounds for statute of frauds).[545] Federal law governs the potential to create an implied non-exclusive copyright license, however, state contract law governs whether or not the copyright owner actually granted such a license.[546] Moreover, at least in the Ninth Circuit, an oral transfer for unspecified duration may not be terminated absent a material breach of the license except as provided in §203 of the Copyright Act.[547]

A second exception, or so it appears at first glance, occurs under the 1909 Act and the preceding 1878 Copyright Act wherein a series

---

[541] *See* N. Y. Times Co. v. Tasini, 533 U.S. 483; Warner Bros. Pictures v. CBS, Inc., 216 F.2d 945 (9th Cir. 1954), *cert. denied,* 348 U.S. 971 (1955); *see generally* Cohen v. Paramount Picture Corp., 845 F.2d 851 (9th Cir. 1988); *But see* Greenberg v. Nat'l Geographic Soc'y, 488 F.3d 1331 (11th Cir. 2007), reh'g en banc granted, opinion vacated, 497 F.3d 1213 (11th Cir. 2007).

[542] *See* Zyla v. Wadsworth, 360 F. 3d 243 (1st Cir. 2004); Greenfield, slip op., 750 N.Y.S.2d 565; Bartsch v. Metro-Goldwyn-Mayer, Inc., 391 F.2d 150, 155 (2d Cir.), *cert. denied* 393 U.S. 826 (1968); Batiste v. Island Records, 179 F.3d 217(5th Cir. 1999), *cert. denied,* 528 U.S. 1076 (2000); Maljack Prods. v. Good Times Home Video Corp., 81 F.3d 881, 885 (9th Cir. 1996).

[543] 17 U.S.C. §101.

[544] *See* Gracen v. Bradford Exch., 698 F.2d 300 (7th Cir. 1983).

[545] *See* Myers v. Waverly Fabrics, 475 N.Y.S.2d 860 (N.Y. App. Div. 1984), *order afff'd as modified,* 489 N.Y.S.2d 891 (N.Y. 1985).

[546] Foad Consulting Group, Inc. v. Azzalino, 270 F.3d 821 (9th Cir. 2001).

[547] Rano v. Sipa Press, 987 F.2d 580 (9th Cir. 1993).

of cases held that transfer of the manuscript or unpublished work prior to registration of copyright or publication with notice served to transfer the underlying copyright.[548] This is in spite of the fact that §28 of the 1909 Act required a writing and §27 of the 1909 Act (reflected in §202 of the 1976 Act) recognized that copyright exists separately from the object in which it is embodied. This apparent anomaly arose from the fact that copyright under the 1909 Act did not commence until after publication with notice or registration. The transfer was, in effect, a transfer of common law copyright or the inchoate right to a statutory copyright.[549] Because, under the current law, copyright commences on the work's embodiment in tangible form, this line of cases has been effectively outdated except for those rare instances where a common law copyright may yet exist.[550] Of course, these cases still hold authority over parole transfers that took place under the 1909 Act.[551]

Finally, under a variation of the transfer of a copy of a work representing a transfer of rights, a number of court decisions have resurrected the formerly obscure doctrine of the "Implied License."[552] Under this doctrine, a putative purchaser who has contributed no more than unprotectable ideas towards the creation of a new work by a non-employee creator may acquire immunity from suit by the creator by obtaining physical possession of the work even though the purchaser has obtained no written or oral authorization for the use of that work. While previously this doctrine was limited to an equitable action by the court to avoid "absurd result,"[553] it has more recently been held that the transfer of physical possession of the works to the defendant created an implied license for the use of those works despite the defendant's

---

[548] *See* Callaghan, 128 U.S. 617, M. Witmark & Sons v. Galloway, 22 F.2d 412 (E.D. Tenn. 1927).
[549] *See* Black v. Henry G. Alien Co., 42 F. 618 (C.C.S.D.N.Y 1890).
[550] *See supra* §1.2.4.1.
[551] *See* Jerry Vogel Music Co. v. Warner Bros., Inc., 535 F. Supp. 172 (S.D.N.Y. 1982).
[552] Effects Assocs. v. Cohen, 908 F.2d 555 (9th Cir. 1990), *cert. denied sub nom.*, Danforth v. Cohen, 498 U.S. 1103 (1991); Maclean Assocs., Inc. v. Mercer-Meidinger-Hansen, Inc., 952 F.2d 769 (3d Cir. 1991).
[553] *See, e.g.*, Brunswick Beacon v. Schock-Hopchas Publishing Co., 810 F.2d 410 (4th Cir. 1987); Gracean v. Bradford Exchange, 698 F.2d 300 (7th Cir. 1983); Oddo, 743 F.2d 630.

admitted failure to pay the creator for those works.[554] In applying this doctrine, courts have overcome the §202 proscription of the Copyright Act that provides that the "[t]ransfer of any material object including the copy ... does not of itself convey any rights in the copyrighted work embodied in the object" by construing the implied license as being a non-exclusive license and thus, in a strict sense, not being the conveyance of a "right."

The concept of an implied license tends to ameliorate at least some of the consequences of what happens when an independent contractor or commissioned party is paid to create. For example, an unsophisticated lay person pays an independent contracting author to create a writing, artwork, website design or audiovisual work. The layperson's assumption is likely that the person who pays for the creation of the work owns its copyright. But under the Copyright Law, that is not normally true. Unless rather specific aspects of the Copyright Act are adhered to or additional actions taken, the creator, not the person who pays for it, still owns it. Nevertheless, an implied license to use the work is typically created, and even if the commissioning party does not own the copyright, he or she does own the right to use it at least for its intended purpose.

1.10.1.2. Subsequent Transfers of Exclusive Rights

As noted above, transfers of exclusive rights in a copyrighted work are regulated by the copyright statute to require that they must be in writing. The law also limits the ability of subsequent licensees of exclusive rights in copyrighted works to transfer their interests (the exclusive right in the copyright) to other parties without the prior consent of the author or original licensor.[555] On a policy ground, the Ninth Circuit held that this policy was necessary to protect the licensor's interests in monitoring the use of the copyright and its exploitation under the exclusive agreement.

---

[554] Effects Assocs., 908 F.2d 630, *cert. denied sub nom.*, Danforth v. Cohen, 498 U.S. 1103.

[555] Gardner v. Nike, Inc., 279 F.3d 774 (9th Cir. 2002).

1.10.2. Mandatory Licenses

In order to encourage the livelihood of certain industries, the copyright law has created certain mandatory licensing structures for the use of copyrighted works. These include secondary transmissions by cable companies,[556] mechanical royalties for phonorecords (i.e., based on the right to affix a composition in the form of records, tapes, compact discs or other embodied form),[557] juke box uses,[558] non-commercial public broadcasting,[559] private copying by digital audio recording devices,[560] subscription digital audio transmission services[561] and digital transmission of phonorecords services.[562]

In the past, this mandatory licensing was incorporated within a mixed system of statutory licenses (licenses in which the royalty fee and all the terms and conditions of the license are set by statute) and compulsory licenses (in which the owner was obligated to grant a license and where agreement between the owner and user cannot be reached voluntarily, the user has a right to appeal to a government authority). Effective December 1993, the U.S. moved closer to a primarily modified compulsory licensing system. Under this system, alterations in statutory licensing rates and rules of distribution for royalties collected under mandated licensing are handled through an arbitration proceeding, as opposed to the prior tribunal procedure.[563] In practice, based upon the nature of arbitration, this should result in greater room for privately negotiated adjustments to statutory terms and privately negotiated distribution allocations.

There was a slight backward movement in 1998. In the Fairness in Music Licensing Act of 1998,[564] Congress took an area in which voluntary licenses were being negotiated by the musical performing rights societies (subject to being monitored by the courts under existing consent decrees) and (a) exempted some establishments from coverage

---

[556] 17 U.S.C. §111 (2008).
[557] *Id.* at §115.
[558] *Id.* at §115.
[559] *Id.* at §118.
[560] *Id.* at §1003.
[561] *Id.* at §114.
[562] *Id.* at §115.
[563] *Id.* at §§801-803. *See infra* §1.15.
[564] Pub.L. No. 105-298, 112 Stat. 2827, Title 2 (1998).

by the performance right[565] while (b) providing others who owned fewer than seven non-publicly traded establishments with a special right to apply to the courts to set special performance rights royalties for their establishments.[566]

1.10.3. Recordation

Section 205 of the 1976 Act governs the formalities of recordation of transfer. It provides that any document pertaining to transfer of copyright (which would include exclusive licenses, mortgages, and assignments in whole or in part) may be filed for recordation, provided that it properly identifies the pertinent work and is signed by the owner (either with the actual signature or accompanied by a sworn acknowledgment that it is a true copy of the original).[567] On receipt of the document and the appropriate fee (provided under §708), the Register of Copyrights will record the document and return it with a certificate of recordation.[568]

Such recordation will provide constructive notice to all persons, provided that (1) it specifically identifies the pertinent work and (2) the work has been previously registered.[569] Moreover, the registration will create priority over subsequent transfers, as long as it is registered within one month of transfer (two months, if occurring outside the United States) or prior to recordation of a later transfer by a bona fide transferee for value (i.e., taken in good faith, without notice, and for value).[570] Although registration is permissive,[571] failure to do so can result in loss of the copyright to a bona fide purchaser for value who registers first.[572] Moreover, as in the case of registration of the primary work, although rectifiable by recordation during pendency,[573]

---

[565] *See supra*, §1.4.1.4.
[566] 17 U.S.C. §512 (2008).
[567] 17 U.S.C. §205(a) (2008).
[568] *Id.* at §205(b).
[569] *Id.* at §205 (c).
[570] *Id.* at §205(e).
[571] *See* Richcar Music Co. v. Towns, 385 N.Y.S. 778 (N.Y.A.D. 1976).
[572] 17 U.S.C. §205(e) (2008).
[573] Meta-Film Assocs. v. MCA, Inc., 586 F. Supp. 1346 (C.D. Cal. 1984).

registration of the transfer was a prerequisite to the maintenance of an infringement action[574] prior to the implementation of the Berne Act.[575]

A nonexclusive license survives transfer of ownership, provided that the license was issued prior to the execution of the transfer or the license was taken in good faith before recordation and without notice of it.[576] Here again is an incentive for recordation.

1.10.4. Attachments of Other Interests

Like any other property interest, copyright can be both directly hypothecated and made subject to other interests. Recordation of copyright not only provides a means to assure that the rights being conveyed in one transfer have not already been transferred in a prior transaction, it allows for an orderly structuring of financial obligations attaching to a copyright interest, such as a security interest that can be recorded under the copyright law,[577] the Uniform Commercial Code registration system of a particular state, or both.

While the copyright statute governs registration of security interests in registered works, it appears that unregistered works remain subject to state law relating to the perfection of security interests. Because the Copyright Act fails to provide any means to protect security interests in unpublished work, state law is not preempted.[578]

While not directly relating to copyright ownership, a law enacted by Congress provides that a transfer after November 1998 of copyright ownership in a motion picture that has been produced subject to one or more collective bargaining agreements includes an assumption by the purchaser of the obligation to make residual payments and to provide related notice according to the terms of the applicable collective bargaining agreement(s).[579] (This provision does not apply to performance rights transfers or to security interests,[580] nor to other

---

[574] Formerly 17 U.S.C. §205(d) deleted by the Berne Convention Implementation Act of 1988.
[575] Berne Act §§5 and 13.
[576] 17 U.S.C. §205(f) (2008).
[577] Id. at §205. See in re Peregrine Entertainment, Ltd. 116 B.R. 194 (1990) (holding security interest in registered copyright perfected only by Copyright Office filing).
[578] In re World Auxillary Power Co., 303 F.3d 1120 (9th Cir. 2002).
[579] 28 U.S.C. §4001 (2008).
[580] Id. at (b) & (c).

ongoing obligations such as profits participation interests held by directors, actors, or other contributors to the film.)

1.11. RENEWAL AND TERMINATION RIGHTS

1.11.1. The Rationale behind Renewal Rights and Termination Rights

The concept of an initial and a renewal term of copyright was first instituted in the Statute of Anne,[581] and was continued under the first federal copyright law[582] and in every subsequent federal copyright law until 1976. There are two rationales for the renewal concept. First, a majority of copyrighted works fail to achieve or attain an economic worth during the first twenty-eight years of their existence (the period of the "initial term" preceding implementation of the 1976 Act) that justifies an author's expending the time and effort necessary to continue protection of that work through the renewal process. Indeed, while the specific figures vary according to the differing types of works protected by copyright (e.g., maps, motion pictures, fine art, fabric designs, etc.), the Copyright Office reports that overall only approximately twenty percent of all copyrights for pre-1978 works were renewed.[583] Thus, in keeping with the intent that copyright is not primarily intended to reward creators but solely to act as an incentive for the creation of new works for the public good,[584] it was felt that creative works should be dedicated to the public domain as soon as practicable. While the renewal requirement accomplished this goal it also had the unfortunate consequence of depriving some deserving authors of their copyrights who failed to renew their rights out of ignorance or clerical error.[585]

The second rationale for the renewal concept, as explained in the House Report for the 1909 Act,[586] was to protect authors who frequently sold their copyrights for low sums at their inception. The

---

[581] 8 Ann. c. 19 (1710).
[582] Act of May 31, 1790, ch. 15, 1 Stat. 124.
[583] H. REP. No. 102-379, 102d Cong. 2d Sess. 19 (1992).
[584] Twentieth Century Music Corp. v. Aiken, 422 U.S. 151 (1975); Mazer, 347 U.S. 201.
[585] H. REP. No. 102-379, 1-10.
[586] House Report on the Copyright Act of 1909, H. REP. No. 2222, 60th Cong. 2d Sess. 14 (1908).

committee felt that, if the work became a great success, the author should become the beneficiary of that success by being able to claim renewal of the copyright in his own name.

This second rationale was largely emasculated by the courts. The 1909 Act[587] provided that the right to renewal vested in the author, or, if deceased, the author's widow, children, executor, or next of kin (who may be referred to as the author's "statutory beneficiaries")[588] within one year before the end of the initial term. The courts very properly determined that this was a "contingent" interest or expectancy that did not vest in the author (or the author's statutory beneficiaries), unless the author survived (or alternatively predeceased the class of beneficiaries that could ultimately be vested with the right of renewal,[589] whether the spouse and/or children or others).[590] Unfortunately, using the rationale that copyright rights should be freely alienable, the court in *Fred Fisher Music Co. v. M. Witmark & Sons*[591] held that an author could assign his or her renewal right and, if it ultimately vested (i.e., the author survived until renewal was effected), the assignment would be binding on the author. Thereafter, it became routine to use language in all original transfers of the copyright assigning "all renewals and extensions thereof."

Such an assignment is not valid against surviving statutory beneficiaries if the author is not living at the time of renewal.[592] However, here again the courts weakened the power of the renewal right by allowing contingent-successor beneficiaries of the renewal right to assign their contingent interests *apart from the author*.[593]

It was against this background that Congress elected to eliminate the renewal provision for all copyrights created on or after January 1, 1978, and in its stead developed the concept of the termination right as a "provision safeguarding authors against unremunerative transfers."[594]

---

[587] Copyright Act of 1909, §24.
[588] *See id.*
[589] *See* Miller Music Corp. v. Charles N. Daniels, Inc., 362 U.S. 373 (1960). *See also* Copyright Act of 1909, §24.
[590] *See* Miller Music Corp., 362 U.S. 373.
[591] Fred Fisher Music Co. v. M. Witmark & Sons, 318 U.S. 643 (1943).
[592] *See* Shapiro, Bernstein & Co. v. Jerry Vogel Music Co., 161 F.2d 406 (2d Cir. 1946), *opinion clarified*, 73 U.S.P.Q. 5 (2d Cir.), *cert. denied*, 331 U.S. 820 (1947).
[593] *See* Fisher v. Edwin H. Morris & Co., 113 U.S.P.Q. 251 No. 97-203, 1957 WL 7177 (S.D.N.Y. Mar. 19, 1957).
[594] H. REP., *supra* note 39, at 124.

The concept avers that, due to "the unequal bargaining position of authors, resulting in part from the impossibility of determining a work's value until it has been exploited,"[595] the author should be *able* to terminate a transfer and reclaim the copyright during some portion of its term.

1.11.2. The Renewal Right

The renewal provision often failed to accomplish its aim of protecting the author, whether by penalizing many authors who inadvertently lost their copyrights through clerical or ignorant failure to renew, or through the systemic failure to protect the author's renewal interest against encroachment by copyright users. Nonetheless, except for a change extending the renewal term from 28 to 47 years, the 1976 Act[596] preserved the renewal concept with respect to all *existing* copyright licenses, reasoning that a great many of these expectancies "are the subject of existing contracts and it be unfair and immensely confusing to cut off or alter these interests."[597] It wasn't until the Copyright Renewal Act of 1992[598] that the most punitive aspect of the renewal provision, the loss of copyright upon failure to renew, was removed from the law. It is noteworthy, and in keeping with recent copyright revision acts, that the Copyright Renewal Act is carefully drafted to limit its impact to eliminating the loss of copyright on pre-1978 filings based upon failure to renew while preserving all other aspects of the judicial and legislative gloss on the nature and rights of renewal.[599] Moreover, because it is believed that renewal registration is beneficial, the law has been drafted to include "incentives" for renewal registration in the same manner as the law provided incentives for the initial registration of copyright.[600] These incentives require the filing of a renewal application in order for a copyright claimant to sue for statutory damages or attorney's fees,[601] or to prevent the continued use of a derivative work during the renewal term (if it is otherwise

---

[595] *Id.*
[596] *See* 17 U.S.C. §203 (2008).
[597] H. REP., *supra* note 39, at 139.
[598] Pub. L. No. 102-307, 106 Stat. 264 (1992) (hereinafter cited as Copyright Renewal Act).
[599] *Id.* at §102 (c).
[600] *See supra* §1.8.4.3.
[601] Copyright Renewal Act §102 (b)(2).

preventable).[602] Statutory damages and attorney's fees are not available for claims arising during the renewal term prior to the renewal registration. It also provides that certificate of renewal registration shall constitute *prima facie* evidence as to the validity of the copyright during its renewal term and the information contained on such renewal registration certificate.[603] Therefore, copyrights existing in their initial term may be renewed within one year prior to the expiration of the original term by the author (or, for works made for hire, by the employer, who for copyright purposes is deemed the author) or, if the author is dead, by the surviving spouse or the author's children or, if they are not living, by the author's executors or next of kin. While the failure to file for renewal registration in the time proscribed by law prior to June 1992 resulted in the loss of copyright protection for those copyright works,[604] failure to file for renewal subsequent to June 1992 results only in the loss of certain proscribed benefits, such as the right to sue for statutory damages.[605] These renewal rights remain subject to the provisions of assignment of the expectancy by the claimant who survives to the vesting of the renewal right, which occurs at the end of the twenty-eighth year.[606]

Absent a prior assignment of the renewal right, the renewal of the copyright by the original author "creates a new estate, and ... the new estate is clear of all rights, interests or licenses granted under the original copyright."[607] Likewise, renewal by a statutory beneficiary where the author dies before the renewal date and the beneficiary has not separately assigned their right creates a new estate in that beneficiary.[608] Moreover, in contrast to a termination under the current 1976 Act[609] renewal acts as a termination of rights with respect to a derivative work (such as a motion picture) based on that work (e.g.,

---

[602] *Id.* at §102 (a)(4)(A).
[603] *Id.* at §102 (a)(4)(B).
[604] 1976 Copyright Act §304(a).
[605] Copyright Renewal Act §102(b)(2).
[606] *See supra* §1.11.1.
[607] G. Ricordi & Co. v. Paramount Pictures, Inc., 189 F.2d 469, 471 (2d Cir.), *opinion clarified*, 89 U.S.P.Q. 564 , No. 157, 1951 WL 81540 (2d Cir. June 1), *cert. denied*, 342 U.S. 849 (1951).
[608] Miller Music Corp., 362 U.S. 37.
[609] *See infra* §§1.11.3-4. *See* Mills Music, Inc. v. Snyder, 469 U.S. 153 (1985).

story, novel, etc.),[610] provided that the copyright claimant has registered his or her claim for renewal rights.[611]

Special provision under the 1976 Act and continued under the Copyright Renewal Act of 1992 is made for a "posthumous work" authorizing the proprietor of the posthumous work, rather than the surviving spouse, children, or other beneficiary class, to file for renewal. The House of Representatives Report states that this term refers not simply to a work published after the author's death but rather to a work for "which no copyright assignment or other contract for exploitation of the work has occurred during an author's lifetime."[612]

1.11.3. Termination during the Extended Renewal Term

The 1976 Act extended the then-current fifty-six-year term to a term of seventy-five years by adding nineteen years to the renewal term (then extended an additional twenty years in 1998).[613] With respect to this additional extended period of the term, Congress applied the concept of termination allowing the author or author's beneficiaries to terminate any grant made by the author or the author's surviving beneficiaries for that extended period of the term. Under §304(c) of the 1976 Act, termination is effected by (1) giving written notice of termination to the grantee (2) signed by the author or a majority of authors or surviving statutory beneficiaries controlling more than one-half of the copyright interest.

The statutory beneficiaries are (1) the surviving spouse, (2) the surviving spouse taking one-half and the surviving children and/or surviving children of a deceased child sharing one-half per stripes (i.e., each child sharing the interest equally, while the grandchildren share in equal portions the share that would have accrued to the dead child, their parent), (3) the surviving children and grandchildren per stripes, or (4) in the event the author's widow, widower and his or her children or grandchildren are deceased, the author's executor, administrator,

---

[610] Abend, 863 F.2d 1465, aff'd sub nom. Stewart v. Abend, 495 U.S. 207. See infra §7.1.8.
[611] 17 U.S.C. §304(a)(4)(A) (2008).
[612] H. REP., supra note 39, at 139. The report specifically cites and ratifies the holding in Bartok v. Boosey & Hawkes, Inc., 523 F.2d 941 (2d Cir. 1975).
[613] 17 U.S.C. §304(a), (b) (2008).

personal representative, or trustee as owner of the author's entire termination interest.[614]

Termination may be effected at any time during a period of five years beginning at the end of fifty-sixth year after copyright was secured. With respect to copyrights in their renewal term for which the author's or the author's beneficiaries' termination rights had expired on or before October 1998, they have an *additional* termination right with respect to the twenty-year extension provided by the Sonny Bono Copyright Extension Act exercisable within the five-year period beginning at the end of seventy-five years from the date copyright was originally secured.[615] Notice must be given not less than two nor more than ten years before the effective date of termination in a form required by the Register of Copyrights with a copy to be filed in the Copyright Office prior to its effective date. Termination may be effected notwithstanding an agreement to the contrary. Termination reverts all rights to all parties entitled to exercise termination rights, whether or not they join in signing the termination notice.

Notwithstanding termination, a derivative work (e.g., a movie or a record) prepared under the authority of the grant prior to its termination may continue to be utilized under the authority of the grant.[616] Moreover, such termination does not result in the author's receiving sole benefit of the continuing use, where, for example, continuing royalties are paid. Such continuing use remains subject to the exact terms of the original grant to create the derivative work, so that if the grant provides an interest to an intermediary grantee (i.e., an agent or a publisher), the intermediary would continue to receive the benefit of that interest after termination.[617] Finally, while musical performing rights in a derivative work, such as a motion picture, a recording or an audiovisual work, that include a song are part of the derivative work and survive termination, performance royalties for radio performances of post termination sound recordings, print royalties and unidentified TV performance royalties are not.[618]

If the grant is not terminated according to §304(c) requirements, the grant will continue for the remainder of the copyright term.

---

[614] *Id.* at §304(c)(2).
[615] *Id.* at §304(d).
[616] *Id.* at §304(c)6(a).
[617] Mills Music, Inc., v. Snyder, 469 U.S. 153 (1985).
[618] Woods v. Bourne Co., 60 F.3d 978 (2d Cir. 1995).

While the Sonny Bono Copyright Extension Act did not alter the law with respect to the ongoing validity of assignments and copyrights relating to audiovisual works, it did note that it was "the sense of the Congress that copyright owners of audiovisual works for which the term of copyright protection [was] extended ... and the screenwriters, directors, and performers of those audiovisual works, should negotiate in good faith in an effort to reach a voluntary agreement or voluntary agreements with respect to the establishment of a fund or other mechanism for the amount of remuneration to be divided among the parties for the exploitation of those audiovisual works."[619] This was clearly intended to prod negotiations in this direction or face the risk of legislation, although to date no such voluntary agreement has been achieved.

Clearly, as provided in the statute, the individual creator of a work would not retain termination rights where the work was created as a work made for hire[620] since, effectively, the individual is not the "author" – the employer is. However, efforts to circumvent the termination right by, for example, entering into an agreement with the author subsequent to creation and asserting that the work was created as a work made for hire will fail as "agreements to the contrary" prohibited under the statute.[621]

1.11.4. Termination of Transfers Made after January 1, 1978

Section 203 of the 1976 Act provides that "in the case of any work other than a work made for hire, the exclusive or nonexclusive grant of a transfer or license of copyright or of any right under a copyright executed by the author on or after January 1, 1978, otherwise than by will, is subject to termination." Because a written transfer which on its face is drafted to end at a date earlier than the dates set forth in §203 will terminate according to its own terms, the obvious intent of this language is to reach those agreements drafted to transfer a copyright interest "forever," "for the full term of copyright protection," or "for the life of the copyright" (all common terms of transfer).[622]

---

[619] Pub. L. No. 105-298, 112 Stat. 2827, Sec. 105 (1998).

[620] *See supra* §1.7.3.

[621] Marvel Characters, Inc., v. Simon, 310 F.3d 280 (2d Cir. 2002).

[622] *See, e.g.*, Screenwriter's Contract (Chapter 8) ¶9, Trade Book Publishing Agreement (Chapter 9) ¶ 1, *infra*.

Interestingly, in the Ninth Circuit, an oral non-exclusive license of indeterminate duration is not terminable at will (as one might expect and as explicitly provided by California statutory law), but is instead interpreted as a life of the copyright transfer subject only to §203 termination (in the absence of a material breach by licensee).[623]

The provisions of §203 are substantially similar to those provided under §304(c) highlighted above, except with respect to the period of time in which termination may be effectuated. Termination is effected by giving written notice of termination to the grantee signed by the author or by a majority of co-authors or surviving statutory beneficiaries controlling more than one-half of the copyright interest. The statutory beneficiaries are (1) the surviving spouse, (2) the surviving spouse taking one-half and surviving children and/or surviving children of a deceased child sharing one-half per stirpes (i.e., each child sharing their interest in equal portions while the grandchildren share in equal portions the share that would have accrued to a dead child, if any, their parents), (3) the surviving children and/or children of a dead child per stirpes or (4) in the event the author's widow, widower and his or her children or grandchildren are deceased, the author's executor, administrator, personal representative, or trustee as owner of the author's entire termination interest.[624]

Termination may be effected at any time during a period of five years beginning at the end of thirty-five years from the date of execution or, with respect to publication licenses, thirty-five years after publication or forty years after execution, whichever will occur first. Notice must be given not less than two nor more than ten years before the effective date of termination in a from required by the Register of Copyrights with a copy to be filed in the Copyright Office prior to the effective date.

Termination may be effected notwithstanding an agreement to the contrary. Termination reverts all rights to all parties entitled to exercise termination rights, whether or not they join in signing the termination notice. Here again, the individual creator of a work would not retain termination rights where the work was created as a work made for hire[625] since, effectively, the individual is not the "author" – the employer is. However, efforts to circumvent the termination right by,

---

[623] Rano v. Sipa Press, Inc., 987 F.2d 580 (9th Cir. 1993).
[624] 17 U.S.C. § 304(c)(2) (2008).
[625] See supra §1.7.3.

for example, entering into an agreement with the author subsequent to creation and asserting that the work was created as a work made for hire will fail as "agreements to the contrary" prohibited under the statute.[626]

Notwithstanding termination, a derivative work (e.g., a movie or a record) prepared under the authority of the grant prior to its termination may continue to be utilized under the authority of the grant. Moreover, such termination does not result in the author's receiving sole benefit of the continuing use, where, for example, continuing royalties are paid. Any continuing use would remain subject to the exact terms of the original grant to create the derivative work, so if the grant provides an interest to an intermediary grantee (i.e., an agent or a publisher), the intermediary would continue to receive the benefit of that interest, even after termination.[627]

If the grant is not terminated according to §203 requirements, the grant will continue for the remainder of the copyright term.

1.11.5. Restoration of Copyright

Effective as of December 8, 1994, with the enactment of the Uruguay Round Agreements Act[628] which amended §104A of the Copyright Act, the authors or initial rights holders of copyrights from countries who are members of the Berne Convention, the World Trade Organization, or countries that extend similar rights to United States rights holders will have the right to file for the restoration of copyright protection for all works which are not in the public domain in their country of origin due to an expiration of term but which have fallen into the public domain due to a failure to comply with copyright formalities[629] (such as notice, or registration), manufacturing clause compliance,[630] a failure to make a timely application for renewal,[631]

---

[626] Marvel Characters, Inc., 310 F.3d 280. However, a British Court has refused to recognize this provision in a breach of contract action brought against Duran Duran for exercising its § 203 termination right under U.S. Copyright Law, which includes the phrase "notwithstanding any agreement to the contrary." The agreement with Sony/ATV's Gloucester Place Music would probably have been such an agreement. The British Court held that UK contract law applied and noted that no expert on U.S. copyright law provided guidance to the court.
[627] Mills Music, Inc. 469 U.S. 153.
[628] Pub. L. No. 103-465, 108 Stat. 4809 (1994).
[629] *See supra* §1.8.
[630] *See id. at infra* §1.14.1.

lack of available protection due the type of work involved (i.e., lack of subject matter protection), as was the case of sound recording fixed before February 15, 1972, or where the author(s)/initial rights owner(s) were not residents, domiciliaries, or beneficial owners under the laws of a country with which the United States had a copyright treaty as of the date in which the work was initially made public.[632] These works were restored on January 1, 1996 where the source countries were members of Berne or a World Trade Organization member, or upon the date of the Presidential proclamation recognizing a reciprocal protection provision in a particular country, and protection continues until the end of the term of protection "that would have otherwise been granted in the United States if the work [had] never entered the public domain..."[633]

Because this potentially involves a significant number of works and affects a large number of rights users, this section has been carefully drafted to address a variety of situations. First, with respect to people caught in the transition, it makes unenforceable any warranty of non-infringement made before January 1, 1995 that is made inaccurate due to the restoration of a copyright, and voids any performance agreement entered into before January 1, 1995 that would entail the infringement of a restored copyright.[634] Second, the act requires that the Registrar of Copyrights maintain a listing of all restored works and all notices of an intent to enforce rights of restored copyrights on a timely basis.[635] The copyright office will also publish notice whenever a new country becomes eligible for restoration.[636] Third, with respect to all users who have commenced using a work prior to its restoration, the restored-rights owner must submit a notice of intent to enforce his/her rights in the restored work prior to enforcement against that person (and subject to certain time limits), and allows for a sell-off of existing inventories of books or phonograms printed before restoration.[637] Finally, where a rights user has created a derivative work based upon a work subject to restoration, the law imposes an obligation upon the derivative-work owner to pay "reasonable compensation" and, in the event the parties cannot reach agreement upon such compensation,

---

[631] *See id. at supra* §1.11.2.
[632] *See id. at supra* §1.2.6.
[633] 17 U.S.C. §104A(a)(1)(B) (2008).
[634] *Id.* at §104A(a)(f).
[635] *Id.* at §104A(e)(1)(B).
[636] *Id.* at §104A(e)(1)(B)(i).
[637] *Id.* at §104A(d)(2).

states that it "shall be determined by an action in United States district court, and shall reflect any harm to the actual or potential market for or value of the restored work from the [derivative-work owner's] continued exploitation of the work, as well as compensation for the relative contributions of expression of the author of the restored work and the [contributions of the derivative-work author]."[638] This latter provision places significant pressure upon the derivative-work rights owner to reach an agreement with the restored-copyright rights owner.

Provisions of this section do not allow for the restoration of a copyright which has fallen into the public domain, where the author or initial rights owner is a United States citizen or domiciliary or where the work was simultaneously published in its country of origin and in the United States.[639]

1.12. INFRINGEMENT

1.12.1. In General

Section 501(a) of the 1976 Act declares that "anyone who violates any of the exclusive rights of the copyright owner is an infringer of the copyright." This statement appears to be very clear, but it fails to illuminate the complexity of an infringement action. For that we must look to the courts.

There are eight essential elements of a cause of action for copyright infringement: (1) The original work was copyrightable;[640] (2) all formalities required to secure copyright were complied with;[641] (3) the plaintiff is the proprietor of the copyright;[642] (4) the defendants have copied the protected work;[643] and the (5) the defendants have utilized the protected work in violation of the owner's exclusive

---

[638] *Id.* at §104A(d)(3). See application of this provision relating to a reliance party and appropriate license fees in Peter Mayer Publishers, Inc. v. Shilovskaya, 11 F.Supp. 3d 421 (S.D.N.Y. 2014).

[639] *Id.* at §104A(h)(6)(D).

[640] *See Id.* at §102. *See also U.S. Copyright Law, supra* §1.2.

[641] *See* 17 U.S.C. §§401 *et seq.* and 205 (recordation of transfer).

[642] *Id.* at §501(b).

[643] Universal Athletic Sales Co. v. Salkeld, 511 F.2d 904 (3d Cir.), *cert. denied sub nom.,* Universal Athletic Sales Co. v. Pinchock, 423 U.S. 863 (1975).

rights,[644] (6) without permission,[645] (7) excuse or (8) defense.[646] These elements bear closer examination.

1.12.2. Essential Elements of a Cause of Action for Copyright Infringement

1.12.2.1. Copyrightability of the Original Work

This element looks to the requirements of originality and authorship.[647] Where the work merely reproduces a work already in the public domain, it is not entitled to protection.[648] Nor does protection extend to facts,[649] historical events,[650] or ideas.[651] Even if other elements of the original work are protectable, nonprotectable elements (e.g., facts and events) may be used by succeeding works.

1.12.2.2. Formalities of Copyright

The next element examines whether or not the owner has complied with the formalities of obtaining copyright protection, such as publication with notice,[652] if required,[653] (or, in its absence, compliance with the cure provisions of §405),[654] and registration of the original work[655] or transfer instrument.[656] The Court may also examine when and how an unpublished work was deposited, and whether the deposited copy was identical to the original or a recreation.[657] Failure to observe these conditions could result in the work's being dedicated

---

[644] *See* 17 U.S.C. §§106-116, 501(a), 602 (2008).
[645] *See* Lawlor v. Nat'l Screen Serv. Corp., 270 F.2d 146 (3d Cir. 1959), *cert. denied*, 362 U.S. 922 (1960).
[646] *See* 17 U.S.C. §§107-116, 602(a)(1)-(3) (2008).
[647] *See supra* §1.2.
[648] *See* L. Batlin & Son, Inc. 536 F.2d 486, *cert. denied*, 429 U.S. 857.
[649] *See* Higgins v. Baker, 309 F. Supp. 635 (S.D.N.Y. 1969).
[650] *See* Rosemont Enters., Inc. 366 F.2d 303, *cert. denied*, 385 U.S. 1009.
[651] *See* Welles v. CBS, Inc., 308 F.2d 810 (9th Cir. 1962).
[652] 17 U.S.C. §§401 *et seq.(2008) See also U.S. Copyright Law, supra* §1.8.
[653] *See* changes made by the Berne Act, U.S. Copyright Law, *supra* §1.8.
[654] *See supra* §1.8.
[655] 17 U.S.C. §§411-412 (2008). *See supra* §1.8.
[656] 17 U.S.C. §201 (2008). *See supra* §1.8.
[657] Coles, 283 F.3d 798.

to the public domain, such as publication without notice or cure,[658] and therefore being unprotectable, or these conditions may be considered in mitigation of potential damages.[659]

1.12.2.3. Ownership of Copyright

Only the legal or beneficial owner of the copyright or of an exclusive right under that copyright is entitled to institute an action for infringement.[660] The Ninth Circuit has held that a bare assignment of claims and causes of action is not sufficient to provide standing for a copyright infringement claim. The actual copyright interest must also be assigned.[661] Because of the principle of division of ownership of exclusive rights under §201(d) of the 1976 Act, the owner of a particular right who is bringing an action for infringement to protect that right may be required to serve notice (with an option of joinder or intervention as determined by the court) on all others who have an interest or claim to the copyright as shown by the Copyright Office records and whose interests may be affected by the action.[662]

1.12.2.4. Copying of the Protected Work

In order "to establish copyright infringement [the owner] must prove that the defendant has copied the protected work."[663] This is one of the primary differences between patent infringement and copyright infringement. One may infringe a patent by the innocent recreation of a patented work, but the law imposes no liability on those who, without copying, independently arrive at the precise combination of words or notes that have been copyrighted.[664]

Copying, except with respect to "pirated works" (i.e., works that purport to be authorized reproductions, such as albums by a particular artist), is inherently difficult to prove directly because in most cases the

---

[658] *See, supra* §1.8.
[659] *Id.*
[660] 17 U.S.C. §501(b) (2008).
[661] Silvers v. Sony Pictures Entertainment, Inc., 402 F.3d 881 (9th Cir. 2005)(*en banc* decision with dissenting opinions).
[662] *Id. See also* H. REP., *supra* note 39, at 158.
[663] Universal Athletic Sales Co., 511 F.2d 904, *cert. denied sub nom*, Universal Athletic Sales Co. v. Pinchock, 423 U.S. 863.
[664] Fred Fisher, Inc. v. Dillingham, 298 F. 145 (S.D.N.Y. 1924).

courts will not have objective evidence as to how the questioned work was created.[665] Although it may be thought that a test of independent creation would seek to determine the state of mind of the alleged infringer (i.e., did the infringer have the original work in mind when creating the new work), such is not the case.[666] Instead, copying must be inferred[667] or proven by showing that defendant had access to the copyrighted work and that defendant's work is substantially similar to the plaintiffs work.[668] Although exact replication is not required for infringement,[669] it must satisfy a two-prong test: first, the extrinsic or objective test requires a substantial similarity at the level of the general ideas expressed in that work;[670] second, the intrinsic or subjective inquiry requires that the similarity must be visible to the ordinary observer[671] or, in cases where the intended audience of the work has specialized expertise relevant to the purchasing decision on the work, it must be visible to such an expert audience member.[672] In considering this similarity, the nature of the works must be considered as well. In a category of works in which the underlying idea(s) limits the way it may be expressed, small variations may be more significant than the number of similarities between two works of that type.[673] (Determining substantial similarity is a question for the jury and the jury's findings are subject to the same deferential review under Federal Rules of Civil Procedure 50 that applies to other jury findings.[674] The jury must be instructed to consider not only similarity and access but also the

---

[665] Ideal Toy Corp. v. Kenner Prods. Div. of Gen. Mills Fun Group, Inc., 443 F. Supp. 291 (S.D.N.Y. 1977).
[666] *See* Weissmann, 868 F.2d 1313, *cert. denied*, 493 U.S. 883.
[667] Ideal Toy Corp., 443 F. Supp. 291.
[668] Schuchart & Assocs. v. Solo Serve Corp., 540 F. Supp, 928 (W.D. Tex. 1982). *See also* Fogerty v. MGM Group Holdings Corp., Inc., 379 F.3d 348 (6th Cir. 2004), *cert denied*, 543 U.S. 1120 (2005); Jorgensen v. Epic/Sony Records, 351 F.3d 46 (2d Cir. 2003); Metcalf v. Bochco, 294 F. 3d 1069 (9th Cir. 2002).
[669] *See* Williams v. Kaag Mfrs., 338 F.2d 949 (9th Cir. 1964).
[670] Litchfield v. Spielberg, 736 F.2d 1352 (9th Cir. 1984), *cert. denied*, 470 U.S. 1052 (1985).
[671] *See* Berlin v. E.C. Publ'ns , 219 F. Supp. 911 (S.D.N.Y. 1963), *aff'd*, 329 F.2d 541 (2d Cir.), *cert. denied*, 379 U.S. 822 (1964).
[672] Dawson v. Hinshaw Music, Inc., 905 F.2d 731 (4th Cir.), *cert. denied*, 498 U.S. 981 (1990).
[673] Howard v. Sterchi, 974 F.2d 1272 (11th Cir. 1992).
[674] Yurman Design, Inc. v. PAJ, Inc., 262 F.3d 101 (2d Cir. 2001).

defense of independent creation.⁶⁷⁵) Nor is it required that the totality of the protected work is appropriated or that a substantial portion of the infringing work is copied. The real question is one of quality and value as well as quantity.⁶⁷⁶

Proof of motive or intent is not required⁶⁷⁷ (indeed the *unconscious* copying of a protected work is nonetheless actionable⁶⁷⁸), although a showing of motive or intent may be used to support a finding that the infringement was "willful"⁶⁷⁹ and thus affect the determination of damages.⁶⁸⁰ Combined with a significant degree of access, it may justify a lower standard of proof of substantial similarities of the works.⁶⁸¹ Equally, where the dissimilarities between the works appear to be quite obviously the result of a studied effort to make minor distinctions, such effort in itself constitutes evidence of copying.⁶⁸² However, even where substantial similarities are apparent in completed works, the courts may determine that material portions of these similarities predate an alleged infringer's exposure to the other work, and the remaining similarities may consequently be deemed insufficient to sustain an infringement claim. On the other hand, the courts have also determined that unauthorized use of an idea by a production company may not itself constitute a copyright infringement, where the idea was furnished to the company by a professional writer with the expectation that, if the concept was utilized, the writer would be entitled to some continuing involvement and compensation in the process, the writer/contributor may be entitled to protection under a

---

⁶⁷⁵ Susan Wakeen Doll Co. v. Ashton-Drake Galleries, 272 F.3d 441 (7th Cir. 2001).
⁶⁷⁶ *See* Markham v. A. E. Borden Co., 108 F. Supp. 695 (D. Mass. 1952), *rev'd on other grounds*, 206 F.2d 199 (1st. Cir. 1953); Harper & Row Publishers, Inc., 471 U.S. 539; Salinger, 811 F.2d 90, *opinion supplemented on denial of reh'g*, 818 F.2d 252, *cert. denied*, 484 U.S. 890.
⁶⁷⁷ *See* Lottie Joplin Thomas Trust v. Crown Publishers, Inc., 456 F. Supp. 531 (S.D.N.Y. 1977), *aff'd*, 592 F.2d 651 (2d Cir. 1978).
⁶⁷⁸ *See* ABKCO Music, Inc. v. Harrisongs Music, Ltd, 722 F.2d 988 (2d Cir. 1983).
⁶⁷⁹ *See* Lauratex Textile Corp. v. Allton Knitting Mills Inc., 519 F. Supp. 730 (S.D.N.Y. 1981).
⁶⁸⁰ *See* 17 U.S.C. §504(c)(2) (2008).
⁶⁸¹ Sid & Marty Krofft Television Prods., Inc. v. McDonald's Corp., 562 F.2d 1157 (9th Cir. 1977).
⁶⁸² Scarves by Vera, Inc. v. United Merchants & Mfrs., Inc., 173 F. Supp. 625 (S.D.N.Y. 1959).

theory of implied-in-fact contract even where copyright law would offer no protection[683], or might otherwise be argued to preempt such a contract or quasi-contract right.[684]

1.12.2.5. Violation of Exclusive Right

As we have seen, copyright creates for the owner a "bundle" of five rights[685] (or six rights, if one counts the ability to confer territorial exclusivity[686]). Those rights are the rights of (1) reproduction, (2) adaptation, (3) publication, (4) performance, and (5) display. It must be shown that the infringer used the protected work in a way that violated one or more of these exclusive rights.

1.12.2.6. Permission

Incidental to the ownership of copyright is the capacity to lease or license the use thereof on stipulated terms[687] or to sell or transfer title to the work[688] or any of the separate, exclusive rights contained therein.[689] Therefore, one must determine if permission was given and/or whether the actual use exceeded the scope of the grant.[690] It also seeks to determine whether or not the party granting the permission had the right to do so.[691] Good faith is not a defense against infringement. Permission given by one without the right to do so is invalid, even if that party had "apparent authority" to confer such permission. Previously, permission obtained from one copyright owner was sufficient to avoid a charge of copyright infringement. A recent decision, however, found otherwise where a defendant obtained

---

[683] Grosso v. Miramax Film Corp., 383 F. 3d 965 (9th Cir. 2004), *opinion amended on denial of reh'g*, 400 F.3d 658 (9th Cir.), *cert. denied*, 546 U.S. 824 (2005).
[684] *See* Montz v. Pilgrim Films & Television, Inc., 649 F.3d 975 (9th Cir. 2011)
[685] *See supra* §1.4.
[686] *See infra* §1.14.2.2.
[687] Westway Theatre v. Twentieth Century-Fox Film Corp., 30 F. Supp. 830 (D. Md.), *aff'd*, 113 F.2d 932 (4th Cir. 1940).
[688] Pellegrini v. Allegrini, 2 F.2d 610 (E.D. Pa. 1924).
[689] *See supra* §1.4.
[690] *See* Twentieth Century-Fox Film Corp. v. Peoples Theatres of Ala., 24 F. Supp. 793 (M.D. Ala. 1938); Loew's Inc., 131 F. Supp. 165, *aff'd sub nom.* Benny v. Loew's Inc., 239 F.2d 532, *cert granted sub nom.* CBS, Inc., 353 U.S. 946, *aff'd*, 356 U.S. 43, *reh'g denied*, 356 U.S. 934.
[691] *See* Chappell & Co. v. Frankel, 285 F. Supp. 798 (S.D.N.Y. 1968).

permission after an infringement suit was filed from a copyright co-owner not involved in the suit.[692]

As between the copyright owner and an "innocent" infringer, courts have found that the infringer was the one in the position to assure themselves of the rights of his/her licensor and to seek protection through the inclusion of an indemnification agreement in its license with that licensor and/or insurance protection.[693] An infringement may also occur as to one element embodied in a work while an adequate license is in place for usage of the remainder of the work even when permission for use has properly been obtained with respect to the broader work (e.g., a musical composition contained in a sound master may be infringed by a sampled appearance in another recording, even though a license with respect to the master itself was properly obtained).[694]

1.12.2.7. Excuse

The inquiry into the element of excuse seeks to determine if there is some privilege or excuse for the use of the protected work. The copyright law specifically places certain limitations on the rights of copyright that allow others to use the protected work in ways that, without such statutory privilege, would infringe the rights of the copyright owner.[695] The broadest and most significant of these privileges is inherent in the doctrine of fair use as a defense against infringement.[696]

1.12.2.8. Defense

The final element of an infringement action is whether or not the defendant can allege and prove any defenses against the alleged infringement. Statutorily, the Copyright Act provides for the defense of the expiration of a three-year statute of limitations.[697] Other defenses

---

[692] Davis v. Blige, 505 F.3d 90 (2d Cir. 2007), *cert. denied*, 129 S. Ct. 117 (2008).

[693] Pinkham v. Sara Lee Corp., 983 F.2d 824 (8th Cir. 1992).

[694] Newton v. Diamond, 349 F. 3d 591 (9th Cir. 2003), *opinion amended & superseded on denial of reh'g*, 388 F.3d 1189 (9th Cir. 2004), *cert. denied*, 545 U.S. 1114 (2005). Notably, the court found in favor of the defendants on the basis that the allegedly infringing use was *de minimis* as it consisted of only three notes.

[695] *See supra* §1.4. 17 U.S.C. §§107 *et seq.* (2008).

[696] *See supra* §1.5.

[697] 17 U.S.C. §507 (2008).

commonly used in other types of actions and equally applicable to actions under copyright include: res judicata and collateral estoppel;[698] unclean hands;[699] laches;[700] fair use;[701] *de minimis* use;[702] and estoppel.[703] Defenses unique to copyright, and intellectual property in general, are: *abandonment*, where the copyright owner has manifested an intent to abandon the copyright to the public domain;[704] and *copyright misuse*, where the copyright owner has improperly used a desirable copyright, through the inclusion of a certain condition in its license, to obtain an improper benefit or advantage from its licensee.[705]

---

[698] Rohauer v. Killiam Shows, Inc., 379 F. Supp. 723 (S.D.N.Y. 1974), *rev'd on other grounds*, 551 F.2d 484 (2d Cir.), *cert. denied*, 431 U.S. 949 (1977).

[699] Midway Mfg. Co. v. Artic Int'l, Inc., 547 F. Supp. 999 (N.D. Ill. 1982), *aff'd*, 704 F.2d 1009 (7th Cir.), *cert. denied*, 464 U.S. 823 (1983).

[700] New Era Publications International, 884 F.2d at 661. Petrella v. Metro-Goldwyn-Meyer, 134 S.Ct. 1962 (2014) (held that laches cannot be used to cutoff a 3 year look back of a claim where a fixed statutory limitations period appears in the copyright statute).

[701] *See* §1.5. 17 U.S.C. 107. The fair use doctrine original based on common law, was incorporated into the Copyright Act of 1976. Section 107 provides a preamble followed by four specific facts which must be considered in determining whether fair use exists, none of which need be determinative. Traditionally, the most important factor was the extent to which the would-be copyright was harmed by the defendant's use. Since the U.S. Supreme Court case of Two Live Crew's parody of the Pretty Woman composition in a rap song, the test has gradually focused on whether the would-be infringement was sufficiently transformative and if so, the defense of fair use may be available. A somewhat extreme example of fair use involves the use of photographs of Rastafarians in their native habitat in Jamaica used to create derivative works by an artist altering those photographs by putting the works in incongruous positions. *See also* Carriou v. Prince, 714 F.3d 694 (2d Cir. 2013).

[702] Newton v. Diamond, 388 F.3d 1189 (9th Cir. 2004). Bridgeport Music, Inc. v. Dimension Films, 410 F.3d 792 (6th Cir. 2005) (held that sampling of sound recordings no matter how small cannot be fair use while VMG Salsoul, LLC v. Ciccone, 824 F.3d 871 (9th Cir. 2016) held that one .23 second sample in Madonna's Vogue was de minimus when applied to sound recordings since the average audience would not recognize the appropriation).

[703] Hampton v. Paramount Pictures Corp., 279 F.2d 100 (9th Cir.), *cert. denied*, 364 U.S. 882 (1960).

[704] Rohauer, 379 F. Supp. 723, *rev'd on other grounds*, 551 F.2d 484, *cert. denied*, 431 U.S. 949.

[705] Lasercomb Am., Inc. v. Reynolds, 911 F.2d 970 (4th Cir. 1990). *See* Omega S.A. v. Costco Wholesale Corp., 776 F.3d 692 (9th Cir. 2015) in which misuse considered a defense to copyright infringement where significant purpose of a globe copyright design on watches was used to control importation.

Some courts hold that the 3 year statute commences when the first act of infringement occurs. Others hold that infringement occurs begins anew for each act of infringement in a materially different form. A dispute over authorship or ownership claims has a 3 year statute of limitations which prevents the issue being raised in a future infringement incident.[706]

For a period of time, the courts were divided over the question of whether a state, its officials, or instrumentalities could be held liable for copyright infringement. While some courts held the Copyright Act should be read expansively to embrace coverage of the states,[707] other courts in more recent cases took the position that the copyright statute as drafted was too vague to overrule a state's traditional Eleventh Amendment immunity from suit, which could not be considered abrogated without the consent of the state or a clear showing that Congress intended its law to make the states liable.[708] This confusion has now been ended by the Copyright Remedy Clarification Act,[709] in which Congress specifically states that "any State, any instrumentality of a State, and any officer or employee of a State or instrumentality of a State acting in his or her official capacity" may be held liable for copyright infringement and that the Eleventh Amendment immunity is specifically abrogated.[710] Or so Congress thought. The Fifth Circuit disagrees[711] arguing that, under Supreme Court precedent, Congress cannot abrogate the sovereign immunity of the States except under the authority of Section 5 the Fourteenth Amendment based upon a showing that Congress is remedying an abuse by the states. Since Congress made no factual findings of widespread copyright infringement by the states, the law fails to meet the Constitutional threshold for action under the Fourteenth Amendment. A final solution to this problem depends upon the Supreme Court.

---

[706] Consumer Health Info Corp. v. Amylin Pharms, Inc., 819 F.3d 992 (7th Cir. 2016); Simmons v. Stanbury, 810 F.3d 114 (2d Cir. 2016)(ownership claims barred by 3 year statute of limitations once issue arises, where an exclusive licensee was denied a license).

[707] See, e.g., Mills Music, Inc. v. Ariz., 591 F.2d 1278 (9th Cir. 1979); Johnson v. University of Va., 606 F.Supp. 321 (W.D. Va. 1985).

[708] See, e.g., BV Eng'g v. Univ. of Cal., L. A., 858 F.2d 1394 (9th Cir. 1988), cert. denied, 489 U.S. 1090 (1989); Lane v. Nat'l Bank of Boston, 687 F.Supp. 11 (D. Mass. 1988), aff'd, 871 F.2d 166 (1st Cir. 1989).

[709] Pub. L. No. 101-553, 104 Stat. 2749 (1990).

[710] Id. at §2 (amending 17 U.S.C. §§501, 511).

[711] Chavez v. Arte Publico Press, 204 F.3d 601 (5th Cir. 2000).

1.12.3. Actions for Infringement

The Copyright Act provides for both civil actions based in tort[712] and criminal actions.[713] Both types of actions are subject to a three-year statute of limitations.[714] Notice of all filings, whether criminal or civil, outlining the claims identified in the filing as well as notice of final judgment or order will be sent by the court clerk to the United States Copyright Office for entry in the public record.[715]

1.12.4. Criminal Offenses

In addition to the elements required to sustain a civil infringement action, as identified in §1.11.2 hereinabove, criminal infringement requires that the infringement be *willful*[716] and for purposes of commercial advantage or private gain[717] (including the receipt of other copyrighted works[718]), or that the infringer reproduce or distribute within any 180-day period copies or phonorecords of copyrighted works with a total retail value of more than $1,000.[719] Specifying that the receipt of other copyrighted works is included within the definition of financial gain clearly reflects an effort to criminalize "barter" type operations, where people trade electronic copies of copyrighted works with each other. In order to make it clear that criminal liability attaches to acts on the Internet or other electronic media, the law specifically states that it applies to "reproduction or distribution, *including by electronic means*"[720] (emphasis added).

The Copyright Act also provides criminal sanctions for use of false notice of copyright with a fraudulent intent,[721] the removal or alteration of a notice with a fraudulent intent,[722] and the making of false

---

[712] *See* Leo Feist, Inc. v. Young, 138 F.2d 972 (7th Cir. 1943).
[713] 17 U.S.C. §506 (2008).
[714] *Id.* at §507.
[715] *Id.* at §508.
[716] *See* United States v. Wise, 550 F.2d 1180 (9th Cir.), *cert. denied*, 434 U.S. 929 (1977).
[717] *Id. See also* 17 U.S.C. §506(A) (2008).
[718] *Id.* at §101 (definition of "financial gain.").
[719] *Id.* at §506(a)(2).
[720] *Id.*
[721] *Id.* at §506(c).
[722] *Id.* at §506(d).

representations of material facts in applications for copyright or statements filed in connection with an application.[723]

1.13. DMCA PROVISIONS

The Online Copyright Infringement Liability Limitations Act of the Digital Millennium Copyright Act sought to strike a balance between copyright rights holders and service providers. Service providers would not be overburdened with copyright infringement claims when they had limited involvement other than providing the tools for carrying out infringement by others while providing useful services to the public. In a detailed manner, the DMCA provided "safe harbors" so that if the service provider undertook certain acts mandated by the statute, it would be shielded from claims of contributory and vicarious liability for copyright infringement.[724]

Content rights holders had an interest in being able to go after service providers for secondary liability of copyright infringement. Secondary liability may be found from either vicarious liability or contributory infringement where the safe harbors are not effectuated. Vicarious liability occurs based on the tort concept of *respondeat superior* or enterprise liability and imputed intent. Vicarious liability arises when a defendant has the right and ability to supervise infringing conduct and has a direct financial interest in the infringing activity. Contributory infringement occurs when a defendant engages in personal conduct that encourages or assists infringement, thus, the combination of knowledge combined with either a material contribution to that infringement or inducement of that infringement. The safe harbors are built on the foundations of defining boundaries for secondary liability for service providers.

Essentially four safe harbors are provided under the DMCA:

a. The safe harbour provision "Transitory Digital Network Communications," essentially for content traveling through intermediate and transient storage of content while being transmitted, routed or providing connections;[725]

---

[723] *Id.* at §506(e).
[724] 17 U.S.C. § 512 (2015).
[725] 17 U.S.C. § 512(a) (2015).

b. System caching, where there is temporary storage of content on a system or network;[726]
c. Information residing on systems or networks at the direction of users;[727] and
d. Information location tools.[728]

The specifics of the implementation and scope in the statute are complex and the statute and case law must be reviewed carefully to meaningfully evaluate particular situations.[729]

One of the requirements to take advantage of the safe harbors was to have agents of service providers provide contact information to the Copyright Office to create a Directory of Service Provider Agents for Notification of Claims of Infringement. Originally, this was accomplished by mail, however, as of 2017, this must be completed online and resubmitted during 2017 if previously submitted by mail.[730]

Another requirement was that sites have provisions to ban "repeat infringers."[731]

Separate subjects of the DMCA are anti-circumvention provisions and copyright information management provisions. The Anti-circumvention provisions prohibit the use of means for circumventing protective measures for prevention of copyright infringement.[732] Information management provisions prohibit removal of copyright management information such as the name of a rightsholder in a copyright notice.[733]

---

[726] 17 U.S.C. § 512(b) (2015).
[727] 17 U.S.C. § 512(c) (2015).
[728] 17 U.S.C. § 512(d) (2015).
[729] Thus, these safe harbor provisions have been held to apply to copyright infringement under state law for pre-72 sound recordings as well as federal copyright. Capitol Records LLC v. Vimeo LLC, 826 F.3d 78 (2d Cir. 2016).
[730] Copyright Office Regulations. Information regarding registration is available on the Copyright Office website at www.copyright.gov.
[731] See Capitol Records Inc. v. MP3tunes LLC, 48 F. Supp. 3d 703 (2014) (in which the failure to terminate repeat infringers was a basis for loss of the safe harbor).
[732] 17 U.S.C. § 1201; See Chapter 1.16.
[733] 17 U.S.C. § 1202.

1.13.1. Takedown Notices

In order for service providers to be brought under safe harbors to avoid copyright liability for infringements by third parties using their services, they must expeditiously remove or disable access to material claimed to be infringing when they are provided notification. Such notices are required to provide specific information to be effective. Essentially, it must include the following six elements:

1. A physical or electronic signature.
2. Identification of the work claimed to be infringed.
3. Identification of the material to be removed.
4. Specific contact information of the complaining party.
5. A stated good faith belief that the use is not authorized.
6. A statement that the information is accurate and that the complaining party is authorized to act.

If the statute is followed, there is no liability for good faith takedowns by the service provider.[734] Where the owner of a hosted website disputes the complaint, a counter-notification procedure is available requiring that the service provider replace the material and again relieving the service provider from liability if the statute is followed.[735]

The public has a duty to consider the fair use defense when submitting take down notices to service providers and the failure to do so could alter an attorney's fees award in infringement litigation.[736]

1.14. REMEDIES

1.14.1. Criminal Sanctions

Actions for criminal infringement provide penalties of fines and/or imprisonment[737] and for forfeiture and destruction of infringing copies

---

[734] 17 U.S.C. § 512(g).
[735] 17 U.S.C. § 512(g)(3).
[736] Lenz v. Universal Music Corp., 801 F.3d 1126 (9th Cir. 2015)(the failure to do so when music of Prince appeared in the background of the "dancing baby" video on YouTube resulted in the court assessing an attorneys' fee award against the plaintiff music rightsholder).
[737] *Id.* at §506(a).

and all equipment used in their manufacture.[738] Actions for fraud or false representation carry penalties of fines.[739]

1.14.2. Civil Remedies

The act provides a number of remedies in a civil action for copyright infringement. A number of these are discretionary and are predicated on the nature of the infringement (whether willful or not)[740] and technical requirements (such as registration).[741]

1.14.2.1. Injunctions

Any federal court having jurisdiction over a civil action arising under the act (subject to the provisions of §1498 of Title 28, judiciary and Judicial Procedures Law governing infringement actions against the United States) may grant temporary and final injunctions on such terms as it may deem reasonable to prevent or restrain infringement of a copyright.[742] These injunctions may be "'preliminary,' 'temporary' 'interlocutory' 'permanent' or 'final.'"[743] While a court may enjoin future infringements by an identified infringer of existing works, it may not enjoin a defendant from infringing works that are not yet created because such works cannot possibly be "fixed" as required by §101.[744]

The granting of an injunction is an equitable action[745] that rests within the discretion of the court.[746] The court will consider a temporary injunction on a showing of (1) likelihood of success on the merits, (2) irreparable harm to the copyright owner if an injunction is not issued (or where there is no adequate remedy at law for money damages), (3) comparative hardship to the defendant resulting from the

---

[738] *Id.* at §§506(b), §509.
[739] *Id.* at §506(c)-(e).
[740] *Id.* at §504(c)(2).
[741] *See supra* §1.8.4.3.
[742] 17 U.S.C. §502(a) (2008).
[743] H. REP., *supra* note 39, at 160.
[744] Cable News Network, Inc. v. Video Monitoring Servs. of Am., Inc., 940 F.2d 1471 (11th Cir.), *reh'g granted and opinion vacated*, 949 F.2d 378 (11th Cir. 1991), *on reh'g,* 9959 F.2d 188 (11th Cir. 1992).
[745] Tempo Music, Inc. v. Myers, 407 F.2d 503 (4th Cir. 1969).
[746] Trifari, Krussman & Fishel, Inc. v. B. Steinberg-Kaslo Co., 144 F. Supp. 577 (S.D.N.Y. 1956).

injunction being less than it would cause the plaintiff,[747] and (4) the injunction not being adverse to the public interest.[748]

As a rule, irreparable harm was presumed once a *prima facie* case of copyright infringement has been established. Plaintiffs should no longer rely on its existence in view of the Ebay case.[749] The conduct of the plaintiff copyright owner may, however, be considered as negating this presumption where, for example, that plaintiff has acquiesced to prior acts of infringement similar to those complained of in the new suit.[750] Any such injunction may be served and enforced anywhere in the United States by way of proceeding in any federal court having jurisdiction over that defendant.[751]

1.14.2.2. Impoundment and Disposition of Infringement Articles

During the pendency of an action the court is empowered to order the impoundment of all copies or phonorecords claimed to have been made or used in violation of the copyright owner's exclusive rights along with all equipment (such as plates, molds, and masters) by means of which such copies may be reproduced.[752] Such an order will be issued on the same basis and subject to the same conditions as is required for the issuance of a preliminary injunction.[753] Impoundment may occur prior to the issuance of an injunction[754] under the now

---

[747] *See* Universal Athletic Sales Co., v. Salkeld, 340 F. Supp. 899 (W.D. Pa. 1972), *vacated*, 511 F.2d 904 (3d Cir. 1975), *cert. denied*, 423 U.S. 863 (1975).

[748] *See* Metro-Goldwyn-Mayer, Inc. v. Showcase Atlanta Co-op Prods., 479 F. Supp. 351 (N.D. Ga. 1979).

[749] Ebay v. Mercexchange, L.L.C. 547 U.S. 388 (2006).

[750] Bourne v. Tower Records, Inc., 976 F.2d 99 (2d Cir. 1992), *aff'd sub nom.* Bourne Co. v. Walt Disney Co., 68 F.3d 621 (2d Cir. 1995), *cert. denied*, 517 U.S. 1240 (1996). However, the presumption of irreparable harm is no longer presumed. Some showing of irrepable harm will go far in having an injunction granted since the case of Ebay v. Mercexchange, L.L.C., 547 U.S. 388 (2006). Although Ebay was a patent case, its concepts have been carried through in other IP cases. *See* Salinger v. *Coting*, 607 F.3d 68 (2d Cir. 2016)(preliminary injunction by J.D. Salinger against author of work based on William Holden character from Catcher in the Rye reversed for not considering irreparable harm as required in Ebay v. Mercexchange).

[751] 17 U.S.C. §502(b) (2008).

[752] *Id.* at §503(a).

[753] Martin Luther King, Jr. Ctr. for Social Change, Inc. v. Am. Heritage Prods., Inc., 296 S.E. 697 (Ga. 1982), *rev'd on other grounds*, 694 F.2d 674 (11th Cir. 1983).

[754] *See* H. REP., *supra* note 39, at 160.

probably inoperative Rules of Practice adopted by the Supreme Court of the United States. Under those rules, a plaintiff files with the court clerk an acceptable bond and sworn affidavit stating to the best of his or her knowledge and belief the number and location of alleged infringing copies and equipment and the value of same.[755] Thereupon, the clerk would issue a writ directed to the marshal of the district where the infringing goods are located directing their seizure.[756] However, these rules have been abrogated by FRCP Rule 65(f)(2001) as a result of the apparent inconsistency with those procedures under the 1976 Act.[757]

As a part of a final judgment or decree, the court may order the destruction or other reasonable disposition of all infringing goods.[758] The term "other reasonable disposition" includes ordering that the infringing goods be delivered to the plaintiff or sold or disposed in some other way that would avoid needless waste and best serve the ends of justice.[759]

1.14.2.3. Damages and Profits

The copyright owner may elect either of two forms of damages: (1) the actual damages suffered by the owner along with the infringer's profits, or (2) statutory damages provided by the Copyright Act.[760]

a. Actual Damages and Profits.

The copyright owner is entitled to recover his or her actual damages caused by the infringement.[761] Such damages may include a diminution in the fair market value of the copyright,[762] lost sales (which may be shown by a diminution in plaintiff's sales or by

---

[755] Copyright Rules of Practice Rule 3.
[756] Copyright Rules of Practice Rule 4.
[757] 17 U.S.C. §503(a). FRCP Rule 65(f) states: "This rule applies to copyright-impoundment proceedings."
[758] 17 U.S.C. §503(b) (2008).
[759] H. REP., *supra* note 39, at 160.
[760] 17 U.S.C. §504(a) (2008).
[761] *Id.* at §504(b). *See* Pfanenstiel Architects, Inc. v. Chouteau Petroleum Co., 978 F.2d 430 (8th Cir. 1992).
[762] *See* Szekely v. Eagle Lions Films, 242 F.2d 266 (2d Cir.), *cert. denied*, 354 U.S. 922 (1957).

showing defendant's sales which could have been sold by plaintiff),[763] costs of a change of plans necessitated by the infringement (where, for example, a magazine must alter its publication schedules because an article is misappropriated prior to its scheduled publication),[764] and punitive damages for any remaining common law copyright claims (at the discretion of the court).[765] U.S. Courts may refrain from awarding actual damages for infringement occurring outside the United States.[766]

In addition to damages, the copyright owner is entitled to recover the infringer's profits (where those profits are not used in determining the owner's damages).[767] In establishing the infringer's profits, the plaintiff must present proof only of the infringer's gross revenue, and the infringer must prove deductible expenses and elements of profit attributable to factors other than the copyrighted work,[768] with any doubt resolved in favour of the plaintiff.[769] With respect to indirect profits (i.e., where the infringer uses the copyrighted work to generate income for other sources, such as using artwork to advertise a concert) in order to recover the plaintiff must offer some non-speculative evidence that the infringed work in fact generated a particular amount of the profits earned.[770]

b. Statutory Damages

Provided the infringed work was duly registered for copyright prior to the infringement, the plaintiff may elect to recover statutory damages in lieu of actual damages and profits at any time prior to the court rendering its final judgment.[771] The plaintiff may elect to seek statutory damages in situations in which there are no actual damages or

---

[763] *See* Stevens Linen Assocs., Inc. v. Mastercraft Corp., 656 F.2d 11 (2d Cir. 1981).
[764] *See* Atlantic Monthly Co. v. Post Publishing Co., 27 F.2d 556 (D. Mass. 1928).
[765] *See* MacMillan Co. v. I.V.O.W. Corp., 495 F. Supp. 1134 (D. Vt. 1980). (This was a common law copyright case, not based on U.S. copyright law. Punitive damages are not available in federal copyright cases.) *See also* On Davis v. The Gap, Inc., 246 F.3d 152 (2d Cir. 2001).
[766] *See* L. A. News Servs. v. Reuters Television Int'l Ltd., 340 F. 3d 926 (9th Cir. 2003), *cert. denied*, 541 U.S. 1041 (2004).
[767] 17 U.S.C. §504(b) (2008).
[768] *Id.*
[769] *See* Frank Music Corp. v. Metro-Goldwyn-Mayer, Inc., 772 F. 2d 505, 514 (9th Cir. 1985).
[770] Mackie v. Rieser, 296 F.3d 909 (9th Cir. 2002), *cert. denied*, 537 U.S. 1189 (2003); Andreas v. Volkswagen of Am., Inc., 336 F. 3d 789 (8th Cir. 2003).
[771] 17 U.S.C. §504(c)(1) (2008).

profits[772] or in which it is extremely difficult to ascertain actual damages and profits.[773] In the event that the plaintiff attempts to prove actual damages and profits and fails, the court is obligated to award statutory damages.[774] However, even if actual damages and profits are proved, the court in its discretion may nonetheless award statutory damages.[775] Determining the amount of statutory damages is a jury question.[776]

For all infringements of one work by the defendant, the court may award as statutory damages a sum of not less than $750 nor more than $30,000 as the court considers just,[777] except for the following situations: (1) where the plaintiff sustains the burden of proving that the infringement was *willful*, the court, in its discretion, may increase the award to a sum of not more than $150,000;[778] (2) where the infringer sustains the burden of proving that he or she had no knowledge or reason to believe that the claimed acts constituted an infringement, the court may reduce the award to not less than $200;[779] or (3) where the infringer was an agent or employee of a nonprofit educational institution, library, or archives acting within the scope of his or her employment and the infringer believed and had reasonable grounds for that belief that his or her use of the copyright was a fair use, or a public broadcasting entity performed a nondramatic literary work, the court will remit statutory damages.[780]

Under the rules of statutory damages, a single infringer (whether one person or an affiliated group who may be singly or jointly liable) of a single work (irrespective of multiple ownership of that work or the

---

[772] *See* Russell v. Price, 612 F.2d 1123 (9th Cir. 1979), *cert. denied,* 446 U.S. 952 (1980).
[773] *See* RSO Records, Inc. v. Peri, 596 F. Supp. 849 (S.D.N.Y. 1984).
[774] *See* Shapiro, Bernstein & Co. v. 4636 Vermont Ave., Inc., 367 F.2d 236 (9th Cir. 1966).
[775] *See* Sid & Marty Krofft Television Prods. Inc., 562 F.2d 1157 (9th Cir. 1977).
[776] Feltner v. Columbia Pictures Television, Inc., 523 U.S. 340, 118 S.Ct. 1279, 140 L.Ed. 2d 438 (1998). There has been criticism of permitting the jury to determine statutory damages to the extent that they may be awarded for punishment rather than compensation. The wide scope of discretion permits awards that may result in a windfall to plaintiffs in some cases and judges tend to have greater experience than laypersons in connection with awards that deter unlawful activity and punish unlawful activity.
[777] 17 U.S.C. §504(c)(I) (2008).
[778] *Id*. at §504(c)(2).
[779] *Id*.
[780] *Id*.

divisible rights therein) is liable for a single amount no matter how many acts of infringement are involved and regardless of whether or not the acts were separate, isolated, or occurred in a related series.[781] Suits in which more than one work is infringed or in which two or more defendants (who are not jointly and severally liable) are joined are subject to separate awards of statutory damages. For purposes of determining statutory damages, each episode and/or broadcast of a television series is a work.[782] The multiplying of statutory damages could lead to absurd results where the number of infringers is massive.[783] The Ninth Circuit has taken a different approach. Although downstream infringers who might be jointly liable for infringement must be named as defendants in order to recover an award, the full statutory damage award against each infringer appears possible.[784]

1.14.2.4. Costs and Attorney's Fees

In its discretion the court may allow the recovery of full costs by or against any party (other than the United States).[785] The court may also award reasonable attorneys' fees to the prevailing party.[786] In the past, when attorney's fees have been awarded to a prevailing defendant, it has been held that they represent a penalty for institution of a frivolous action,[787] and when awarded against a defendant, they have been held to penalize the losing party as well as compensate the plaintiff.[788] In practice, this has commonly resulted in plaintiff's routinely recovering costs and attorney's fees. This dual standard was overruled by the Supreme Court when it was held that plaintiffs and defendants were to be subject to the same standards.[789] The Court argued that the intent of the Copyright Act was not to benefit authors

---

[781] H. REP., *supra* note 39, at 162.
[782] Columbia Pictures Television, Inc. v. Krypton Broad. of Birmingham, Inc., 259 F.3d 1186 (9th Cir. 2001), *cert. denied sub nom.* Feltner v. Columbia Pictures Television, Inc., 534 U.S. 1127 (2002).
[783] *See* Bouchat v. Champion Products, Inc., 327 F. Supp. 2d 537 (D.Md. 2003).
[784] Friedman v. Live Nation Merchandise, Inc., 833 F.3d 1180 (9th Cir. 2016).
[785] 17 U.S.C. §505 (2008). Under §116 of the 1909 Act, such an award of costs was mandatory.
[786] 17 U.S.C. §505 (2008).
[787] *See* Jartech, Inc. v. Clancy, 666 F.2d 403 (9th Cir.), *cert. denied*, 459 U.S. 826, 879 (1982).
[788] *See* Boz Scaggs Music v. KND Corp., 491 F. Supp. 908 (D. Conn. 1980).
[789] Fogerty v. Fantasy, Inc., 510 U.S. 517 (1994).

(typically plaintiffs in these types of actions), but rather to support the Constitutional mandate "to promote the Progress of Science and the useful Arts" (Const. Arts. I, 8, §8). Hence, §505 must be applied to encourage both defendants and plaintiffs to fully litigate their rights.

The Court stressed that an award of costs and attorney's fees remains a matter of equitable discretion and it denied any congressional intention to adopt the "British Rule," allowing for the automatic recovery of attorney's fees by the prevailing party. Thus, requirement that attorney's fees must be reasonable is continued. Moreover, in making its decision, courts can continue to consider factors such as the novelty of the legal issues, the experience of counsel, and the nature of the infringement (whether it is willful or not).[790] For example, it has been held that the prevailing party in a copyright case in which the stakes are small and the infringement willful should have a presumptive entitlement to attorney's fees.[791] Furthermore, a prevailing defendant may not be entitled to attorney's fees in some cases where the plaintiff's claim is found to have been reasonable, albeit unsuccessful. The Supreme Court continued to adopt a flexible standard in awarding attorney's fees finding that objective reasonableness in prosecuting a claim for infringement can be only an important factor in assessing attorney fee applications, but not the only one.[792]

1.15. MANUFACTURE AND IMPORTATION

1.15.1. Manufacturing Requirement

Section 601 of the 1976 Act is a continuation of a provision of the law that first appeared in 1891 in an effort to protect the American printing industry.[793]

Although this section expired on July 1, 1986, and its reimplementation is generally precluded by U.S. adherence to the Berne Convention (which prohibits any required formalities for copyright recognition[794]), it bears review at this time to understand its

---

[790] *See* Blendingwell Music, Inc. v. Moor-Law, Inc., 612 F. Supp. 474 (D. Del. 1985).
[791] Gonzales v. Transfer Techs., Inc., 301 F.3d 608 (7th Cir. 2002).
[792] Kirtsaeng v. John Wiley & Sons, Inc., 136 S. Ct. 1979, 1988 (2016)(Kirtsaeng II).
[793] *See* Boz Scaggs Music, 491 F. Supp. 908; Blendingwell Music, Inc., 612 F. Supp. 474.
[794] Berne Convention for the Protection of Literary and Artistic Works (1971), Art. 5.

possible impact on existing copyrights (or where it has been used to preclude protection of copyrights). Section 601 basically provided that in order for a nondramatic literary work in the English language to receive United States copyright protection, that work must have been manufactured in the United States or Canada. The manufacturing requirement is satisfied if the printing plates are created in the United States or Canada and the binding and finishing of the copies are performed in the United States or Canada.

This provision does not apply where the author/owner is a non-United States national or domiciliary; where no more than 2,000 copies are imported; where copies are imported for use and not sale; or where the work is published solely outside of the United States and there is no authorized United States edition.

Although §601 does not invalidate the copyright of the work, it essentially precludes its protection against infringement.

The provision has been attacked as an infringement of First Amendment protection for freedom of speech and Fifth Amendment protection of due process. However, the courts have to date sustained its validity.[795]

1.15.2. Importation Restrictions

Totally separate from the issue of the manufacture clause requirement is the issue of importing copies of copyrighted works presented under §602.

Section 602 of the 1976 Act deals with two restrictions on import: (1) restricting importation of copies that, under United States law, were illegally made, and (2) restricting importation of copies that were legally made but by license were restricted from export.[796] Both of these restrictions rest on the owner's exclusive right of distribution under §106.[797] The second restriction, that of export, may now be relatively meaningless because it is subject to the resale doctrine.[798]

---

[795] Author's League of Am., Inc. v. Assoc. of Am. Publishers v. Ladd, 619 F. Supp. 798 (S.D.N.Y. 1985), *aff'd sub nom.*, Authors League of Am., Inc. v. Oman, 790 F.2d 220 (2d Cir. 1986).
[796] H. REP., *supra* note 39, at 169.
[797] 17 U.S.C. §602(a) (2008).
[798] *See* Quality King Distribs. Inc. v. L'Anza Research Int'l, Inc., 523 U.S. 135 (1998)(hair care products with copyrighted label affixed; authorized for export from the United States but not authorized for reimport); *See* Kirtsaeng v. John Wiley &

1.15.2.1. Piratical Copies Exclusion

The first element of this restriction is the prohibition on importing "piratical" copies of a protected work. The operative phrase of this element describes such works as being "where the making of the copies or phonorecords would have constituted an infringement of copyright *if this title had been applicable*" (emphasis added).[799] The House Report suggests that this provision empowers the Customs Service to exclude copies that were unlawful in the country where they were made,[800] but its primary application is where the manufacture of copies would be an infringement under United States law. Thus, copies made in a country that does not recognize copyright or where the work may be in the public domain, and thus legally made in that country, may yet be prevented from being imported.[801]

Other than the importation of a limited number of copies by a governmental entity, private acquisition by a single party for private use, or acquisition by an educational institution for archival or library lending, the Customs Service is authorized to exclude and/or seize the violating goods.[802] Unless the importing party can show to the satisfaction of the Secretary of the Treasury that there were no reasonable grounds for the importer to believe that such importation violated the law, seized goods are subject to forfeiture.[803] Because of the continuing prevalence of piracy issues, Congress passed the Prioritizing Resources and Organization for Intellectual Property (PRO-IP) Act. The PRO-IP Act creates new enforcement provisions for the protection of intellectual property rights, including the appointment of an Intellectual Property Enforcement Coordinator (IPEC) who will serve within the Office of the President.[804]

Sons, Inc., 133 S. Ct. 1351 (2013)(sometimes referred to as Kirtsaeng I; textbooks authorized for sale outside of the United States but not authorized for import into the United States)
[799] 17 U.S.C. §602(b) (2008).
[800] H.. REP., *supra* note 39, at 170.
[801] *Id.*
[802] 17 U.S.C. §603(c) (2008).
[803] *Id.*
[804] *See* Pub. L. No. 110-403, 122 Stat 4256 (2008).

1.15.2.2. Territorial Exclusivity

The second element of this restriction recognizes the copyright owner's right to restrict the exercise of those rights to a given territory. Thus, a copyright owner may grant one party the exclusive right to copy and distribute the work in one territory, such as the United States, and a second party the exclusive right to make copies and distribute the work in another, such as Canada and/or Great Britain. The copies made in Canada or Great Britain would be "lawfully made,"[805] but their importation would violate the exclusive nature of the grant to the United States party and would therefore be "without the authority of the owner of copyright."[806] Such importation, commonly referred to as "parallel importing,"[807] is prohibited under §602 of the 1976 Act.[808]

By statute, this restriction does not apply to importation under the authority of or for use by the federal, state or local governments, limited importation by citizens for private use, nor limited importations by scholarly, educational and religious organizations.[809]

While this restriction would appear to remain applicable to a licensed manufacturer or producer, in 1998 the Supreme Court ruled that the "first sale doctrine"[810] applies to the products of these licensees.[811] Anyone who buys copies of the copyrighted work from a licensed manufacturer or producer (so that the production of the work in the first instance is "legal") is then free to export those copies back into the United States. In effect, the territorial restriction in §602 becomes meaningless because it can easily be circumvented through the intervention of a separate intermediary distributor.

---

[805] *Id.* at §602(b).

[806] *Id.* at §602(a).

[807] *See* Feingold, Parallel Importing under the Copyright Act of 1976, 32 J. COPR. Soc'y 211 (1985).

[808] A different approach appears to be now taken in the European Union where the general approach is a doctrine of exhaustion similar to the first sale concept through the territory. This is significant as at least in the past, the traditional manner of distribution of media such as theatrical motion pictures was to sell off split rights by specific territories. That approach however, may be limited to digital rights rather than copyright embodied in physical objects. Case C-419/13 Art&Allposters (CJEU 2015).

[809] 17 U.S.C. §602 (a)(1)-(3) (2008).

[810] *See supra* 1.4.1.3.

[811] *See* Quality King Distributors, Inc., 523 U.S. 135.

The enforcement of this prohibition is left to the owner of copyright as an action for infringement.[812] Although the Customs Service has no authority to prevent their importation (absent a concurrent violation of §601 manufacturing requirements), parties claiming interest in a copy-right may file an application along with the applicable fee with the Customs Service to be notified of the importation of copies of the work.[813]

In 2013, the Supreme Court modified broadened the scope of the first sale doctrine in an international context. Essentially it found that goods, in this case, college textbooks, acquired lawfully abroad could be imported lawfully without permission of the copyright proprietor.[814]

1.16. COPYRIGHT ROYALTY DISTRIBUTION

In December 1993, with the enactment of the Copyright Royalty Tribunal Reform Act of 1993,[815] the United States, in relation to its limited system of mandatory copyright licensing, moved closer to a predominantly compulsory licensing system from its current mixed system of statutory and compulsory licenses.[816] In reaching this point, Congress dissolved the then existing Copyright Royalty Tribunal System and in its place instituted an arbitration system.[817] In 2004 Congress enacted the Copyright Royalty and Distribution Reform Act of 2004,[818] which phased out the Copyright Arbitration Royalty Panel and established a Copyright Royalty Board.

The Copyright Royalty Board determines the rates and terms for copyright statutory licenses and distribution of royalties collected. Members of the Copyright Royalty Board are full-time employees who are appointed for six years and have the opportunity for reappointment to the Board. Additional information on the Copyright Royalty Board is available on the Copyright Royalty Board web site.[819]

---

[812] H.R. REP, *supra* note 398, at 170. Hearst Corp. v. Stark, 639 F. Supp. 970 (N.D. Cal. 1986); CBS, Inc. v. Scorpio Music Distributors, 569 F.Supp. 47 (E.D. Pa. 1983), *aff'd without opinion,* 738 F.2d 424 (3d Cir. 1984).
[813] 17 U.S.C. §602(b) (2008).
[814] Kirtsaeng I, 133 S.Ct. 1351 (2013).
[815] Pub. L. No. 103-198, 107 Stat. 2304 (1993).
[816] *See supra* §1.10.2.
[817] 17 U.S.C. §§801-803 (2008).
[818] Pub. Law 108-419 (Nov. 30, 2004).
[819] Copyright Royalty Board, http://www.loc.gov/crb/

1.17. COPYRIGHT PROTECTION AND MANAGEMENT SYSTEMS

In an age when copyrights were embodied as tangible works of art (e.g., books, paintings, printed sheets of music), affixing a notice of copyright and the maintenance of printed records of copyright may have been an adequate method of protection and management. One could not easily reproduce copies of the copyrighted work (at least not in commercial quantities), and if one did one had to confront the need to have a copyright notice in the expected place. Moreover, this type of management was the limit of what technology provided at that time.

As creative technology developed it became more difficult to protect copyrights because the protected work could be reproduced far more easily in forms where a visible notice would not be expected. At the same time it became technologically possible to protect products better through the emergence of encryption technologies. The two technologies in which this came to a head in the United States were those of computer software and digital audio recording, with Congress becoming active in digital audio recording.[820] In the area of digital home recording, a means of protecting copyrighted works from reproduction emerged at the beginnings of an industry before it had developed to a stage where regulation was precluded because of the entrenched interests of an established industry. The principle was therefore established in the law through passage of the Audio Home Recording Act, amending the Copyright Act through adoption of Chapter 10. The principle could equally be applied to technologies such as computer software, video recording and a host of others.

The WIPO Copyright Treaty[821] and the WIPO Performance and Phonogram Treaty[822] have both accepted this principle and required that all signatories protect copyright management systems and provide technological protections. The WIPO Implementation Act[823] implemented this requirement through a revision incorporating a new Chapter 12 into the Copyright Act. In Chapter 12, the challenge is to protect management systems and safeguards while at the same time encouraging the development of new copyrighted works (such as computer software) and the dissemination of knowledge. The law now

---
[820] *See* §7.4.3.1b in THE ESSENTIAL GUIDE TO ENTERTAINMENT LAW: DEALMAKING.
[821] Arts. 11 & 12.
[822] Art. 18.
[823] Pub. L. No. 105-304, 112 Stat. 2860 (1998).

proscribes the circumvention of copyright protection systems through technological means or the manufacture, importation and/or distribution of such technologies[824] and requires the preservation of the integrity of copyright management information by precluding, for example, dissemination of false copyright information or the deletion or alteration of copyright information that may be electronically encoded in the copyrighted work.[825] At the same time, the law authorizes some circumventions of protection, including those related to legitimate research on encryption technologies,[826] reverse engineering of computer software to assure compatibility for independently created software programs[827] or so that a nonprofit library, archive, or educational institution can examine the work for possible purchase.[828]

Violation of these protections is subject to both civil[829] and criminal remedies, where the violation is willful and for financial gain.[830] Moreover, enforcement efforts are subject to all laws protecting the privacy of individuals using the Internet.[831]

The concept of copyright management has come under intense scrutiny and attack. Computer hackers have developed programs that will break the encryption and allow them to copy and share copyrighted works over the Internet. They have also made these decrypting programs freely available, and when producers have sought to obtain judicial relief, they argued that their distribution of decrypting programs was protected as an exercise of free speech. There is now some disagreement on this point. While a California appellate court did agree with this argument,[832] the Second Circuit categorically rejected

---

[824] 17 U.S.C. §1201 (20008).
[825] *Id.* at §1202.
[826] *Id.* at §1201(g).
[827] *Id.* at §1201(f).
[828] *Id.* at §1201(d).
[829] *Id.* at §1203. As to statutory damages, *See* §1203(c)(3)(b) whereby statutory damages range from $200 to $2,500 per act of circumvention of copyright protection systems in violation of §1201, and from $2,500 to $25,000 per violation of §1202 in relation to copyright information management systems.
[830] *Id.* at §1204.
[831] *Id.* at §1205.
[832] DVD Copy Control Ass'n. v. Bunner, 41 P.3d 2 (Cal. 2002), rev'd, 75 P.3d 1 (Cal. 2003).

this defense.[833] Indeed, the Second Circuit went further. Recognizing that publicizing the existence and Internet address for these decryption programs promotes their use in copyright infringement, the Court enjoined a journalist, in a news story on decryption programs, from identifying or linking to a web site where a decryption program was available.[834] The knowledge that copyright management information has been removed even if a defendant did not remove it creates a triable issue of fact.[835]

---

[833] Universal City Studios, Inc. v. Reimerdes, 111 F. Supp. 2d 294 (S.D.N.Y.), aff'd sub nom. Universal City Studios, Inc. v. Corley, 273 F.3d 429 (2d Cir. 2001).
[834] Id.
[835] Friedman v. Live Nation Merchandise, Inc., 833 F.3d 1180 (9th Cir. 2016)(knowledge that copyright management information had been removed even if defendant did not remove it creates a triable issue of fact and thereby downstream infringers who might be liable jointly for infringement must be named as defendants in order to recover award).

— CHAPTER 2 —

THE LAW OF IDEAS

2.1. General Principles
2.2. Subject Matter of Protectable Ideas
2.3. Exclusive Rights in Ideas
2.4. Fair Use
2.5. Creation and Commencement of Protection
2.6. Ownership
2.7. Formalities
2.8. Duration
2.9. Transfers
2.10. Infringement
2.11. Remedies

2.1. GENERAL PRINCIPLES

U.S. copyright law specifically precludes the protection of ideas as a part of copyright.[1] This has in many instances lead to the unfortunate and generally erroneous conclusion that ideas, unless they are protected as a part of patent law,[2] are not protectable; that "ideas are as free as the air."[3] However, as one Justice has noted, "[T]here can be circumstances when neither air nor ideas may be acquired without cost. The diver who goes deep in the sea ... knows full well that for life itself he, or someone on his behalf, must arrange for air ... to be specially provided at the time and place of need."[4]

The need to protect ideas in the entertainment industry is obvious. Creators regularly go into meetings with executives to "pitch" ideas for programs of films. Writers propose book ideas to publishers. Television producers and programmers regularly purchase the ideas for programs from other programmers.[5] The question is how to

---

[1] 17 U.S.C. §102(b) (1990).
[2] *See, e.g.*, Alfred Bell & Co. v. Catalada Fine Arts, Inc., 191 F.2d 99 (2d Cir. 1951).
[3] *See, e.g.*, Int'l News Serv. v. A.P., 248 U.S. 215, 250 (1918); Rokos v. Peck, 227 Cal. Rptr. 480 (Cal. App. 2 Dist. 1986); Fendler v. Morosco, 171 N.E. 56 (N.Y. 1930).
[4] Desny v. Wilder, 299 P.2d 257, 265 (Cal. 1956).
[5] *See, e.g.*, Carter, *"ABC's 'Home Videos' Pays Off Big,"* N.Y. Times, Feb. 19, 1990, D1 at D5 ("ABC pays a fee to Tokyo Broadcasting each week for use of the idea for the show ...").

protect creators without limiting the free flow of ideas that may be independently created.

To balance these interests, the protections accorded ideas are limited, but they do exist. Protection arises under a number of differing legal theories that, unfortunately, vary according to the jurisdiction in which enforcement is sought.

Most commentators categorize the protection of ideas in one of two ways. One way categorizes protections as arising under theories of contract or property law.[6] The second identifies three general theories of protection: contracts, property, and misappropriation.[7] It should be noted that both groups of commentators classify quasi-contracts or contracts in law as arising under the law of contracts. For reasons that will be seen, a better classification system is one that divides protection between express and implied-in-fact contracts, on the one hand, and fair practices protections on the other. While the label *misappropriation* may accurately describe this latter category of protection, misappropriation is often thought of in terms of a specific tort, whereas a variety of causes of action can be pleaded and categorized under the broader and less defined label of fair practices.

There are three principle reasons for this categorization system. First, the single category for express and implied-in-fact contracts is self-evident. There is very little difference between an express and an implied-in-fact contract. Both represent agreements voluntarily entered into between the parties, with the sole difference between them being the formalities of acceptance and, perhaps, the necessity of establishing the exact terms of the agreement as an element of the court action. With respect to categorizing quasi-contractual protections under the general heading of fair practices, as opposed to the contract heading, while quasi-contracts are described as contract remedies, they are not in fact true contracts, in the sense of voluntary agreements between two or more parties. A quasi-contract is a legal obligation imposed by law for reasons of justice and equity.[8]

---

[6] *See, e.g.*, Paul Goldstein, GOLDSTEIN ON COPYRIGHT §15.8 (2008).

[7] Melville B. & David Nimmer, NIMMER ON COPYRIGHT §16.01 *et seq.* (2008).

[8] *See, e.g.*, Decorative Aides Corp. v. Staple Sewing Aides Corp., 497 F. Supp. 154 (S.D.N.Y. 1980), *aff'd*, 657 F.2d 262 (2d Cir. 1981); Weitzenkorn v. Lesser, 256 P.2d 947 (Cal. 1953); Downey v. Gen. Foods Corp., 323 N.Y.S.2d 578 (N.Y.A.D. 1971), *rev'd on other grounds*, 334 N.Y.S.2d 874 (N.Y. 1972).

Second, although the courts often discuss their decisions in the context of property law theories,[9] this discussion masks and confuses the true rationale behind many if not most of those decisions. Under a theory of property law, a person is assumed to have a proprietary interest in their ideas; that is, that the idea is a species of property. The problem with this approach is that it directly conflicts with a long-standing belief about the protectability of ideas. As Prof. Nimmer has written, "The concept that ideas are 'free as air' is of ancient origin and is well rooted in our jurisprudence [footnotes omitted]."[10] Indeed, it is significant that if, in a particular jurisdiction, a deserving plaintiff can be protected under an express or an implied-in-fact contract[11] or is subject to protection by statutory or common law copyright,[12] courts appear to be quite willing to state that a creator has no property rights (in the same sense as personal property) in his or her ideas. Difficulties arise, however, when the courts are confronted with situations in which it seems unfair to allow certain individuals to commercially exploit and profit from the ideas of others. It is in these latter situations where confused and occasionally contorted discussions of property interests in ideas are most problematic.[13]

While a number of courts have discussed the possibility of a property right in certain ideas in submission of ideas cases,[14] in practice such a right is rarely found when applied to the facts,[15] and when it is found it appears that an alternate contract theory would be

---

[9] *See, e.g.*, Int'l. News Serv., 248 U.S. 215; Bromhall v. Rorvik, 478 F. Supp. 361 (E.D. Pa. 1979); Fenton McHugh Prods., Inc. v. WGN Cont'l Prods. Co., 434 N.E.2d 537 (Ill. App. 1982); Downey, 323 N.Y.S.2d 578, *rev'd on other grounds*, 334 N.Y.S.2d 874.

[10] Nimmer, NIMMER ON COPYRIGHT at §16.01.

[11] *See, e.g.*, Desny v. Wilder, 299 P.2d 257, 265 (Cal. 1956); Weitzenkorn, 256 P.2d 947.

[12] *See, e.g.*, Dellar v. Samuel Goldwyn, Inc., 150 F.2d 612 (2d Cir. 1945), cert. denied., 327 U.S. 790 (1946); Fendler v. Morosco, 171 N.E. 56 (N.Y. 1930).

[13] *See, e.g.*, Int'l News Serv., 248 U.S. 215; Bromhall, 478 F. Supp. 361; Rokos, 227 Cal. Rptr. 480; Fenton McHugh, 434 N.E.2d 537.

[14] *See, e.g.*, Murray v. Nat'l Broad. Co., 844 F.2d 988 (2d Cir.), *cert. denied*, 488 U.S. 955 (1988), *abrogated sub nom.*, Nadel v. Play-By-Play Toys & Novelties, Inc., 208 F.3d 368 (2nd Cir. 2000); J. Irizarry y Puente v. President & Fellows of Harvard College, 248 F.2d 799 (1st Cir. 1957), *cert. denied*, 356 U.S. 947 (1958); Kurlan v. CBS, Inc., 256 P.2d 962 (Cal. 1953).

[15] *See, e.g.*, J. Irizarry v Puente, 248 F.2d 799, *cert. denied*, 356 U.S. 947; Moore v. Ford Motor Co., 28 F.2d 529 (S.D.N.Y. 1928), *aff'd.*, 43 F.2d 685 (2d Cir. 1930).

more appropriate.[16] Moreover, many of the more important of these decisions were rendered prior to the 1976 Copyright Act,[17] a time when "common law copyright" (also known as a "literary property right"[18]) had not yet been absorbed into the copyright law system.[19] It appears that many of these decisions may be more properly described as common law copyright cases that are now largely preempted by the copyright law.

Third, with respect to the proposed category of fair practices, while the causes of action used to protect ideas outside the realm of express and implied contracts varies greatly, from quasi-contract to misappropriation and so on, there are strong similarities among them which are focused and clarified by categorizing them in one group. These protections all rest on a sense of fairness, equity, and justice.[20] The essential feature of each is that the defendant's taking and use of the plaintiff's idea is unfair. In these cases the primary focus is not (or at least conceptually should not be) whether the plaintiff has a property interest in his or her ideas. Instead, the court is free to base its judgment on a plaintiff's right to profit from his or her ideas, whether that right be based on the plaintiff's expenditures of time and effort,[21] harm caused by the breach of a confidential relationship,[22] or that the defendant was

---

[16] *See, e.g.*, Cole v. Phillips H. Lord, Inc., 28 N.Y.S.2d 404 (N.Y.A.D. 1941) (plaintiff conceived and communicated radio program format to defendant – direct connection suggests possibility of implied contract).

[17] *See, e.g.*, Belt v. Hamilton Nat'l Bank, 108 F. Supp. 689 (D.D.C. 1952), *aff'd*, 210 F.2d 706 (D.C. Cir. 1953) (radio program format) (*NB* subsequent DC court decisions do not appear to have followed this case); Kurlan 256 P.2d 962 (radio program format); Kovacs v. Mut. Broad. Sys., 221 P.2d 108 (Cal. App. 2 Dist. 1950) (radio program format); Healey v. R. H. Macy & Co., 14 N.E.2d 388 (N.Y. 1938) (advertising slogan protected).

[18] *See, e.g.*, Buckley v. Music Corp. of Am., 2 F.R.D. 328 (D. Del. 1942); Fenton McHugh, 434 N.E.2d 537; Healey, 14 N.E.2d 388.

[19] *See supra* §1.2.4.

[20] *See, e.g.*, Vantage Point, Inc. v. Parker Bros. Inc., 529 F. Supp. 1204 (E.D.N.Y. 1981), *aff'd sub nom.*, Vantage Point, Inc. v. Milton Bradley Co., 697 F.2d 301(2d Cir. 1982); Downey, 323 N.Y.S.2d 578, *rev'd on other grounds*, 334 N.Y.S.2d 874; Werlin v. Reader's Digest Ass'n, Inc., 528 F. Supp. 451 (S.D.N.Y. 1981); Robbins v. Frank Cooper Assocs., 241 N.Y.S.2d 259 (N.Y.App. Div. 1963), *rev'd on other grounds*, 252 N.Y.S.2d 318 (N.Y. 1964).

[21] *See, e.g.*, Int'l News Serv., 248 U.S. 215.

[22] *See e.g.*, Blaustein v. Burton, 88 Cal. Rptr. 319 (Cal. App. 2 Dist. 1970); Thompson v. Cal. Brewing Co., 12 Cal. Rptr. 783 (Cal. App. 1 Dist. 1961).

somehow unjustly enriched by the taking of the idea.[23] The remedy in these cases is shaped not by the negotiated or market value of the ideas, but by the wrong done as measured by the defendant's profits.[24]

2.1.1. Contract Law Protections

The most common and well-accepted theory of noncopyright, non-trademark idea protection[25] is that an idea may be protectable based on some form of contract theory; that is, the idea should be protected according to the terms of an express or an implied-in-fact contract. These theories are most frequently applied to "submission of ideas" cases. The importance of these theories varies from a somewhat general recognition of protectability under express agreements to a much more limited recognition of implied-in-fact contractual protection,[26] even where the underlying idea or material which is exploited might not independently be protectible under copyright law theory.[27]

2.1.1.1. Express Contracts

In theory, an idea creator should be able to protect his or her idea under the terms and conditions of an express contract whenever it can be shown that the idea creator has (1) voluntarily submitted his or her idea (2) to an idea user (3) in consideration for an express promise by the user to either pay for its disclosure[28] or to pay for its use if used.[29] The "consideration" for the agreement is the voluntary act of disclosure.

---

[23] *See, e.g.*, Werlin, 528 F. Supp. 451; Robbins 241 N.Y.S.2d 259, *rev'd on other grounds*, 252 N.Y.S.2d 318.

[24] *Id.*

[25] Note: The term "idea protection" as used in the text hereinafter should be understood as addressing only those situations in which copyright, trademark, and/or patent law do not apply unless the context requires otherwise.

[26] *See, e.g.*, Goldstein, GOLDSTEIN ON COPYRIGHT at §15.8; Nimmer, NIMMER ON COPYRIGHT at §16.01 *et seq*.

[27] *See, e.g.*, Grosso v. Miramax Film Corp., 383 F.3d 965 (2004), 400 F.3d 658 (2005), *opinion amended on denial of reh'g*, 400 F.3d 658 (9th Cir.), *cert. denied*, 546 U.S. 824 (2005).

[28] *See, e.g.*, Blaustein 88 Cal. Rptr. 319; Buck v. City of Eureka, 56 P. 612 (Cal. 1899); People's Nat'l Bank v. Geisthardt, 75 N.W. 582 (Neb. 1898) (discussing obligation to pay lawyer for his advice and opinion).

Some courts impose the additional requirement that the idea submitted must be a protectable idea, that is, that it must meet certain standards of *novelty*,[30] *concreteness*,[31] and/or *nonpublication*[32] in order for the contract to be enforceable. This is based on an argument that the protectability of the idea itself is required in order for there to be valid consideration for the contract.[33]

2.1.1.2. Implied-in-Fact Contracts

An implied-in-fact contract differs from an express contract only by the fact that the acceptance of the proposed agreement or promise to pay by the user is conveyed by actions rather than by words.[34] Thus, an idea creator should be able to protect an idea under the terms of an implied-in-fact contract whenever it can be shown that the creator has (1) voluntarily submitted an idea to an idea user[35] (2) with a reasonable expectation that he or she will be compensated for its use,[36] and (3) under circumstances that justify such an expectation[37] that the user (4) knew of that expectation and had an opportunity to reject receipt of the idea (so as not to "trap" the user),[38] and that (5) the user used the idea under circumstances evidencing agreement to the contract offer made by the creator through his or her submission of the idea.[39]

It must be stressed that "[t]he law will not imply a promise to pay for an idea from the mere facts that an idea has been conveyed, is valuable, and has been used for profit; that is true even though the

---

[29] *See, e.g.*, Whitfield v. Lear, 751 F.2d 90 (2d Cir. 1984); Vantage Point, 529 F. Supp. 1204, *aff'd sub nom.*, Vantage Point, Inc. v. Milton Bradley, 697 F.2d 301; Desny v. Wilder, 299 P.2d 257, 265 (Cal. 1956).

[30] *See infra* §2.2.1.1.

[31] *See id.* at §2.2.1.2.

[32] *See id.* at §2.2.1.3.

[33] *See id.* at §2.2.2.1.

[34] Stanley v. CBS, Inc., 221 P.2d 73 (Cal. 1950). *See also* Blaustein, 88 Cal. Rptr. 319; Chandler v. Roach, 319 P.2d 776 (Cal. App. 2 Dist. 1957).

[35] *See, e.g.*, Giangrasso v. CBS, Inc., 534 F. Supp. 472 (E.D.N.Y. 1982); Mann v. Columbia Pictures, Inc., 180 Cal. Rptr. 522 (Cal. App. 2 Dist. 1982).

[36] *See, e.g.*, Chandler v. Roach, 319 P.2d at 780.

[37] *Id.*

[38] *See, e.g.*, Klekas v. EMI Films, Inc., 198 Cal. Rptr. 296 (Cal. App. 1984); Donahue v. Ziv Television Programs, Inc., 54 Cal. Rptr. 130 (Cal. App. 2 Dist. 1966); Thompson, 12 Cal. Rptr. 783.

[39] *See, e.g.*, Stanley, 221 P.2d 73; Blaustein, 88 Cal. Rptr. 319; Chandler, 319 P.2d 776.

conveyance has been made with the hope or expectation that some obligation will ensue"[40] unless it can also be shown that there is a custom or practice in the industry that justifies that expectation,[41] or where agreement can be shown through other facts such as through a course of prior dealings or a confidential relationship between the parties.[42] An invitation by the defendant for the creator to present his or her ideas, whether or not the presentation was originally solicited by the creator, may be offered as evidence of an implied promise justifying protection.[43]

Here again, as with express contracts, some courts impose the additional obligation that the idea must be a protectable idea.[44] Indeed, although it is a generally accepted principle of the law that the only difference between an express and an implied-in-fact contract is the means of consent or agreement,[45] it has been suggested, though rarely followed, that the idea should have a higher level of novelty, concreteness, and/or nonpublication than that required for protection under an express contract.[46]

2.1.2. Fair Practices Protections

Fair practices actions are generally less well recognized and, concomitantly, less successful than are contract actions in protecting ideas. The four principle fair practice theories are: quasi-contracts, misappropriation or unfair competition, breach of confidential relationship, and trade secrets.

---

[40] Desny v. Wilder, 299 P.2d 257, 265 (Cal. 1956). *See also* Faris v. Enberg, 158 Cal. Rptr. 704 (Cal. App. 2 Dist. 1979); Blaustein, 88 Cal. Rptr. 319.

[41] *See, e.g.*, Whitfield, 751 F.2d 90; Davies v. Krasna, 54 Cal. Rptr. 37 (Cal. App. 2 Dist. 1966).

[42] *See, e.g.*, Landsberg v. Scrabble Crossword Game Players, Inc., 736 F.2d 485 (9th Cir.), *cert. denied*, 469 U.S. 1037 (1984); Vantage Point, 529 F. Supp. 1204, *aff'd sub nom.*, Vantage Point, Inc. v. Milton Bradley, 697 F.2d 301; Rokos, 227 Cal. Rptr 480; Cole, 28 N.Y.S.2d 404.

[43] Gunther-Wahl Prods., Inc. v. Mattel, Inc., 128 Cal. Rptr.2d 50 (Cal. App. 2 Dist. 2002).

[44] *See, e.g.*, Murray, 844 F.2d 988, cert denied 488 U.S. 955, *abrogated sub nom.*, Nadel, 208 F.3d 368; Stevens v. Cont'l Can, Co., 308 F.2d 100 (6th Cir. 1962), *cert. denied*, 374 U.S. 810 (1963).

[45] *See, e.g.*, Stanley, 221 P. 2d 73; Blaustein, 88 Cal. Rptr. 319; Chandler, 319 P.2d 776.

[46] *See, e.g.*, Stanley, 221 P. 2d 73 (Traynor, C.J., dissenting). *Contra*, Desny v. Wilder, 299 P.2d 257, 265 (Cal. 1956); Minniear v. Tors, 72 Cal. Rptr. 287 (Cal. App. 1968).

2.1.2.1. Quasi-Contract

Protection for an idea is sometimes accorded on the basis of a quasi-contract or a contract implied-in-law[47] in situations in which there is no express or implied-in-fact contract but the circumstances make it inequitable for the idea user to profit from the use of the creator's idea or material.[48] The label for this action is unfortunate. First, a quasi-contract is not a true contract in the sense of representing any kind of agreement, either tacit or express, between the parties. It is a legal obligation imposed by law for reasons of justice and equity.[49] Second, "[c]onfusion has resulted from the practice of referring to both implied-in-fact and implied-in-law contracts as 'implied contracts.'"[50] It is therefore better practice, as is done herein, to refer to implied-in-law contracts solely by the label quasi-contracts and to use the term implied contracts to refer solely to implied-in-fact contracts.

In order to establish quasi-contract protection, an idea creator must prove (1) that the idea user was enriched by the use of the creator's idea and (2) that the circumstances were such that it would be unjust, in equity and good conscience, to permit the idea user to refuse to make any restitution to the creator.[51] In order to establish enrichment, the creator must demonstrate that his or her idea was protectable (i.e., novel and concrete)[52] and that it was the creator's idea that was actually appropriated by the idea user in its use.[53]

---

[47] *See, e.g.*, Matarese v. Moore-McCormick Lines, Inc., 158 F.2d 631 (2d Cir. 1946); Buckley. 2 F.R.D. 328; Seymore v. Reader's Digest Ass'n, Inc., 493 F. Supp. 257 (S.D.N.Y. 1980); Belt, 108 F. Supp. 689, *aff'd*, 210 F.2d 706.

[48] *See, e.g.*, Werlin, 528 F. Supp. 451; Stanley, 221 P.2d 73; Robbins, 241 N.Y.S.2d 259, *rev'd on other grounds* 252 N.Y.S.2d 318.

[49] *See, e.g.*, Decorative Aides, 497 F. Supp. 154 (S.D.N.Y.), *aff'd.*, 657 F.2d 262; Weitzenkorn, 256 P.2d 947; Downey, 323 N.Y.S.2d 578, *rev'd on other grounds*, 334 N.Y.S.2d 874.

[50] Nimmer, NIMMER ON COPYRIGHT at §16.03.

[51] Werlin, 528 F. Supp. at 465. *See also* Marine Designs, Inc. v. Zigler Shipyards, 791 F.2d 375 (5th Cir. 1986) (adding additional requirement that under Louisiana law, idea user must appreciate benefit conferred); Seymore, 493 F. Supp. 257; Weitzenkorn, 259 P.2d 947.

[52] *See infra* §2.2.2.1.

[53] Werlin, 528 F. Supp. at 465. *See also* Seymore, 493 F. Supp. 257; Galanis v. Procter & Gamble Corp., 153 F. Supp. 34 (S.D.N.Y. 1957), *For additional opinion, see* 30 Fed. App'x 726 (9th Cir. 2002); Weitzenkorn, 256 P.2d 947; Fink v. Goodson-Todman Enters., Ltd., 88 Cal. Rptr. 679 (Cal. App. 1970).

To establish that it would be unjust for the user not to make restitution is, on its face, an issue of equity that will depend on the specific circumstances of the case. As a general rule, it would appear that at a minimum this will require that the idea creator show some sort of preexisting relationship between the creator and the user that justified his or her disclosure of the idea in the first place.[54] Some courts have extended this concept to require that an idea creator must be able to establish an express or implied-in-fact agreement between the parties in order to justify that creator's expectation of payment.[55] However, given the fact that there would be no need for a quasi-contract remedy if either an express or implied contract could be proved, most courts properly do not impose such a requirement.[56]

2.1.2.2. Misappropriation or Unfair Competition

An idea may be protectable under a theory of misappropriation or the more broadly defined tort of unfair competition.[57] Though this tort is often discussed in terms of an unfair taking of property,[58] and thus it might not be thought to protect ideas where it is questionable as to whether an idea is susceptible to being defined as property,[59] a close reading of these cases reveals that the courts have used this tort to protect not property in a strict sense, but rather something which has been described as "quasi-property."[60] This may more accurately be described as a protectable right or interest, such as a person's right to their own labor, efforts, and expenditures made to develop an idea.[61]

---

[54] *See, e.g.*, Matarese, 158 F.2d 631; Werlin, 528 F. Supp. 451; Trenton Indus. v. A.E. Peterson Mfg., 165 F. Supp. 523 (S.D. Cal. 1958).

[55] *See, e.g.*, Hampton v. La Salle Hat Co., 88 F. Supp. 153 (S.D.N.Y. 1949); Davis v. Gen. Foods Corp., 21 F. Supp. 445 (S.D.N.Y. 1937); Grombach Prods., Inc. v. Waring, 59 N.E. 2d 425 (N.Y. 1944).

[56] *See, e.g.*, Buckley, 2 F.R.D. 328; Werlin, 528 F. Supp. 451; Seymore, 493 F. Supp. 257; Belt, 108 F. Supp. 689, *aff'd*, 210 F.2d 706; Stanley, 221 P.2d 73.

[57] *See, e.g.*, Werlin, 528 F. Supp. 451; Warner Bros. v. Gay Toys, Inc., 513 F. Supp. 1066 (S.D.N.Y.), *rev'd on other grounds*, 658 F.2d 76 (2d Cir. 1981); Decorative Aides, 497 F. Supp. 154, *aff'd.*, 657 F.2d 262.

[58] *See, e.g.*, Int'l News Serv., 248 U.S. 215; Pocket Books v. Dell Pub. Co., 267 N.Y.S.2d 269 (N.Y. Sup. Ct. 1966); Dior v. Milton, 155 N.Y.S.2d 443 (N.Y. Sup. Ct.), *aff'd*, 156 N.Y.S.2d 996 (N.Y.App. Div. 1956).

[59] *See* discussion at *supra* §2.1.2.

[60] Int'l News Serv., 248 U.S. 215.

[61] *See, e.g.*, Int'l News Serv., 248 U.S. 215; Werlin, 528 F. Supp. 451.

To establish the tort of misappropriation, the idea creator must show (1) that the user obtained access to the idea through an abuse of fiduciary or confidential relationship with the creator or via some sort of fraud or deception,[62] and (2) that the user's use of the idea deprived the creator of the opportunity to reap its due profits on the idea.[63] Alternately, an idea may be protected when its use will entail the misappropriation of another protectable interest in connection with that use, such as the exploitation of another's name and/or reputation in association with the idea.[64]

2.1.2.3. Breach of a Confidential Relationship

Ideas are sometimes protected on the theory of a breach of confidential relationship, a theory that closely resembles the protections accorded to trade secrets.[65] The law requires that one who receives a work in confidence is obligated to guard it.[66] A confidential relationship exists in a traditional employee-employer relationship.[67] It also exists in any relationship in which "one [party] has gained the confidence of the other and purports to act or advise with the other's interest in mind."[68]

A confidential relationship is not created from the mere submission of an idea; there must be evidence of communication of the confidentiality of the submission[69] or other evidence showing a confidential relationship, such as proof of an implied-in-fact contract,[70]

---

[62] *See, e.g.*, Warner Bros., 513 F. Supp. 1066, *rev'd on other grounds*, 658 F.2d 76; Bromhall, 478 F. Supp. 361; Dior, 155 N.Y.S.2d 443, *aff'd*, 156 N.Y.S.2d 996.

[63] *See, e.g.*, Werlin, 528 F. Supp. 451; Decorative Aides, 497 F. Supp. 154, *aff'd*, 657 F.2d 262.

[64] *See, e.g.*, Bromhall, 478 F. Supp. 361; Pocket Books., 267 N.Y.S.2d 269; Dior v. Milton, 155 N.Y.S.2d 443, *aff'd*, 156 N.Y.S.2d 996.

[65] *See, e.g.*, Moore, 28 F.2d 529, aff'd., 43 F.2d 685; Capital Films Corp. v. Charles Fries Prods., Inc., 628 F.2d 387 (5th Cir. 1980); Faris, 158 Cal. Rptr. 704; Dior, 155 N.Y.S.2d 443, *aff'd*, 156 N.Y.S.2d 996.

[66] Fink, 88 Cal. Rptr. 679. *See also* Davies, 54 Cal. Rptr. 37; Thompson, 12 Cal. Rptr. 783.

[67] *See, e.g.*, Am. Visuals Corp. v. Holland, 261 F.2d 652 (2d Cir. 1958); Radium Remedies Co. v. Weiss, 217 N.W. 339 (Minn. 1928).

[68] Davies, 54 Cal. Rptr. 37.

[69] *See, e.g.*, Faris, 158 Cal. Rptr. 704.

[70] *See, e.g.*, Davies, 54 Cal. Rptr. 37.

proof of novelty and concreteness,[71] or proof of a particular relationship, such as partners, joint venturers, principal and agent, or buyer and seller, under certain circumstances.[72]

2.1.2.4. Trade Secrets

"A trade secret may consist of any formula, pattern, device or compilation of information which is used in one's business, and which gives him an opportunity to obtain an advantage over competitors who do not know or use it" (emphasis added).[73] A trade secret is protected against disclosure or use if knowledge of that trade secret was acquired by improper means, breach of confidence, via a third party who acquired the secret through improper means or breach of confidence (with notice to that effect), or acquired through mistaken disclosure (with notice of that mistake).[74]

This broad definition is obviously capable of protecting "ideas" that are useful and have been reduced to practice. The problem with respect to submission of idea cases is finding a way to satisfy the requirement that the secret be in use in one's trade or practice.[75] While inventors, whose business is said to be inventing new, marketable products, have found protection for their ideas that have been reasonably well developed and reduced to a material form,[76] comparable protections have not to date been found applicable to professional writers or other idea creators (who are arguably analogous to professional inventors).[77] Nonetheless, notice of this theory should be made as an area ripe for possible future development.

---

[71] *See, e.g.*, Fink, 88 Cal. Rptr. 679.

[72] *See, e.g.*, Blaustein, 88 Cal. Rptr. 319; Thompson, 12 Cal. Rptr. 783.

[73] RESTATEMENT OF TORTS §757 comment b (1937). N.B. The Restatement is considered authoritative in all of the industrial (and most other) states. Roger M. Milgram, MILGRAM ON TRADE SECRETS §2.01 (4 vols. 1987).

[74] RESTATEMENT OF TORTS §757 (1937).

[75] *Id.* comment b.

[76] *See, e.g.*, Aronson v. Quick Point Pencil Co., 440 U.S. 257 (1979); Sinclair v. Aquarius Elecs., Inc., 116 Cal. Rptr. 654 (Cal. App. 1 Dist. 1974).

[77] Milgram, MILGRAM ON TRADE SECRETS at §8.03.

2.2. SUBJECT MATTER OF PROTECTABLE IDEAS

What is a protected or protectable idea depends in large part on the specific facts and circumstances in which protection is sought, the theory of protection being applied, and, unfortunately, on where protection is sought. An express contract protects more than an implied contract,[78] while California more readily accords protection to ideas[79] than will New York[80] or Pennsylvania.[81] Though summary of this area of law is difficult, certain general principles appear to apply according to the theory followed.

2.2.1. Requirements of Novelty, Concreteness, and Nonpublication

In almost all cases in which an effort is being made to protect or enforce rights relating to ideas, questions regarding the novelty and concreteness of those ideas are raised. Unfortunately, the meaning of those terms is rarely explicitly defined. In most cases, it seems that if the issue is raised by the court, the court finds the ideas discussed as failing to attain standards of novelty and concreteness that would justify protection.[82] Prof. Ralph S. Brown has suggested that these terms reflect an attempt by troubled judges to find more secure footholds for their decisions in idea cases.[83]

In these cases, courts are being asked to directly confront the conflict between the rights of individuals with respect to their ideas and

---

[78] Whitfield, 751 F.2d 90; *compare with* Murray, 844 F.2d 988, *cert. denied*, 488 U.S. 955, *abrogated sub nom.*, Nadel, 208 F.2d 368.

[79] California even has a statute to protect works of the mind not protected by any other form of protection. *See* CAL. CIV. CODE §980.

[80] *Compare* Whitfield, 751 F.2d 90, *with* Murray, 844 F.2d 988, *cert. denied*, 488 U.S. 955, *abrogated sub nom.*, by Nadel, 208 F.3d 368.

[81] *See, e.g.*, Thomas v. R.J. Reynolds Tobacco Co, 38 A.2d 61 (Pa. 1944)

[82] *See, e.g.*, Murray, 844 F.2d 988, *cert. denied*, 488 U.S. 955, *abrogated sub nom.*, Nadel, 208 F.3d 368; Lueddecke v. Chevrolet Motor Co., 70 F.2d 345 (8th Cir. 1934); Soule v. Bon Ami Co., 195 N.Y.S. 574 (N.Y.A.D. 1922), aff'd., 139 N.E. 754 (N.Y. 1923).

[83] Ralph S. Brown & Robert C. Denicola, CASES ON COPYRIGHT: UNFAIR COMPETITION AND RELATED TOPICS BEARING ON THE PROTECTION OF WORKS OF AUTHORSHIP, 633 (4th ed. 1985).

the public's rights as embodied in the first amendment.[84] To decide these cases, the courts appear to be attempting to ground their decisions within the framework of other more defined areas of creative rights laws (i.e., copyright and patents) by requiring that the idea that is to be protected must bear some of the, indicia of these recognized rights- namely, novelty or originality. It is not clear that such a requirement is appropriate. Moreover, the need for novelty and concreteness, or the level of novelty and concreteness needed for protection, logically should and practically does vary according to the theory of law under which the decision is to be decided.

Also relevant in almost all cases is whether an idea has been published prior to its "unauthorized" expropriation. That is, has the idea creator limited other people's access to his or her idea, or has he or she made it widely available to many others?

2.2.1.1. Novelty

A requirement that an idea be "novel" or "original," terms that are frequently used interchangeably,[85] accords with our general understanding of creative rights and properties (i.e., copyright,[86] trademarks,[87] and patents[88]) and appears quite reasonable. However, any attempt to define novelty in the abstract is extremely problematic. First, one must address the problem that any measure of creative effort is a relative term. While copyright will protect works exhibiting a very low degree of "original expression," patent law requires that a work be a "new" invention or discovery of the patent applicant.[89] Indeed, the difference between the two standards – copyright "originality" and patentable "novelty" – is so great as to be virtually a difference in kind as well as degree. In the area of ideas, though many courts recite the necessity for an idea to be "novel," there is no consensus as to the degree of "newness" that may be required to render an idea novel and protectable. Some courts have held that an idea is novel if the idea user

---

[84] *See, e.g.*, Swanson, Copyright Versus the First Amendment, 7 LOYOLA ENTERTAINMENT L.R. 263 (1987).
[85] *See, e.g.*, Sellers v. Am. Broad. Co., 668 F.2d 1207 (11th Cir. 1982); Bergman v. Electrolux Corp., 558 F. Supp. 1351 (D.C. Nev. 1983); Belt, 108 F. Supp. 689, *aff'd*, 210 F.2d 706.
[86] *See U.S. Copyright Law, supra* §1.2.2.
[87] *See U.S. Trademark & Unfair Competition Law, infra* §3.2.
[88] *See, e.g.*, 35 U.S.C. §102.
[89] *See supra* §1.2.2.

would not have known about the idea but for the disclosure by the idea creator.[90] Other courts use the terms "novel" and "original" interchangeably, thus suggesting, without always clearly stating, that protection requires some level of creative effort in line with those required by copyright.[91] Others, more confusingly require that an idea be both novel and original,[92] thus, presumably requiring a degree of newness or originality higher than copyright requires.[93] Lastly, some courts require that an idea's novelty must be similar to, if not identical with, the degree of novelty required under the law of patents.[94]

A second problem is that the specific facts of the case and/or the theory of protection used affect the need for a novelty requirement, or at least the degree of novelty appropriate to be required. For example, in the context of an express agreement, a court that imposes a novelty requirement is concerned by the fact that the purchaser of an idea will not know what he or she is buying until the idea is disclosed. What happens when the idea is so obvious that it would be unfair to enforce an obligation to pay for such an "idea"? A proposal that a defendant raise its prices as a way to increase profits is, on its face, so obvious, it is understandable that a court would find the idea lacking in novelty, thus making the agreement unenforceable.[95] However, the results of such a case should be different if the party making this recommendation (regardless of its lack of novelty) is a marketing expert whose services were expressly contracted for by the defendant.[96] The work rendered by an expert is clearly a valuable form of consideration for a contract.

It appears that because courts cannot readily define novelty what they have left is a question of fact to be determined by the fact finder,[97]

---

[90] *See, e.g.*, Werlin, 528 F. Supp. 451.

[91] *See, e.g.*, Sellers, 668 F.2d 1207; Bergman, 558 F. Supp. 1351; Silver v. Television City, Inc., 215 A.2d 335 (Pa. Super. 1965).

[92] *See, e.g.*, Ed Graham Prods., Inc. v. Nat'l Broad. Co., 347 N.Y.S.2d 766 (N.Y. Sup. Ct. 1973); Downey, 323 N.Y.S.2d 578, *rev'd on other grounds*, 334 N.Y.S.2d 874.

[93] As Prof. Nimmer has noted, this requirement is somewhat redundant in that if novelty is a higher requirement than originality, then, of necessity, an idea will be original whenever it is found to be novel. Nimmer, NIMMER ON COPYRIGHT at §16.08.

[94] *See, e.g.*, Educ. Sales Programs, Inc. v. Dreyfus Corp., 317 N.Y.S.2d 840 (N.Y. Sup. 1970); Lueddecke 70 F.2d 345.

[95] Soule 195 N.Y.S. 574, *aff'd.*, 139 N.E. 754.

[96] *See, e.g.*, Desny v. Wilder, 299 P.2d 257, 265 (Cal. 1956).

[97] *See, e.g.*, Anderson v. Liberty Lobby, Inc., 477 U.S. 242 (1986); Dezendorf v. Twentieth Century-Fox Film Corp., 32 F. Supp. 359 (S.D. Cal. 1940), *aff'd*, 118 F.2d

though some courts continue to aver that novelty is in the first instance a question of law.[98] It would appear that the best approach is one which defines novelty as a low threshold test of protectability. Obviously, if the user has taken and used an idea, that user has found it uniquely valuable and novel.[99] Nonetheless, "[n]ovelty, by its very definition, is highly subjective."[100] Thus, at its most basic, if there is no evidence that a defendant knew about or would have discovered the idea except through the plaintiff's proposal, then the idea would be novel in so far as that defendant is concerned.[101] Thereafter, the *degree* of novelty found with respect to a particular idea may be considered relative to other equitable factors in actions based on fair practice theories of protection.[102]

2.2.1.2. Concreteness

The requirement of "concreteness" is an even more problematic issue than the issue of novelty. Very few courts have ever attempted to resolve or define exactly what is meant by this term. Though some courts have held to the contrary,[103] the better view is that a requirement of concreteness does not require that the idea be fixed in writing.[104] Indeed, the fact that an idea is written down does not give any assurance that that idea is in any way developed beyond a vague generality, while the fact that an idea has been communicated verbally does not mean that the idea has not been fully developed. In fact, the opposite is quite possible. Moreover, it is suggested that writings may fall prey to issues of copyright pre-emption.[105]

---

561 (9th Cir. 1941); Yadkoe v. Fields, 151 P.2d 906 (Cal. App. 2 Dist. 1944); Downey v. Gen. Foods, 334 N.Y.S.2d 874 (N.Y. 1972); Burgess v. Coca-Cola, Co., No. D47343 (Fulton Co. Super. Ct. Ga., April 1999); *aff'd,* 536 S.E. 2d 764 (Ga. App. 2000)

[98] *See, e.g.,* Weitzenkorn, 256 P.2d 947; Golding v. R.K.O. Pictures, 221 P.2d 95 (Cal. 1950); Stanley, 221 P.2d 73.

[99] *See, e.g.,* Fink, 88 Cal. Rptr. 679.

[100] Murray, 844 F.2d at 1003 (J. Pratt, dissenting), *cert. denied,* 488 U.S. 955, *abrogated sub nom.,* Nadel, 208 F.3d 368.

[101] Werlin, 528 F. Supp. 451.

[102] *See infra* §2.2.3.

[103] *See, e.g.,* Bailey v. Haberle Congress Brewing Co., 85 N.Y.S.2d 51 (N.Y. Mun. Ct. 1948); Silver, 215 A.2d 335.

[104] *See, e.g.,* Jones v. Ulrich, 95 N.E.2d 113 (Ill. App. 1950).

[105] *See* the discussion to follow at the end of this section.

Common sense suggests that concreteness requires that the idea be developed with a certain degree of detail and specificity. The question is, how much? While it has been suggested that an idea must be so fully developed that it is capable of immediate implementation,[106] few courts actually require this.[107] It appears that concreteness is, again, a question of fact.

In practice, this requirement has resulted in wildly contradictory results. For example, is an advertising slogan concrete? Some courts have said yes,[108] while others have said no.[109] In *Liggett & Meyers v. Meyer*,[110] a general advertising concept for cigarettes where two men in hunting or working clothes are involved in a conversation and one offers a cigarette to the other who responds, "No thanks, I smoke Chesterfields," was held to have been concrete and to have been misappropriated in two different ads involving two golfers and a caddie, and a second involving two women and a man in each of which the response to the offer of a cigarette was "I'll stick to Chesterfields." In contrast, in *Plus Promotions, Inc. v. RCA Mfg. Co.*,[111] a substantially developed marketing plan for the sale and distribution of classical recordings outside the normal channels of distribution, which was subsequently used by the defendant, was held not to have been developed with sufficient concreteness.

A second problem with the issue of concreteness is determining when the case crosses over into the realm, of copyright or patents. Specifically, if an idea is substantially developed and articulated, would it not at some point reach a level of detail and specificity that would be protectable under copyright law or patents? Moreover, if the idea does reach a level of expression protectable by copyright, it would appear that there is a risk that the copyright pre-emption doctrine[112]

---

[106] *See, e.g.*, Bergman, 558 F. Supp. 1351.

[107] *See, e.g.*, Yadkoe, 151 P.2d 906; Buchwald v. Paramount Pictures Corp., 13 U.S.P.Q.2d 1497, 1504 (Cal. App. Super. 1990); Downey, 323 N.Y.S.2d 578, *rev'd on other grounds*, 334 N.Y.S.2d 874.

[108] *See, e.g.*, Healey, 14 N.E.2d 388.

[109] *See, e.g.*, Bailey, 85 N.Y.S.2d 51.

[110] Liggett & Meyer Tobacco Co. v. Meyer, 194 N.E. 206 (Ind. App. 1935).

[111] Plus Promotions Inc. v. RCA Mfg. Co., 49 F. Supp. 116 (S.D.N.Y. 1943).

[112] 17 U.S.C. §301 (1998). *But see* Whitfield v. Lear, 582 F.Supp. 1186 (E.D.N.Y.), *rev'd on other grounds*, 751 F.2d 90 (2d Cir. 1984).

would come into play demanding that only the expression of the ideas be protectable, not the ideas themselves.[113]

2.2.1.3. Nonpublication

Though not often specifically addressed, a number of decisions have required that an idea creator not have previously published or publicly disclosed his or her idea.[114] In part, it would appear that this requirement may have been an outgrowth of the traditional publication restriction on common law copyrights, that is, that a work protected by common law copyright lost that protection on its "publication" (i.e., public dissemination).[115] There are, however, justifications for such a requirement specific to the law of ideas.

First, it has been suggested that publication destroys the novelty of an idea.[116] Where an idea has become widely known, it can no longer be considered novel in the sense of being unknown by others.[117] In this sense a nonpublication requirement should be coextensive with the requirement of novelty and its concomitant limitations.[118]

A second and obviously fundamental restriction on publication would apply where protection for an idea is sought under the rubric of trade secrets.[119] In trade secret litigation, the secrecy of the idea is a necessary element of the cause of action.[120]

Third, evidentiary considerations and considerations of standards of proof argue for the imposition of a nonpublication requirement. The protections accorded ideas are very limited. All such protections rest on protecting an idea creator against an unfair taking of that creator's ideas by one to whom or through whom the creator disclosed an idea. Without a nonpublication restriction, an effort to protect an idea

---

[113] *See supra* §1.2.

[114] *See, e.g.*, Decorative Aides, 497 F. Supp. 154 , *aff'd.*, 657 F.2d 262; Desny v. Wilder, 299 P.2d 257, 265 (Cal. 1956); Shaw v. Williamsville Manor, Inc., 330 N.Y.S.2d 623 (N.Y.A.D. 1972); Hemingway's Estate v. Random House, Inc., 296 N.Y.S.2d 771 (N.Y. 1968).

[115] *See, e.g.*, Ferris v. Frohman, 223 U.S. 424 (1912); Capitol Records v. Mercury Records Corp., 221 F.2d 657 (2d Cir. 1955).

[116] *See, e.g.*, Decorative Aides, 497 F. Supp. 154, *aff'd.*, 657 F.2d 262.

[117] *See supra* §2.2.1.1.

[118] *See* discussion at *id., infra* §2.2.2 *et seq.*

[119] *See id., supra* §2.1.2.4.

[120] *See* RESTATEMENT OF TORTS §757 (1939).

becomes extremely difficult in terms of identifying and proving the source of the idea. Just like starting a rumor, within a very few tellings, the source of the rumor is lost and the rumor simply becomes "general knowledge."

Fourth, in all creative rights (i.e., copyright, common law copyright, patents) publication or nonpublication rules reflect a consideration of public policy. That is, the goal of creative rights laws in the United States is not to protect abstract "natural rights" of creators, it is to encourage the development and dissemination of ideas and creative works for the public good.[121] The traditional approach to the law is that unless a creator takes affirmative steps to protect his or her interests by either limiting publication or seeking the protection of copyright or patent laws, then the law will presume an intent to dedicate the work in question to the public domain.[122] In the case of ideas, voluntarily failing to preserve the confidentiality of an idea by widely disclosing it is an act that can readily be interpreted as an act of dedication to the public domain.

Last, and perhaps most persuasively, the law of ideas is, at best, one of strict limits. In no cases has it ever been the intent of a court to confer an exclusive proprietary interest in an idea on one party as against the claims of all others.[123] If one allows a creator to be protected against use by anyone to whom that creator has divulged the idea, then a creator could, arguably, gain absolute ownership of an idea by widely disclosing that idea.[124] Moreover, as has previously been suggested, because the source of an idea rapidly becomes lost when it is widely disclosed, it is an unreasonable restriction on the market in ideas to impose liability on a user who, though he or she may have in fact had direct dealings with the creator, assumes that an idea is in the

---

[121] Mazer v. Stein, 347 U.S. 201 (1954).

[122] *See, e.g.*, Wheaton v. Peters, 33 U.S. (8 Pet.) 591 (1834) (common law copyright); King Instrument Corp. v. Otari Corp., 767 F.2d 853 (Fed. Cir. 1985), *cert. denied*, 475 U.S. 1016 (1986) (patents). Note, this rationale has been weakened or altered by U.S. adherence to the Berne Act under which a copyright owner is not required to comply with any formalities in order to obtain the benefits of copyright protection. *See* Pub. L.No. 100-586, 102 Stat 2853, §§5 *et seq.*; Atl. Monthly Co. v. Post Publishing Co., 27 F.2d 556 (D. Mass. 1928) (requirement of invoking copyright law protections).

[123] *See, e.g.*, Fendler v. Morosco, 171 N.E. 56 (N.Y. 1930); Int'l News Serv., 248 U.S. 215; Desny v. Wilder, 299 P.2d 257, 265 (Cal. 1956); Weitzenkorn v. Lesser, 256 P.2d 947 (Cal. 1953).

[124] *See, e.g.*, Glane v. Gen. Mills, Inc., 298 P.2d 626 (Cal. App. 1956).

public domain because he or she may have heard the same idea discussed by many others due to its previous wide dissemination.

It must be noted that nonpublication requirements do not demand absolute secrecy, any more than does the law of trade secrets.[125] They merely demand that the idea not be disclosed beyond a reasonably limited number of people.[126]

2.2.2. Ideas Protected by Contract

Because there are no legal differences between express contracts and implied-in-fact contracts, save the manner of their formation, it would appear that there should be no difference between the ideas that are protectable under either form of contract. Unfortunately, in practice that is not the case.

2.2.2.1. Ideas Protected by Express Contract

In the best of all possible worlds, the person submitting an idea and the person receiving that idea would sit down, negotiate, and memorialize an agreement covering all of the terms and conditions relating to the submission, use, and compensation for an idea creator's idea. In such a case, the agreement should be absolutely controlling, and whether the submitted idea must be novel, concrete, or unpublished would be relevant only if the agreement required such characteristics.[127] Of course, this is not the best of all possible worlds, and agreements are frequently made on an informal, incomplete manner. It is in the context of these later situations that definitional requirements frequently arise and become important.

In general, an express contract, absent proof of fraud, should protect virtually any idea submitted by one party to another. The consideration for the contract is the agreement by one party to convey

---

[125] *See* RESTATEMENT OF TORTS §757 (1939).

[126] *See, e.g.*, Decorative Aides, 497 F. Supp. 154, *aff'd.*, 657 F.2d 262; Furr's, Inc. v. United Specialty Adver. Co., 338 S.W.2d 762 (Tex. Civ. App. 1960). *Cf.* RESTATEMENT OF TORTS §757 comment b (1939) (secrecy under trade secrets law).

[127] *See, e.g.*, Krisel v. Duran, 258 F. Supp. 845 (S.D.N.Y. 1966), *aff'd.*, 386 F.2d 179 (2d Cir. 1967), *cert. denied*, 390 U.S. 1042 (1968); Kurlan, 256 P.2d 962; Blaustein, 88 Cal. Rptr. 319.

to another certain ideas in exchange for money.[128] There are, however, a number of jurisdictions that require not only an express agreement, but also require that the idea being submitted must be "novel and concrete" in order for there to be valid consideration for the agreement.[129] These jurisdictions are concerned with the fact that the purchaser of an idea will not know what he or she is buying until the idea is disclosed and the idea may be so obvious that it would be unfair to enforce an obligation to pay for such an idea. The problem with this approach is that it misdefines "consideration" for "condition,"[130] that is, a court is imposing its judgment that the defendant intended to impose a condition that he or she would not be bound by the contract unless the idea that was submitted was novel and concrete. It is almost universally agreed that any promise to do or not to do something that the promissor is otherwise free to do is valid consideration for a contract.[131] Clearly, an idea creator agreeing to submit an idea to an idea user is a discretionary act that should support a contract.

This is not to say that the standard of novelty is totally irrelevant. Given the fact that most agreements are incompletely negotiated, and the courts will be called on to complete those agreements, novelty may be a factor to consider. For example, when a client engages a lawyer to give the client an opinion, in many, if not most, cases the client will hope that the ideas conveyed by that attorney are not novel (in the sense of being discoveries not made by the courts). The contract should be strictly enforced if the lawyer simply rendered the opinion properly.[132] The same should apply if a client engages any other professional idea creators.[133] However, when the agreement is vague and arises between an idea user and a novice or unknown idea creator,

---

[128] *See, e.g.,* Whitfield, 751 F.2d 90; Desny v. Wilder, 299 P.2d 257, 265 (Cal. 1956); Fink , 88 Cal. Rptr. 679; Cole, 28 N.Y.S.2d 404.

[129] *See, e.g.,* Lueddecke., 70 F.2d 345; Bergman., 558 F. Supp. 1351; Thomas., 38 A.2d 61. (Pa. 1944).

[130] *See* John D. Calamari and Joseph M. Perillo, Calamari & Perillo's HORNBOOK ON CONTRACTS, §§4.3, 11.1 et seq. (5th ed. Thomson/West 2003).

[131] *Id.* at §4.3.

[132] *See e.g.,* Buck, 56 P. 612; People's Nat'l Bank, 75 N.W. 582; Elfenbein v. Luckenbach Terminals, Inc., 166 A. 91 (N.J. Err. & App. 1933); High v. Trade Union Currier Publ'g Corp., 69 N.Y.S.2d 526 (1946), *aff'd.*, 89 N.Y.S.2d 527 (N.Y.A.D. 1949).

[133] *See, e.g.,* Desny, 299 P.2d 257; Blaustein, 88 Cal. Rptr. 319.

imposing a condition of limited novelty[134] may be appropriate in order to avoid frivolous litigation.

Equally, the issue of the concreteness of the idea also appears to be one that should have very limited application in an action based on express contract. Indeed, courts will not generally introduce a concreteness requirement into an express agreement.[135]

2.2.2.2. Ideas Protected by Implied-in-Fact Contracts

Because there is no legal difference between an express and an implied-in-fact contract except for the method of acceptance, there is no logical reason to require that an idea exhibit any greater degree of novelty or concreteness in order to be protected by one rather than by the other.[136] Nonetheless, many courts require that the subject ideas attain a higher standard of novelty and/or concreteness in order for protection to adhere under an implied-in-fact contract than that required for protection under an express contract.[137]

Notably, California, a particularly important jurisdiction in the entertainment industry, does *not* adopt such a requirement. As the home of the motion picture and television industries where "pitch meetings" (the purpose of which is to discuss ideas or concepts) are a standard practice, the degree of creativity is largely irrelevant so long as an implied contract can be determined.[138] As a consequence, creative submissions to major companies in most instances are now preceded by the required execution of a submissions release restricting the scope of remedies for those delivering creative "pitches" to a recipient creative company in the event the creator subsequently believes his or her ideas have been appropriated by the recipient for commercial purposes without an agreement as to the terms of such use, including without limitation proper credit or compensation (whether or not the recipient can establish independent origins for its similar project).

---

[134] *See supra*, at §2.2.1.

[135] *See, e.g.*, Weitzenkorn, 256 P.2d 947; Blaustein, 88 Cal. Rptr. 319 *Contra* Yadkoe, 151 P.2d 906.

[136] *See, e.g.*, Osborn v. Boeing Airplane Co., 309 F.2d 99 (9th Cir. 1962); Desny, 299 P.2d 257; Chandler, 319 P.2d 776.

[137] *See, e.g.*, Murray, 844 F.2d 988 (2d Cir.), *cert. denied*, 488 U.S. 955, abrogated sub nom., Nadel, 208 F.3d 368; Yadkoe, 151 P.2d 906.

[138] *See, e.g.*, Desny, 299 P.2d at 266-67; Gunther-Wahl, 128 Cal. Rptr.2d 50.

2.2.3. Ideas Protectable under Fair Practices Standards

Though it is often stated in fair practices cases that an idea must attain a higher degree of novelty and/or concreteness than that required for protection under contract,[139] in practice many courts quite properly consider the degree of novelty and/or concreteness of an idea (if they discuss it at all) as merely one factor among many.[140] This is entirely in line with and appropriate to the equitable nature and character of these types of actions.

Nonpublication requirements in fair practices cases are equally variable, with some cases appearing to hold that publication destroys any possibility of protection, while others hold publication virtually irrelevant[141] in the face of other factors that that court deems unfair and inequitable.[142]

2.2.3.1. Ideas Protectable under Quasi-Contract

Among all the fair practices actions, it is arguably appropriate that quasi-contract action require the highest standard of novelty and concreteness.[143] Where an express agreement in these instances cannot be shown, this cause of action requires proof that what was taken unfairly enriched the taker. The fact that an idea is novel and concrete is obviously persuasive of the fact that what the idea user took (i.e., the idea) did in fact "enrich" the idea user,[144] as opposed to other factors independent of the use of the idea, such as the contribution and

---

[139] *See, e.g.*, Bromhall, 478 F. Supp. 361; Educ. Sales Programs, Inc., 317 N.Y.S.2d 840; Kurlan, 256 P.2d 962; Fink, 88 Cal. Rptr. 679.

[140] *See, e.g.*, Int'l News Serv., 248 U.S. 215; Werlin, 528 F. Supp. 451; Metro. Opera Ass'n v. Wagner Nichols Recorder Corp., 101 N.Y.S.2d 483 (N.Y. Sup. Ct. 1950), *aff'd.* 107 N.Y.S.2d 795 (N.Y. App. Div. 1951).

[141] *See, e.g.*, Decorative Aides, 497 F. Supp. 154, *aff'd.*, 657 F.2d 262; Boop v. Ford Motor Co., 177 F. Supp. 522 (S.D. Ind. 1959), *aff'd*, 278 F.2d 197 (7th Cir. 1960); Furr's, 338 S.W.2d 762; Kurlan, 256 P.2d 962.

[142] *See, e.g.*, Int'l News Serv., 248 U.S. 215; N. Y. Bond Buyer v. Dealers Digest Publ'g Co., 267 N.Y.S.2d 944 (N.Y.App. Div. 1966); Metro. Opera Ass'n., 101 N.Y.S.2d 483, *aff'd.* 107 N.Y.S.2d 795.

[143] *See, e.g.*, Seymore, 493 F. Supp. 257; Educ. Sales Programs, Inc., 317 N.Y.S.2d 840; Fink 88 Cal. Rptr. 679.

[144] *See, e.g.*, Warner Bros. 513 F. Supp. 1066 , *rev'd on other grounds*, 658 F.2d 76; Galanis, 153 F. Supp. 39; Weitzenkorn, 256 P.2d 947; Fink, 88 Cal Rptr. 679.

combination of other ideas with that submitted by the idea creator.[145] Yet, in fact, this is nothing more than requiring that the idea creator prove that it was the idea creator's actual idea that was taken and that formed the primary basis for the questioned work. The novelty of the idea and its concreteness are useful in proving its identity and the fact that the idea creator is the source of that idea.[146]

Nonpublication requirements appear to be more strictly applied in quasi-contract actions as opposed to contract actions.[147] Yet, here again, if the idea user was unaware of that publication, it would seem that the publication should be deemed irrelevant to the action because, while others might be free to exploit that idea, the idea user was "enriched" not by the idea, but by that idea creator's *communication* of that idea to the idea user.[148]

2.2.3.2. Ideas Protected against Misappropriation or Unfair Competition

Because the tort of misappropriation is normally considered a property-based action, it might be thought that the law would demand that ideas protectable under this theory must attain the highest possible standard of novelty and concreteness. Courts that have directly addressed the issue of recognizing a property right or interest in ideas have generally stated it was possible only in dicta,[149] and have almost uniformly denied property protection under the facts of the case because those ideas failed to attain the high level of novelty and concreteness demanded for protection as property – to the point that one wonders if attaining such a level of novelty and concreteness is possible.[150] However, courts have not blindly followed this property dictate. Instead of basing their decisions solely on the basis of novelty and/ or concreteness, they have protected ideas based on, among other

---

[145] *See, e.g.*, Burtis v. Universal Pictures Co., 256 P.2d 933 (Cal. 1953); Stanley, 221 P.2d 73.
[146] *See, e.g.*, Werlin, 528 F. Supp. 451.
[147] *See, e.g.*, J. Irizarry y Puente, 248 F.2d 799, *cert. denied*, 356 U.S. 947; Desny, 299 P.2d 257; Kurlan, 256 P.2d 962.
[148] Werlin, 528 F. Supp. 451.
[149] *See, e.g.*, Desny, 299 P.2d 257.
[150] *See, e.g.*, Murray, 844 F.2d 988 , *cert. denied*, 488 U.S. 955, *abrogated sub nom.*, Nadel, 208 F.3d 358; Lueddecke., 70 F.2d 345; Kurlan, 256 P.2d 962.

factors, the creator's effort and expense used in developing the idea[151] (arguably a form of concreteness requirement, in that in practice the quasi-property taken in these cases were fully developed works in their own right) and whether the use involves the taking of another protectable interest, such as an idea creator's name and/or reputation.[152]

The issue of publication or nonpublication in these cases focuses not on whether the idea has or has not been published, but rather on whether the idea creator has had an opportunity to fully profit from his or her publication of the idea(s).[153]

2.2.3.3. Ideas Protected through a Confidential Relationship

Most jurisdictions do not impose a novelty and concreteness requirement in order to protect ideas under the theory of a breach of a confidential relationship,[154] nor do they elect to apply the requirement at a low level.[155] The crucial factor in these cases is not the idea but the unfairness of allowing the idea user to breach a relationship of trust.[156]

Because the breach of a confidential relationship is a relative of trade secret actions, the issue of nonpublication is concomitantly higher.[157] As previously stated, the issue is not whether the idea is strictly secret, but rather whether the disclosure of the idea rises to the level of a publication.[158] Thus, disclosure of the idea to a limited or even a large number of persons who are aware of the confidential

---

[151] *See, e.g.*, Int'l News Serv., 248 U.S. 215; N.Y. Bond Buyer, 267 N.Y.S.2d 944; Metropolitan Opera Ass'n, 101 N.Y.S.2d 483, aff'd. 107 N.Y.S.2d 795.

[152] *See, e.g.*, Bromhall, 478 F. Supp. 361; Pocket Books, 267 N.Y.S.2d 269; Dior, 155 N.Y.S.2d 443, *aff'd*, 156 N.Y.S.2d 996.

[153] *See, e.g.*, Int'l News Serv., 248 U.S. 215; N. Y. Bond Buyer, 267 N.Y.S.2d 944.

[154] *See, e.g.*, A.O. Smith Corp. v. Petroleum Iron Works Co., 73 F.2d 531 (6th Cir. 1934), *opinion modified*, 74 F.2d 934 (6th Cir. 1935); Blaustein, 88 Cal. Rptr. 319; Davies, 54 Cal. Rptr. 37; Thompson, 12 Cal. Rptr. 783. *Contra* Murray, 844 F.2d 988, *cert. denied*, 488 U.S. 955, abrogated sub nom., Nadel, 208 F.3d 368; Pittman v. Am. Greeting Corp., 619 F. Supp. 939 (W.D. Ky. 1985).

[155] *See, e.g.*, Fink, 88 Cal. App. 679.

[156] *See supra* §2.1.2.3.

[157] *See, e.g.*, J. Irizarry y Puente, 248 F.2d 799, *cert. denied*, 356 U.S. 947; Boop, 177 F. Supp. 522 , *aff'd*, 278 F.2d 197; Furr's, 338 S.W.2d 762.

[158] *See, e.g.*, J. Irizarry y Puente, 248 F.2d 799 *cert. denied*, 356 U.S. 947; Kurlan, 256 P.2d 962.

nature of the disclosure will not be deemed a publication destructive of the idea's protectability.[159]

2.2.3.4. Ideas Protectable as Trade Secrets

Novelty, in terms of newness, is not a critical element in protections arising under the law of trade secrets.[160] The law merely requires that the secret not be generally known within an industry at a given time and place.[161] The law of trade secrets does require that a protectable idea must be concrete (i.e., well developed) as a part of the requirement that a trade secret be in "use" in one's trade or business.[162] Clearly, a vague or ill-formed idea cannot be in use by anyone.

As the name of the action avers, trade secret law does require that the idea to be protected be a secret, that is, that it be unpublished.[163] This does not require absolute secrecy, but merely that the trade secret owner must exercise all reasonable efforts to protect the secrecy of the idea and communicate it only on condition that the person to whom it is communicated should maintain and respect that secrecy.[164]

2.3. EXCLUSIVE RIGHTS IN IDEAS

Unlike copyright, where a copyright owner is deemed to hold a "bundle of rights" (i.e., publication, performance, etc.),[165] the idea creator's rights to an idea are indivisible and personal.[166] This means that an idea creator cannot assign one right to one user, such as a right to make a motion picture based on the idea, while retaining or assigning a right to create a book based on the same idea to another idea user. This also reflects on the limited right of control held by an idea creator over his or her idea. Under the theory of contract law,

---

[159] *See, e.g.,* Capital Films Corp., 628 F.2d 387; D.C. Comics Inc. v. Filmation Assocs., 486 F. Supp. 1273 (S.D.N.Y. 1980); Faris, 158 Cal. Rptr. 704; Dior, 155 N.Y.S.2d 443, *aff'd*, 156 N.Y.S.2d 996.

[160] *See, e.g.,* Extrin Foods, Inc. v. Leighton, 115 N.Y.S.2d 429 (N.Y.Sup. Ct. 1952); Sealectro Corp. v. Tefco Elecs., Inc., 223 N.Y.S.2d 235 (N.Y.Sup. Ct. 1961).

[161] *See* Milgram, MILGRAM ON TRADE SECRETS at §2.07.

[162] *See, e.g.,* Aronson., 440 U.S. 257; Sinclair, 116 Cal. Rptr. 654.

[163] *See* Milgram, MILGRAM ON TRADE SECRETS at §2.04.

[164] *Id.*

[165] *See supra* §1.5.

[166] *See, e.g.,* Rokos, 227 Cal. Rptr.480; Chandler, 319 P.2d 776.

"unlike copyright, a contract creates no monopoly; it is effective only between the contracting parties; it does not withdraw the idea from general circulation. Any person not a party to the contract is free to use the idea without restriction."[167] Similarly, an action brought under a fair practices theory is based on a personal relationship between the idea creator and the idea user or the person through whom the idea user obtained the idea (i.e., where the user obtained the idea through a breach of a confidential relationship).[168]

2.4. FAIR USE

Unlike the law of copyright[169] and/or trademarks,[170] there is no doctrine of fair use in the law of ideas. The doctrine of fair use, in large part, reflects an attempt to balance the rights of creators with the countervailing interests of society in promoting free speech. Because the rights of an idea creator are so limited, that is, they are restricted to persons bound by contract or personal relationship with the idea creator,[171] there appears to be no need for a fair use doctrine.

2.5. CREATION AND COMMENCEMENT OF PROTECTION

Unlike copyright, an idea does not have an independent existence; that is, it does not become an independent protectable work on creation, as is the case with a copyright.[172] An idea creator cannot enforce any rights against anyone who independently comes up with the same idea, or even someone who becomes aware of the idea creator's idea outside a contractual or personal relationship[173] or through methods which society deems inherently unfair.[174] Thus, an idea creator's rights with respect to his or her idea(s) commences on

---

[167] Stanley, 221 P.2d 73.
[168] *See, e.g.*, Rokos, 227 Cal. Rptr 480. *See supra* §2.1.2.
[169] *See supra* §1.5.
[170] *See infra* §3.4.
[171] *See supra* §2.3.
[172] *See supra* §1.5.
[173] *See, e.g.*, Weitzenkorn, 256 P.2d 947; Rokos, 227 Cal. Rptr. 480; Fink, 88 Cal. Rptr. 679.
[174] *See, e.g.*, Int'l News Serv., 248 U.S. 215; Dior, 155 N.Y.S.2d 443, *aff'd*, 156 N.Y.S.2d 996.

the creation of an enforceable contractual relationship,[175] on the disclosure of his or her idea(s) to someone via a confidential relationship, or where that idea(s) is unfairly taken.[176]

2.6. OWNERSHIP

It is logically incorrect to characterize an idea creator as "owning" his or her ideas, in that ideas cannot be owned in the sense of personal property.[177] What the law of ideas recognizes is an idea creator's right with respect to his or her ideas, whether that right arises under contract or fair practices theories of protection.[178]

2.7. FORMALITIES

There are no formalities required for the protection of an idea (i.e., in terms of notice, registration) except that in a few jurisdictions the courts require, as a part of the concreteness requirement,[179] that an idea be in writing to be protectable.[180]

2.8. DURATION

There is no fixed durational limit to how long an idea may be protected.

2.9. TRANSFERS

Unlike copyright, where a copyright owner is deemed to hold a "bundle of rights" (i.e., publication, performance, etc.),[181] an idea creator's rights to an idea are indivisible and personal.[182] This means that an idea creator cannot assign one right to one user, such as a right to make a motion picture based on the idea, while retaining or assigning a right to create a book based on the same idea to another

---

[175] *See supra* §2.1.1.
[176] *See, e.g. supra* §2.1.2.
[177] Int'l News Serv., 248 U.S. 215.
[178] *See, e.g.*, Rokos, 227 Cal. Rptr. 480.
[179] *See supra* §2.2.1.2.
[180] *See, e.g.*, Bailey, 85 N.Y.S.2d 51; Silver, 215 A.2d 335.
[181] *See supra* §1.5.
[182] *See, e.g.*, Rokos, 227 Cal. Rptr.480; Chandler, 319 P.2d 776.

idea user. This approach resembles the traditional approach to assignments of copyrights prior to the 1976 Act[183] and the traditional requirement that a trademark cannot be assigned "in gross."[184]

2.10. INFRINGEMENT

While proving infringement of an idea creator's rights will require the specific allegation and proof of all the elements of the action required by the theory of law on which protection is based,[185] there are three key factors common among all such actions: copying, who can be sued, and infringement defenses.

2.10.1. Copying

Establishing the fact that an idea user has copied the idea creator's idea is a universally recognized prerequisite to any recovery in idea cases.[186] Thus, an idea creator's idea is infringed, or in other words, an obligation to pay the idea creator for the use of his or her idea arises if the idea user's work is "based on a material element of or was inspired by" the creator's idea.[187] This requires that the creator show that the user has "appropriated and used a quantitatively important part of [creator's] material in such a way that features discernible in [the user's work] are substantially similar [to the creator's idea]."[188] The same test applies whether the action is based on contract or noncontract grounds.[189]

---

[183] *See* Abraham L. Kamenstein, *Divisibility of Copyrights*, 1 STUDIES ON COPYRIGHT 623 (1963).

[184] *See* J. Thomas McCarthy, MCCARTHY ON TRADEMARKS AND UNFAIR COMPETITION §18.1 et seq. (4th. Ed. 2003-2008). *Also, see supra* §2.3.

[185] *See supra* §2.1.1, §2.1.2.

[186] *See, e.g.*, Amberley Co. v. Brown Co., 408 F.2d 1358 (6th Cir. 1969); Bolt Assocs., Inc. v. Alpine Geophysical Assocs., Inc., 365 F.2d 742 (3d Cir. 1966); Donahue, 54 Cal. Rptr. 130; Flemming v. Ronson Corp., 258 A.2d 153 (N.J. Super. 1969), *aff'd.*, 275 A.2d 759 (N.J. Super. 1971); Downey, 323 N.Y.S.2d 578, *rev'd on other grounds*, 334 N.Y.S.2d 874.

[187] Buchwald, 13 U.S.P.Q.2d 1497, 1504. *See also*, Fink, 88 Cal. Rptr. 679; Donahue, 54 Cal. Rptr. 130; Flemming, 258 A.2d 153, aff'd. 275 A.2d 759.

[188] Fink, 88 Cal. Rptr. at 688.

[189] *Id.*

These tests are substantially similar to those required for proof of copyright infringement copying,[190] save that whereas copyright cases specifically exempt the copying of ideas,[191] the copying of ideas is the essence of this complaint.[192]

2.10.2. Against Whom an Idea Creator's Rights May Be Enforced

An idea creator's rights to an idea are considered personal rights,[193] and in most cases this means that the idea creator is restricted to actions against parties with whom that creator has entered into a contractual[194] or confidential (a/k/a fiduciary) relationship,[195] or where the taking of the idea is considered so unfair as to be deemed unfair competition.[196] Thus, for example, a corporation will not be liable for its infringement if an employee to whom the idea creator submitted the idea was not authorized to act on behalf of the corporate idea user.[197]

There are exceptions to this general rule. First, an idea user may be obligated to an idea creator based on the relationship between that user and the party who directly received the idea from the idea creator. For example, a corporate officer will be personally bound by an implied contract with respect to a particular idea that is binding on his or her corporation.[198] Similarly, a corporation that clothes an employee with the appearance of authority to receive and contract for ideas on its behalf will be bound by that employee's actions.[199] Second, an idea user may be liable for inducing a breach of contract whenever the user knowingly induces the person who has directly received the idea to give it to that user.[200] Third, one who has acquired the idea from

---

[190] *See supra* §1.13.2.4.
[191] *See supra* §1.2.3.
[192] *See, e.g.*, Whitfield, 751 F.2d 90; Donahue, 54 Cal. Rptr. 130.
[193] *See, e.g.*, Rokos, 227 Cal. Rptr. 480; Chandler, 319 P.2d 776.
[194] *See, e.g.*, Stanley, 221 P.2d 73; Rokos, 227 Cal. Rptr. 480; Fink, 88 Cal. Rptr. 679.
[195] *See, e.g.*, Rokos, 227 Cal. Rptr. 480; Fink , 88 Cal. Rptr. 679.
[196] *See, e.g.*, Int'l News Serv. , 248 U.S. 215; Metropolitan Opera Ass'n, 101 N.Y.S.2d 483, *aff'd*. 107 N.Y.S.2d 795.
[197] *See, e.g.*, Matarese, 158 F.2d 631; Herwitz v. Nat'l Broad. Co., 210 F. Supp. 231 (S.D.N.Y. 1962); Curtis v. United States, 168 F. Supp. 213 (Ct. Cl. 1958).
[198] *See, e.g.*, Davies, 54 Cal. Rptr. 37.
[199] *See, e.g.*, Donahue, 54 Cal. Rptr. 130.
[200] *See, e.g.*, Minniear, 72 Cal. Rptr. 287.

another who, by revealing said idea, is in breach of a confidential relationship will be liable to the idea creator (1) when the user had knowledge of that confidential relationship[201] or (2) when the user is given notice of the wrongful disclosure provided that prior to receiving notice that the disclosure of the idea was wrongful, the user has not changed his or her position such that subjecting the user to liability would be inequitable.[202]

2.10.3. Defenses

A defendant in an idea case has all of the defenses available under the particular theory under which idea protection is sought. Among others, a defendant will not be found liable if it can be shown that the similarity between the submitted idea and the idea used by the user was coincidental or achieved independently of the idea creator.[203] (This, of course, is nothing more than showing that the idea user did not copy the idea creator's idea.) Idea cases are also subject to the statute of limitations applicable to the theory of law concerned.[204] Lastly, an idea action under a theory of fair practices will be subject to laches.[205]

2.11. REMEDIES

Although in appropriate cases an idea creator may be able to obtain an injunction against an infringing idea user,[206] the most common remedy claimed in idea cases is monetary damages. The amount of those damages depends on the theory under which protection is sought. In an action based on an express contract, the

---

[201] *See, e.g.*, Bevan v. CBS, Inc., 329 F. Supp. 601 (S.D.N.Y. 1971); Donahue, 54 Cal. Rptr. 130.

[202] *See, e.g.*, Vantage Point, Inc., 529 F. Supp. 1204, *aff'd, sub nom.* Vantage Point, Inc. v. Milton Bradley, 697 F.2d 301.

[203] *See, e.g.*, Mann, 180 Cal. Rptr. 522; Fink, 88 Cal. Rptr. 679.

[204] *See, e.g.*, Rokos, 227 Cal. Rptr. 480.

[205] *See, e.g.*, Vantage Point, Inc., 529 F. Supp. 1204, *aff'd, sub nom.* Vantage Point, Inc. v. Milton Bradley, 697 F.2d 301. In a recent suit, Francis Ford Coppola was denied relief after waiting 20 years to sue Carl Sagan over a breach of contract suit over the book and subsequent movie, *CONTACT. See*, Shprintz, *"Coppola Loses 'Contact' Suit,"* The Washington Post (April 13, 2000).

[206] *See, e.g.*, Int'l News Serv., 248 U.S. 215; Dior, 155 N.Y.S.2d 443, *aff'd*, 156 N.Y.S.2d 996.

damages will be the contracted for value of the idea.[207] In an implied-in-fact contract, the damages will be what the parties are presumed to have contracted for, namely, the reasonable value of the material.[208] In a quasi-contract action, the damages are the defendant's unjust enrichment – what that defendant profited from the use of the material.[209] Lastly, in a misappropriation action, the damages will be the value of the idea to the appropriating party.[210]

---

[207] *See, e.g.*, Kurlan, 256 P.2d 962 (though often, as here, contracted price term will be absent, and there will be assumed term of reasonable value for idea deemed incorporated in agreement).

[208] *See, e.g.*, Robbins, 241 N.Y.S.2d 259 , *rev'd on other grounds*, 252 N.Y.S.2d 318.

[209] *See, e.g.*, Werlin, 528 F. Supp. 451.

[210] *See, e.g.*, Stanley, 221 P.2d 73; Liggett , 194 N.E. 206; Alexander & Assocs. v. Cheyenne Neon Sign Co., 417 P.2d 921 (Wyo. 1966).

— CHAPTER 3 —

U.S. TRADEMARK AND UNFAIR COMPETITION LAW

3.1. General Principles
3.2. Subject Matter of Trademark
3.3. Exclusive Rights of Trademark
3.4. Fair Use of Trademarks
3.5. Creation and Commencement of Protection
3.6. Ownership
3.7. Formalities of Registration and Notice
3.8. Duration
3.9. Transfers
3.10. Renewals and Termination
3.11. Unfair Competition
3.12. Infringement
3.13. Remedies

Although not commonly thought of as part of entertainment law, the areas of trademark and unfair competition offer significant protection for parties involved in entertainment. For example, much of the moral rights protection demanded by the United States by its adherence to the Berne Convention exists (if at all) under the general rubric of unfair competition.[1] Product endorsements, limited protection of titles, characters and rights of publicity come within this area. Opportunities are thus offered for the further development in the protection of entertainment properties.

3.1. GENERAL PRINCIPLES

3.1.1. Jurisdiction

Unlike copyright, over which the federal government has exclusive jurisdiction,[2] jurisdiction over trademark and unfair competition is concurrent with the state and federal governments (with the usual

---

[1] *See supra* §1.5.2.
[2] *See supra* §1.1.

caveat that, where a conflict between the two bodies of the law exists, the federal law will take precedence).[3] Federal law is codified in the Lanham Act.[4] The common law of unfair competition and other statutory laws apply only at the state level.[5] (Our focus with respect to trademarks will be based primarily on federal law as embodied in the Lanham Act unless otherwise noted.)

3.1.2. Rationale for Protection

Two rationales point to the difference between trademark and unfair competition. The first is that protection of a trademark protects the interests of the public by designating the source of a particular product or service, thus facilitating the development of a market reputation for quality (either good or bad).[6] The second focuses on the reputation of the creator or producer of the goods or services. This latter rationale recognizes that creators expend a great deal of effort in cultivating a positive reputation in the public mind (i.e., good will),[7] which should be protectable against the depredations of others.[8] Trademark law is predominantly focused on the first rationale, while the law of unfair competition strongly supports the latter.[9]

3.1.3. Terminology

The Lanham Act[10] identifies a number of "marks" entitled to protection and registration under the act. They are

> *Trademark.* The term "trademark" includes any word, name, symbol or device or any combination thereof adopted and used by a manufacturer or merchant to identify his goods and distinguish them from those manufactured or sold by others.

---

[3] *See* J. GILSON ON TRADEMARKS §7.04 (2008) [herein after cited as GILSON].
[4] 15 U.S.C. §§1051 *et seq.* (2002).
[5] *See* GILSON, *supra* note 3, §1.04.
[6] *Id.* at § 1.03.
[7] *See* Beech-Nut Packing Co. v. P. Lorillard Co., 273 U.S. 629 (1927).
[8] *See* Mishawaka Rubber & Woolen Mfg. Co. v. S. S. Kresge Co., 316 U.S. 203 (1942).
[9] The law of unfair competition is much broader than this rationale suggests; however, this brief overview is sufficient to support the general area of focus of this book.
[10] 15 U.S.C. §1127 (2006).

Service Mark. The term "service mark" means a mark used in the sale or advertising of services to identify the services of one person or distinguish them from the services of others. Titles, character names and other distinctive features of radio or television programs may be registered as service marks.

The act also identifies "certification marks" (such as the "Good Housekeeping Seal of Approval," "Underwriter's Laboratory Seal," etc.) and "collective marks" (such as union affiliations like "Screen Actors Guild," etc.).

There is no substantive legal significance to the various categories of marks, except that the Commissioner of Patents and Trademarks may establish separate registers for each type of mark.[11]

3.2. SUBJECT MATTER OF TRADEMARK

3.2.1. In General

By definition, a trademark includes any word, name, symbol, or device or any combination thereof that identifies its owner.[12] This listing is not exhaustive, so that other designations, such as slogans, numerals, pictures, and letters, may also qualify as trademarks.[13] And in proper limited circumstances, titles, character names and character images, performer names and nicknames may also qualify.[14]

3.2.2. Conflicting Marks

In order to be protectable, a mark must not be confusingly similar to marks or trademarks previously used by others,[15] when applied to goods,[16] services,[17] or the application of collective or certification marks[18] and whether or not registered.

---

[11] *Id.* 15 U.S.C. §§1053 (1999) and 1054 (1999). Unless the context indicates otherwise, the terms *trademark* and *mark* (hereinafter used interchangeably) should be taken to include all forms of marks.
[12] 15 U.S.C. §1127 (2006).
[13] *See* Application of Tobias Kotzin, 276 F.2d 411 (C.C.P.A. 1960).
[14] *See infra* §§3.2.7 and 3.2.8.
[15] 15 U.S.C. §1052(d) (2006).
[16] 15 U.S.C. §1052(d) (2006).
[17] 15 U.S.C. §1053.
[18] 15 U.S.C. §1054.

Marks which are found by the Examining Attorney at the Trademark Office to be confusingly similar to *previously* registered marks will be rejected by the Trademark Office under Section 2(d) of the Lanham Act. Marks which are found by the Examining Attorney at the Trademark Office to be potentially confusingly similar to *pending* marks applied for in the Trademark Office will likely result in a suspension of the newer application and may later result in a refusal to register in the event that the application matures into a registration. Marks which are confusingly similar to marks in use, which could be blocked in a court under common law will not be refused registration by the Trademark Office in the initial examination process. However, those common law rights established by use of a mark without registration may be used as a basis for their owner to (1) later filing an opposition proceeding to block registration or (2) a cancellation proceeding to revoke a registered mark.

Confusing similarity is often determined in part by reviewing a checklist of twelve prescribed "Dupont Factors."[19]

In the Trademark Office, the determination as to whether a mark is confusingly similar to an existing registration is made by comparing the marks and the specific identification of goods and services identified in the registration and pending application. A word mark is considered to be a broad form of a mark and it is assumed that could be used in any matter, form, size or typeface. Thus, one word of a registered mark might be used in a very large typeface and the remaining words in a very small font.[20]

---

[19] In re E. I. du Pont de Nemours & Co., 476 F.2d 1357 (CCPA 1973). There, the court identified a dozen factors to consider, none of which were exclusive or necessarily determinative to evaluate likelihood of confusion. In the context of determining trademark infringement in a court proceeding, some courts follow this decision and other follow different decisions, notably, the 8-factor matrix in AMF Inc. v. Sleekcraft Boats, 599 F.2d 341 (9th Cir. 1979).

[20] *E.g.* In re Mr. Recipe, LLC (TTAB 2016) finding that the application for the word mark JAWS DEVOUR YOUR HUNGER was confusingly similar to the well-known film title JAWS. The TTAB pointed out that the word JAWS in the pending application could be displayed in a large typeface with the remaining words in a small typeface. Even though the identification of services in the pending application was for "Entertainment, namely, streaming of audiovisual material via an Internet channel providing programming related to cooking," the registered mark for JAWS for "video recordings in all formats featuring motion pictures" was deemed broad enough to include video recordings featuring cooking.

3.2.3. Distinctiveness

Trademarks may be placed in categories according to strength and the corresponding amount of protection that will be accorded them. From the lowest to the highest they are: (1) generic (the name of a particular class of things); (2) descriptive (the mark describes the product or service itself; (3) suggestive (the mark describes or suggests a characteristic of the product or service); (4) arbitrary (the mark is a word in common use but is applied to a product or service unrelated to its meaning, so that the word neither describes nor suggests the product or service); or (5) coined or fanciful (the mark is a word devised or invented for the purpose of identifying the product or service, e.g., Exxon, Xerox or Kleenex).[21]

Descriptive marks are not initially protectable. Suggestive marks are on the "protectable" side of protection. When a mark is descriptive or generic, it may be refused registration, and if registered may be vulnerable to cancelation. By definition, generic marks can never be registered. A mark involving a generic name (such as "desk" as used in connection with a desk, "table" for furniture, or "piano" for a musical instrument with a mechanical keyboard, etc.) is virtually unprotectable and unregisterable[22] and may, in fact, serve as the basis of cancellation of registration where a previously protected mark becomes generic.[23] In seeking to determine whether a mark is generic, one must first consider the mark as a whole. While the inclusion of generic or descriptive words as an element of a mark may tend to lessen the distinctiveness of that mark, public perception evidence may nonetheless justify protection of an otherwise unprotectable element of that mark when considered as a whole.[24] Second, the primary test for generic-ness is one which considers the significance of the mark to the relevant consuming public, evidence in support of which will preferably include direct evidence (such as consumer surveys and

---

[21] *See* Tisch Hotels v. Americana Inn, Inc. 350 F.2d 609 (7th Cir. 1965); McGregor-Doniger, Inc. v. Drizzle, Inc., 599 F.2d 1126 (2d Cir. 1979).

[22] Kellogg Co. v. Nat'l Biscuit Co., 305 U.S. 111 (1938); *see also* E. Air Lines v. N. Y. Air Lines, Inc., 559 F. Supp. 1270 (S.D.N.Y. 1983) ("air shuttle" means back and forth air services).

[23] 15 U.S.C. §1064 (2006).

[24] Opryland USA, Inc. v. Great Am. Music Show, Inc., 970 F.2d 847 (Fed. Cir. 1992).

testimonials) as well as indirect evidence (such as the use of general publications, dictionaries, etc.).[25]

3.2.4. Secondary Meaning

Related to the issue of distinctiveness of a mark is evidence that the mark has gained secondary meaning. Whereas marks that are suggestive, arbitrary, or fanciful are protectable from the moment they are adopted,[26] the Lanham Act proscribes registration (and protection) of marks that are merely (1) descriptive, (2) geographic, or (3) a surname *unless* those marks have become distinctive through their use in commerce.[27] A title of a single creative work is not subject to trademark registration under most circumstances. A literary title, for example, may be registered, but if not used in connection with a series, it will require proof of secondary meaning before it becomes protectable.[28] Publication of a single volume, even when followed by sales of a large number of copies, does not alone prove secondary meaning has been established justifying protection.[29]

Secondary meaning arises when the mark becomes associated in the public mind as the source of a particular product or service.[30] Intentional copying of a mark may be considered as presumptive evidence that the mark has acquired secondary meaning and that there is a likelihood of consumer confusion.[31]

In part because of the difficulty of protecting titles, the major studios through their Title Registration Bureau support a private registration system on a voluntary basis for studio members (and those outside of the studios should they voluntarily choose to participate) through the Motion Picture Association of America (MPAA). The members register or list their proposed titles with the Bureau and the

---

[25] Berner Int'l Corp. v. Mars Sales Co., 987 F.2d 975 (3d Cir. 1993).

[26] *See* Armco, Inc. v. Armco Burglar Alarm Co. 693 F.2d 1155 (5th Cir. 1982); Feathercombs, Inc. v. Solo Prods. Corp., 306 F.2d 251 (2d Cir.), *cert. denied*, 371 U.S. 910 (1962).

[27] 15 U.S.C. §1052 (2006).

[28] *See* Int'l Film Servs. Co. v. Associated Producers, 273 F. 585 (S.D.N.Y. 1921); McGraw-Hill Book Co. v. Random House, Inc., 225 N.Y.S.2d 646 (N.Y. Sup. Ct. 1962).

[29] Herbko Int'l, Inc. v. Kappa Books, Inc., 308 F.3d 1156 (Fed.Cir., 2002).

[30] *See* Levi Strauss & Co. v. Blue Bell, Inc., 632 F.2d 817 (9th Cir. 1980).

[31] *See* Osem Food Indus. Ltd. v. Sherwood Foods, Inc., 917 F.2d 161, 1646 (4th Cir. 1990).

members agree to abide by a dispute resolution mechanism through contract. It is generally believed not beneficial for the independent producer to participate.

3.2.5. Unique Characteristics of Entertainment Industry Marks

Certain types of marks used in and arising through the entertainment industry may be claimed to take advantage of publicity generated through film, media and music. Not all are protectable through the trademark laws, however. For example, a brief phrase made popular in a motion picture may not be sufficiently protectable through the trademark laws to stop use in an advertisement alluding to the film and motion picture.[32] Animated characters may be difficult to protect through trademark laws depending upon whether the mark is a physical embodiment of a character and if so, the manner in which it will be used outside of a creative work.

3.2.6. Unprotectable Marks

Certain marks are unprotectable and proscribed by the Lanham Act irrespective of secondary meaning. These are marks that (1) are immoral, slanderous, or disparaging of persons, beliefs, or national symbols[33]; (2) embody the flag or symbol of a governmental entity (foreign or domestic); or (3) consist of the name, portrait, or signature of a living individual (without his or her written consent) or a deceased president of the United States during the life of his widow (without her written consent).[34]

---

[32] Lions Gate Entertainment Inc. v TD Ameritrade Services Company, Inc., 170 F Supp. 3d 1249 (CD Cal 2016)(no claim stated by motion picture company against advertising agency in commercial which alluded to the film *Dirty Dancing* by use of the phrase "NOBODY PUTS YOUR OLD 401(k) IN A CORNER" referencing "NOBODY PUTS BABY IN A CORNER" comprised in the dialogue from *Dirty Dancing*).

[33] However, at least the disparagement clause was held to violate the Free Speech Clause of the First Amendment in Matal v. Tam, 137 S. Ct. 1744 (2017) (where registration for the mark THE SLANTS was initially denied by the Trademark Office, finding it derogatory to Asian-Americans.)

[34] 15 U.S.C. §1052(a)-(c) (2006). Written consents authorizing registration and use signed by the personality are typically filed in connection with these applications.

A mark that may falsely suggest a connection with an individual, living or dead is a basis for rejecting a trademark.[35]

Registration of a mark involving a living person whose name or identity is made a part of that mark without disclosing same to the Patent and Trademark Office (PTO) is considered a fraud upon the PTO and voids the rights of all but the person associated with the mark (or his/her privities).[36]

In addition, functional or utilitarian features of a product (even if they have obtained a secondary meaning as to the source and could therefore serve the trademark purpose of identifying the source of the product) are not protectable under trademark law.[37] Such protection as may exist would arise under patent law.[38]

The fact that a mark involves religion (referred to as "beliefs" in the statute) does not mean that the mark is unprotectable. So long as the mark bears the characteristics of protectability, it violates neither the statute nor the First Amendment to protect the mark against infringement by another religious organization.[39]

3.2.7. Famous Marks

In 1995, Congress enacted the Federal Trademark Dilution Act of 1995[40] and introduced the concept of famous marks, in part to create a reciprocal form of protection for the concept of famous names recognized in other countries and in a number of international treaties, where well-known marks which were not marketed within a particular

---

[35] 15 USC § 1052 (a) (2006). TWIGGY on children's clothing would point to petitioner, a famous British model and consumers would assume an association with petitioner, granting petition to cancel registration and thus creating a false connection with persons in violation of Section 2(a) of the Lanham Act. Hornby v. TJX Companies, Inc., 87 USPQ 2d 1411 (TTAB 2008).

[36] Gilbert/Robinson, Inc. v. Carrie Beverage-Mo, Inc., 989 F.2d 985 (8th Cir. 1993), cert. denied sub nom. Carrie Beverage, Inc. v. Gilbert/Robinson, Inc., 510 U.S. 928 (1993).

[37] See Vaughan Novelty Mfg. Co. v. G. G. Greene Mfg. Co., 202 F.2d 172 (3d Cir.), cert. denied, 346 U.S. 820 (1953).

[38] See 35 U.S.C. §171. (1952).

[39] Te-Ta-Ma Truth Found. – Family of URI, Inc. v. World Church of the Creator, 297 F.3d 662 (7th Cir. 2002), cert. denied, 537 U.S. 1111 (2003).

[40] P.L. 104-98.

country could still receive protection in that country.[41] The 1995 Act, however, was interpreted as requiring actual dilution rather than a likelihood of dilution[42] and, in certain instances, recognized "niche" fame as sufficient to establish the requisite fame for a mark.[43] Following this interpretation, Congress passed the Federal Trademark Dilution Revision Act (FTDRA) in 2006 to clarify the requirements for a dilution action.[44] The 2006 FTDRA lists four factors to consider when determining whether there is sufficient fame for there to be dilution: (1) the duration, extent and geographic reach of advertising and publicity of the mark, whether advertised or publicized by the owner or third parties; (2) the amount, volume and geographic extent of sales of goods or services offered under the mark; (3) the extent of actual recognition of the mark; and (4) whether the mark was registered under the Principal Register.[45] Also, the 2006 FTDRA explicitly establishes the test as a likelihood of dilution and eliminates niche fame as a basis for establishing the requisite fame of a mark. The statute does not define exactly what a famous mark is, leaving it to the discretion of the courts. It does offer a set of factors for the courts to consider (though not limiting the courts to these factors.)[46] They include:

(1) the degree of inherent or acquired distinctiveness of the mark;

(2) the duration and extent of use of the mark in connection with the goods or services with which the mark is used;

(3) the duration and extent of advertising and publicity of the mark;

(4) the geographical extent of the trading area in which the mark is used;

---

[41] *See* J. Thomas McCarthy, MCCARTHY ON TRADEMARKS AND UNFAIR COMPETITION §§39.26-29.29, Thomson/West (4th Ed. 2008).

[42] Moseley v. Secret Catalogue, Inc. 537 U.S. 418 (2003).

[43] Times Mirror Magazines v. Las Vegas Sports News, LLC, 212 F.3d 157 (3d Cir. 2000), *cert. denied*, 531 U.S. 1071 (2001).

[44] Section 1125(c)(3) (2006).

[45] Times Mirror Magazine, Inc. v. Las Vegas Sports News, LLC, 212 F.3d 157 (3rd Cir. 2000), *cert. denied*, 531 U.S. 1071 (2001).

[46] Amending §15 U.S.C. §1125 (2006).

(5) the degree of recognition of the mark in the trading areas and channels of trade used by the marks' owner and the person against whom an injunction is sought;

(6) the nature and extent of use of the same or similar marks by third parties; and

(7) whether the mark was registered under the Act of March 3, 1881, or the Act of February 20, 1905, or on the principal register.[47]

3.2.8. The Anticybersquatting Consumer Protection Act

In 1999, Congress enacted the Anticybersquatting Consumer Protection Act.[48] This act elaborates on the protections accorded to famous names, protecting names that are trademarked as well as those otherwise protected by statute.[49] While traditional trademark offers some protection under the traditional standards of an infringement action,[50] the Anticybersquatting Act offers an enhancement of that protection.

The problem confronting Congress and the owners of famous marks (including the names of well-known individuals) was that as the internet developed, the assignment of domain names or tags was not handled by a governmental entity, but was instead administered by a private company, Network Solutions, Inc., pursuant to a license from the United States commerce department.[51] In turn, while Network Solutions maintains the central registry for domain names, the industry created the Internet Corp. for Assigned Names and Numbers (ICANN), a nonprofit private-sector corporation set up to oversee Web-name assignments and resolve domain-name disputes, which in turn appoints smaller private company intermediaries to act as registrars of domain names and address.[52] During the early days of the Internet craze, many enterprising individuals filed a multitude of applications for domain names using the names of famous individuals and corporations. They would then either turn around and offer to sell those domain names to

---

[47] 15 U.S. C. §1125 (d)(1)(A) (2006).
[48] Amending §43 of the Trademark Act, 15 U.S.C. §1125.
[49] 15 U.S.C. §1125 (d)(1)(A).
[50] Brookfield Commc'ns, Inc. v. W. Coast Entm't Corp., 174 F.3d 1036 (9th Cir. 1999).
[51] See their web page at: http://www.icann.org.
[52] See their web page at: http://www.networksolutions.com.

the individual or the corporation whose name they had appropriated at an inflated price or they might attempt to use that name to sell their own products or services to all of the customers where were lured to that site when they performed an internet search using the name of the well-known company or individual.

In order to address this problem, Congress created a new cause of action. The plaintiff can proceed either *in rem* (i.e., against the registration as a "thing"), with the remedies limited to a court order forfeiting or cancelling the infringing domain registration or transferring the registration to the mark owner,[53] or *in personam* against the infringer for damages or other remedies. Provided that the plaintiff acted willfully with the knowledge that the mark was protected and the intent to profit from its use, under the personal action the plaintiff may not only seek injunctive relief and cancellation or transfer of the domain name but also profits, proven damages, or statutory damages (not less than $1,000 nor more than $100,000 per domain name at the determination of the court, along with attorney's fees and expenses).[54]

While the Anticybersquatting Consumer Protection Act specifically protects the actual name of the mark claimant as a domain name, cases addressing the act have also protected against misspellings or "typosquatting."[55] The misspelled domain names may be cancelled and, if the misspelling is indeed intentional, statutory damages and attorneys' fees may be awarded against the defendant.

Of particularly interest in the entertainment industry is an explicit right of publicity provision, in Section (b) of the Anticybersquatting Consumer Protection Act found at Section 47 of the Lanham Act.[56] Section 47 prohibits registration of domain names consisting of the name of another living person without consent, with the specific intent to profit by selling that name for financial gain.[57]

3.2.9. ICANN/WIPO Arbitration of Domain Names

The problem of cybersquatting (both in terms of actual use of protected names and intentionally misspelled versions) has also been

---

[53] 15 U.S.C. §1125 (d)(2)(A) (2006).
[54] *Id.* 15 U.S. C §1116.
[55] Shields v. Zuccarini, 254 F.3d 476 (3d Cir. 2001).
[56] 15 U.S.C. 1129 (2006).
[57] For more on the right of publicity, *see infra* §4.1.2.

recognized by the Internet Corporation for Assigned Names and Numbers (ICANN). On October 24, 1999 ICANN promulgated the Uniform Policy for Domain Name Dispute Resolution (the Policy) and Rules (the Rules) in association with the World Intellectual Property Organization. By registering with ICANN, every domain name claimant agrees to be bound by the Policy and Rules and to submit to binding arbitration under the Rules and the rules of WIPO's Arbitration and Mediation Center. Because the Internet is an international undertaking by ICANN, it is a major forum for international complaints – despite some courts finding that these arbitrations are not binding on U.S. courts.[58] However, these "arbitrations" are not traditional arbitrations as practiced in the United States. Everything is done on paper and there is no opportunity to present live testimony by way of an arbitration hearing. The rules specifically contemplate that the determinations are not binding on courts.

Management of the manner in which domain names are controlled was originally conducted by the Internet Assigned Numbers Authority (IANA, an agency affiliated with the Department of Commerce of the United States government). That contract was transferred to a private consortium in October 2016 away from U.S. government oversight.

As is the case with the United States Anticybersquatting Act, the burden for the Complainant under paragraph 4(a) of the ICANN Policy is to prove: (1) that the domain name registered by the Respondent is identical or confusingly similar to a trademark or service mark in which the Complainant has rights; and (2) that the Respondent has no rights or legitimate interests in respect of the domain name; and (3) that the domain name has been registered and used in bad faith.[59] Registration and use in bad faith can be shown where the following are present:

---

[58] Weber-Stephen Prods. Co. v. Armitage Hardware & Bldg. Supply, Inc., 54 U.S.P.Q.2d 1766, No. 00 C 1738, 2000 WL 562470 (N.D. Ill. 2000).

[59] This prong tends to be the one most difficult of proof as a practical matter. Decisions in these proceedings are generally published on the internet. The assigned arbitrators are not bound to follow these decisions although they may be persuasive. The arbitration may also be handled by the Arbitration Forum in the Midwest, www.adrforum.com. Keep in mind that since the procedure and rights are worldwide, there must be some sensitivity to rights outside of the United States and their laws rather than simply traditional U.S. rights. Registrations can be much more important than the concept of common law rights in the United States in order to be successful.

U.S. TRADEMARK AND UNFAIR COMPETITION LAW 167

(1) Acquisition of the domain for selling it at a profit to other than to the mark owner;
(2) Registering the domain to prevent the mark owner from using it where the domain owner has engaged in a pattern of such conduct;
(3) Registering the domain for disrupting the business of a competitor; and
(4) Intentionally and for commercial gain attempting to create confusion as to source, sponsorship or affiliation.

Ownership of a trademark registration for the affected name is *prima facie* evidence of the validity of the mark.[60] Domain names that are intentionally similar to a protected name (either as an intentional misspelling or a use that incorporates the mark/name with logically related names) is prohibited as being virtually identical or confusingly similar.[61] Finally use of these domain names to divert users to unrelated advertisements is classic bad faith. As one recent court has stated, "[t]aking advantage of consumers' known disposition to misspell domain names, Zuccarini has diverted Internet traffic to his web sites, thereby earning substantial revenue from advertisers."[62]

WIPO/ICANN arbitration does not result in financial penalties or damages. The affected domain names are simply cancelled, suspended or reassigned to the proper owner.

3.3. EXCLUSIVE RIGHTS OF TRADEMARK

3.3.1. In General

Trademarks, like copyrights and patents, are forms of intellectual property that may be licensed[63] and bought, sold, or assigned.[64]

---

[60] *See* Miller v. Zuccarini, WIPO Case No. D2001-0064 (April 25, 2001) §5b; *see also* Minolta Co., Ltd. v. Cupcake City, WIPO Case No. D2000-1291 (Jan. 18, 2001) §6.

[61] *See* Backstreet Productions, Inc. v. John Zuccarini, WIPO Case No. D2001-0654 (Aug. 24, 2001) §8.A.

[62] Encyclopedia Britannica, Inc. v. Zuccarini, WIPO Case No. 2000-0330 (June 7, 2000) (finding bad faith under the U.S. Anticybersquatting Consumer Protection Act, Section 43(d) of the Lanham Act).

[63] *See* Sheila's Shine Prods, Inc. v. Sheila Shine, Inc., 486 F.2d 114 (5th Cir. 1973).

[64] 15 U.S.C. §1060 (2002).

However, unlike copyrights or patents, it is not a property right that exists in the abstract, separate from its use in commerce, to identify and embody the good will of the owner's trade or business.[65] Thus, there must be some degree of transfer of good will as associated with that mark.[66]

Moreover, the degree of protection that the mark is given varies according to the strength of the trademark.[67] Although the owner of a mark involving a surname that has acquired secondary meaning may receive protection, a second person of the same surname may be entitled to the use of his or her surname with a disclaimer of non-affiliation with that mark's owner.[68] A stronger mark will be given broader protection.

3.3.2. Exclusive Market

The basic right of trademark is the exclusive right to use the registered mark in commerce in connection with the product or services specified in the registration and subject to any conditions or limitations stated therein.[69] This applies as well to unregistered marks. There are two factors to consider in this right: the territory of use and the type or character of use.

3.3.2.1. Territory

Federal trademark law ordinarily presumes national registration or coverage. However, under certain conditions, such as where prior to federal registration two or more parties have been using the same mark in different territories, each may apply for federal registration concurrently with each party's rights defined according to geographic limitations.[70]

---

[65] *See* Hanover Star Milling Co. v. Metcalf, 240 U.S. 403 (1916), *superceded by statute sub nom.* Park 'N Fly, Inc. v. Dollar Park & Fly, Inc. 469 U.S. 189 (1985).
[66] 15 U.S.C. §1060 (2002).
[67] *See supra* §3.2.3.
[68] *See* L. E. Waterman Co. v. Modern Pen Co., 235 U.S. 88 (1914).
[69] 15 U.S.C. §1115(a) (2002).
[70] *See* Anderson v. Capitol Records, No. 274080, 1973 WL 19895, 178 U.S.P. Q. 238 (Cal.App.Super. 1973)(obtaining a geographically limited registration is not necessarily a simple procedure and requires approval by the Trademark Trial and Appeal Board (TTAB), the administrative law tribunal within the Trademark Office.)

3.3.2.2. Competing Products or Services

A second limitation exists with regard to products or services identified with the mark. The owner is given a protectable exclusive right to use the mark in association with an identified product or service.[71] The level of protection against use of the mark in association with products or services different from those that are protected depends in part on the strength of the mark used[72] and the product relationship (e.g., whether or not they are of the same class or genre or family of products).[73] The test is whether or not there is a likelihood of confusion in the mind of the consumer as to the source of the goods or services.[74]

3.3.3. Well-Known Marks

The "well-known" marks doctrine may extend protection to trademarks even when such marks may not otherwise be entitled to protection in the United States, although courts have the soundness of this doctrine.[75] Trademark rights are based upon use of a mark in commerce and such use, generally, must occur within the United States under the territoriality rule.[76] Under the territoriality rule, use of a mark that occurs in a foreign country is not relevant to establishing trademark rights in the United States.[77]

The "well-known" marks doctrine, however, may protect international marks even when such marks may not be used in United States commerce in the trademark sense. The degree of reputation that

---

The TTAB must find in a concurrent use proceeding that mistake, confusion or deception is not likely to occur. 15 USC §1052(d).

[71] *See* 15 U.S.C. §§1052, 1114(1) (2006).

[72] *See* In HMH Publishing Co. v. Brincat, 342 F. Supp. 1275 (N.D. Cal. 1972). *aff'd in part & rev'd in part*, 504 F.2d 713 (9th Cir. 1974).

[73] Kiki Undies Corp. v. Promenade Hosiery Mills, Inc. 411 F.2d 1097 (2d Cir. 1969).

[74] 15 U.S.C. §1114(1) (2005).

[75] See ITC Ltd. v. Punchgini, Inc., 482 F.3d 135 (2d. Cir., March 28, 2007) (refusing to recognize the "well-known" marks doctrine as part of federal trademark law, but leaving open its possible application under New York state law).

[76] Grupo Gigante S.A. de C.V. v. Dallo & Co., 119 F. Supp. 2d 1083, 1089 (C.D. Cal. 2000).

[77] Grupo Gigante, 119 F. Supp. at 1089 (citing *Scholastic, Inc. v. Macmillan, Inc.*, 650 F. Supp. 866, 873 n. 6 (S.D.N.Y. 1987)..

is necessary to protect a mark as "well-known" is that the trademark is sufficiently "well-known" in the relevant sector of the public in the United States that the defendant's use is likely to cause confusion. Numerous factors are considered in determining whether a mark is "well-known" and merits protection.[78]

3.4. FAIR USE OF TRADEMARKS

Just as with the law of copyright, rights arising under the rubric of trademarks and unfair competition are subject to third party use under a "fair use" doctrine.[79] A party asserting a fair use defense is not required to also prove that the use is not likely to cause confusion.[80]

A statutory fair use defense appears in the Lanham Act stating that "the use of the name, term, device charged to be an infringement is a use, otherwise than as a mark, of the party's individual name in his own business ... or of a term ... which is descriptive of and used fairly and in good faith only to describe the goods or services of such party or their geographical origin...."[81]

There also appears to exist a limited right to create parodies based on the marks of others, such as a parody of the television program *Miami Vice* printed on T-shirts with a logo named *Miami Mice*,[82] so long as the parody is not too literal[83] or too derogatory to the mark.[84]

---

[78] *See* Frederick W. Mostert, FAMOUS AND WELL-KNOWN MARKS, pp. 1-13 – 1-17 (INTA 2nd Ed. 2004) (listing factors including the degree of recognition of the mark, extent of use, extent and duration of publicity including the mark, the degree of exclusivity of use of the mark, and the economic value of the mark).

[79] KP Permanent Make-Up, Inc. v. Lasting Impression, Inc., 543 U.S. 111, 122 (2004).

[80] *Id.*, at 124.

[81] 15 U.S.C. § 1115(b)(4). This particular section only appears to apply as a defense to an incontestable registration though it is referenced in other contexts.

[82] Universal City Studios, Inc. v. T-Shirt Gallery, Ltd., 634 F. Supp. 1468 (S.D.N.Y. 1986).

[83] Dallas Cowboys Cheerleaders, Inc. v. Pussycat Cinema, Ltd., 467 F. Supp. 366 (S.D.N.Y. 1979), *aff'd*, 604 F.2d 200 (2d Cir. 1979).

[84] Coca-Cola Co. v. Gemini Rising, Inc. 346 F. Supp. 1183 (E.D.N.Y. 1972); Eastman Kodak Co. v. Rakow, 739 F. Supp.116 (W.D.N.Y. 1989) (decided on state law anti-dilution grounds). It should be noted that there is significant conflict over parodies of marks which may appear to defame or ridicule the original marks, with decisions frequently turning on whether or not the court finds the parody humorous. *See* Kent, "Proposed Changes to Lanham Act" N.Y.L.J. Vol. 199-No. 102 3-4 (May 27, 1988). Basic principles of trademark law are used in determining whether a parody

Even famous marks may be subject to parody.[85] Like copyright, the parody can involve a significant use of material associated with a mark, such as the pattern, format or story line of a commercial or ad. For example, in the 2000 Presidential Election, Ralph Nader created ads based on MasterCard's "Priceless" ad campaign. In the MasterCard ads, a series of goods or services along with their costs are displayed followed by an intangible good followed by the word and/or voice-over "Priceless." The tag line of the ad is "There are some things that money can't buy. For everything else, there's MasterCard." Nader's ads, focusing on the need for campaign finance reform, list a series of questionable political practices (fund raisers, campaign ads, promises to special interest groups) with price tags and "finding out the truth – priceless." The tag line is "There are some things that money can't buy."[86] Similarly, using the Charles Atlas ads involving a skinny young man being provoked to acquire a muscular body after having sand kicked in his face (along with visual images inspired by the ad) as the basis for a comic book story can be protected as a parody.[87]

Incidental and non-derogatory uses of a mark may also be deemed fair use, although it would be more accurate to describe this as noninfringing use in so far as the use does not reflect on the source of any goods or services.[88] The law also recognizes as fair use a good faith non-trademark use by an individual of his or her own surname

---

is trademark infringement, i.e., whether there is a likelihood of confusion. In other words, would a consumer really be likely to believe that the parody was endorsed or sponsored by the plaintiff? Thus, HERE'S JOHNNY was not held to be trademark infringement of the mark JOHNNY CARSON for various goods, even though it was considered a violation of his publicity rights. Carson v. Here's Johnny Portable Toilets, Inc., 698 F.2d 831 (6th Cir. 1983); Mutual of Omaha Ins. Co. v. Novak, 648 F.Supp. 905 (D. Neb. 1986), *aff'd* 836 F.2d 397 (8th Cir. 1987)(MUTANT OF OMAHA merchandise mocking Mutual of Omaha's advertising; court held that this was more of a satire than a parody, making a statement about the potential for nuclear war, rather than specifically directing it against the insurance company as a target; survey suggested that there was 10% that thought that plaintiff went along with the message of defendant's products, supporting plaintiff's contention of likelihood of confusion or trademark infringement; no trademark disparagement found).

[85] 15 U.S.C. § 1125(c); *see also,* Louis Vuitton Malletier S.A. v. Haute Diggity Dog, LLC, 507 F.3d 252 (4th Cir. 2007).

[86] In a case in the SDNY adjudicated by Judge George B. Daniels – see *http://www.lawpublish.com/a1-3.html.*

[87] Charles Atlas Ltd. v. DC Comics Inc., 112 F. Supp. 2d 330 (S.D.N.Y. 2000).

[88] *See* Anne Gilson Lalonde, GILSON ON TRADEMARKS (2008), Sec. 1.03 *et seq.*; Packman v. Chicago Tribune Co., 267 F.3d 628 (7th Cir. 2001).

(i.e., by that person, or one with whom he or she is in privity), or the use of a descriptive or geographic term to describe the users of such goods or service or their geographic origin.[89] Whether or not the use is a trademark use (i.e., intended to distinguish those goods or services from others) is a question of fact for the trial court.[90]

A variation of this is the nominative fair use, in which the defendant uses the plaintiff's mark as a means of describing his own product or service.[91] This would, for example, protect the use of the Playboy and Playmate of the Year marks on the website of a former Playmate of the Year – because the use of these marks is descriptive of her independent of the owner.[92] Similarly, a maker of personality related products could market personality products that have lost their protection under the law of publicity/privacy (for example, after expiration of post-mortem rights (if any)) even though another marketer may hold trademark rights to its own versions of such personality objects. For example, the Franklin Mint was allowed to market its "Princess Diana" ceramics using the "Princess Diana" name to identify those products despite the objections of the owner of the Princess Diana mark.[93] Using the Princess Diana mark did not reflect an endorsement or an identification of source for the products; it merely described the ceramics produced by Franklin Mint. The nominative fair use defense would not, however, apply to the use of a band's name even by an original member of the band, if the use suggested some connection or endorsement by the original band and owner of the mark,[94] as opposed to incidental reference merely in a biographical context.

In order to establish a nominative fair use defense, a defendant must prove the following three elements: first, the plaintiff's product or

---

[89] *Id.* 15 U.S.C. §1115b(4); 2002 KP Permanent Make-Up, Inc. v. Lasting Impression, Inc., 543 U.S. 111 (2004) (recognizing descriptive fair use as a defense even where some confusion may occur).

[90] See Pure Foods v. Minute Maid Corp., 214 F.2d 792 (5th Cir.), *cert. denied*, 348 U.S. 888 (1954).

[91] *See, e.g.*, New Kids on the Block v. News Am. Publ'g., Inc., 971 F.2d 302 (9th Cir. 1992); WCVB-TV v. Boston Athletic Ass'n, 926 F.2d 42 (1st Cir. 1991).

[92] Playboy Enters. v. Welles, 279 F.3d 796 (9th Cir.), *aff'd.*, 30 Fed. Appx 734 (9th Cir. 2002).

[93] Cairns v. Franklin Mint Co., 292 F.3d 1139 (9th Cir. 2002).

[94] Brother Records, Inc. v. Jardine, 318 F.3d 900 (9th Cir.), *cert. denied*, 540 U.S. 824 (2003).

service in question must be one not readily identifiable without use of the trademark; second, only so much of the mark or marks may be used as is reasonably necessary to identify the plaintiff's product or service; and third, the user must do nothing that would, in conjunction with the mark, suggest sponsorship or endorsement by the trademark holder.[95]

With respect to famous marks, a special fair use provision has been included in the law which provides that the following shall not be actionable as dilution:.

(1) Fair use of a famous mark by another, including nominative or descriptive fair use other than as trademark use by a person in comparative commercial advertising or promotion to identify the competing goods or services of the owner of the famous mark or identifying, parodying, criticizing or commenting on famous mark owner or its goods or services;
(2) all forms of news reporting and news commentary; and
(3) noncommercial use of a mark[96]

While all of these fair uses are generally supported under the existing law, to the extent they are not one can anticipate their use by the courts as guides.

An interesting variation on the fair use doctrine has arisen in relation to an effort not to display a trademark. Specifically, in a couple of cases involving the filming or broadcast of productions shot in Time Square, the producers blocked out advertisements on the side of a building and superimposed images of their own choosing masking those advertisements to viewers. In one such instance, the owners of the building sued for trademark infringement and unfair competition. In addition to denying the owner the status of trademark owner (because the building in no way reflected the source of the films as goods), the court added that the creative manipulation of the environment by the producers of the film *Spiderman* reflected a creative blending of fact and fiction justifying First Amendment protection.[97]

---

[95] Cairns v. Franklin Mint Co., 292 F.3d 1139 (9th Cir. 2002); *see also* Century 21 Real Estate Corp. v. Lendingtree, Inc., 425 F.3d 211, 220 (3rd Cir. 2005) (applying modified test in nominative fair use analysis).

[96] *See* 15 U.S.C. §1125(c)(3)(2).

[97] Sherwood 48 Assocs. v. Sony Corp. of Am., 213 F. Supp. 2d 376 (S.D.N.Y 2002), *aff'd in part, vacated in part, remanded*, 76 Fed. App's. 389 (2nd Cir. 2003).

3.5. CREATION AND COMMENCEMENT OF PROTECTION

A trademark is created under both common law and the Lanham Act by the use of the mark in commerce in association with the goods or services, so that the mark becomes associated with the marketer/creator of the goods or services.[98] Use in commerce requires that the mark be affixed in a tangible form on goods, containers or displays, or in advertising associated with those goods or services in transactions occurring in more than one state.[99] This would, for example, include a title or the names of characters distributed for sale in the form of a book or movie.[100] Use in commerce in order to gain protection over the internet would also be achieved by free distribution of a product over the internet identified by a mark (without an immediate intent to market the product),[101] and acting to prevent others from obtaining or using the trademark holder's goods or services, or using the mark as a domain name and using that site to link to the other's goods or services.[102]

For protection to commence there is the added requirement that the mark become associated in the public's mind with the source of those goods or services.[103] Although, as a rule, the use of an *identifiable* trademark (particularly one that is novel or fanciful) immediately establishes some protectable rights[104] (with novel or fanciful marks

---

[98] *See* In Re Trade-Mark Cases, 100 U.S. 82 (1879). *See also* 15 U.S.C. §1051 (2002).

[99] 15 U.S.C. §1127 (2006).

[100] Protection of character names embodied within a creative work such as a book or motion picture may not be easy to obtain. Simply reciting the name within a book is not likely to result in protection without more. Trademark registration for character names must be identified in connection with specific goods and services. The manner of use of the mark with those services may determine whether protection is available. Marks that merely identify a character in a creative work whether used in a series or in a single work are not registrable. In re Scholastic Inc., 223 USPQ 431 (TTAB 1984)(THE LITTLES used in the title of each book in a series of children's books does not function as a mark where it merely identifies the main characters in the books); In re Frederick Warne & Co., Inc., 218 USPQ 345 (TTAB 1983)(holding that an illustration of a frog used on the cover of a single book served only to depict the main character in the book and not function as a trademark). Trademark Manual of Examining Procedure § 1202.10. Character marks as other marks must be used in a manner to specifically identify and distinguish the source of goods or services to gain protection.

[101] Planetary Motion, Inc. v. Techsplosion, Inc., 261 F.3d 1188 (11th Cir. 2001).

[102] People for Ethical Treatment of Animals, Inc. v. Doughney, 263 F.3d 359 (4th Cir. 2001).

[103] *See* United Drug Co. v. Rectanus Co., 248 U.S. 90 (1918).

[104] *See* In Re Trade-Mark Cases, 100 U.S. 82 (1879). *See also* 15 U.S.C. §1052.

creating quite strong rights),[105] other marks may create negligible protection (e.g., merely "descriptive" marks) until secondary meaning has attached.[106] It is presumed that a distinctive mark will easily translate into consumer identification. The Trademark Law Revision Act of 1988[107] has created an exception to this general practice by allowing limited protection of marks intended for use, but not yet in use. Specifically, a person who has a bona fide intent to use a mark in circumstances showing good faith may file an application for registration of the mark on the principal register.[108] While this application establishes the applicant's priority of filing,[109] the actual registration of the mark is not completed until the mark has been put to use in interstate commerce.[110]

It should be noted that federal or state registration does not create a trademark.[111] Registration applies only to a mark in *existence* and, under the Lanham Act, used in interstate commerce.[112]

3.6. OWNERSHIP

Ownership ordinarily vests in the first person or entity to use the mark in commerce.[113] It is possible, however, for ownership to be held by two or more unrelated parties, where, for example, prior to federal registration, the marks were developed under state law in different parts of the country and where they were consequently not in direct competition. For this reason, the Lanham Act creates a mechanism for registering co-ownership with use by each party restricted to a certain specified territory.[114] Moreover, the courts recognize agreements by two or more parties allowing concurrent use of marks on closely related products.[115]

---

[105] *See supra* §3.2.2.
[106] *See supra* §3.2. *See also* 15 U.S.C. §1051(e).
[107] P.L. 100-667.
[108] 15 U.S.C. §1051(b) (2002).
[109] 15 U.S.C. §1057(c) (2000).
[110] 15 U.S.C. §1051(b) (2002).
[111] *See* United Drug Co. v. Rectanus, 248 U.S. 90 (1918).
[112] *See* 15 U.S.C. §1051 (2002).
[113] *See* In Re Trademark Cases, 100 U.S. 82 (1879).
[114] *See supra* §3.3.2.1.
[115] *See* Waukesha Hygeia Mineral Springs Co. v. Hygeia Sparkling Distilled Water Co., 63 F. 438 (7th Cir. 1894).

3.7. FORMALITIES OF REGISTRATION AND NOTICE

3.7.1. Federal Registration

A mark may be registered in the federal registers by filing a written application including verified statements of when the mark was first used in commerce, the goods or services in connection with which it was used, a drawing of the mark plus specimens (or facsimiles) of the mark as used as required by the Trademark Office and payment of the required fee.[116] Information on this process, including forms for registration and instructions as to their completion, may be obtained from the Trademark Office website (www.uspto.gov). The forms are completed online and the Trademark Office provides incentives for conducting all business online discouraging the use of paper filings. If the applicant is not a United States domiciliary, he or she must designate a resident agent for the service of process.[117] The mark is examined by an Examining Attorney at the Trademark Office to evaluate whether or not it can be registered, and the mark is then published in the *Official Gazette of the Patent and Trademark Office*.[118] It is then subject to opposition by any person who believes that he or she may be damaged by the issuance of registration.[119] Typical bases for an opposition, as well as the initial determination by the Examining Attorney, are that the mark sought to be registered is confusingly similar with a mark used prior to the filing of the pending application.[120] Other bases for refusal to register, or for opposition or cancellation, include but are not limited to the following: the mark is

---

[116] 15 U.S.C. §1051 (2002). The Trademark Office can be very particular in accepting or declining a particular specimen of a mark for a specific service. E.g., an application to file for registration of the mark WORLDS BIGGEST SMALL GROUP for broadcasting services was refused on the grounds that the specimen submitted showed use of the mark as a title of a radio program which would fall within a different class, class 41. In re Way Media, Inc., Serial No. 86325739 (TTAB June 3, 2016).
[117] *Id.*
[118] 15 U.S.C. §§1062(a) 1066.
[119] 15 U.S.C. §1063 (2006).
[120] MAYARI for wine sufficiently dissimilar in appearance, sound, meaning and commercial impression from opposer's mark MAYA to avoid the TTAB sustaining an opposition. Oakille Hills Cellar, Inc. v. Georgallis Holdings, LLC, 826 F.3d. 1376 (2016).

descriptive or generic,[121] the mark is primarily merely a surname,[122] the mark comprises matter that, as a whole, is functional,[123] there was no bona fide intent to use mark in commerce for identified goods or services,[124] failure to function as a mark,[125] applicant is not the rightful owner of mark for identified goods or services,[126] the mark carries a false suggestion of a connection with persons, living or dead, institutions, beliefs, or national symbols, or brings them into contempt, or disrepute,[127] consists of or comprises a name, portrait, or signature of a living individual without written consent, or the name, portrait, or signature of a deceased president without the written consent of the surviving spouse,[128] fraud on the USPTO,[129] or is the title of single creative work.[130] The fact that the complainant may have been aware of the applicant's prior use of the mark without making objection does not preclude his or her opposition to registration or prosecution of a cancellation action on grounds of laches as might be the case with an

---

[121] E.g., Patty's Original Cheese Zombies, Inc. v. Dumploads on Us, Cancellation 92058966 (TTAB 2016)(CHEEZE ZOMBIES descriptive but not generic for filled bakery products where that type of product was previously referred to by that term).

[122] Adlon Brand GmbH & Co. KG c/o Fundus Fonds, 120 USPQ2d 1717 (TTAB 2016)(rare name ADLON primarily merely a surname); however, rejection is may be less likely to be based on any requirement for secondary meaning where the mark is a "personal name" as opposed to a surname. Christopher Brooks v. Creative Arts by Calloway, LLC, 93 USPQ 2d 1823 (TTAB 2009)(CAB CALLOWAY did not require proof of secondary meaning).

[123] See International Association of Job's Daughters v. Lindeburg & Co., 633 F.2d 912 (9th Cir. 1980)(aesthetic functionality prevented organization from asserting valid claim against jewelry company where court found that students purchased class rings to show their affiliation with organization, rather than because of concern over manufacturing source); followed in Fleischer Studios, Inc., 636 F.3d 1115 (9th Cir. 2010)(BETTY BOOP held aesthetically functional; this opinion was withdrawn, yet on remand the District Court followed its reasoning, essentially stating that although the images were in the public domain by copyright, the use of the words BETTY BOOP was the only way that the public domain images could be described).

[124] Lanham Act Section 1(b).

[125] See In re Hechinger Inv. Co. of Del., 24 USPQ2d 1057, 1059 (TTAB 1991); In re McDonald's Corp., 229 USPQ 555, 555 (TTAB 1985); TMEP §§904.07(b), 1301.02(b).

[126] Trademark Act Section 1.

[127] Trademark Act Section 2(a).

[128] Trademark Act Section 2(c).

[129] In re Bose Corp., 580 F.3d 1240, 91 USPQ2d 1938 (Fed. Cir. 2009).

[130] Trademark Act Sections 1, 2 and 45, Mattel Inc. v. Brainy Baby Co., 101 USPQ2d 1140 (TTAB 2011).

infringement action.[131] An examining attorney acting on behalf of the Trademark Office evaluates such claims and the validity of proposed registration.[132] His or her determination is subject to review by the Trademark Trial and Appeal Board,[133] and is thereafter appealable to the United States Court of Appeals for the Federal Circuit.[134]

A mark that might otherwise be rejected based upon the likelihood of confusion with a prior registered mark may be registered with the consent of the owner of the prior registration. Such consent must be more than a "mere naked consent" and should involve detailed provisions to minimize potential confusion.[135]

Where a mark has not been used in interstate commerce but the mark's owner has a bona fide intent to use the mark under conditions that show good faith, the person can apply to register the trademark on the principal register by making written application, accompanied by a drawing of the mark, a verified statement avowing that the person or the entity he or she represents intends to use the mark, that he or she knows of no obstruction to that intended use, and payment of the required application fee.[136]

---

[131] Nat'l Cable Television Ass'n, Inc. v. Am. Cinema Editors, Inc., 937 F.2d 1572 (Fed. Cir. 1991).

[132] 15 U.S.C. §1068 (2000). The determination is primarily based on the Lanham Act, 15 U.S.C. 1051 et seq, the Rules of Practice, Title 37, Code of Federal Regulations, 2.1 et seq., and the Trademark Manual of Examining Procedure (TMEP), tmep.uspto.gov.uspto.gov/sites/default/files/documents/tmlaw.pdf., each of which are available to the public online. Also helpful is the U.S. Acceptable Identification of Goods and Services Manual. This online resource identifies descriptions of goods and services, which descriptions are generally acceptable to examining attorneys. The United States is a member of the Nice Convention, which has its own identification of goods and services, which member countries are required to use to reference specific classes of goods and services, which serves to harmonize somewhat the manner in which goods and services are classified across international jurisdictions.

[133] 15 U.S.C. §1070 (1958).

[134] 15 U.S.C. §1071 (2000).

[135] In re Four Seasons Hotels, Ltd., 987 F.2d 1565 (Fed. Cir. 1993)(not every consent to register will be accepted at face value). The Examining Attorney refused to accept a consent agreement for the marks TIME TRAVELER BLONDE and TIME TRAVELER (both for beer) in In re Bay Street Brewing Co., Inc., 117 USPQ 2d 1958 (TTAB 2016). The TTAB found a high likelihood of confusion and even though consent agreements are frequently entitled to great weight, registration was denied.

[136] 15 U.S.C. §1051(b) (2002). Lack of bona fide intent is a basis for opposing or cancelling a registration. Intent must generally be demonstrable and more than merely a subjective belief. Inconsistent oral testimony and lack of documentary evidence suggested that intent was to reserve a right in the mark rather than to use the mark in commerce, resulting in sustaining an opposition to the mark. M.Z. Berger & Co. v.

After appropriate examination and review, the Commissioner, through the Examining Attorney, will issue a notice of "allowance"[137] that, in essence, preserves the applicant's filing priority.[138] Either during the pendency of the initial application, within six months of the issuance of the allowance, or within a permitted extension of the said six months which may be granted pursuant to written application and payment of an appropriate fee (but in any event not more than a cumulative twenty-four months following the initial extension), the applicant must file a Statement of Use revealing (1) that the mark is being used in commerce,[139] (2) the products or services it is being used in connection with, and (3) the initial date of that use, accompanied by samples or facsimiles of the mark as actually used and payment of the appropriate fee.[140] The mark will then be registered and published in the *Official Gazette of the Patent and Trademark Office*[141] where it will be subject to the same challenges and oppositions as would be applied to the registration of an already used mark. Failure to file a Statement of Use within the specified time period will result in the abandonment of the application.[142]

In addition to federal registration, a mark may be registered in a state register or in a foreign country.[143]

Swatch AG, 787 F.3d 1368 (Fed. Cir. 2015); Commodore Electronics Ltd. v. CBM Kaushiki Kaisa (TTAB 1993); Swiss Grill Ltd. et al. v. Wolf Steel Ltd. (TTAB 2015)(post filing documentation and lack of documents may be the basis of sustaining an opposition to an application to register a mark).

[137] 15 U.S.C. §1063(b)(2) (2006).

[138] 15 U.S.C. §1057(c) (2000).

[139] Commerce including interstate commerce is essentially any type of commerce which Congress regulates or could regulate and thus provides a basis for filing federally. Since Heart of Atlanta Motel v. United States, 85 S. Ct. 348 (1964), the scope of what is considered acceptable commerce tends to be broad, though not unlimited. In re Ponderosa Motor Inns., 156 USPQ 474 (TTAB 1968); but see Larry Harmon Pictures Corp. v. The Williams Restaurant Corp., 929 F.2d 663 (Fed. Cir. 1991)(restaurant not on interstate highway, not listed in restaurant guide and had no liquor license not sufficient to support claim that there was interstate commerce or business that affected interstate commerce); In Christian Faith Fellowship Church v. Adidas AG, 841 F. 3d 986 (Fed. Cir. 2016) (the sale of 2 hats within Illinois to an individual who resides out of state may be sufficient commerce to support federal registration avoiding cancellation).

[140] 15 U.S.C. §1051 (2002).

[141] 15 U.S.C. §1051(d) (2002).

[142] 15 U.S.C. §1051(d)(4) (2002).

[143] *See* Gilson, *supra* note 3, §3.01, for the process of doing a trademark search to determine the availability of the mark.

3.7.2. State Registration

Individual States maintain their own registries for trademarks and service marks. They are generally administered by the Secretary of State offices. Forms can be obtained online for downloading and completion. It is rare when there is a substantial benefit to obtain state registrations. They may be useful when the issue of commerce, whether interstate or other commerce regulable by Congress is weak, where activity is entirely within a single state and where a conflict with other registrations is anticipated. However, this may not create a complete solution to the issue of concern. Registration is based on actual use of the mark within the state. Generally, there may be no substantive advantage which is available for federal registration, and the benefits are not necessarily analogous to federal registration on a statewide scale.

The Model State Trademark Bill promulgated by the International Trademark Association has attempted to create some consistency in state trademark registrations, enhancing some features of the registrations and limiting others. While adopted in some jurisdictions, it has not been universally accepted. Some of the characteristics of the Model Trademark Bill are to set the registration term at 5 years, to create a *prima facie* presumption of ownership, but to require the applicant to provide information to the applicant's Secretary of State regarding refusal of federal registration of the mark.

3.7.3. Registration Outside of the United States

Enforcement of trademarks, with a few minor exceptions, are territorial. Trademark rights must be established in each territory in which enforcement is desired. Unlike copyright, that usually means registration in each such territory. The requirement of use of a mark as a basis for registration is somewhat unique to the United States. Registration in most countries tends to be based on first to file an application, though there are some saving features to prevent trademark piracy and permit actions for unfair competition and palming off even in the absence of a valid registration. Nevertheless, a different mindset is beneficial in understanding the differences. Absent a prior filing and especially prior use in a particular territory, it may be virtually impossible to overcome a prior filing by a third party having no other apparent rights in a mark.

Three primary international conventions and treaties should be considered in approaching international filing, depending on the territories of interest.[144] The first is the Paris Convention, which among other features, permits the filing of a trademark in most countries within six months of the filing date in a home country, yet preserving the home country filing date for the foreign filing.

The next is the Madrid Protocol which allows one to obtain an international registration based on a home country application or registration in designated member countries. Close to 100 countries are currently members, though few in Latin America. Canada is expected to adhere to the Madrid Protocol shortly. China is a member, but Hong Kong is not. The procedure is that an international application is filed through the home country intellectual property office, which for the United States is the United States Patent and Trademark Office. The application is filed online referencing one or more home filed applications and registrations on which to base the international registration. The applicant designates one or more countries to be covered by the international registration, pays various fees online usually by credit card or deposit account, and the application is forwarded to the International Bureau (IB) of the World Intellectual Property Organization (WIPO) in Geneva. Once the IB finds it acceptable, the application is forwarded to the IP offices of the designated countries. Those countries have either 12 months or 18 months in which to reject the application.[145] If the application is not rejected by a particular country it remains in force.

One limitation of the Madrid Protocol registration is that the scope of the registration cannot be greater than the scope of the home application or registration(s) on which it is based. Thus, if the scope of the U.S. application is narrow, or narrowed during the scope of the registration process, the Madrid Protocol registration will be similarly limited. And if the home registrations or applications are abandoned or cancelled, the Madrid Protocol registration will also be cancelled unless the Madrid Protocol registration has been in existence for over 5

---

[144] Several additional geographically based trademark treaties and protocols not yet matured may be useful many years from now.

[145] The 12 or 18 month period is determined by how the country signed the treaty.

years. From that period on, the Madrid Protocol registration maintains its own status independent of the base application or registration.

The third treaty of importance is that creating the Community Trademark, formerly referred to at a CTM or European mark. The primary feature of the CTM is that it covers the entire European Union, currently 28 territories in Western and Central Europe.[146] It remains to be seen what will happen with the UK in this regard. The CTM is an affordable way to gain trademark protection in numerous developed countries. A single application is filed with EUIPO, the European Intellectual Property Office, which is located in Alicante, Spain. Its location is largely irrelevant as applications are filed by licensed attorneys throughout the EU. The CTM application is reviewed on "absolute grounds" only, not "relative grounds." This means that EUIPO will not reject a pending application on the ground that it conflicts with an existing registration. It is up to owners of registrations to file opposition proceedings based on relative or other grounds if they choose. Once issued, the CTM is effective, in varying degrees, in each of the member countries as a basis for suit for infringement claims. The European Union is a member of the Paris Convention and also the Madrid Protocol.

Application for registrations can also be filed nationally, which means on a country by country basis. This tends to be the most expensive, but sometimes more desirable way to proceed in obtaining trademark protection abroad.

3.7.4. Registration of Entertainment and Creative Industry Marks

A growing number of performers and sports figures, among them Tiger Woods, Charlie Sheen and the artist formerly known as Prince, have begun to trademark their names in order to protect their use within the growing celebrity endorsement market.[147] Obtaining trademark registrations, for celebrities may be challenging. The use of the name must act as more than simply the name of the celebrity. Specimens of use must show that the mark actually designates a source

---

[146] Keep in mind that neither Norway nor Switzerland are members of the EU.

[147] *See, e.g.*, ETW Corp. v. Jireh Publ'g, Inc., 332 F.3d 915 (6th Cir. 2003) (finding use of Woods' image (rather than name) in a limited-edition artwork did not violate trademark rights).

of the goods or services sought to be registered. The applicant must demonstrate permission to register if it is an entity or person other than the celebrity that seeks to register the celebrity identity.[148]

There are hurdles to registering entertainment marks. The title of a single creative work is not subject to registration.[149] However, the titles of a series may be registered.[150] Phantom marks may not be registered. A "phantom mark" is one which has a changing element, word or feature that varies from one use to another. For example, "THE ADVENTURES OF BIG GRASHOPPER JUMPS TO ..." where the ellipses represents a varying geographic region or other component which is subject to change would be considered to be a phantom mark and could not be registered in that manner.[151] A mark solely used as a domain name is not registrable.[152] Simply identifying an author or performer may be difficult to register.[153] A mark solely to identify a character is not registrable. It must function as a mark to identify and distinguish the applicant's services from those of others and to indicate the source of applicant's services.[154] The name of a character is registrable as a service mark only where the record shows that it is used in a manner that would be perceived by consumers as identifying the services in addition to identifying the character.[155] Marks used as mere ornamentation are not registrable.[156] Marks simply spread across the front of a t-shirt may not be permitted registration if they do not tell the public who sponsored the article. The applicant may need to show a source identifying function to the use of the mark.[157]

---

[148] 15 USC §1052(c); TMEP 813, 1206.04(a).
[149] TMEP 1202.08(c).
[150] TMEP 1202.08(b).
[151] TMEP 1214.
[152] TMEP 1215.02.
[153] TMEP 1202.09(a).
[154] 15 U.S.C. §§1051-1053, 1127; *see* In re Hechinger Inv. Co. of Del., 24 USPQ2d 1057, 1059 (TTAB 1991); In re McDonald's Corp., 229 USPQ 555, 555 (TTAB 1985); TMEP §§904.07(b), 1301.02(b).
[155] In re Fla. Cypress Gardens Inc., 208 USPQ 288, 292 (TTAB 1980); TMEP §1301.02(b).
[156] *See* TMEP 1202.03.
[157] In re Paramount Pictures Corp., 213 USPQ 1111 (TTAB 1982) (Mork & Mindy would reference television series to a prospective purchaser).

3.7.5. Principal versus Supplemental Register

The Patent and Trademark Office maintains two registers: the *Principal Register*[158] and the *Supplemental Register*.[159] Marks registrable on the *Supplemental Register* are primarily those marks that are sufficient to identify the source of goods or services but are not suitable for registration on the *Principal Register* (where, for example, "secondary meaning" is required).[160] Registration in the *Supplemental Register* does not preclude subsequent registration on the *Principal Register*.[161] However, they now show up on the publicly accessible Trademark Office database known as TSDR, available at tsdr.uspto.gov.

Registration on the *Principal Register* carries certain advantages over the *Supplemental Register*. For example, it creates nationwide constructive notice;[162] it constitutes *prima facie*[163] or conclusive[164] evidence of the ownership in interstate commerce of the rights in the mark; and it allows the mark to be registered with the United States Treasury Department in order to block importation of goods bearing an infringing mark.[165] Registration on the *Principal Register* (as well as registration under the two prior trademark acts) also acts as a complete bar against any suit for the infringement of a mark under the common law or a state statute seeking to prevent the dilution of a mark.[166] Presumably this also applies against a claim by an owner of a famous mark.

Supplemental registration does serve to provide notice of use to anyone who searches the records of the Patent and Trademark Office and affords a basis for federal jurisdiction.[167] It also allows the owner to use the registration notice ®;[168] and it can be used to block registration of a confusingly similar mark.[169]

---

[158] *See* 15 U.S.C. §1052 *et seq.* (2006).
[159] 15 U.S.C. §§1091-1096.
[160] 15 U.S.C. §1091 (2002).
[161] 15 U.S.C. §1095 (1988).
[162] 15 U.S.C. §1072 (1946).
[163] 15 U.S.C. §§1057(b), 1115(a) (2000).
[164] 15 U.S.C. §§1065, 1115(b) (2002).
[165] 15 U.S.C §1124.
[166] 15 U.S.C. §1125(c)(3) (2006).
[167] 15 U.S.C. §1121 (1998).
[168] 15 U.S.C. §1111 (1998).
[169] 15 U.S.C. §1052(d) (2006).

3.7.6. Notice

There is no requirement that trademark notice be given to the public. The law merely provides that if notice (i.e., ® or "Reg. U.S. Pat. & Tm. Off.") is not placed on the mark, no profits or damages are recoverable in an infringement action unless the infringer had actual notice of registration.[170] Use of the marks *TM* (i.e., "Trademark") or *SM* (i.e., "Service Mark") although commonly used on nonregistered marks, do not by themselves confer any protection under the Lanham Act, although such use may discourage some degree of intentional infringement.

3.8. DURATION

There is no fixed term for trademark protection, and a trademark will, in fact, remain the exclusive property of its owner forever if it is not abandoned.[171] *Abandonment* is a technical term referring to the discontinuance of use with an intent to abandon the mark,[172] or when any course of conduct (including acts of commission or omission) causes the mark to lose its significance as an identification of origin.[173] Under the Lanham Act, failure to use a mark for three consecutive years will be *prima facie* evidence of abandonment.[174] Abandonment is a heavily fact-based analysis and decisions are not entirely consistent. The concept of residual goodwill sometimes comes in conflict with the doctrine, holding that where the public perceives continuing goodwill, it may be possible to prevent a ruling of abandonment, especially when there is deception to the public.[175]

---

[170] 15 U.S.C. §1111 (1998).

[171] *See* Diamond, *Properly Used, Trademarks Are Forever*, 68 A.B.A.J. 1575 (1982).

[172] Saxlehner v. Eisner & Mendelson Co., 179 U.S. 19 (1900). *See also* 15 U.S.C. §1127 (2006).

[173] 15 U.S.C. §1127.

[174] 15 U.S.C. § 1127 (2006) Major League Baseball Properties, Inc. v. Sed Non Olet Denarius, Ltd., 817 F. Supp. 1103 (S.D.N.Y. 1993), *vacated*, 859 F.Supp 80 (S.D.N.Y. 1994).

[175] Cumulus Media, Inc. v. Clear Channel Communications, Inc., 304 F.3d 1167 (11th Cir. 2002)(single business card for radio station name THE BREEZE sufficient to avoid abandonment claim on motion for preliminary injunction where defendant specifically used name to try to divert audience); Grondin v. Rossington, 690 F.Supp. 200 (SDNY 1988)(post death recordings of Van Zant had right to require that recent

Abandonment is not "cured" by the resumption of use by a mark's former owner. Instead, the mark itself is treated as though it were a new mark with the mark's owner acquiring trademark rights in the same manner and to the same extent as if that mark were a newly created mark effective as on the date on which the mark owner resumes use of that mark.

3.9. TRANSFERS

3.9.1. In General

Transference of trademark rights may occur in two ways: either by assignment, where ownership of the mark is vested in the assignee, or by license, in which case the licensee is granted the exclusive or nonexclusive right to use the mark in commerce.

3.9.2. Assignments

In order to transfer title in the mark validly, a trademark assignment must be joined with a conveyance of the goodwill that the mark symbolizes.[176] Thus, if the mark has lost its good will through misuse or abandonment, the assignment confers no rights on the assignee.[177]

There is no legal requirement that trademark assignment of common law rights be in writing to be effective,[178] and those rights will be deemed automatically transferred in a sale of the entire business in which the mark is used.[179]

Assignment of a registered work must be in a duly executed writing.[180] Although recordation of the assignment is not required for a

---

recording not use original band name LYNYRD SKYNYRD despite death of key performer Van Zant 12 years earlier); Kingsman v. K-Tel International Ltd., 557 F. Supp. 178 (SDNY 1983) (Performing group that ceased performing in 1967 did not abandon rights in band name KINGSMAN)..

[176] *See* SMI Indus. Canada Ltd v. Caelter Indus., Inc., 586 F. Supp. 808 (N.D.N.Y. 1984). Although true in the United States, not that not all countries require a formal assignment of goodwill with a trademark to be effective or result in loss of trademark rights.

[177] *See* Haymaker Sports Inc. v. Turian, 581 F.2d 257 (C.C.P.A. Cir. 1978).

[178] *See* Speed Prods. Co. v. Tinnerman Prods., 179 F.2d 778 (2d Cir. 1949).

[179] *See* United States Ozone Co. v. United States Ozone Co., 62 F.2d 881 (7th Cir. 1932).

[180] 15 U.S.C. §1060 (2002).

valid transfer, recordation is required prior to the assignee's being allowed to deal with the Trademark and Patent Office with respect to that mark[181] and in order to protect against loss of the mark to a subsequent good faith purchaser of the mark for value and without notice.[182] Assignments are kept in a separate register in the Trademark and Patent Office.[183]

3.9.3. Licenses

A trademark may be licensed to one party on an exclusive basis or, as the basis of a franchise system (such as McDonald's or Carvel) to hundreds, if not thousands, of licensees.[184] In order to avoid abandonment of the mark, such licenses should be in writing and must include provisions to ensure the maintenance of a certain level of quality by the licensee as determined by the owner (under the theory that if the mark does not, in fact, identify the source, it at least functions as a guarantee of uniform quality).[185]

A license is not required for a middleman merchant, reseller, or distributor of finished goods because he or she is not the source identified by the mark.[186]

Because a mark trades on and embodies the good will associated with that name, a licensee is expected to do nothing that would harm it. To do so is grounds for terminating the license. For example, when the licensees of Michael Jordan, who were using his name for a restaurant in Chicago, publicly disparaged Jordan for not visiting the restaurant often enough, their license was terminated upon a showing that as a result of their comments a restaurant licensee in New York suffered a loss of income.[187]

---

[181] 37 C.F.R. § 3.73(b).
[182] 15 U.S.C. §1060 (2002).
[183] *Id.*
[184] *See* Susser v. Carvel Corp., 206 F. Supp. 636 (S.D.N.Y. 1962), *aff'd*, 332 F.2d 505 (2d Cir.), *cert. granted*, 379 U.S. 885 (1964), *cert. dismissed*, 381 U.S. 25 (1965).
[185] *See* FreecycleSunnyvale v. Freecycle Network, 626 F.3d 509 (9th Cir. 2010)(naked licensing resulting in abandonment of mark supported motion for summary judgment); E.I. Du Pont De Nemours & Co. v. Celanese Corp. of Am, 167 F.2d 484 (C.C.P.A. 1948).
[186] *See* Champion Spark Plug Co. v. Sanders, 331 U.S. 125 (1947).
[187] MJ & Partners Rest. Ltd. P'ship & 23 Food v. Zadikoff & Jordan v. 23 Food, Inc., 126 F. Supp. 2d 1130 (N.D. Ill. 1999).

3.10. RENEWALS AND TERMINATION

A trademark endures for as long as it is properly used,[188] but trademark *registration* is usually for a set period of years.

State registration terms vary from a term of five years (Oregon) to a perpetual registration (West Virginia), with the many set at ten years and all terms being renewable.[189] Some states have adopted the Model State Trademark Bill which provides a term of 5 years.[190] Federal registration exists for a period of ten years and may be renewed indefinitely after issuance, provided that the mark is still used in commerce.[191] Renewal may be made at any time within twelve months of its expiration by application showing current use (or explaining extraordinary circumstances for current nonuse with intent to resume use) accompanied by a proper fee.[192] In addition, federal registration requires an interim filing between the fifth and sixth year of issuance of the registration of the affidavit declaration of continuing use.[193] A six month grace period of the date to file the sixth year declaration and a six month grace period of the date to file the renewal is possible by paying a slightly greater filing fee.

Failure to renew or file the six-year affidavit of use can result in the termination of the registration.[194] (The termination of registration does not terminate the protection of the mark itself but merely the protections of registration.)[195] The Lanham Act also provides the ability to file a statement that the mark has been in continuous use for a period of 5 years following registration, in which event the registration becomes incontestable for certain purposes.[196]

---

[188] *See supra* §3.8.
[189] *See* Gilson, *supra* note 3, §10.12.
[190] *See* e.g. California Business and Professions Code §§14200 et seq. This Act allows registration based only on actual use, rather than intent to use as permitted under the Federal Act. California requires that information be provided to the California Secretary of State who administers the Act, relating to any prior refusal of a federal registration, and requires the signer of the application to state under penalty of perjury and a $10,000 civil penalty that the statements in the trademark application are true.
[191] 15 U.S.C. §1059 (2002).
[192] *Id.*
[193] *Id.* §1058.
[194] *Id.* §§1058-1059.
[195] *See supra* §3.7.
[196] Lanham Act §15.

3.11. UNFAIR COMPETITION

3.11.1. Common Law and State Statutory Law

Although competition in the market place has always been favored at common law, it is not without restriction.[197] Actions for unfair competition have developed under common law as a broad-based tort encompassing any type of economic/competitive practice that society has deemed unfair.[198] Among those of particular interest in the entertainment practice would be disparagement of a person's goods and business methods[199] and the related statutory development of false advertising[200] and "palming off" (the making of some misrepresentation that would induce the public to believe the goods or services are those of another party).[201] It should be noted that "palming off" has served as the primary basis for a large portion of the law of trademarks.[202]

Much of the common law of unfair competition has been codified in state law, including its broad standards in which acts are determined to be fair or unfair according to principles of equity.[203]

Unfair competition actions have been used to protect titles,[204] and trademarks (even where they are not registered either federally or state),[205] as well as commercial reputations.[206]

3.11.1.1. Vocal Performance Imitations in Commercials

Recent decisions have extended actions for unfair competition to protect against the intentional imitation of the vocal performance style

---

[197] *See* Martell v. White, 69 N.E. 1085 (1904).

[198] *See* W. PROSSER, HANDBOOK OF THE LAW OF TORTS §130 (4th ed. 1971).

[199] *See* Paramount Pictures v. Leader Press, 106 F.2d 229 (10th Cir. 1939).

[200] *See* N.Y. GEN. BUS. LAW §350.

[201] *See* Dixi-Cola Labs. v. Coca Cola Co., 117 F.2d 352 (4th Cir.), *cert.denied*, 314 U.S. 629 (1941).

[202] *See supra* §3.1.2.

[203] *See* Santa's Workshop v. Sterling, 153 N.Y.S.2d 839 (N.Y. App. Div. 1956), *aff'd*, 163 N.Y.S.2d 986 (N.Y. 1957) (interpreting N.Y. Gen. Bus. Law § 368d). *See also* Orion Pictures Co. v. Dell Publ'g. Co., 471 F. Supp. 392 (S.D.N.Y. 1979).

[204] *See* Nat'l Lampoon v. Am. Broad. Cos., 376 F. Supp. 733 (S.D.N.Y. 1974), *aff'd*, 497 F.2d 1343 (2d Cir.1974). *See also* Metro-Goldwyn-Mayer v. Lee, 27 Cal Rptr. 833 (Cal. App. 2 Dist. 1963).

[205] *See* Dawn Donut Co. v. Hart's Food Stores, Inc., 267 F.2d 358 (2d Cir. 1959).

[206] *See* Dallas Cowboys Cheerleaders Inc. v. Pussycat Cinema, Ltd. 467 F. Supp. 366 (S.O.N.Y.), *aff'd*, 604 F.2d 200 (1979).

of well-known musical performers in connection with commercial endorsements.[207] This is a controversial application of the law[208] and might be thought of as an issue more appropriately decided under the rubric of publicity/privacy,[209] although several courts have specifically denied application of those doctrines[210] or have left the decision in an ambiguous middle ground between a statutory right of publicity and unfair competition that may or may not exist as a common law right of publicity.[211]

The tort itself in these decisions is now fairly specific. It protects against the deliberate misappropriation for commercial purposes of (1) a voice that is (2) distinctive and (3) widely known.[212] In considering the nature of the "voice," the imitation should be so good that people who are familiar with the plaintiffs voice would, on hearing the commercial, "believe [ ] plaintiff performed it" (emphasis in original).[213] To be distinctive, the voice need only be identifiable, while the criteria of "widely known" requires not that the performer be a superstar, but only that the person be known to a large number of people throughout a relatively large geographic area.[214]

---

[207] Midler v. Ford Motor Co., 849 F.2d 460 (9th Cir. 1988), *appeal after remand sub non*, Midler v. Young & Rubican Inc. 944 F.2d 909, No. 90-55027,90-55028,1991 WL 185170, 22 U.S. P. Q. 2d 1478 1991), *cert. denied*, 503 U.S. 951 (1992) Bette Midler v. Ford Motor Co. and Young & Rubicam No. 86-2683 (C.D. Cal. 1987) *rev'd* 849 F.2d 460 (9th Cir. 1988), *cert. denied*, 112 S. Ct. 1513 (1992); Waits v. Frito-Lay, Inc., 978 F.2d 1093 (9th Cir. 1992) (actually decided on false endorsement grounds), *cert. denied*, 506 U.S. 1080 (1993).

[208] Lahr v. Adell Chem. Co., 300 F.2d 256 (1st Cir. 1962) (reinstating on appeal Burt Lahr's claim for the imitation of his vocal style in an animated commercial as stating a valid cause of action); *contra* Sinatra v. Goodyear Tire & Rubber Co., 435 F.2d 711 (9th Cir. 1970), *cert. denied*, 402 U.S. 906 (1971).

[209] *See supra* §3.2.

[210] Lahr v. Adell Chem. Co., 300 F.2d 256 (1st Cir. 1962); Sinatra v. Goodyear Tire & Rubber Co., 435 F.2d 711 (9th Cir. 1970); Booth v. Colgate-Palmolive Co., 362 F. Supp. 343 (S.D.N.Y. 1973).

[211] Midler v. Ford Motor Co., 849 F.2d 460 (9th Cir. 1988), *cert. denied was after appeal after remand. See B 2-24 for full cite*, 112 S. Ct. 1513 (1992); Waits v. Frito-Lay, Inc., 978 F.2d 1395 (9th Cir. 1992).

[212] Midler v. Ford Motor Co., 849 F.2d 460 (9th Cir. 1988), *cert. denied*, 112 S. Ct. 1513 (1992); Waits v. Frito-Lay, Inc., 978 F.2d 1395 (9th Cir. 1992).

[213] Waits v. Frito-Lay, Inc., 978 F.2d 1395 (9th Cir. 1992).

[214] Midler v. Ford Motor Co., 849 F.2d 460 (9th Cir. 1988), *cert. denied*, 112 S. Ct. 1513 (1992); Waits v. Frito-Lay, Inc., 978 F.2d 1395 (9th Cir. 1992).

Remedies available for this tort include compensatory damages for: (1) fair market value of services; (2) injury to peace and happiness; (3) goodwill, professional standing, and future publicity value.[215]

3.11.2. Section 43(a)

Section 43(a) of the Lanham Act[216] has incorporated a substantial amount of unfair-competition protection within the ambit of federal trademark law.[217] Its protections extend not only to registered trademarks[218] but to titles,[219] screen credit to a limited extent,[220] the names of musical groups,[221] and the use of look-alikes[222] and sound-alikes[223] in advertising. Invocation of §43(a) requires proof of three elements: (1) involvement of goods or services, (2) effect on interstate commerce, and (3) false designation of origin or false description of goods or services,[224] or a false association of the sponsoring person with another person.[225]

The Trademark Law Revision Act of 1988[226] represents a legislative endorsement and expansion of the rights of well-known personalities and others to prevent the commercial use of their names and reputations in the commercial arena. Section 43(a) was amended to specifically prohibit representations that likely will cause confusion, mistake, or deceive consumers as to "the affiliation, connection, or association of [the representing] person with another person [the celebrity or other person]"[227] or that likely will confuse, cause

---

[215] Waits v. Frito-Lay, Inc., 978 F.2d 1395 (9th Cir. 1992).

[216] 15 U.S.C. §1125(a) (2006).

[217] *See* Gilson, *supra* note 3, §7.01-7.02.

[218] *Id.*

[219] *See* Brandon v. Regents of the Univ. of Cal., 441 F. Supp. 1086 (D. Mass. 1977).

[220] *See* Perin Film Enter. v. Two Prods., 400 P.T.C.J. A-13 (Oct. 19) (S.D.N.Y. 1978) (no written decision); *but see* Dastar Corp. v. Twentieth Century Fox Film Corp., 539 U.S. 23, 123 S. Ct. 2041, 156 L.Ed. 2d 18 (2003)(Section 43(a) held not to prevent unaccredited copying of a work in the public domain).

[221] *See* Noone v. Banner Talent Assocs., Inc. 398 F. Supp. 260 (S.D.N.Y. 1975).

[222] *See* Allen v. Nat'l Video, 610 F. Supp. 612 (S.D.N.Y. 1985); Alien v. Men's World Outlet Inc., 678 F. Supp. 360 (S.D.N.Y. 1988).

[223] *See* Motown Record Corp. v. George A. Hormel & Co., 657 F. Supp. 1236 (C.D. Cal. 1987).

[224] *Id.*

[225] 15 U.S.C. §1125(a) as amended by P.L. 100-667 (1988) (2006).

[226] P.L. 100-667.

[227] 15 U.S.C. §43(a)(1) (1914).

mistakes, or deceive consumers "as to the origin, sponsorship or approval of his or her goods, services, or commercial activities by another person."[228] A §43(a) action may thus be used as an alternate method of protecting the so-called rights of publicity and privacy.[229]

In considering the issue of confusion or deception in relation to artistic credit, the form of the credit given can be decisive. Possessory credit, that is, credit asserting that an artistic work is the creation of an identified individual (e.g., Alfred Hitchcock's *Psycho*) requires that the party being given credit for the work must have had some minimal involvement in its creation. Use of a person's name without such involvement may be enjoined.[230] In contrast, a credit indicating that a work is "based upon" another work involves both a quantitative (i.e., "how much?") and qualitative analysis of the two works in question before a determination of fair or unfair competition can be made.[231] However, the failure to credit a work may no longer be attacked by use of the Lanham Act.[232]

While §43(a) will protect the "trade dress" of a product (i.e. its unique packaging that associates that product with its manufacturer), it will not protect the product's design unless that design has acquired "secondary meaning" in the eyes of consumers. For example, even with proof of intentional copying of a line of clothing, the courts will not protect clothing designs without proof that consumer's may have been confused as to the origin of that clothing as a product of the original designers.[233]

Consumers have no standing to sue under Section 43(a).[234] These issues therefore arise only where the person affected by the credit is unhappy with that credit to the extent that remedy may still be available in view of *DaStar*.

---

[228] *Id.*
[229] *See infra* Chapter 4.
[230] King v. Innovation Books, 976 F.2d 824 (2d Cir. 1992);
[231] *Id.*
[232] *See* Dastar Corp. v. Twentieth Century Fox Film Corp., *supra*.
[233] Wal-Mart Stores, Inc. v. Samara Bros., Inc., 529 U.S. 205 (2000).
[234] Serbin v. Ziebart Int'l Corp., 24 U.S.P.Q.2d 1957, No. Civ. A. 92-1762, 1992 WL 415248 (W.D. Pa. 1992), *aff'd.*, 11 F.3d 1163 (3d Cir. 1993).

3.12. INFRINGEMENT

3.12.1. In General

An infringement of a federally registered trademark may give rise to causes of action under a multiplicity of legal grounds, including §32(a) (15 U.S.C. §1114(i)) for federal trademark infringement; §43(a) (15 U.S.C. §1125(a)) for federal unfair competition; §43(c) (15 U.S.C. §1125(a)) for federal trademark dilution for famous marks; §44 (15 U.S.C. §1126) for federal unfair competition in some jurisdictions; state common law of unfair competition; or a state statute.[235] Nonregistered marks and elements of identification not qualifying as marks (such as titles or publicity) may also be protected on several different bases, including previously noted federal unfair-competition statutes (§§43(a) and 44), state common law of unfair competition, and state statutes.[236] Both registered marks and unregistered (or unregisterable) marks start with the same rationale for protection (i.e., to protect the public from a "likelihood of confusion" as to their source or quality).[237]

3.12.2. Elements of an Action

While each jurisdiction applies a separate test for likelihood of confusion, these tests generally adhere to the following six factors: (1) the strength of the mark (including "secondary meaning"), (2) similarity, (3) proximity of the competing products (e.g., "fashion goods" and "cosmetics"), (4) evidence of actual confusion as to the source, (5) the sophistication of the audience, and (6) the defendant's good or bad faith.[238] Intentional copying of a mark may be considered as presumptive evidence that the mark has acquired secondary meaning and that there is a likelihood of consumer confusion.[239] The fact that an application for trademark registration has been rejected in a cancellation proceeding based upon likelihood of public confusion is

---

[235] *See* GILSON, *supra* note 3, §7.01(4).
[236] *See supra* §3.10.
[237] *See supra* §3.1.
[238] *See* Alien v. Nat'l Video, Inc., 610 F. Supp. 612 (S.D.N.Y. 1985); Alien v. Men's World Outlet, Inc. 679 F. Supp. 360 (S.D.N.Y. 1988).
[239] *See* Osem Food Indus. Ltd. v. Sherwood Foods, Inc., 917 F.2d 161 (4th Cir. 1990).

not sufficient evidence for an infringement action which requires a greater specificity of evidence regarding actual use.[240]

If a registered mark is infringed, an action is much simpler. Under §33(a) (15 U.S.C. §1115(a)) the basic elements are that (1) the plaintiff owns a valid registered mark and (2) the defendant has used the mark in commerce on goods or services specified in the registration.[241] The action is subject to equitable defenses (such as laches) and defects that might have been asserted if the mark had not been registered,[242] including such defenses as abandonment,[243] use by permission,[244] and obtaining registration of the mark by fraud.[245] The test for dilution of famous marks is similar in that a plaintiff must show a likelihood of dilution by blurring or tarnishment of the plaintiff's famous mark.[246]

3.12.3. Defenses

As previously noted, a defendant may assert a number of defenses falling under the rubric of fair use.[247] In addition, the defendant may offer equitable defenses such as laches or estoppel.[248] Procedural defenses such as collateral estoppel or issue preclusion could be available.[249] Failure to seek protection against a use after knowledge or constructive knowledge of an infringing use while allowing the

---

[240] Jim Beam Brands Co. v. Beamish & Crawford Ltd., 937 F.2d 729 (2d Cir. 1991). *cert. denied*, 502 U.S. 1094 (1992).
[241] 15 U.S.C. §1115(a) (2002).
[242] *Id.*
[243] *See supra* §3.8. *See also* 15 U.S.C. §1115(b) (2002).
[244] 15 U.S.C. §1115(b) (2002).
[245] *Id.*
[246] 15 U.S.C. §1125(c) (2006).
[247] *See supra*, §3.4.
[248] *See* Chattanoga Mfg., Inc. v. Nike, Inc., 301 F.3d 789 (7th Cir. 2002).
[249] A final decision in a Trademark Trial and Appeal Board proceeding may result in collateral estoppel in a federal court litigation. B&B Hardware, Inc. v. Hargis Industries, 135 S. Ct. 1293 (2015) held that in the right circumstances, a TTAB decision could be considered collateral estoppel. Cases since then have used this case as a basis of granting the defense of collateral estoppel in determinations of likelihood of confusion in infringement litigation. TTAB proceedings tend to involve somewhat different issues and the application to federal court litigation proceedings is not always appropriate. The significance is that one should be careful about ignoring what appears to be a less important proceeding as it could prove determinative in a more important case.

defendant to proceed to his or her prejudice will preclude recovery or enforcement.

3.13. REMEDIES

Remedies under the trademark law are substantially similar to those afforded under the copyright law, including injunctive relief;[250] recovery of (1) the defendant's profits,[251] (2) the plaintiff's damage, and (3) the costs of the action;[252] attorney's fees;[253] and the destruction of infringing goods and their means of manufacture.[254] Importation of goods bearing marks that infringe federally registered marks may also be prohibited.[255]

---

[250] *Id.* at §1116 (2002).

[251] Profits are not generally available when infringement is not willful. A 1999 amendment to the Lanham Act added the word "willful" to monetary claims for dilution relief but not with respect to trademark infringement. The Federal Circuit rejected plaintiff's claim for profits in Romag Fasteners, Inc. v. Fossil, Inc., 817 F.3d 782 (Fed. Cir. 2016) noting that there is a split among the circuits on this issue and that an amendment in 1999 to the Lanham Act did not mean that Congress intended to make any change to a willful requirement for violations of Section 43(a). *See* George Basch Co. v. Blue Coral, Inc., 968 F.2d 1532 (2d Cir. 1992); Int'l Star Class Yacht Racing Ass'n v. Tommy Hilfiger, U.S.A., Inc., 80 F.3d 749 (2d Cir. 1996); Lindy Pen Co. v. Bic Pen Corp., 982 .2d 1400 (9th Cir. 1993)(accounting of profits not justified where trademark was weak and Bic's infringement was unintentional).

[252] *Id.* at §1117 (2004).

[253] Attorney fees were rarely granted in trademark infringement disputes though there is statutory authority for granting attorney's fees for exceptional cases. "The court in exceptional cases may award reasonable attorney fees to the prevailing party." 15 § U.S.C. 1117 (Lanham Act § 35). Courts have more recently have become more liberal in attorney fee awards in view of Octane Fitness, LLC v. Icon Health & Fitness, Inc., 134 S. Ct. 1749 (2014). Although patent infringement case Octane has been followed in trademark infringement litigation matters. This means that both prevailing plaintiffs and defendants could be awarded attorney fees depending on a variety of factors. This was followed in Baker v. DeShong, 821 F.3d 620 (5th Cir. 2016) in which an exceptional case was considered to be one where (1) in considering both governing law and the facts of the case, the case stands out from others with respect to the substantive strength of a party's litigating position; or (2) the unsuccessful party has litigated the case in an "unreasonable manner."

[254] *Id.* at §1118 (1999).

[255] *Id.* at §1124 (1999). Note that importation of goods manufactured under license but restricted to foreign territories (i.e., grey market goods) may not be prosecuted as an infringement except where the fundamental character of the use becomes misleading. *See* Original Appalachian Artworks, Inc. v. Granada Elec., Inc., 229 U.S.P.Q. 54 (S.D.N.Y. 1986), *aff'd*; 816 F.2d 68 (2nd Cir. 1987), *cert. denied*, 484 U.S. 847 (1987).

The First Circuit has identified four criteria for determining monetary damages under the Lanham Act.[256] First, absent extenuating circumstances, a plaintiff seeking damages must prove actual harm, such as a diversion of sales. Second, where a plaintiff is seeking an accounting of the defendant's profits, the plaintiff must demonstrate that the infringing product or service directly competes with that of the plaintiff such that the profits would have gone to the plaintiff if there had been no infringement. (In essence, the court appears to be requiring proof of actual harm and only shifting the measurement from the plaintiff having a decrease in existing business to the defendant where the defendant's profits represent an increase in the total market.) Third, the rule of direct competition is loosened where the defendant acted fraudulently or palmed off inferior goods. In such cases, actual harm is presumed. Finally, in cases of gross inequitable conduct, damages may be assessed on an unjust enrichment or deterrence theory.

Counterfeiting claims under the Lanham Act are potentially valuable in the entertainment industry in the context of touring merchandising and as a companion to claims of copyright piracy. A "counterfeit" is a spurious mark which is identical with, or substantially indistinguishable from, a registered mark.[257] The mark must also be federally registered.[258]

Section 1117(b) of the Lanham Act mandates treble damages and attorney's fees for intentional infringement of marks and discretionary prejudgment interest.

As an alternative to actual damages and profits, the Lanham Act includes an election of substantial statutory damages where a finding of counterfeiting is had. There are two levels of civil counterfeiting liability. The statute provides for up to $200,000 statutory damages for each type of goods infringed. If counterfeiting is willful, the amount of statutory damages rises to up to $2,000,000 for each type of goods or services sold, offered for sale or distributed. The main prerequirement on the part of the plaintiff is that the mark be federally registered. An example of a counterfeiting act that might not be willful could be a shopkeeper that was not aware of the counterfeit nature of the goods

---

[256] Aktiebolaget Electrolux v. Armatron Int'l, Inc., 999 F.2d 1, 27 U.S.P.Q.2d 1460 (1st Cir. 1993).
[257] 15 U.S.C. 1127(b), (c).
[258] 15 U.S.C. 1116(d)(1)(B)(i).

being sold in his or her store, while the manufacturing of the product might be more likely to be liable for the full amount of statutory damages.

Action for trademark infringement and §43(a) unfair competition are subject to a limiting defense of "innocent infringement."[259] Innocence, in this sense, requires the absence of malicious intent. An innocent infringer is one who acts in an objectively reasonable manner in the use of the mark,[260] in which case the plaintiff's remedies will be limited to injunctive relief.

With respect to famous marks, actions under the trademark act are limited to injunctive relief "unless the person against whom the injunction is sought willfully intended to trade on the owner's reputation or to cause dilution of the famous mark. If such willful intent is proven, the owner of the famous mark shall also be entitled to the remedies [accorded other trademark owners] at the discretion of the court and the principles of equity."[261]

---

[259] 15 U.S.C. §1114(2).
[260] Dial One of the Mid-South, Inc. v. BellSouth Telecomm., Inc., 269 F.3d 523 (5th Cir. 2001).
[261] 15 U.S.C. §1127(c)(2) (2006).

— CHAPTER 4 —

PUBLICITY AND PRIVACY*

4.1. In General
4.2. Subject Matter
4.3. Exclusive Rights
4.4. Fair Use – Limitations to Publicity and Privacy Rights
4.5. Creation and Commencement
4.6. Ownership
4.7. Formalities
4.8. Duration
4.9. Transfer
4.10. Infringement
4.11. Remedies

4.1. IN GENERAL

The rights of publicity and privacy are closely related, sharing a common genesis[1] and concurrent development.[2] This commonality, however, unfortunately has led to a great deal of confusion as to the nature of these rights,[3] which are, in fact, quite different.

The right of privacy is most accurately described as a personal defensive right, like slander and defamation, protecting an individual's privacy.[4] This right has been described as "the right to be left alone."[5]

The right of publicity, on the other hand, is most accurately described as an exploitative right, resembling copyright and trademark, wherein an individual maintains the right to exploit the economic value

---

* The authors wish to thank Andrews Kurth Kenyon LLP associate Susanna P. Lichter for her valuable assistance in the preparation of this chapter.

[1] *See* Samuel D. Warren and Louis D. Brandeis, *The Right of Privacy*, 4 HARV. L. REV. 193 (1890).

[2] *See* Pavesich v. New England Life Ins. Co., 50 S.E. 2d (Ga. 1905); Munden v. Harris, 153 Mo. App. 652 (1911).

[3] *See* Jerome Gilson, TRADEMARK PROTECTION AND PRACTICE §2.15(a) (1985), discussing the conflict as to whether or not the rights of Publicity and Privacy are personal rights or property rights.

[4] *See* William Prosser and Robert E. Keeton, PROSSER AND KEETON, LAW OF TORTS §117 (5th ed. 1988) (hereinafter "Prosser").

[5] Thomas M. Cooley, TORTS A Treatise on the Law of Torts or the Wrongs which Arise Independent of Contract, 29 (2d ed. 1888).

of his or her personality.[6] (The use of the term personality is intended to embrace that person's name, likeness or image, signature, performance, and all other aspects that are exploitable under the right of publicity.)[7]

4.1.1. The Right of Privacy

Perhaps the most influential law review article ever written on the subject of privacy appeared in 1890 in the Harvard Law Review.[8] Written by Samuel D. Warren and Louis D. Brandeis, The Right of Privacy argued that the growing excesses of the press demanded the recognition of the right of a private individual to be protected against unjustified infliction of mental pain and distress by the press. Although, in retrospect, a number of cases[9] and commentaries[10] presaged the development of this right, prior to 1890 no English or American court had ever granted relief expressly based on the invasion of such a right.[11]

The first state to confront the possible existence of the privacy right directly was New York in the case of *Robertson v. Rochester Folding-Box Co.*[12] The court in *Robertson* rejected the existence of such a right, holding that, if such a right were to exist, its proper forum for creation was the legislature and not the courts. In the next legislative session, the New York legislature enacted a statute[13] making it both a misdemeanor and a tort to use the name, portrait, or picture of any person for the purpose of advertising or trade without his or her prior written consent.

Three years after the New York courts rejected the existence of a common law right of privacy, the courts of Georgia, in the case of

---

[6] *See* Zachini v. Scripps-Howard Broadcasting Co., 433 U.S. 562 (1977); *see also* Haelan Labs. v. Topps Chewing Gum, 202 F.2d 866 (2d Cir.), *cert. denied*, 346 U.S. 816 (1953).

[7] *See Publicity and Privacy, infra* §§4.3.1-4.3.5.

[8] Warren and Brandeis, *supra* note 1, at 193.

[9] *See* DeMay v. Roberts, 9 N.W. 146 (Mich. 1881) (intrusion on childbirth); Lord Byron v. Johnston, 2 Mer. 29 (1816) (attribution of authorship of a spurious poem).

[10] *See* Cooley, TORTS 29 (2d ed. 1888).

[11] *See* Prosser, *supra* note 4, §117.

[12] Roberson v. Rochester Folding Box Co., 64 N.E. 442 (1902).

[13] 1903 N.Y. Laws ch. 132 §§1-2, as amended in 1921 N.Y. CIV. RIGHTS LAW §§50-51.

Pavesich v. New England Life Ins. Co.,[14] accepted the Warren-Brandeis arguments and recognized a right of privacy. This became the leading right-of-privacy case, and since that time all jurisdictions have recognized a right of privacy in one form or another.[15] At that time (1971) Professor Prosser wrote that only four states (Nebraska, Rhode Island, Texas and Wisconsin) had specifically rejected the existence of this right. All of those states have since recognized the right either by statute (Nebraska,[16] Rhode Island[17] and Wisconsin[18]) or court decision (Texas[19]). Minnesota once rejected a common law right of privacy,[20] but has since recognized one.[21]

One significant result of the different ways in which this right was created (i.e., by statute in New York and at common law in Georgia) has been with the restriction of the right's development under a statutory system such as New York's,[22] as opposed to the more fluid growth and expansion of the right at common law.[23]

In analyzing hundreds of cases described on privacy grounds, Dean William Prosser[24] found that there is not one tort but a complex of four that deal with four different interests:

1. *Appropriation:* appropriation of the plaintiff's name or likeness for the defendant's benefit;[25]
2. *Intrusion:* intrusion on the plaintiff's physical solitude or seclusion;
3. *Public disclosure of private facts*: Publicizing of private information, even though it may be true, in a highly

---

[14] Pavesich v. New England Life Ins. Co., 50 S.E. 2d (Ga. 1905).
[15] *See* Prosser, *supra* note 4, §117.
[16] NEB. REV. STAT. §§20-201-20-2-11 (2008).
[17] R.I. GEN. LAWS. §§9-1-28-9-1-28.1 (2008).
[18] WIS. STAT. §895.50 (Renumbered 995.50 by 2005 Act 155 § 51) (2008).
[19] Billings v. Atkinson, 489 S.W.2d 858 (Tex. 1973).
[20] Hendry v. Conner, 226 N.W. 2d 921 (Minn.1975).
[21] Lake v. Wal-Mart Stores, Inc., 582 N.W.2d 231 (Minn. 1998).
[22] *See* Delan by Delan v. CBS, Inc., 458 N.Y.S.2d 608 (N.Y. App. Div. 1983).
[23] *Id.* Nonetheless, it should be noted that, although this has restricted the recognition of the right of publicity in New York (see *infra* §4.1.2), the statutory right of privacy in New York is in substantial conformity with the common law right of privacy in other states. Prosser, *supra* note 4, §117.
[24] *Id.* §117.
[25] This is the primary focus of the New York statute, N.Y. Civil Rights Law §§50-51, and is the right most closely related to the right of publicity (*see infra* §4.1.2).

objectionable manner (such as revealing the past of a former prostitute);[26] and
4. *False light*: publicity that places the plaintiff in a false light in the public view (such as using a person's picture in connection with an article in which no reasonable connection exists, with the implication that such a connection exists).[27]

4.1.2. The Right of Publicity

The right of publicity has developed under the twin rubrics of the appropriation tort of privacy (the earliest of the privacy torts to be recognized)[28] (hereinafter referred to as privacy-appropriation) and the tort of unfair competition[29] (with the influence of the latter causing some confusion as to the protectability of the right, particularly in the area of its descendibility).[30] In spite of its subsequent recognition as a right that is separate from the right of privacy-appropriation,[31] it continues to be protected in some areas as a cause of action under the right of privacy-appropriation[32] and/or unfair competition[33]

Although the right of privacy-appropriation is founded on the concept of the right of a private individual to be "left alone"[34] early decisions in this area recognized that "if there is a value in [a name] sufficient to excite the cupidity of another, why is it not the property of him *who gives it value and from whom the value springs?*[35] (emphasis added). It is this concept of proprietary value as opposed to protection from infliction of harm (as identified by Warren and Brandeis)[36] that distinguishes the right of publicity from the right of privacy-

---

[26] Melvin v. Reid, 297 P. 91 (Cal. App. 4 Dist. 1931).

[27] *See* Peay v. Curtis Publ'g. Co., 78 F. Supp. 305 (D.D.C. 1948).

[28] *See* Pavesich v. New England Life Ins. Co., 50 S.E. 68 (Ga. 1905).

[29] *See* Madison Square Garden Corp. v. Universal Pictures, 7 N.Y.S.2d 845 (N.Y.App.Div. 1938) See also *U.S. Trademark and Unfair Competition Law,* supra §3.10.

[30] *See infra* §4.8.

[31] *See* Haelen Labs. v. Topps Chewing Gum, 202 F.2d 866 (2d Cir.), *cert. denied*, 346 U.S. 816 (1953).

[32] *See* N.Y. CIV. RIGHTS LAW §§50-51.

[33] *See* Allen v. Nat'l Video, Inc., 610 F. Supp. 612 (S.D.N.Y. 1985) (an action brought under §43(a) of the Lanham Act for federal unfair competition). *See supra* §3.11.2.

[34] *See supra* §4.1.1.

[35] Munden v. Harris, 153 Mo. App. 652, 659 (1911).

[36] *See supra* §4.1.1.

appropriation. The basic function of privacy is to protect the anonymity of private figures,[37] whereas the right of publicity, as ultimately recognized, is designed to protect the rights of celebrities, who, by their very nature, are far from anonymous.[38]

Thirty-three states currently recognize some form of a right of publicity either at common law or by statute (which may or may not properly distinguish between "privacy" or "publicity"). Those states are:

State	Common Law	Statute
Arizona	X[39]	—
Alabama	X[40]	—
California	X[41]	CA. CIV. CODE §§4344 & 990 (amending and replacing §990 effective 1999)
Connecticut	X[42]	—
District of Columbia	X[43]	—
Florida	X[44]	FLA. STAT. TIT. 31 TRAD. COM. & INV. §540.08
Georgia	X[45]	—
Hawaii	X[46]	—

---

[37] *See* Pavesich v. New England Life Ins. Co., 50 S.E. 2d (Ga. 1905).
[38] *See* Haelen Labs. v. Topps Chewing Gum, 202 F.2d 866 (2d Cir.), *cert. denied*, 346 U.S. 816 (1953).
[39] Pooley v. Nat'l Hole-in-One Ass'n, 89 F. Supp. 2d 1108 (D. Ariz. 2000).
[40] Allison v. Vintage Sports Plaques, 136 F3d 1443 (11th Cir. 1998).
[41] Motschenbacher v. R. J. Reynolds Tobacco Co., 498 F.2d 821 (9th Cir. 1974).
[42] Bi-Rite Enters, Inc. v. Bruce Miner Co., 757 F.2d 440 (1st Cir. 1985).
[43] Tripp v. United States, 257 F. Supp. 2d 37, 43 (D. D.C. 2003); Lane v. Random House, Inc., 985 F. Supp. 141 (D. D.C. 1995).
[44] Zim v. W. Publ'g Co., 573 F.2d 1318 (5th Cir. 1978).
[45] Martin Luther King Jr., Cent For Social Change, Inc. v. Am. Heritage Prods., Inc.296 S.E. 697 (1982).
[46] Fergerstrom v. Hawaiian Ocean View Estates, Inc., 441 P.2d 141 (Haw. 1968) (labeled as "privacy").

Illinois	X[47]	765 ILCS 1075/1-60
Indiana	—	IN Code §42-13-1-8
Kentucky	X[48]	KY. REV. STAT. ANN. §491.170
Louisiana	—	La. Rev. Stat. Ann. 14:102.21
Massachusetts	—	MASS. GEN. L. Ch. 214 §§4A, 1B
Michigan	X[49]	—
Minnesota	X[50]	—
Missouri	X[51]	—
Nebraska	—	NEB. REV. STAT. §§20-201 to 20-211
Nevada	—	NEV. REV. STAT. CH. 598
New Hampshire	X[52]	—
New Jersey		
	X[53]	—
New York	—	N.Y. CIV. RIGHTS LAW §§50-51
Ohio	X[54]	OH REV CODE §2741.01-.09
Oklahoma	—	OKLA. STAT. TIT. 21 §§839.1-.3, 1448,1449
Oregon	X[55]	

[47] Douglass v. Hustler Mag., Inc., 769 F.2d 1128 (7th Cir. 1985), cert. denied, 475 U.S. 194 (1986).
[48] Cheatham v. Paisano Publication. Inc., 891 F. Supp. 381 (W.D.Ky. 1995).
[49] Carson v. Here's Johnny Portable Toilets, Inc., 698 F.2d 831 (6th Cir. 1983).
[50] Uhlaender v. Henrickson, 316 F.Supp. 1277 (D. Minn. 1970).
[51] Munden v. Harris, 153 Mo. App. 652 (1911); Cepeda v. Swift & Co., 415 F.2d 1205 (8th Cir. 1969).
[52] Doe v. Friendfinder Network, Inc., 540 F.Supp 2d 288 (D.N.H. 2008).
[53] Palmer v. Schonhorn Enters, Inc., 232 A.2d 458 (N.J. Super. Ct. 1967); Estate of Elvis Presley v. Russen, 513 F. Supp. 1339 (D. N.J. 1981).
[54] Zacchini v. Scripps-Howard Broad. Co., 433 U.S. 562 (1977). *But see* Reeves v. United Artists Corp., 765 F.2d 79 (6th Cir. 1985).
[55] Anderson v. Fisher Broadcasting Co., 712 P.2d 803 (Ore. 1986); Hinish v. Meier & Frank Co., 113 P.2d 438 (Ore. 1941); Rogers v. Grimaldi, 875 F.2d 994 (2d Cir. 1989).

Pennsylvania	X[56]	42 Pa.C.S.A. §8316
Rhode Island	—	R.I. GEN. LAWS. §§9-1-28-9-1-28.1
South Carolina	X[57]	
Tennessee	—	TENN. CODE ANN. §§47-25-1101-1108
Texas	X[58]	4 TEX.STAT.CH.26
Utah	X[59]	UTAH CODE ANN. §§45-3-1-6
Virginia	—	VA. CODE. ANN. §§8.01-40 & 18.2-216.1
Washington	—	WA ST 63.60.010
Wisconsin	X[60]	WIS. STAT. §895.50

4.1.3. Publicity versus Privacy

It is analytically appropriate to suggest that actions brought by celebrities should always be brought under the rubric of the right of publicity and that actions for privacy-appropriation be brought only by private nonpublic figures. However, due to the confusion of the courts and statutes in various jurisdictions (in some that do not distinguish among the rights[61] and in others that confuse the distinction between the two)[62] this is not practical or advisable. Moreover, although the rights are analytically distinguishable (and this chapter focuses primarily on what is correctly identified as the right of publicity), individual jurisdictions must be consulted as to which label is to be applied.

---

[56] Hogan v. A.S. Barnes & Co., 114 U.S.P.Q. 314, No. 8645, 1957 WL 7316 (Pa. Commw. Ct. June 19, 1957).
[57] Gignilliat v. Gignilliat, Savitz & Bettis L.P., 684 S.E.2d 756 (S.C. 2009)
[58] Kimbrough v. Coca-Cola/USA, 521 S.W.2d 719 (Tex. Civ. App. 1975) (labeling it "privacy"); Nat'l Bank of Commerce v. Shaklee Corp., 503 F. Supp. 533 (W.D. Tex. 1980).
[59] Nature's Way Prods., Inc. v. Nature-Pharma Inc., 736 F. Supp. 245 (D. Utah 1990).
[60] Hirsh v. S.C. Johnson & Sons, Inc., 280 N.W. 2d 129 (Wis. 1979).
[61] *See* Delan by Delan v. CBS, 91 A.D.2d 255 (1983).
[62] *See* In Nat'l Bank of Commerce v. Shaklee Corp., 503 F. Supp. 533 (W.D. Tex. 1980) (in which the court used "the right of privacy" and "misappropriation" interchangeably, although the context suggested that "misappropriation" was actually the right of publicity).

4.1.4. Publicity/Privacy versus Trademark

One of the most significant problems with publicity/privacy protection is that it is a product of state law and the amount of protection accorded under those laws varies significantly from state to state. For example, while one of the early precedent setting cases in the law of publicity and privacy was *Haelan Labs. v. Topps Chewing Gum*[63] recognizing the right of baseball players to license their pictures for use on baseball cards, in 1996 a court in Oklahoma found that Oklahoma's right of publicity statute was unconstitutional when applied to baseball cards as a form of protected free speech.[64] As a consequence, a number of performers have registered their names as trademarks.[65] As a federal law, trademark avoids this problem and provides uniform protection across the country.

Trademark law may also offer a level of protection for publicity/privacy rights that have lost their protection due to the death of the individual involved. For example, while the beneficiary of a public figure could not prevent someone else from creating personality products based upon that public figure after the expiration of their postmortem rights (if any) nor could they prevent the incidental use of the public figure's name in identifying and selling those personality products, the beneficiary may nonetheless obtain trademark rights in the name and its use to identify the source of "officially licensed" personality products.[66]

4.1.5. Publicity, Privacy, and State Jurisdiction

The rights of publicity and privacy are created and protected by the states. However, commerce in these rights is national and/or international. The question then arises as to what is being protected and where. For example, the nature and duration of a person's publicity

---

[63] Haelan, 202 F.2d 866 (2d Cir.), *cert. denied*, 346 U.S. 816 (1953).

[64] Cardtoons, L.C. v. Major League Baseball Players Ass'n, 95 868 F. Supp. 1266 (N.D. Okla. 1994), *aff'd* 95 F. 3d 959 (10th Cir. 1996).

[65] *See, e.g.*, United States Registration Nos. 3,468,196, TIGER WOODS for various services; 1,640,320, PRINCE for compact discs and related products; and 1,487,719, MICHAEL JORDAN for various services.

[66] Cairns v. Franklin Mint Co., 292 F.3d 1139 (9th Cir. 2002); *see also* A.V.E.L.A. v. Estate of Marilyn Monroe, 1:12-cv-04828 (S.D.N.Y. Sept. 18, 2015) (the Estate or Marilyn Monroe, unable to assert post-mortem publicity rights, could assert that goods featuring Monroe violate its trademark rights).

privacy rights may vary enormously between the state of the person's domicile, the state in which an infringement may occur and/or the state of domicile of the infringer. As yet no clear guidelines exist on which law applies under questions of venue or choice of law, although in cases involving post-mortem rights, courts have looked to the decedent's domicile.[67]

4.2. SUBJECT MATTER

4.2.1. In General

The subject matter for both the rights of privacy-appropriation and publicity are essentially the same and, as articulated under the earliest statute, include the "name, portrait or picture of any living person."[68] This has been interpreted to accord protection against such use as a person's name and signature,[69] and use of any type of images or likenesses (including drawing, cartoon, or robots)[70] through which an individual is "capable of identification."[71]

Protection has also been accorded the use of a person's name and biography in a fictionalized biography.[72] However, a factual biography[73] (even though unauthorized)[74] or a fictional biography that does not hold itself out as true[75] would be privileged.[76]

---

[67] *See infra* §4.10.4.

[68] *See* N.Y. CIV. RIGHTS LAW §50.

[69] *See* U.S. Life Ins. Co. v. Hamilton, 238 S.W.2d 289 (Tex. Civ. App. 1951).

[70] White v. Samsung Elecs. Am., Inc., 971 F.2d 1395 (9th Cir. 1992); Wendt v. Host Int'l, Inc., 129 F.3d 806 (9th Cir. 1997), *reh'g & suggestion for reh'g en banc denied*, 197 F. 3d 1284 (9th Cir. 199), *cert. denied sub nom.*, Paramount Pictures Corp. v. Wendt, 531 U.S. 811 (2000).

[71] Cohen v. Herbal Concepts, 482 N.Y.S.2d 457 (N.Y. 1984) (rear view of nude woman recognizable from "dimples over nude buttocks"). *See also* Motchenbacher v. R. J. Reynolds Tobacco Co., 498 F.2d 821 (9th Cir. 1974) (distinguishing marks of race car made him recognizable-although barely visible behind the wheel).

[72] *See* Spahn v. Julian Messener, Inc., 286 N.Y.S.2d 832 (N.Y. 1967), *appeal dismissed*, 393 U.S. 1046 (1969).

[73] *See* Time, Inc. v. Hill, 385 U.S. 374 (1967).

[74] *See* Rosemont Enters, v. Random House, 58 Misc. 2d 1, 294 N.Y.S.2d 122 (Supp. Ct. 1968), *aff'd mem.*, 32 A.D.2d 892, 301 N.Y.S.2d 948 (1969).

[75] *See* Hicks v. Casablanca Record & Ballentine Books, 464 F. Supp. 426 (S.D.N.Y. 1978).

[76] *See infra* §4.4.

Advances in technology relating to digital editing may present some interesting problems in the near future. In movies like *Forrest Gump*, the leading character was digitally edited into photographs and scenes with a number of historical figures. Director Robert Zemeckis took this step further, digitally editing images of then President Clinton and excerpts from some of his speeches into the movie *Contact*. When White House counsel protested this use, Zemeckis responded that the President was "in the public domain" and he was free to proceed as he wished.[77] While clearly an inaccurate statement of the term "public domain," it would appear quite likely that Zemeckis' specific use, absent other circumstances, would be privileged under the First Amendment.[78] Nonetheless, this incident suggests the possibility of litigation in the near future where the digitized inclusion of deceased celebrities and public figures occurs absent the express consent of the portrayed person or that person's estate.

4.2.2. Publicity/Privacy and Copyright

The rights of publicity and privacy intersect with copyright law in a number of different and, in some cases puzzling ways. To begin with, most of the expressions upon which rights of publicity/privacy attach (e.g. photographs, drawings, figurines, etc.) are themselves copyrightable works. Neither the embodiment nor a registered claim for ownership of the copyright to that work affects the publicity/privacy rights of the individual embodied in the work. For example, the transfer of ownership in that work, by itself, does not convey any of the rights of the subject.[79] Thus, the owner of a sound recording of a famous singer cannot, without the permission of the performer, effectively license that work for use in a commercial. The owner could make its own commercial use of it, but cannot convey that right to others.[80]

The right of publicity (and presumably privacy) also protects a celebrity's right to his or her act or performance.[81] However, given the broad scope of copyright that protects not only dramatic, pantomime

---

[77] Joseph J. Beard, *"Will the Reel, er, Real Bill Clinton Please Stand Up: The Unauthorized Use of the Presidents Image – A New 'Contact' Sport,"* 15(4) ENT SPORTS LAWYER 3-6 (1998).

[78] *See infra* §4.4.

[79] Downing v. Abercrombie & Fitch, 265 F.3d 994 (9th Cir. 2001).

[80] Olivieira v. Inc., 251 F. 3d 56 (2d Cir. 2001).

[81] *See* Zacchini v. Scripps-Howard Broad. Co., 433 U.S. 562 (1977).

and choreographic works (as copyrightable works in themselves)[82] and musical performances, which between them would appear to encompass almost all types of public performances, and the copyright statute's preemption of any state law regulation of a subject equivalent to copyright, this form of publicity privacy subject matter protection may be significantly limited.

In both of the foregoing situations, to some extent the rights of the individual pre-exist the work that is subject copyright. But what happens when elements of the copyrightable work pre-exist the involvement of the individual. For example, what are the rights of an actor when they are performing a role created and written by another?

In *Hoffman v. Capital Cities/ABC*[83] Dustin Hoffman sued Los Angeles Magazine after it superimposed an image of Hoffman's face made up for his role in the movie *Tootsie* onto the picture of a fashion model as a part of a fashion spread entitled "Grand Illusions." Hoffman was awarded approximately $3 million dollars in compensatory and punitive damages, based upon the judge's finding that Hoffman and the other celebrities featured in "Grand Illusions" were being "commercially exploited and ... robbed of their dignity, professionalism, and talent" and "violated by technology."[84] Although it appears that the *Tootsie* character owned by the studio might otherwise have been used in this photographic feature based upon a fair use-copyright defense, that did not apply as a defense to the use of Hoffman's image.

However, what happens when the use is licensed by the producer/owner of the copyrighted audiovisual work and/or the characters in it? Here again, the rights of the individual performer prevail. Assuming the film's producers have not secured express permission to use the actor's name and likeness for broad advertising and promotional purposes, "an actor or actress does not lose the right to control the commercial exploitation of his or her likeness by portraying a fictional character."[85]

Finally, a related question is what happens when the image of the celebrity is embodied in a copyrighted work and that work falls into the

---

[82] 17 U.S.C. §102 (2008).

[83] Hoffman v. Capital Cities/ABC, Inc., 33 F. Supp.2d 867 (C.D. Cal. 1999), rev'd., 255 F.3d 1180 (9th Cir. 2001).

[84] *Id.* at 873.

[85] Wendt v. Host Int'l, 125 F.3d 806 (9th Cir. 1997) *cert. denied* 531 U.S. 811 (2000); Lugosi v. Universal Pictures, 603 P.2d 425, 431 (1979).

public domain? Clearly, the work itself can be exploited,[86] but can excerpts be taken from the work and used to promote an otherwise unrelated product? In *Astaire v. Best Film & Video Corp.*[87] the widow of Fred Astaire sued the producers of a dance video who had included clips drawn from some of Fred Astaire's films that had fallen into the public domain. Under California law, it was held that this use was exempted under the then applicable statute (which has since been amended and, it would appear, would now preclude this use).[88]

4.3. EXCLUSIVE RIGHTS

Although they are not separately identified in case law, a review of relevant decisions suggests that the right of publicity (and privacy-appropriation) may be broken down into five separate rights – namely, performance, adaptation, personality products, endorsement, and reputation. These rights are closely related, and as was the case in copyright law,[89] although analytically separable, an infringement may simultaneously involve more than one of the rights. It must be stressed that case law does not recognize these distinctions. They are set forth here to provide a framework in which to understand the nature of the exclusive right of publicity.

4.3.1. Performance

The right of performance relates to an individual's exclusive right to perform the services by which that person earns his or her living and to exploit those services. Although rarely litigated as such, it has been held that a person has the exclusive right to exploit his or her "act or performance"[90] and to preclude others from appropriating the act in its entirety (to be performed in the same manner as the personality).[91] Moreover, the right of performance includes the right

---

[86] *See* Ca Civ Code §4344.1 (2008).
[87] Astaire v. Best Film & Video Corp., 116 F.3d 1297 (9th Cir. 1997) *opinion amended*, 136 F.3d 1208 (9th Cir.) *cert. denied* 525 U.S. 868 (1998).
[88] *See*, Ca Civ Code §4344.1 (2008).
[89] *See U.S. Copyright Law, supra* §1.4.
[45] *See* Zacchini v. Scripps-Howard Broad. Co., 433 U.S. 562 (1977).
[91] *See* Estate of Presley v. Russen, 513 F. Supp. 1339 (D.N.J. 1981); Bette Midler v. Ford Motor Co., 849 F.2d 460 (9th Cir. 1988) (decided on unfair competition grounds).

to control and determine the media through which the performance may be exploited.[92]

This right was given a statutory gloss when Congress enacted a new Chapter 10 of the Copyright Act, entitled "Digital Audio Recording Devices and Media."[93] Under the provisions of this chapter, performers are now entitled to share in the income from a statutory license governing the private home recording of phonograms by means of digital audio tape (DAT) technology.[94] What is significant here is that performers are not entitled to *copyright* their performances, but are nonetheless recognized as possessing some form of protectable right independent of their contract with their recording company (the basis upon which they are entitled to payment for all other uses of their performances in that recorded media).

Continuing this trend, in 1994 Congress enacted the Uruguay Round Amendments Act, which included a new Chapter 11 for the Copyright Act, creating and/or recognizing certain rights for musical performers.[95] Under the terms of this amendment to the copyright act, musical performers have the right to control the fixation, reproduction, transmission, or distribution of copies of a live musical performance.[96] It is unclear whether, in fact, this is a new form of copyright or simply a new form of neighboring rights.[97] What is clear is that this enactment does not preempt other laws in this area (either common or statutory), thus allowing the continuing evolution of the laws of publicity and privacy and unfair competition in this area.

4.3.2. Adaptation

The right of adaptation relates to an individual's exclusive right to authorize others to create derivative works embodying the performance of the individual, either as performed by the individual[98]

---

[92] *See* Ettore v. Philco Television Broad. Corp., 229 F.2d 481 (3d Cir.), *cert. denied*, 351 U.S. 926 (1956). *See also* Zacchini v. Scripps-Howard Broad. Co., 433 U.S. 562 (1977).
[93] 17 U.S.C. §§1001-1010 (2008).
[94] *Id.* § 1006(b)(1) (2004).
[95] 17 U.S.C. §1101.
[96] *See supra* §§1.3.2 & 1.4.4.
[97] 17 U.S.C. §1101(d) (2008).
[98] *See* Zacchini v. Scripps-Howard Broadcasting, 433 U.S. 562 (1977).

or as performed by imitators of the individual.[99] One court, however, has determined that use of players' names and statistics is protected under the First Amendment when used in connection with fantasy sports leagues.[100] A New York district court determined that a video game maker who had created a character using a celebrity's outfit, hair, jewelry, and cell phone — but not her name, portrait, picture or voice -- was entitled to First Amendment protection, and the celebrity's claim failed.[101] The New York State Court of Appeals has agreed to hear the celebrity's case on appeal.[102]

4.3.3. Personality Products

The right to create and sell personality-products relates to the exploitation of products based on a person's name, likeness, or image. These would include posters,[103] bubblegum cards,[104] and motion pictures and stills therefrom.[105]

4.3.4. Endorsement

The right of endorsement relates to the use of an individual's name, image, likeness, and reputation in connection with the

---

[99] *See* Estate of Presley v. Russen, 515 F. Supp. 1339 (D.N.J. 1981). Note the decision in Groucho Marx Prods, v. Day & Night Co., 523 F. Supp. 485 (S.D.N.Y. 1981), *rev'd*, 689 F.2d 317 (2d Cir. 1982). The district court, we believe, correctly acknowledged this right. Nonetheless, it was overturned on determination that the California law of publicity would not recognize this right as descendible (and may or may not recognize the right itself being that the decision was founded on the question of descendibility). California has subsequently modified its law to provide for the descendibility of the right of publicity.

[100] *See* C.B.C. Distribution & Mktg., Inc. v. Major League Baseball Advanced Media, L.P., 505 F.3d 818 (8th Cir. 2007), *cert. denied*, 553 U.S. 1090 (2008). Notably, the NFL was involved in a similar challenge against CBS in CBS Interactive, Inc. v. Nat'l Football League Players Ass'n, 259 F.R.D. 398 (D. Minn. 2008).

[101] Lohan v. Take Two Interactive Software Inc., 2016 NY Slip Op 05942 (App. Div. 1st Dept. Sept. 1, 2016).

[102] Lohan v. Take-Two Interactive Software, Motion No. 2017-74 (Feb. 16, 2017).

[103] *See* Factors Etc. Inc. v. Pro Arts, 579 F.2d 215 (2d Cir. 1978), *cert. denied*, 440 U.S. 908 (1979), *on remand*, 496 F. Supp. 1090 (S.D.N.Y. 1980), *rev'd*, 652 F.2d 278 (2nd Cir.1981), *cert denied*, 456 U.S. 927 (1982).

[104] *See* Haelan Labs. v. Topps Chewing Gum, Inc., 202 F.2d 866 (2d Cir.), *cert. denied*, 346 U.S. 816 (1953).

[105] *See* Price v. Hal Roach Studios, 400 F. Supp. 836 (S.D.N.Y. 1975).

advertising of goods or services.[106] *Implied* endorsements of goods or services are also encompassed within this right.[107] Professional basketball player Michael Jordan successfully sued a grocery store for infringing his right of publicity when the store used his name in a magazine advertisement. The ad appeared in a magazine commemorating Jordan's induction into the Basketball Hall of Fame, congratulating him alongside the store's logo. It did not expressly promote the store's services. Nevertheless, the court held that "an ad congratulating a famous athlete can only be understood as a promotional device."[108]

In California, nonpublic figures have found protection under that state's right of publicity statute where their names and images have been integrated into sponsored advertisements for certain brands without their consent, based on their interaction with those brands over social media.[109]

The use of look-alikes and/or sound-alikes of celebrities in product endorsement cases (because in a strict sense it does not involve the actual image or voice of the celebrity) has found protection under laws governing unfair competition rather than being protected as a publicity right[110] Moreover, in order to obtain additional protection of this right, a number of performers and sports figures, like Tiger Woods and the artist formerly known as Prince, have begun to trademark their names.[111]

One area in which the rights of personality products and endorsements are bridged occurs when the name of the individual is attached to the product (in a fashion similar to the attachment of a

---

[106] *See* Pavesich v. New England Life Ins. Co., 50 S.E. 2d (Ga. 1905). *See also* Allen v. Nat'l Video, Inc., 610 F. Supp. 612 (S.D.N.Y. 1985); Lombardo v. Doyle Dane & Bernbach, Inc., 396 N.Y.S.2d 661 (N.Y. App. Div. 1977); Onassis v. Christian Dior N.Y., Inc., 472 N.Y.S.2d 943 (N.Y. Sup.Ct. 1984), aff'd, 488 N.Y.S.2d 943 (N.Y.App.Div. 1985).

[107] *See* Motschenbacher v. R.J. Reynolds Tobacco Co., 498 F.2d 821 (9th Cir. 1974).

[108] Jordan v. Jewel Food Stores, Inc., 743 F.3d 509 (7th Cir. 2014).

[109] *See* Fraley v. Facebook, Inc., 830 F. Supp.2d 785 (N.D. Cal. 2011) (social media company Facebook settled a class action lawsuit brought by users for use of their names and images in connection with "Sponsored Stories").

[110] *See supra* §3.11.2.

[111] *See e.g.*, United States Registration Nos. 3,468,196, TIGER WOODS for various services; 1,640,320, PRINCE for compact discs and related products; and 1,487,719, MICHAEL JORDAN for various services.

trademark).[112] Because one of the rationales for trademark is to warrant quality[113] (a form of endorsement), it seems reasonable to place such use within this right.

4.3.5. Reputation

The right of reputation represents a means of protecting the reputation of an individual against subsequent misuse *even though the use was otherwise authorized*.[114] This is a little-used right, in some ways resembling the concept of droit moral or an author's right not to have his or her reputation damaged by the "emasculation" of his or her work, which developed in copyright under the Berne Convention.[115] It recognizes that the ongoing market of an artist's past work has a continuing effect on that artist's reputation. (Droit moral, except for limited statutory recognition in the field of fine arts,[116] receives only limited recognition in the United States under the Visual Artists Rights Act of 1990.[117]) Applied here it seeks to protect the reputation of the personality from damaging misuse.

4.4. FAIR USE – LIMITATIONS TO PUBLICITY AND PRIVACY RIGHTS

Throughout the development of the rights of privacy and publicity there have arisen certain limitations to those rights which can be referred to as fair use. At present, there is no single, coherent doctrine of fair use in this area, unlike that which has evolved in the law of copyright. Instead, the courts and the legislatures approach the issue of establishing the appropriate limits from a variety of perspectives. In

---

[112] *See* Cepada v. Swift Co., 415 F.2d 1205 (8th Cir. 1969).

[113] *See infra* §4.3.3.

[114] *See* Russell v. Marlboro Books, 18 Misc. 2d 166, 183 N.Y.S.2d 8 (N.Y. Sup. Ct. 1959) (alteration of the photograph of a model known for wholesome family-oriented work so that she appeared as a prostitute). *See also* Eastwood v. Superior Court, 198 Cal.Rptr. 342 (Cal. App. 2 Dist. 1983) [*superseded by statute sub nom.* KNB Enters. V. Matthews, 92 Cal. Rptr. 2d 713 (Cal App. 2 Dist. 2000)]; Sellack v. Nat'l Enquirer, No. C441-180 (Cal. App. Super. 1983) (use of a photograph on the cover of a magazine where the article inside was false).

[115] *See supra* §1.4.2 ("droit moral").

[116] *See* N.Y. ARTS & CULTURAL AFFAIRS LAW art. 14A; California Arts Preservation Act, CAL. CODE §987.

[117] *See supra* §1.4.2.

some cases, fair use is a result of the narrowness of the right that is recognized either by the courts or the legislature.[118] For example, in some jurisdictions the right exists only to protect against the use of the name, likeness, or image for purposes of advertising or trade.[119] In general, fair use type limitations on the right of publicity/privacy cluster around a few types of analysis.

4.4.1. First Amendment

The largest single exception has been based on consideration of the First Amendment. Indeed, First Amendment concerns underlie almost all the fair use limitations, however framed. The First Amendment exception has been justified in different ways at different times. For example, it has been held that *publication* of the name or likeness in connection with a newsworthy event is not a use[120] for the purposes of "trade or advertising,"[121] regardless of the fact that the press is an advertiser-sponsored medium.[122] In other cases, it has been more bluntly held that freedom of speech and press under the First Amendment transcends the right to privacy[123] before which the right of privacy must "bow."[124] Courts have also held that a statutory right of publicity must bow to the First Amendment where the use is considered to be a form of speech (i.e., baseball cards).[125] Using a

---

[118] *See supra* §4.1.

[119] *See* N.Y. CIVIL RIGHT LAW §§50-51 (precluding use in "advertising or purposes of trade" only).

[120] *See* Sidis v. F-R Pub. Corp., 34 F. Supp. 19 (S.D.N.Y. 1938), *aff'd*, 113 F.2d 806 (2d Cir.), *cert. denied*, 311 U.S. 711 (1940); Montana v. San Jose Mercury News, Inc., 34 Cal. App. 4th 790, 793 (Cal. App. 6 Distr. 1995).

[121] *See* Paulsen v. Personality Posters. Inc., 299 N.Y.S.2d 501 (N.Y. Sup. Ct. 1968).

[122] *See* Sidis v. F-R Pub. Corp., 34 F. Supp. 19 (S.D.N.Y. 1938), *aff'd*, 113 F.2d 806, *cert. denied*, 311 U.S. 711 (1940). *See also* Ann-Margaret v. High Soc'y Magazine, 498 F. Supp. 401 (S.D.N.Y. 1980).

[123] Namath v. Sports Illustrated, 363 N.Y.S.2d 276 (N.Y.Sup.Ct.), *aff'd*, 371 N.Y.S.2d 10 (1975), *aff'd*, 386 N.Y.S.2d 397 (N.Y.App.Div. 1976), aff'd, 386 N.Y.S.2d 397 (N.Y. 1976).

[124] *See* Rosemont Enters, v. Random House, 58 Misc. 2d 1, 294 N.Y.S.2d 122, *aff'd*, 32 A.D.2d. 892 (1968), *aff'd*, 301 N.YS.2d (1969).

[125] Cardtoons, L.C. v. Major League Baseball Players Ass'n, 868 F. Supp. 1266 (N.D. Okla. 1994), *aff'd* 95 F. 3d 959 (10th Cir. 1996). *See also* C.B.C. Distribution & Marketing, Inc. v. Major League Baseball Advanced Media, L.P., 505 F.3d 818 (8th

prominent figure's name or likeness as a part of a fictional work may also be privileged under the First Amendment as a form of protected speech and also because it is highly unlikely that anyone would mistake the fictional character for the original.[126] Finally, protection is lost by "people who, by their accomplishments, mode of living, professional standing or calling, create a legitimate and widespread attention to their activities."[127]

Nonetheless, First Amendment protection may be lost if, for example, the use is tainted with libelous material,[128] a "fictional" biography is presented as fact[129] (although a fictional biography not holding itself out as true still remains protected),[130] where there is a false attribution on authorship,[131] or where the use is misleading.[132] Also, incidental use in association with promotional efforts for a news media (such as subscription ads) is allowed[133] unless the use identified in the promotion is false or misleading with respect to that publication.[134]

Finally, continued commercial use of a picture which was originally constitutionally protected as a news item, may become an infringing use after the passage of sufficient time.[135]

Cir. 2007), *cert. denied*, 553 U.S. 1090 (2008). *But see*, Haelan Laboratories v. Topps Chewing Gum, 202 F.2d 866 (2d Cir.) *cert. denied*, 346 US 816 (1953).

[126] Doe v. TCI Cablevision, No. 972-09415, 2000 WL 35715278 (Mo. Cir. Oct. 31, 2000), *aff'd in part, rev'd in part and remanded*, 110 S.W. 3d 363 (Mo. 2003), *cert denied sub nom*, McFarlane v. Twist, 540 U.S. 1106 (2004).

[127] *See* Eastwood v. Superior Court, 198 Cal.Rptr. 342 (Cal. App. 2 Dist. 1983) [*superseded by statute sub nom*. KNB Enters. v. Matthews, 92 Cal. Rptr. 2d 713 (Cal App. 2 Dist. 2000)].

[128] *See* Ali v. Playgirl, Inc., 447 F. Supp. 723 (S.D.N.Y 1978).

[129] *See* Spahn v. Julian Messner, Inc., 286 N.Y.S.2d 832 (N.Y. 1967), *appeal dismissed*, 393 U.S. 1046 (1969).

[130] *See* Hicks v. Casablanca Record & Ballentine Books, 274 N.Y.S.2d 877, 221 N.E.2d 543, 464 F. Supp. 426 (S.D.N.Y. 1978).

[131] Dempsey v. Nat'l Enquirer, 702 F. Supp. 935 (D. Me. 1988).

[132] *See* Grant v. Esquire, Inc., 367 F. Supp. 876 (S.D.N.Y. 1973).

[133] *See* Namath v. Sports Illustrated, n. 65, *supra*; New York Times Magazine v. The Metro. Transp. Auth., 136 F.3d 123 (2nd Cir. 1998).

[134] *See* Cher v. Forum Int'l Ltd., 692 F.2d 634 (9th Cir. 1982), *cert. denied*, 462 U.S. 1120 (1983).

[135] Mendonsa v. Time. Inc. 678 F. Supp. 967 (D.R.I. 1988) (supporting a claim by the sailor in Eisenstadt's famous 1946 "Kissing Sailor Photo" against Time's selling of prints).

4.4.2. Mimicry and Imitation

A second exception, although much less litigated, appears in the area of mimicry or imitation. Whereas the characterizations performed by such entertainer impressionists as Rich Little and Marilyn Michael are generally not considered as infringing on the rights of publicity or privacy of their subjects, a complete appropriation of the subject performer's act may be penalized.[136] Imitation of a vocal performance style in the context of creating a commercial may also cross the border of fair use into an action for unfair competition,[137] or a common-law tort of publicity.[138]

4.4.3. Fair Use Doctrine Test

Courts have applied in this area a test for fair use similar to that set forth in the law of copyright.[139] Use of such a test analyzing the purpose and character of the use, the nature of the protected right, the substantiality of the amount used, and the potential effect on the market value of the holder of the rights of publicity or privacy appropriation (tempered by the rules of equity) can, in many instances, be applied to support the current law.

Despite the intellectual promise offered by the copyright fair use doctrine, the courts have not followed up upon its initial promise. For example, while a lower court adopted a fair use analysis to protect a "parody" set of baseball card (i.e. using cartoon figures resembling the images of real players), the appellate court affirming that decision relied solely upon a First Amendment balancing test.[140]

---

[136] *See* Estate of Presley v. Russen, 513 F. Supp. 1339 (D.N.J. 1981).

[137] M'Lahr v. Adell Chem. Co., 300 F.2d 256 (1st Cir. 1962) (reinstating on appeal Burt Lahr's claim for the imitation of his vocal style in an animated commercial as stating a valid cause of action). Note that an action under New York's law of privacy was denied and the action was brought under unfair competition standards.

[138] Bette Midler v. Ford Motor Co. & Young & Rubicam No. 86-2683 (C.D. Cal 1987) *rev'd* 849 F.2d 460 (9th Cir. 1988), *appeal after remand*, 944 F.2s 909 (9th Cir. 1991), *cert. denied*, 503 U.S. 951 (1992) (Note – the ruling held that the statutory right of publicity did not apply). *See* §2.11.1 *supra* at n. 102.1.

[139] *See* Apple Corps. v. Leber, 229 U.S.P.Q. 1015 (Cal. App. Super. 1986). *See also supra* §1.4.

[140] Cardtoons, L.C. v. Major League Baseball Players Assn., 868 F. Supp. 1266 (N.D. Okla. 1994), *aff'd* 95 F. 3d 959 (10th Cir. 1996).

Different circuit courts also disagree on whether to apply a copyright-based fair use test, or to follow a trademark-based approach. An example involves three cases bought by football players against the makers of sports video games. In one California case (affirmed by the 9th Circuit on appeal), the court followed a trademark law-based approach and held that the plaintiff football player's likeness was artistically relevant to the games, and that the facts did not sufficiently allege that consumers would be misled as to the player's involvement with the games.[141] The player's case was therefore dismissed.[142] In a second California case (brought as a class action and also affirmed on appeal), the court followed the copyright fair use-based test, and ruled in favor of the players.[143] It held that the video game maker had not added sufficient creative characteristics to the likenesses of the player avatars to warrant First Amendment protection.[144] In the third New Jersey case (also brought as a class action and affirmed by the 3rd Circuit on appeal), the court likewise followed the copyright fair use-based test, and ruled in favor of the players.[145] The court found that the context in which the players' avatars appeared, specifically playing in a football game, did not transform the players' identities.

4.4.4. Fine Arts Exception

Courts have also recognized what might be referred to as a fine arts exception. An artist who creates a work of fine art (a painting, drawing, lithograph etc.) depicting even a well-known person will probably not be liable to that person, even if the artist makes fine art multiples of the work or a number of different fine art portraits of the person.[146] The artist loses this protection, however when that work of fine art is converted into a mass marketed work by transferring it to a mass-market medium, such as imprinting it on a T-shirt.[147]

The courts have not clearly defined what constitutes a "mass market" in this context. In practice, celebrities have had some success against mass marketers of porcelain representations by producers like

---

[141] Brown v. Elec. Arts Inc., 724 F.3d 1235 (9th Cir. 2013).
[142] *Id.* at 1248.
[143] Keller v. Elec. Arts. Inc., 724 F.3d 1268 (9th Cir. 2013).
[144] *Id*,
[145] Hart v. Elec. Arts. Inc., 717 F. Supp. 3d 141 (3rd Cir. 2013).
[146] *See, e.g.* ETW Corp v. Jiher Publ'g, Inc. , 332 F.3d 915 (6th Cir. 2003).
[147] Comedy III Prods., Inc. v. Saderup, 21 P.3d 797 (Cal. 2001).

the Franklin Mint.[148] But what about multiple copies of lithographs or serigraphs which can run into the hundreds? These have been accepted as works of fine art by at least one court.[149] Nonetheless, one standard which might be used in the definition of fine arts provided in the Copyright statute which would limit protection to limited edition of 200 or fewer copies.[150]

4.4.5. First Sale

While not an element of traditional fair use analysis, some courts have held the first sale doctrine, as applied to copyrights, trademarks and patents applicable to the rights of publicity.[151] Once the celebrity's likeness is embodied in a tangible product, subsequent owners can resell that copy or adapt it into other forms, such as attaching a trading card to a plaque.

4.4.6. Public Domain Limits

Publicity/privacy rights related to advertisements for the sale and distribution of audiovisual recordings of performances embodied in a copyrighted work, though originally subject to contractual agreement, will be limited when that work falls into the public domain.[152] That is to say, when an audiovisual work falls into the public domain, distributors can freely use excerpts of performances embodied in that work in their marketing of the work.[153] However, while currently unresolved, it would appear that excerpts of a performance cannot be taken and used to promote an unrelated commercial work if not related to original performance or not otherwise subject to exemption as a fair use.[154]

---

[148] See ETW Corp. v. Jiher Publ'g, Inc., 332 F.3d 915 (6th Cir. 2003).
[149] Id.
[150] 17 U.S.C. §§ 101, 106A. Accord, see Comedy III Prods., Inc. v. Saderup, 21 P.3d 797 (Cal. 2001).
[151] Allison v. Vintage Sports Plaques, 136 F.3d 1443 (11th Cir. 1998); Major League Baseball Players Ass'n v. Dad's Kid Corp., 806 F. Supp. 458 (S.D.N.Y. 1992), transferred sub. nom. In re Dad's Kid Corp., Nos. CV-92-04119-WJR (CTX), CV-93-2753-WJR (CTX), 1994 WL 794763 (C.D. Cal. June 30, 1994).
[152] See, e.g. Orioles, Inc. v. Major League Baseball Players' Ass'n, 805 F.2d 663 (7th Cir. 1986); cert. denied, 480 U.S. 941 (1987).
[153] See Astaire v. Best Film & Video Corp., 136 F.3d 1208 (9th Cir. 1998), cert. denied 525 U.S. 868 (1998).
[154] While Astaire v. Best Films, supra, allowed this type of use, it relied upon a provision of California law that has subsequently been amended and would appear to preclude this type of use.

4.4.7 Non-Endorsement Use

The concept of endorsement within the right of publicity resembles trademark law. The right is an effort to protect the public good will of the celebrity, to protect others from trading on that good will and to protect consumers from a mistaken assumption that the celebrity is endorsing a product or service that they have not in fact endorsed.[155] Courts have extended this analysis to publicity/privacy, finding that the right of publicity is not infringed where it is clear that the average consumer would not interpret the use as one in which the celebrity is endorsing the product or service being promoted.[156] Presumably, this is a rebuttable presumption upon a showing of consumer confusion.

4.4.8. Antitrust

Antitrust laws and policies may come into play as well. For example, a federal court in California held that non-professional college athletes are entitled to a right of publicity in their images, finding that a collegiate sports organization's rules limiting compensation to such athletes for the commercial use of their images violated federal anti-trust laws.[157]

4.5. CREATION AND COMMENCEMENT

4.5.1. Privacy

The right of privacy is, by its very nature, an inherent right of an individual that commences at birth.[158] No actions or formalities are necessary to create the right. However, the right may be limited by actions of the individual that might make that individual a public figure.[159]

---

[155] *See supra* §3.1.2.
[156] N.Y. Magazine v. Metro. Transp. Auth., 136 F.3d 123 (2d Cir.), *cert. denied*, 525 U.S. 824 (1998); *see also* Brown v. Elec. Arts Inc., 724 F.3d 1235 (9th Cir. 2013).
[157] O'Bannon v. Nat'l Collegiate Athletic Ass'n, 802 F.3d 1049 (9th Cir. 2015).
[158] *See* N.Y. CIVIL RIGHTS LAW §§ 50-51 (2008) ("any living person").
[159] *See* Time, Inc. v. Hill, 385 U.S. 374 (1966).

4.5.2. Publicity

The distinction between the rights of privacy and publicity suggests that the right of publicity rests on some effort of the individual to create economic value with respect to his or her name, likeness, or image.[160] Particularly insofar as the right touches on the doctrine of unfair competition[161] or in which a claim is to be made under §43a of the Lanham Act,[162] the right of publicity may require that the individual's name, likeness, or image must have acquired some degree of popular recognition.[163] Finally, although not used to define the commencement of protection, decisions relating to the descendibility of the right of publicity (as distinct from the right of privacy, which is never descendible)[164] frequently require not only celebrity status but also some level of exploitation of the right of publicity in association with that celebrity.[165]

A review of state statues in this area is, unfortunately, not particularly illuminating. Most statutes are, if named at all, denominated as rights of privacy[166] and the rights of publicity are "subsumed" in the statute with the assumption that the effort to exploit or not exploit is irrelevant as the statute precludes any use of an individual's likeness.[167] Such an interpretation, while appropriate in statutory construction and in relation to privacy rights, ignores the differences between the two rights. In contrast, among the thirteen state statutes that specifically recognize a post mortem right in one's

---

[160] *See* Munden v. Harns, 153 Mo. App. 652 (1911).

[161] *See* Madison Square Garden Corp. v. Universal Pictures Co., 255 App.Div. 459. 7 N.Y.S.2d 845 (1938); Allen v. Men's World Outlet, Inc., 679 F. Supp. 360 (S.D.N.Y. 1988).

[162] *See* Allen v. Nat'l Video, Inc., 610 F. Supp. 612 (S.D.N.Y. 1985); Allen v. Men's World Outlet, Inc., 679 F. Supp. 360 (S.D.N.Y. 1988).

[163] *See supra* §3.10.

[164] *See* Guglielmi v. Spelling-Goldberg Prods., 603 P.2d 454 (Cal. 1979) (although a cause of action may or may not survive the death of the individual) Prosser, *supra* note 4, §117). It must be noted that this use of the term *privacy* does not apply to those jurisdictions that confuse the distinctions between the two rights or mislabel them.

[165] *See* Hicks v. Casablanca Records & Ballentine Books, 464 F. Supp. 426 (S.D.N.Y. 1978). *See also infra* §4.8.2.

[166] E.g. MASS. GEN. L. Ch. 214 §§4A; N.Y. CIV. RIGHTS LAW §§50-51; OKLA. STAT. tit 21 §§839.1-3 *et. al*.

[167] Stefano v. News Group Publ'ns., Inc., 485 N.Y.S.2d 220 (N.Y. 1984), order amended, 506 N.Y.S.2d 283 (N.Y. App. Div. 1986).

personality,[168] a characteristic appropriate to and in clear conformity with the concept of the right of publicity being an exploitable economic right,[169] five states require some level of celebrity. Kentucky makes its statute applicable to persons who are "public figures"[170] while California,[171] Oklahoma[172] and Texas[173] require that the person's likeness has acquired some commercial values at death, whether or not that person had exploited it during their lifetime. Thus, these statutes suggest that the right commences at the point at which the likeness gains commercial value. Texas[174] also extends protection to persons whose likeness acquires commercial value after death while Tennessee[175] specifies that while all individuals possess a 10-year post mortem right in their likeness, that right expires any time after 10 years if it is shown that it ceases being commercially exploited for any subsequent consecutive two-year period. In each of these latter cases the right could be said to commence after death.

Nevada takes a curious position in this dispute. While it does not require prior use or fame for the protection of this right during a person's lifetime, *if* the individual dies without surviving beneficiaries or successors, then the statute provides that the right is lost unless the decedent previously had licensed his or her persona for use during his or her lifetime.[176] Thus, in this one case, the rights of the licensee are "created" and preserved by the act of "commercial use" during the individual's lifetime.

The degree of fame[177] or the degree of exploitation[178] that is required to create the right of publicity has not been determined. It is suggested that the threshold of such protection should be low, based on the idea that if the name, likeness, or image has sufficient value for someone to attempt to appropriate its use, then that individual should receive

---

[168] *See infra* §4.8.
[169] *See supra* §4.1.2.
[170] KY. REV. STAT. ANN. §491.170.
[171] CAL. CIV. CODE §990(h).
[172] OKLA. STAT. tit. 21 §1448 (H).
[173] 4 TEX. STAT. §26.003 (2).
[174] *Id.*
[175] TENN. CODE ANN. §47-25-1104.
[176] NEV. REV. STAT. CH. 598 §4(2).
[177] *See* Hicks v. Casablanca Records & Ballentine Books, 464 F. Supp. 426 (S.D.N.Y. 1978).
[178] *See* Price v. Hal Roach Studios, 400 F. Supp. 836 (S.D.N.Y. 1975).

protection of the right.[179] Also, the fact that an infringer exploits it commercially generally indicates that it is established and has commercial value.[180]

4.6. OWNERSHIP

4.6.1. Privacy

The right of privacy, by its very nature, is a personal right that is "owned" by that individual at birth.[181] It pertains only to individuals and does not apply to partnerships[182] or corporations.[183] It does not extend to members of the individual's family,[184] nor is it assignable,[185] although a cause of action may[186] or may not[187] survive the individual's death according to the survival rules of a particular state. The right does not exist in one who is dead.[188]

4.6.2. Publicity

As suggested in the preceding section, generally the right of publicity does not accrue until the individual has exerted some efforts to create economic value in his or her name, likeness, or image,[189] at which point "ownership" of that value vests in that individual.[190] The

---

[179] *See* Munden v. Harris, 153 Mo. App. 652 (1911).
[180] *See* Memphis Dev. Found. v. Factors Etc., Inc., 616 F.2d 956 (6th Cir.), *cert. denied.* 449 U.S. 953 (1980) (while, unlike trademark, "secondary meaning" [*see supra* §3.2.3] is required, this use indicates "secondary meaning").
[181] *See* Prosser, *supra* note 4, §117.
[182] *See* Rosenwasser v. Ogoglia, 158 N.Y.S.2d 56 (N.Y. App. Div. 1916).
[183] *See* University of Notre Dame du Lac v. Twentieth Century-Fox Film Corp., 259 N.Y.S.2d 832 (N.Y. 1965).
[184] *See* Kelly v. Johnson Publ'g. Co., 325 P.2d 659 (1958).
[185] *See* Rhodes v. Sperry & Hutchinson Co., 85 N.E. 1097 (1908), *aff'd*, 220 U.S. 502 (1911).
[186] *See* Reed v. Real Detective Pub. Co., 162 P.2d 133 (1945).
[187] *See* Wyatt v. Hall's Portrait Studios, 128 N.Y.S. 247 (N.Y. Sup. Ct. 1911).
[188] *See* Maritote v. Desilu Prods. Inc., 345 F.2d 418 (7th Cir.), *cert. denied*, 382 U.S. 883 (1965). Contra TENN. CODE ANN. §47-25-1104 (a statute labeled as a right of privacy in which there is no requirement of commercial value or exploitation for an initial post mortem term of 10 years.) *See Publicity and Privacy supra* §4.5.2 at note 161 and *Publicity and Privacy, infra*, §4.9.2 at note 238.
[189] *See supra* §4.5.
[190] *See* Munden v. Harris, 153 Mo. App. 652 (1911).

right is transferable or assignable[191] and thus may be owned by a corporation or partnership. It is an interesting question as to whether or not a corporation or partnership may have an independent right of publicity. Decisions rendered under the rubric of privacy have held that corporations and partnerships do not possess such a right.[192] Litigation in the area of unfair competition[193] suggests that such a right, although not defined as a right of publicity, does exist,[194] and ownership of this interest may vest in more than one individual at its commencement.[195] Finally, in some jurisdictions, the right may be descendible.[196]

4.7. FORMALITIES

Unlike copyright or trademark protection, there are no formalities of registration, notice, or protection (such as quality-control restrictions)[197] required to obtain or protect the rights of publicity or privacy.[198] The right of privacy exists simply by virtue of the existence of the individual,[199] while the right of publicity, in most cases, exists on its creation by exploitation.[200]

Four states that recognized a post mortem right of publicity, California,[201] Nevada,[202] Oklahoma,[203] and Texas,[204] provide procedures under which beneficiaries may register claims to a deceased individual's right of publicity. While each of these registration systems provide the benefit of creating public records of the claim of ownership, only Nevada requires registration for protection, and at

---

[191] See *Publicity and Privacy, infra* §4.9.
[192] See Rosenwasser v. Ogoglia, 158 N.Y.S.2d 56 (N.Y. App. Div. 1916); University of Notre Dame du Lac v. Twentieth Century-Fox Film Corp., 22 A.D. 452, 256 N.Y.S. 301, 207 N.E.2d 508 (1965).
[193] See *U.S. Trademark and Unfair Competition Law, supra* §3.10.
[194] See Rare Earth, Inc. v. Hoorelbeke, 401 F. Supp. 26 (S.D.N.Y. 1975); Giammarese v. Delfino, 197 U.S.P.Q. 162, No. 75 C 1051, 1977 WL 22745 (N.D. Ill. 1977).
[195] See Peterson v. Lightfoot, 191 P. 48 (Cal. App. 1 Dist. 1920).
[196] See *infra* §4.8.2.
[197] See Sharman v. C. Schmidt & Sons Inc., 216 F. Supp. 401 (E.D. Pa. 1963).
[198] For example, see N.Y. CIVIL RIGHTS LAW §§50-51.
[199] *Id.*
[200] See *supra* §4.5.
[201] CAL. CIV. CODE §990(f).
[202] NEV. REV. STAT. CH. 598.
[203] OKLA. STAT. tit. 21 §1448 (F).
[204] TEX. STAT. §26.006.

that, the requirement arises only after the post mortem owner learns of (or should have learned) of an infringement of rights,[205] and only the Texas statute specifies that registration provides *prima facie* evidence of the claim made and that the registered claim is superior to a conflicting unregistered claim.[206] Notably, there was some confusion as to whether post-mortem rights in California applied retroactively to individuals who passed away before passage of the California statute. The California legislature amended the statute in 2007 to reflect its intent that the application of the statute be retroactive. This action was taken in response to a dispute involving the publicity rights of Marilyn Monroe.[207]

Although not strictly a right of publicity formality, the owner of that right may register his or her name (which has acquired secondary meaning, a/k/a *celebrity*) as a trademark/service mark,[208] subject to all the formalities of trademark law.[209]

4.8. DURATION

4.8.1. Privacy

The right of privacy is a personal right commencing at birth[210] and ending on the death of the person asserting it.[211] A cause of action accruing prior to an individual's death may survive death,[212] but no new cause of action may arise after that death.[213]

4.8.2. Publicity

Duration of the right of publicity at common law is problematic and varies from jurisdiction to jurisdiction. It clearly exists during the

---

[205] NEV. REV. STAT. CH. 598 §4(4), (5).
[206] 4 TEX. STAT. §26.007.
[207] See Shaw Family Archives, Ltd. v. CMG Worldwide, Inc., No. 05 CIV. 3939 (CM), 2008 WL 4127830 (S.D.N.Y. Sept. 2, 2008) (discussing California and New York post-mortem publicity rights).
[208] *See* In re Carson, 197 U.S.P.Q. 554, 1977 WL 22654 (T.T.A.B. Nov. 29, 1977).
[209] *See supra* §3.7.
[210] *See supra*, §4.5.1.
[211] *See* Price v. Hal Roach Studios, 400 F. Supp. 836 (S.D.N.Y. 1975).
[212] *See* Reed v. Real Detective Pub. Co., 63 Ariz. 294 (1945).
[213] *See* Schumann v. Loew's Inc., 135 N.Y.S.2d 361 (N.Y. Sup. Ct. 1954), 144 N.Y.S.2d 27 (N.Y. Sup. Ct. 1955).

lifetime of the individual,[214] and a growing number of cases have held the right to be descendible.[215] A majority of cases holding the right to be descendible require that the right must have been exploited (in fields other than the field that made the individual a celebrity),[216] while a significant minority hold that the right is descendible without exploitation (outside of the area that created the individual's celebrity.[217]

However, despite the support for descendibility of the right, the issue of exact duration, when descendible at common law, has not been decided. The question of indeterminate duration has, in fact, been used as an argument against descendibility.[218] In one prominent California dissent[219] supporting descendibility, a durational limit of the life of the person plus fifty years (the same duration as copyright protection under the current copyright law)[220] has been suggested.

An alternate approach may be through an analogy with the law of trademarks. Because publicity rights are frequently used to endorse products,[221] are registrable as trademarks,[222] and are protectable under the Lanham Act (generally applying §43a unfair competition standards),[223] it appears appropriate to suggest that protection like the protection for trademarks should continue for however long the use continues and effectively embodies the good will that makes it marketable.[224]

---

[214] See Guglielmi v. Spelling-Goldberg Prods., 25 Cal. 3d 860, 603 P.2d 454, 160 Cal. Rptr. 352 (1979).

[215] See Factors Etc., Inc. v. Pro Arts, Inc., 444 F. Supp. 288 (S.D.N.Y. 1977), aff'd, 579 F.2d 215 (2d Cir. 1978), cert. denied, 440 U.S. 908 (1979); Hicks v. Casablanca Record & Ballentine Books, 464 F. Supp. 426 (S.D.N.Y. 1978); Martin Luther King, Jr. Center for Social Change v. American Heritage Prods., 694 F.2d 674 (11th Cir. 1983).

[216] See Lugosi v. Universal Pictures, 603 P.2d 425 (1979).

[217] See Martin Luther King, Jr. Center for Social Change v. American Heritage Prods., 694 F.2d 674 (11th Cir. 1983).

[218] See Memphis Dev. Found. v. Factors, Inc., 616 F.2d 956 (6th Cir.), cert. denied, 449 U.S. 953 (1980).

[219] Lugosi v. Universal Pictures, 603 P.2d at 434-454 (Chief Justice Byrd, dissent) (1979).

[220] 17 U.S.C. §402. See supra §1.10.1.

[221] See Allen v. Nat'l Video, Inc., 610 F. Supp. 612 (S.D.N.Y. 1985).

[222] See In re Carson, 197 U.S.P.Q. 554, 1977 WL 22654 (T.T.A.B. Nov. 29, 1977).

[223] See Allen v. Nat'l Video, Inc., 610 F. Supp. 612, See In re Carson, 197 U.S.P.Q. 554, 1977 WL 22654 (T.T.A.B. Nov. 29, 1977).

[224] See supra §3.8.

The statutory approach is equally varied. Thirteen states, California, Florida, Illinois, Indiana, Kentucky, Nevada, Ohio, Oklahoma, Pennsylvania, Tennessee, Texas, Virginia and Washington, recognize by statute the dependability of a right of publicity for varying terms of protection. Those post mortem periods of protection range from twenty years in Virginia,[225] forty years in Florida,[226] fifty years in Kentucky,[227] Nevada,[228] and Texas,[229] seventy years in California,[230] and up to 100 years in Oklahoma.[231] The adoption of a fixed post mortem term (particularly in Kentucky, Nevada, and Texas with their fifty year terms) is clearly modeled on current protections of copyright, as was previously suggested at common law.[232] Tennessee,[233] in contrast, while providing that every personality receives protection for a period of ten years following their death, goes on to allow continuing protection for howsoever long as someone continues to exploit the right (i.e. until the right is not exploited for two consecutive years), a duration of protection which more closely resembles trademark protection.

4.9. TRANSFER

4.9.1. Privacy

The right of privacy is not assignable[234] or transferable.[235] Nonetheless, its use may be authorized (or protection waived) by written consent[236] or conduct,[237] or where the use is related to or

---

[225] VA. CODE ANN. §8.01-40 (B) (2008).
[226] FLA. STAT. *tit.* 31 (§540.08(4) (2008).
[227] KY. REV. STAT. ANN. §491.170(2) (2008).
[228] NEV. REV. STAT. CH. 598.
[229] 4 TEX. STAT. §26.012(d).
[230] Cal. Civ. Code § 3344.1.
[231] OKLA. STAT. tit. 21 §1448(G).
[232] Lugosi v. Universal Pictures, 603 P.2d at 434-454 (Chief Justice Byrd, dissent).
[233] TENN. CODE ANN. §47-25-1104 (2008).
[234] *See* Rhodes v. Sperry & Hutchinson Co., 85 N.E. 1097, *aff'd*, 220 U.S. 502.
[235] *See* Schumann v. Loews, Inc., 135 N.Y.S.2d 361; Runyon v. United States, 281 F.2d 590 (5th Cir. 1960).
[236] *See* N.Y. CIVIL RIGHTS LAW §§50-51 (2008).
[237] *See* O'Brien v. Pabst Sales Co., 124 F.2d 167 (5th Cir. 1941), *cert. denied*, 315 U.S. 823 (1942). *Contra*: Caesar v. Chem. Bank, 483 N.Y.S.2d 16 (N.Y. App. Div. 1984), *appeal dismissed*, 64 N.Y.2d 886, 1985 WL 308266 (N.Y. Feb. 28), *order affirmed as modified by* 496 N.Y.S.2d 418 (N.Y. 1985) (may only be used in mitigation under N.Y. CIVIL RIGHTS LAW §§50-51).

derived from the individual's services rendered pursuant to an employment agreement[238] (although not where the use is unrelated to that employment).[239]

4.9.2. Publicity

The right of publicity is freely assignable[240] and, unlike trademarks, may be assigned "in gross"[241] (i.e., without the necessity of transferring the associated good will of an ongoing business).[242] Assignment may be effected by a written release,[243] pursuant to an employment contract where the use is incidental thereto[244] or, unless otherwise restricted by law,[245] waived by a course of conduct.[246] It must be noted that courts are reluctant to imply assignments even in written agreements where the facts are less than conclusive[247] unless an ambiguous assignment is coupled with facts clearly evidencing an intent to assign.[248]

---

[238] *See* Dzurenko v. Jordache, Inc., 454 N.Y.S.2d 102 (N.Y.App.Div.), *appeal dismissed*, 454 N.Y.2d 775 (N.Y. 1982), *aff'd as modified*, 464 N.Y. S. 2d 730 (N.Y. 1983); Dahl v. Columbia Pictures Corp., 166 N.Y.S.2d 708 (N.Y. Sup. Ct. 1957), *aff'd*, 183 N.Y.2d 992 (N.Y. App. Div. 1959).

[239] *See* Caesar v. Chem. Bank. 483 N.Y.S.2d 16 (N.Y.App.Div. 1984), appeal dismissed, 64 N.Y.2d 886, 1985 WL 308266 (N.Y. Feb. 28), *order aff'd as modified by* 496 N.Y.S.2d 418 (N.Y. 1985).

[240] *See* Factors Etc., Inc. v. Pro Arts, 579 F.2d 215 (2d Cir. 1978), *cert. denied*, 440 U.S. 908, on remand, 496 F. Supp. 1090, rev'd 652 F.2d 278, cert. denied, 456 U.S. 927.

[241] *See* Haelen Labs. v. Topps Chewing Gum, 202 F.2d 866 (2d Cir.), *cert. denied*, 346 U.S. 816 (1953).

[242] *See supra* §3.1.

[243] *See* Sharman v. C. Schmidt & Sons. 216 F. Supp. 401.

[244] *See* Price v. Hal Roach Studios, 400 F. Supp. 836.

[245] *See* N.Y. CIVIL RIGHTS LAW §§50-51 (2008). New York's law of privacy encompasses, such as exists, the right of publicity. Stephano v. News Group Publ'ns, Inc., 485 N.Y.S.2d 220 (N.Y. 1984), order amended, 506 N.Y.S.2d 283 (N.Y. App. Div. 1986).

[246] *See* O'Brien v. Pabst Sales Co., 124 F.2d 167 (5th Cir. 1941), *cert. denied*, 315 U.S. 823 (1942). Note that this case arose under privacy grounds, but it appears clearly applicable to publicity rights.

[247] *See* Ettore v. Philco Television Broad. Corp., 229 F.2d 481, *cert. denied*, 351 U.S. 926 (1956) (right of theatrical exhibition not extended to include television broadcast).

[248] *See* Factors Etc., Inc. v. Pro Arts, 444 F. Supp. 288 (S.D.N.Y. 1977), *aff'd*, 579 F.2d 215 (2d Cir. 1978), *cert. denied*, 440 U.S. 908 (1979).

A license or assignment may be limited as to the nature of the name or likeness,[249] to a particular version of the name or likeness,[250] a specific product on which they appear,[251] and a specific limited duration,[252] or alternately, it may be unlimited in time and scope.[253]

Finally, in those jurisdictions which recognize a post mortem right of publicity, the right is descendible.[254]

4.9.3. Privacy and Defamation

Defamation and the right of privacy are related in that they both are personal rights protecting an individual's position in society, the right of privacy protecting his or her anonymity, and the law of defamation protecting his or her reputation and good name.[255] A primary difference between the two is that the torts of defamation (either libel or slander) protects against dissemination of falsehoods to members of a community (with truth being an absolute defense),[256] whereas the right of privacy is impinged by publication without regard to truth.[257]

Similarities do exist. In both areas, an accurate identification of a specific living individual is required;[258] the infringement of the rights occurs on any communication to a third party (while privacy involves

---

[249] *See* Ettore v. Philco Television Broad. Corp., 229 F.2d 481 (3d Cir.), *cert. denied*, 351 U.S. 926 (1956).

[250] *See* Price v. Hal Roach Studios, 400 F. Supp. 836 (S.D.N.Y. 1975).

[251] *See* Capeda v. Swift & Co., 415 F.2d 1205 (8th Cir. 1969).

[252] *See* Haelan Labs. v. Topps Chewing Gum, 202 F.2d 866 (2d Cir.), *cert. denied*, 346 U.S. 816 (1953).

[253] *See* Lugosi v. Universal Pictures, 603 P.2d 425 (1979).

[254] *See supra* §4.8.2.

[255] *See* Prosser, *supra* note 4, §§111-117.

[256] *Id*. §116.

[257] In most instances, other than the tort of portrayal in a "false light" (see supra §4.1), publications infringing the right of privacy are true in that they may involve, for example, an accurate presentation of an individual's image or likeness. *See* Prosser, *supra* note 4, §117.

[258] *Compare* Mothersill v. Voliva, 158 Ill. App. 16 (Ill. App. 2 Dist. 1910) (defamation), *with* Motschenbacher v. R.J. Reynolds Tobacco Co., 498 F.2d 821 (9th Cir. 1974) (publicity-privacy). Note that a corporation or partnership may also be defamed in a more limited sense regarding its business reputation only. *See* Prosser, *supra* note 4, §111).

more extensive commercial publication),[259] and both areas are subject to restrictions based on the supremacy of the first amendment and freedom of the press doctrines.[260] Although defamation and privacy are not exploitable rights, such as trademarks or copyright, an individual may consent to an invasion of those rights (with or without monetary compensation therefore) by specific consent[261] or as a part of an employment agreement where the actions impinging those rights directly arise out of such employment.[262]

One area in which these two doctrines touch, arises where use of an individual's publicity rights in a manner that would otherwise be deemed a fair use[263] is coupled with defamatory material and the defamation destroys the fair use privilege, making the user liable for both privacy-publicity infringement and damages for defamation.[264]

4.10. INFRINGEMENT

4.10.1. Privacy-Appropriation

An action for infringement of the right of privacy involves proof of the following four elements:

1. Use of a living[265] individual's name, image, or likeness;[266]
2. For purposes of advertising or trade;[267]

---

[259] *Compare* Notarmuzzi v. Shevack, 108 N.Y.S.2d 172 (N.Y. Supp.Ct. 1951) (defamation), *with* Hill v. Hayes, 240 N.Y.S.2d 286 (N.Y.App.Div. 1963), appeal after remand 260 N.Y.S.2d 7 (N.W. 1965) *judgment set aside sub nom.*, Time, Inc. v. Hill, 385 U.S. 374 (1967) (privacy).

[260] *Compare* Time, Inc. v. Hill, 385 U.S. 374 (1966) (privacy must yield to the first amendment), *with* N.Y. Times Co. v. Sullivan, 376 U.S. 254 (1964) (requiring a higher standard of proof of malice for a public figure in defamation cases).

[261] *Compare* Schneiderman v. N.Y. Post Corp., 220 N.Y.S.2d 1008 (N.Y. Sup. Ct. 1961) (privacy), *with* Shinglemeyer v. Wright, 82 N.W. 887 (Mich. 1900) (defamation).

[262] *Compare* Dzurenko v. Jordache, Inc., 454 N.Y.S.2d 102 (N.Y.App.Div.), *appeal dismissed*, 454 N.Y.2d 775 (N.Y. 1982), *aff'd as modified*, 464 N.Y. S. 2d 730 (N.Y. 1983), *with* Bander v. Metro. Life Ins. Co., 42 N.E. 2d 595 (Mass. 1943).

[263] *See supra* §4.4.
[264] *See* Ali v. Playgirl, 447 F. Supp. 723 (S.D.N.Y. 1978).
[265] *See supra* §4.8.1.
[266] *See supra* §4.2.
[267] *See supra* §4.3.

3. Without permission or consent of that individual[268] (which in New York must be in writing[269] with oral permission considered only in mitigation of damages);[270] and
4. Absent privilege of fair use[271] (an affirmative defense).

4.10.2. Publicity

An action for infringement of the right of publicity involves proof of the following elements:

1. Use of a person's name, likeness, image,[272] or identity;[273]
2. Which name, likeness, or image has attained celebrity status;[274] and
3. If the individual is dead, that he or she exploited that right prior to death;[275]
4. Without permission or consent;[276] and
5. Absent privilege of fair use[277] (an affirmative defense).

4.10.3. Unfair Competition

An alternate cause of action for infringement of the right of publicity may be brought under §43(a) of the Lanham Act[278] or state unfair competition statutes. A cause of action under the Lanham Act requires the establishment of three elements: (1) involvement of goods or services, (2) an effect on interstate commerce, and (3) the false designation of origin or false description of goods or services (including improper endorsement of those goods or services).[279]

---

[268] *See supra* §4.9.1.
[269] *See* N.Y. CIVIL RIGHTS LAW §§50-51 (2008).
[270] *See* Caesar v. Chem. Bank, 460 N.Y.S.2d 235 118 Misc. 2d 118, (1983) *aff'd*, 483 N.Y.S.2d 16 (1984) (N.Y. Supp. 1983) aff'd 432 N.Y.S.2d. (16 N.Y.App.Div. 1984).
[271] *See supra* §4.4.
[272] *See supra* §4.2.
[273] White v. Samsung Electronics America, Inc., 971 F.2d 1395 (9th Cir. 1992).
[274] *See supra* §4.5.2.
[275] *See supra* §4.8.2.
[276] *See supra* §4.9.2.
[277] *See supra* §4.4.
[278] 15 U.S.C. §112s(a). *See supra* §3.10.
[279] *See supra* §3.10; Allen v. Nat'l Video, Inc., 610 F Supp. 612; Allen v. Men's World Outlet, Inc., 679 F. Supp. 360 (S.D.N.Y. 1988).; Bette Midler v. Ford Motor Co.

4.10.4. Venue or Choice of Law

Because an action for violation of the right of publicity involves commerce, the plaintiff should have significant discretion in the choice of venue. Given the wide discrepancy in the level of protection offered, plaintiffs will need to consider the level of protection offered by each possible forum. For example, in connection with a suit by Rosa Parks against the musical group Outkast, of three potential venues, California, New York and Michigan, Parks elected to sue in Michigan.[280] The case ultimately settled. Nonetheless, where the media is involved, it appears that the courts may favor setting the venue within the state in which the publisher is located.[281]

Choice of venue, however, may be limited by the substantive or choice of law provisions of that forum. For example, it has been held in California that the state law which recognizes a post-mortem right of publicity also relies upon a personal property determination statute that applies the law of the domicile of the person in determining postmortem publicity rights.[282] In that case, a beneficiary charitable trust of Princess Diana could not avail itself of the California postmortem publicity rights because the domicile of Princess Diana (Great Britain – before her death) did not recognize a postmortem right of publicity. Following the Princess Diana case, there was still some confusion over post-mortem publicity rights in California, which led to statutory revisions that explicitly made the recognition of post-mortem publicity rights in California retroactive as noted in *Shaw Family Archives, Ltd. v. CMG Worldwide, Inc.*[283] Nevertheless, in Shaw, the court determined that New York applied to the publicity rights of Marilyn Monroe and New York does not recognize post-mortem publicity rights. The court determined the Monroe estate was bound by arguments asserted previously seeking the benefits of New York tax laws.[284]

& Young & Rubicam, No. 86-2683 (C.D. Cal. 1987), *rev'd*, 849 F.2d 460 (9th Cir. 1988), *appeal after remand*, 944 F.2s 909 (9th Cir. 1991), *cert. denied*, 503 U.S. 951 (1992).

[280] Rosa Parks v. Outkast, 76 F.Supp.2d 775 (E.D. Mich. 1999), *aff'd in part, reversed in part, and remanded*, 329 F.3d 437 (6th Cir.), *cert denied*, 540 U.S. 1074 (2003)

[281] *See* Messenger v. Gruner + Jahr Printing and Publishing, 175 F.3d 262, 264 (2d Cir. 1999).

[282] Cairns v. Franklin Mint Co., 292 F.3d 1139 (9th Cir. 2002).

[283] No. 05 CIV. 3939 (CM), 2008 WL 4127830 (S.D.N.Y. Sept. 2, 2008).

[284] *Id.*

4.11. REMEDIES

4.11.1. Privacy

Remedies for an invasion of the right of privacy include injunctive relief[285] (although a preliminary injunction is rarely appropriate);[286] general damages based on mental distress[287] and property interests, if they are inextricably interwoven with an individual's personality;[288] and exemplary or punitive damages (on a showing of bad faith on the part of the defendant).[289]

4.11.2. Publicity

Remedies for an invasion of the right of publicity include injunctive relief;[290] general damages based on injury to feelings where the plaintiff has elected not to exploit his or her personality[291] or has exploited it without profit motive;[292] specific damages based on the fair market value of the use or endorsement[293] or, alternatively, based on the profits earned by the infringer;[294] and punitive damages where bad faith is proven.[295]

---

[285] *See* N.Y. CIVIL RIGHTS LAW §51 (2008).
[286] *See* Paulsen v. Personality Posters, 299 N.Y.S.2d 501 (N.Y. Supp. Ct. 1968).
[287] *See* Time, Inc. v. Hill, 385 U.S. 374 (1967).
[288] *See* Manger v. Kree Inst. of Electrolysis, 233 F.2d 5 (2d Cir. 1956).
[289] *See* Roberts v. Conde Nast Publ'ns, 146 N.Y.S. 493 (N.Y. App. Div. 1955).
[290] *See* Uhlaender v. Henricksen, 316 F. Supp. 1277 (D. Minn. 1970).
[291] *See* Grant v. Esquire, Inc., 367 F. Supp. 876.
[292] *See* Hogan v. A.S. Barnes & Co., 114 U.S.P.Q. 314, No. 8645, 1957 WL 7316 (Pa. Commw. Ct. June 19, 1957).
[293] *See* Hirsch U.S.C. Johnson & Sons, 90 Wis. 2d 379 (1979).
[294] *See* Factors Etc., Inc. v. Pro Arts, 496 F. Supp. 1090 (S.D.N.Y. 1980), *rev'd. on other grounds*, 652 F.2d 278 (2d Cir. 1981), cert denied 456 U.S. 927 (1982).
[295] *See* Nat'l Bank of Commerce v. Shaklee Corp., 503 F. Supp. 533 (W.D. Tex. 1980).

— CHAPTER 5 —

INTERNATIONAL COPYRIGHT TREATIES

5.1. The Berne Convention
5.2. The WIPO Copyright Treat (Geneva 1996)
5.3. The Universal Copyright Convention (UCC)
5.4. The Buenos Aires Convention
5.5. The Convention for the Protection of Producers of Phonograms against Unauthorized Duplication of Their Phonograms (Geneva 1971) (the Phonogram Convention)
5.6. The WIPO Performances and Phonograms Treaty (Geneva 1996)

5.1. THE BERNE CONVENTION

5.1.1. Introduction

The author Victor Hugo was one of the early instigators of the development of the Berne Convention. The Berne Convention was first accepted in Berne Switzerland in 1886 and addresses the rights of authors and artists in their works. The Berne Convention established an early framework for worldwide protection of intellectual property rights. A copy of the Berne Convention text is available at http://www.wipo.org.

5.1.1.1. The Conventions and the Union

The Berne Convention is not a single international treaty but rather a series of treaties commencing with the original Berne Convention (1886) followed by the Additional Act of Paris (1896), the Berlin Revision (1908), the Additional Protocol of Berne (1914), the Rome Revision (1928), the Brussels Revision (1948), the Stockholm Revision (1967), and the Paris Revision (1971). The level of protection has, throughout the history of the Convention, gradually and consistently increased.[1] A signatory to any one of these treaties, although bound only to that level of protection accorded by the specific treaty under

---

[1] STEPHEN M. STEWART, INTERNATIONAL COPYRIGHT AND NEIGHBOURING RIGHTS §5.07 (Lexis Nexis UK 1983) (hereinafter "S. STEWART").

which it joined[2] (e.g., the Rome Act of 1928), automatically makes that member state a member of the Berne Union and establishes international copyright relations with all other members.[3] (It should be noted that a new member may not ratify or accede to an earlier version of the Convention.)[4]

The Berne Union is open to all countries that will agree to accede to the standards of the current act,[5] and although separate levels of protection exist between signatories to prior acts and the current act, there is no separate administration of the different acts; the Union functions as one entity from a legal, administrative, and financial point of view.[6]

5.1.1.2. Minimum Standards of Protection

The convention establishes certain minimum standards of protection for authors in all member states (with certain limited variations)[7] to which the domestic law of that state must conform.[8] While some member states have held that these minimums arise directly from the accession to the convention (i.e. that the rights arise *jure conventionis*),[9] others, most notably the United States, have taken the position that the only way that these minimum standards of protection may exist is when they are implemented by domestic legislation.[10] Member states may enact domestic laws granting greater protection to authors under their jurisdiction than that afforded by the Convention[11] and may enter into bilateral agreements extending those protections to other countries' nationals. Nonetheless, it is a basic

---

[2] Berne Convention for the Protection of Literary and Artistic Works (Paris Act 1971) art. 32. [hereinafter citations to this Berne Convention will refer simply to the article in question as "Art.—", and to the Treaty's Appendix as "App. Art.—".]

[3] *Id.*

[4] Art. 34.

[5] Art. 29.

[6] S. STEWART, *supra* note 1, §5.06.

[7] Art. 30.

[8] Art. 36.

[9] S. STEWART, *supra* note 1, §5.04.

[10] The Berne Implementation Act of 1988 §2 (1) (P.L. 100-568 10/21/88, 102 Stat. 2853). *See U.S. Copyright Law, supra* §1.1.3.

[11] Art. 19.

premise of the convention that, except for certain limited exceptions,[12] authors protected by the convention shall be accorded by all member states the same protections that the member state accords its own authors.[13] This is known as "national treatment."

5. 1.2. Subject Matter of Copyright

5.1.2.1. Protectable Works

Article 2 of the Berne Convention[14] provides a very broad definition of "literary and artistic works" as including "every production in the literary, scientific and artistic domain, whatever may be the mode or form of its expression,"[15] and extends protection to include translations, adaptations, arrangements of music,[16] and collections and encyclopedic works with respect to their arrangement and the author's creative contribution.[17]

It is left to the discretion of the member state as to whether or not the work must be fixed in material form[18] and whether or not governmental publications[19] or political speeches[20] receive protection.

Protections of the Convention do not apply to "news of the day or to miscellaneous facts having the character of mere items of press information."[21]

5.1.2.2. National Eligibility

The Convention protects:[22]

1. Authors who are nationals of a member country for works, whether or not they are published;

---

[12] For example, droit de suite rights under art. 14ter. *See Berne Convention and the WIPO Copyright Treaty, infra* §5.3.3.2.
[13] Art. 5.
[14] Use of the term *Berne Convention* refers to the Paris Act 1971 unless otherwise noted.
[15] Art. 2(1).
[16] Art. 2(3).
[17] Art. 2(5).
[18] Art. 2(2).
[19] Art. 2(4).
[20] Art. 3.
[21] Art. 2(8).
[22] Art. 3.

2. Authors whose works are first published in a member country or simultaneously (i.e., within thirty days) in a country outside of the Union and in a member country;

3. Authors who are not nationals of a member country but who maintain a habitual residence there.

Publication refers to publications by the consent of the author in a manufactured form. Dramatic performance, literary readings[23] or exhibitions of art are not considered publications.[24]

5.1.3. Exclusive Rights in Copyrighted Works

5.1.3.1. Basic Rights

Like United States copyright law, the Berne Convention grants its authors a bundle of basic rights, although they are defined somewhat differently than those provided by United States copyright.[25] Those rights include the exclusive rights of reproduction,[26] translation,[27] adaptation,[28] dramatic and musical-works performance,[29] public recitation of literary works,[30] broadcast rights,[31] and cinematographic adaptation and reproduction rights.[32] Even though these rights are labeled differently than the rights granted under United States copyright law, they are nevertheless functionally the same. For example, such rights as the rights of translation, adaptation, and cinematographic adaptation under the Convention would be protected under the adaptation right of United States copyright.

In addition to these rights, the Rome Convention grants its authors certain moral rights (to be discussed in more detail *infra* §5.3).

---

[23] Art. 3(3).
[24] *Id.*
[25] *See* discussion *supra* §1.4.
[26] Art. 9.
[27] Art. 8.
[28] Art. 12.
[29] Art. 11.
[30] Art. 11^{ier}.
[31] Art. 11bis.
[32] Art. 14.

5.1.3.2. Limitations of the Basic Rights

Unlike the United States, which provides specific limitations to each of the exclusive rights conferred by it (excluding fair use, to be discussed *infra* §5.4), the limitations provided under Berne are limited to certain rights and are drawn to allow individual member countries to determine the extent of those limitations. For example, the right of reproduction may be limited by member countries to permit the reproduction of works in special cases, provided that such reproduction does not harm the interests of the author.[33] Berne provides for the creation of a compulsory license (similar to the United States)[34] for musical works at the election of a member state and subject to the imposition of "equitable remuneration" for the benefit of the author.[35] Broadcast rights are subject to limitations to be determined by the member state (subject to the right of the author to receive "equitable remuneration"), including the rights of making "ephemeral recordings" and archive copies.[36]

5.1.3.3. Droit Moral/Droit de Suite

The Berne Convention provides for two additional classes of exclusive rights for the benefit of authors. Those rights are *droit moral* (or "moral right") and *droit de suite* (the right to follow a work and receive a percentage of the proceeds of sequential sales).[37] (Both of these rights developed under French law, which is why they are frequently referred to by their French names.)[38]

a. Droit Moral or Moral Right

Moral rights recognize that "an author's work is a [continuing] reflection of the personality of the creator,"[39] much the way that a

---

[33] Art. 9(2).
[34] 17 U.S.C. §115 (2006).
[35] Art. 13.
[36] Art. 11bis.
[37] Art. 14ter.
[38] *See* STEWART, *supra* note 1, §5.17 *et. seq.*
[39] *Id.* §5.17 citing WIPO GUIDE TO BERNE 6bis 1.

trademark reflects on the good will encompassed by a trademark. There are three basic moral rights:[40]

1. *The right of publication*, which is the right to decide whether or not the work is to be made public or (under French law)[41] the right to withdraw the work after publication;

2. *The right of paternity*, which is the right to claim authorship of a published work by (a) demanding that the author's name appears in an appropriate place, (b) preventing others from claiming authorship, or (c) preventing the use of the author's name in connection with someone else's work;[42]

3. *The right of integrity*, which is the right of the author to protect his or her reputation by preserving the integrity of the work. The test as to whether or not the integrity of a work is damaged varies among jurisdictions between a subjective test (does the author honestly believe the alterations harm his reputation?) and the objective test (would a reasonable person think the alteration prejudicial to the honor and reputation of the author?).[43]

What makes these rights particularly distinctive is that they exist *independently* of the author's economic rights and may be enforceable *after* the transfer of rights to the work.[44] Droit moral may be enforced by the author or, in some jurisdiction, after his or her death by statutorily defined designees for as long as his or her economic rights survive.[45] Droit moral may or may not be transferable by the author, depending on the law of the member state.[46]

---

[40] *Id.* §5.17.
[41] *Id.* §5.18.
[42] *Id.* §5.19.
[43] Art. $6^{bis}(1)$.
[44] See S. STEWART, *supra* note 1, §5.21.
[45] Art. $6^{bis}(2)$. Enforcement of the right after death may be subject to some limitations in some countries of the Union.
[46] E.g., it is inalienable in France (Law No. 57-298 of March 11, 1957, art. 6) and waivable in the Netherlands (Copyright Law of the Netherlands 1925 [revised October 1972], art. 25).
[47-55] [Reserved.]

b. Droit de Suite

Although applicable to writers and composers with respect to their original manuscripts,[56] the principle of droit de suite primarily allows fine artists (e.g., painters and sculptors) to share in the marketing of their original works as they pass through economic channels. To effectuate this purpose, the Convention provides artists (as well as writers and musicians with respect to their manuscripts) with an *"inalienable* right to share in the proceeds of *any* sale of the work subsequent to the first transfer of the work" by the author (emphasis added)[57] if the country to which the author is a national recognizes such a right and only to the extent permitted by the country where protection is claimed.[58]

Application of this right varies greatly within the Union going from no recognition in Anglo-Saxon countries,[59] to recognition of the right without means of implementation or enforcement[60] in others, to various forms of recognition where variations exist in the amount of the royalty (of 2 to 6 percent of the sales price), to whether or not the royalty is applicable to all sales (3 percent of all sales in France)[61] or only against the appreciated value of the work (Italy).[62]

5.1.4. Fair Use

The Berne Convention does not define the doctrine of fair use with the clarity of United States copyright law[65] but, nonetheless, it recognizes exceptions to an author's exclusive rights similar to those recognized under the United States doctrine of fair use. For example, member countries may permit reproduction "of such works in certain special cases, provided that such reproduction does not conflict with a normal exploitation of the work and does not unreasonably prejudice

---

[56] Art. 14ter(1).
[57] *Id.*
[58] Art. 14ter(2). This is referred to as a standard of material reciprocity.
[59] *See* S. STEWART, *supra* note 1, §5.53.
[60] E.g., Luxembourg, Morocco, and Turkey. *See* S. STEWART *supra* note 1.
[61] *Id.*
[62] *Id.*
[63] [Reserved.]
[64] [Reserved.]
[65] *See supra* §1.5. Admittedly, fair use is one of the most misunderstood doctrines under the U.S. copyright law.

the legitimate interests of the author,"[66] and it allows uses in conjunction with news and current events where such use is not expressly reserved.[67] Moreover, all members are to authorize the use of quotations in news sources and for teaching purposes, subject to the restraint of fair practice.[68] (Such uses in the United States would fall under the doctrine of fair use.) Unlike the United States, where the fact that a work may be unpublished is one, albeit very important, factor in the four-part fair use test,[69] the Berne Convention *requires* that the work have been "lawfully made available to the public" as a prerequisite to any finding of fair use or fair practice.[70] This requirement is in line with the convention's provision of the droit moral of the right of publication.[71]

5.1.5. Creation and Commencement

There are two elements to consider in the creation of copyright: first, when and where the law becomes applicable, and second, when the law recognizes the work. These principles interact as follows in determining creation and commencement of copyright:

1. Protection is automatically afforded to every author who is a national of one of the countries of the Union and to authors whose works are first published in a member country,[72] and both enjoy the rights recognized by the Convention and protection afforded by member countries (in that country) that the member affords to its own nationals.[73]

2. The Convention authorizes member countries to determine by legislation whether or not a work must be embodied in tangible form before protection adheres.[74]

---

[66] Art. 9(2).
[67] Art. 10bis.
[68] Art. 10.
[69] *See supra* §1.5.2.
[70] Art. 10(1).
[71] *See Berne Convention and the WIPO Copyright Treaty, supra* §5.3.3.1.
[72] Art. 3.
[73] Art. 5.
[74] Art. 2(2). *See U.S. Copyright Law, supra* §1.5.

3. Therefore, copyright protection will commence for nationals of a member country for their works *prior* to embodiment[75] in those countries that recognize such protection for their own authors and after embodiment in all other member countries.

4. However, protection for a non-national of the Union will not commence until his or her work is *published* in a member country.[76]

5.1.6. Ownership

The Berne Convention vests original ownership of a work in its author[73] or authors (with respect to joint works).[77] However, it fails to define the term *author*, other than to aver that the person under whose name it appears is deemed to be the author.[78] It is, therefore, left up to the member state where protection is sought to determine who is an author.[79] This ambiguity serves to bridge the gap between those countries that follow the French system in which only individual human beings are recognized as authors and the Anglo-Saxon-based systems that recognize legal entities as authors or original rights owners[80] (under the concept of "works made for hire").[81]

5.1.7. Formalities of Notice and Registration

There are no formalities of notice, registration, or deposit required for the enjoyment of protections under the Convention.[82] Although fixation of the work may be required,[83] this is not deemed a formality in that it becomes part of what is defined as a work rather than a condition for a work's protection. Nonetheless, compliance with formalities may be required by member states for their *own* nationals or works published within their own territory (because this prohibition

---

[75] *See* France, art. 41(3), Law No. 57-298 of March 11, 1957.
[76] Art. 3.
[73] Art. 2(6).
[77] *See* Art. 7bis.
[78] Art. 15(1).
[79] S. STEWART, *supra* note 1, §5.29.
[80] *Id.*
[81] *See supra* §1.7.
[82] Art. 5(2).
[83] Art. 2(2).

applies to the recognition of the rights of the citizens of other member nations)[84] and may be required of others where the formalities that are imposed are administrative or result in additional rights that are offered as incentives for compliance with these formalities.[85]

5.1.8. Duration of Copyright

The basic measure of protection under the Convention is the life of the author plus fifty years[86] (or, with respect to joint works, life plus fifty years from the death of the last surviving co-author).[87] Anonymous, pseudonymous (unless they are claimed by or identified with the author during the term, thus applying the life plus fifty duration), and cinematographic works[88] receive a term of protection of fifty years after the work is made available to the public or created, if not made available to the public. Photographs and works of applied art (if protectable)[89] are protected for twenty-five years from creation.[90]

Member countries may grant terms of protection in excess of those provided in the Convention,[91] and members under the prior Rome act may retain shorter durations although acceding to the other terms of the present act.[92] The term of protection is governed by the legislation of the country where protection is sought. However, unless that country specifically provides to the contrary, the term will not exceed the term fixed in the country of origin.[93] This latter element, which is designed to encourage countries to extend their duration of protection, is the only major exception to the principle of national treatment (i.e., that foreign authors be treated the same as nationals of that country).

---

[84] Art. 5(2).
[85] For example *see supra* §1.8.
[86] Art. 7(1).
[87] Art. 7(3).
[88] Art. 7(2).
[89] Art. 2(7).
[90] Art. 7(4).
[91] Art. 7(6).
[92] Art. 7(7).
[93] Art. 7(8).

5.1.9. Transfers

The Convention does not directly address the issue of transferability of rights except to separate out the right of droit moral from an economic transfer[94] and to make the right of droit de suite nontransferable.[95] Regulation of transfers is left to the legislation of the member states and varies from recognition of free alienability of rights under Anglo-Saxon-influenced laws to strict prohibition of transfer under Continental European laws (e.g., Germany and Austria), which recognize only the granting of a "right to use."

5.1.10. Termination and Renewal Rights

The Convention does not provide for termination or renewal rights. The rationale for those provisions under United States copyright law (i.e., protecting the author from not properly enjoying the fruits of his or her labor by virtue of a "bad deal")[96] are addressed in part by the droit de suite provisions of the Convention and by the legislation of member nations. For example, under French law, payment terms of an assignment are subject to the value of the work,[97] and it requires the author to share in the proceeds of exploitation of unforeseen or unforeseeable methods developed after an assignment.[98]

5.1.11. Infringement

In order to develop a cause of action for infringement under the Convention, the following elements must be determined:

5.1.11.1. Plaintiff

Under the Convention, the author named on the work (absent proof to the contrary) is entitled to institute actions to protect the work.[99]

---

[94] Art. 6bis(1). *See also Berne Convention and the WIPO Copyright Treaty, supra* §5.3.3.1.
[95] Art. 14ter(1). *See also Berne Convention and the WIPO Copyright Treaty, supra* §5.3.3.3.
[96] *See supra* §1.12.
[97] French Law No. 57-298 of March 11, 1957, arts. 35-36.
[98] French Law No. 57-298 of March 11, 1957, art. 38.
[99] Art. 15(1)-(2).

Anonymous or pseudonymous works (where the identity of the true author is not conclusively known) may be prosecuted by the publisher whose name appears on the work.[100] Unpublished *anonymous* works where the author is known to be a national of a Union member are protected by a party to be designated by that country.[101] Assignee-copyright owners as plaintiffs are determined solely under local legislation of a member country.[102]

5.1.11.2. Applicability of the Berne Convention

Applicability of Berne Convention protections is determined by whether or not (1) the author is a national (or resident) of a Union member, or (2) the work was first published in a country of the Union.[103] If either of the foregoing conditions are met, then the work is protected.

5.1.11.3. Applicable Law

The actual procedural rights and remedies accorded in an infringement action are determined by the law of the country in which protection is claimed.[104]

5.1.12. Remedies

The remedies generally may include both criminal actions and civil relief such as injunctive relief, seizure of infringing goods, and damages.[105] The Convention extends the relief of seizure of infringing goods to any country of the Union where the work enjoys legal protection[106] and includes a prohibition on importation of infringing reproductions of the work, even from a country where the work is not protected.[107]

---

[100] Art. 15(3).
[101] Art. 15(4).
[102] *See Berne Convention and the WIPO Copyright Treaty, supra* §5.9.
[103] Art. 3. 99 Art. 5(1).
[104] Art. 5(1).
[105] *See* S. STEWART, *supra* note 1, §§5.42 *et seq.*
[106] Art. 16(1).
[107] Art. 16(2).

5.1.13. Developing Nations

The Berne Convention makes special provision for developing countries (as determined "in conformity with the established practice of the General Assembly of the United Nations")[108] that for as long as they maintain their developing-country status they will have the right to create compulsory licenses with respect to translation[109] and reproduction rights[110] for protected works. The exercise of these rights is limited to a system of nonexclusive and nontransferable licenses to be granted by a competent governmental authority and triggered by the unavailability of the work pursuant to a voluntary license issued by the author/owner.[111]

5.1.14. Members of the Berne Convention

Status as of August 3, 2017 Accessible at:
http://www.wipo.int/treaties/en/ShowResults.jsp?lang=en&treaty_id=15

State	Date on Which Membership in Berne Took Effect	Latest Act by Which the State Is Substantively Bound and Date on Which the Ratification of or Accession to Such Act Became Effective
Albania	March 6, 1994	Paris: March 6, 1994
Algeria	April 19, 1998	Paris: April 19, 1998
Andorra	June 2, 2004	Paris: June 2, 2004
Antigua & Barbados	March 15, 2000	Paris: March 15, 2000
Argentina	June 10, 1967	Brussels: June 10, 1967
Armenia	Oct. 19, 2000	Paris: Oct. 19, 2000
Australia	April 14, 1928	Paris: March 1, 1978
Austria	Oct. 1, 1920	Paris: Aug. 21, 1982
Azerbaijan	June 4, 1999	Paris: June 4, 1999
Bahamas	July 10, 1973	Brussels: July 10, 1973

---

[108] App. Art. I(1).
[109] App. Art. II.
[110] App. Art. III.
[111] App. Arts. II-II.

Bahrain	March 2, 1997	Paris: March 2, 1997
Bangladesh	May 4, 1999	Paris: May 4, 1999
Barbados	July 30, 1983	Paris: July 30, 1983
Belarus	Dec. 12, 1997	Paris: Dec. 12, 1997
Belgium	Dec. 5, 1887	Brussels: Aug. 1, 1951
Belize	June 17, 2000	Paris: June 17, 2000
Benin	Jan. 3, 1961	Paris: March 12, 1975
Bhutan	Nov. 25, 2004	Paris: Nov. 25, 2004
Bolivia	Nov.4, 1993	Paris: Nov. 4, 1993
Bosnia and Herzegovina	March 1, 1992	Paris: March 1, 1992
Botswana	April 15, 1998	Paris: April 15, 1998
Brazil	Feb. 9, 1922	Paris: April 20, 1975
Brunei Darussalam	Aug. 30, 2006	Paris: Aug. 30, 2006
Bulgaria	Dec. 5, 1921	Paris: Dec. 4, 1974
Burkina Faso	Aug. 19, 1963	Paris: Jan. 24, 1976
Burundi	Jan. 12, 2016	Paris: April 12, 2016
Cabo Verde	July 7, 1997	Paris: July 7, 1997
Cameroon	Sept. 21, 1964	Paris: Oct. 10, 1974
Canada	April 10, 1928	Paris: June 26, 1998
Central African Rep.	Sept. 3, 1977	Paris: Sept. 3, 1977
Chad	Nov. 25, 1971	Brussels: Nov. 25, 1971
Chile	June 5, 1970	Paris: July 10, 1975
China	Oct. 15, 1992	Paris: Oct. 15, 1992
Colombia	March 7, 1988	Paris: March 7, 1988
Comoros	April 17, 2005	Paris: April 17, 2005
Congo	May 8, 1962	Paris: Dec. 5, 1975
Cook Islands	May 3, 2017	Paris: Aug. 3, 2017
Costa Rica	June. 10, 1978	Paris: June 10, 1978
Côte d'Ivoire	January 1, 1962	Paris: Articles 1 to 21: Oct.. 10, 1974
Croatia	Oct. 8, 1991	Paris: Oct. 8, 1991
Cuba	Feb. 20, 1997	Paris: Feb. 20, 1997
Cyprus	Feb. 24, 1964	Paris: July 27, 1983

Czech Republic	Jan. 1, 1993	Paris: Jan. 1, 1993
Democratic People's Republic of Korea	April 28, 2003	Paris: April 28, 2003
Democratic Republic of the Congo	October 8, 1963	Paris: Jan. 31, 1975
Denmark	July 1, 1903	Paris: June 30, 1979
Djibouti	May 13, 2002	May 13, 2002
Dominica	Aug. 7, 1999	Paris: Aug. 7, 2000
Dominican Rep.	Dec. 24, 1997	Paris: Dec. 24, 1997
Ecuador	Oct. 9, 1991	Paris: Oct. 9, 1991
Egypt	June 7, 1977	Paris: June 7, 1977
El Salvador	Feb. 19, 2994	Paris: Feb. 19, 1994
Equatorial Guinea	June 26, 1997	Paris: June 26, 1997
Estonia	Oct. 26, 1994	Paris: Oct. 26, 1994
Fiji	Dec. 1, 1971	Brussels: Dec. 1, 1971
Finland	April 1, 1928	Brussels: Jan. 28, 1963
France	Dec. 5, 1887	Paris: Oct. 10, 1974
Gabon	March 26, 1962	Paris: June 10, 1974
Gambia	March 7, 1993	Paris: March 7, 1993
Georgia	May 16, 1995	Paris: May 16, 1995
Germany	Dec. 5, 1887	Paris: Oct. 10, 1974
Ghana	Oct. 11, 1991	Paris: Oct. 11, 1991
Greece	Nov. 9, 1920	Paris: March 8, 1986
Grenada	Sept. 22, 1998	Paris: Sept. 22, 1998
Guatemala	July 28, 1997	Paris: July 28, 1997
Guinea	Nov. 20, 1980	Paris: Nov. 20, 1980
Guinea-Bissau	July 22, 1991	Paris: July 22, 1991
Guyana	Oct. 25, 1994	Paris: Oct. 25, 1994
Haiti	Jan. 11, 1996	Paris: Jan. 11, 1996
Holy See	Sept. 12, 1935	Paris: April 24, 1975
Honduras	Jan. 25, 1990	Paris: Jan. 25, 1990
Hungary	Feb. 14, 1922	Paris: Oct. 10, 1974
Iceland	Sept. 7, 1947	Rome: Aug. 25, 1999

India	April 1, 1928	Paris: May 6, 1984
Indonesia	Sept. 5, 1997	Paris: Sept. 5, 1997
Ireland	Oct. 5, 1927	Paris: Jan. 2, 1990
Israel	March 24, 1950	Brussels: Aug. 1, 1951
Italy	Dec. 5, 1887	Paris: Nov. 14, 1979
Jamaica	Jan. 1, 1994	Paris: Jan. 1, 1994
Japan	July 15, 1899	Paris: April 24, 1975
Jordan	July 28, 1999	Paris: July 28, 1999
Kazakhstan	April 12, 1999	Paris: April 12, 1999
Kenya	June 11, 1993	Paris: June 11, 1993
Korea, Rep. of	Aug, 21, 1996	Paris: Aug 21, 1996
Kuwait	Sept. 2, 1014	Paris: Dec. 2, 2014
Kyrgyzstan	June 8, 1999	Paris: June 8, 1999
Loa People's Democratic Republic	Dec. 14, 2011	Paris: March 14, 2012
Latvia	Aug. 11, 1995	Paris: Aug. 11, 1995
Lebanon	Sept. 30, 1947	Rome: Sept. 30, 1947
Lesotho	Sept. 28, 1989	Paris: Sept. 28, 1989
Liberia	March 8, 1989	Paris: March 8, 1989
Libya	Sept. 28, 1976	Paris: Sept. 28, 1976
Liechtenstein	July 30, 1931	Brussels: Aug. 1, 1951
Lithuania	Dec. 14, 1994	Paris: Dec. 25, 1994
Luxembourg	June 20, 1888	Paris: April 20, 1975
Madagascar	Jan; 1, 1966	Brussels: Jan. 1, 1966
Malawi	Oct. 12, 1991	Paris: Oct. 12, 1961
Malaysia	Oct. 1, 1990	Paris: Oct. 1, 1990
Mali	March 19, 1962	Paris: Dec. 5, 1977
Malta	Sept. 21, 1964	Rome: Sept. 21, 1964
Mauritania	Feb. 6, 1973	Paris: Sept. 21, 1976
Mauritius	May 10, 1989	Paris: May 10, 1989
Mexico	June 11, 1967	Paris: Dec, 17, 1974
Micronesia (Federated States of Moldova)	Nov. 2, 1995	Paris: Nov. 2, 1995
Monaco	May 30, 1889	Paris: Nov. 23, 1974

Mongolia	March 12, 1998	Paris: March 12, 1998
Montenegro	June 3, 2006	Paris: June 3, 2006
Morocco	June 16, 1917	Brussels: May 22, 1952
Mozambique	August 22, 2013	Paris: Nov. 22, 2013
Namibia	Dec. 24, 1993	Paris: Dec. 24, 1993
Nepal	January 11, 2006	Paris: Jan. 11, 2006
Netherlands	Nov. 1, 1912	Brussels: Jan. 7, 1973
New Zealand	April 24, 1928	Rome: Dec. 4, 1947
Nicaragua	Aug. 23, 2000	Paris: Aug. 23, 2000
Niger	May 2, 1962	Paris: May 21, 1975
Nigeria	Sept. 14, 1993	Paris: Sept. 24, 1993
Niue	June 24, 2016	Paris: Sept. 24, 2016
Norway	April 13, 1896	Brussels: Jan. 28, 1963
Oman	July 14, 1999	Paris: July 14, 1999
Pakistan	July 5, 1948	Rome: July 5, 1948
Panama	June 8, 1996	Paris: June 8, 1996
Paraguay	Jan. 2, 1992	Paris: Jan. 2, 1992
Peru	Aug. 20, 1988	Paris: Aug. 20, 1988
Philippines	Aug. 1, 1951	Brussels: Aug. 1, 1951
Poland	Jan. 28, 1920	Paris: Oct. 22, 1994
Portugal	March 29, 1911	Paris: Jan. 12, 1979
Qatar	July 5, 2000	Paris: July 5, 2000
Republic of Moldova	August 1, 1995	Paris: Nov. 2, 1995
Romania	Jan. 1, 1927	Paris: Sept. 9, 1998
Russian Federation	March 13, 1995	Paris: March 13, 1995
Rwanda	March 1, 1984	Paris: March 1, 1984
Saint Kitts & Nevis	April 9, 1995	Paris: April 9, 1995
Saint Lucia	Aug., 24, 1993	Paris: Aug. 24, 1993
Saint Vincent & the Grenadines	Aug. 29, 1995	Paris: Aug. 29, 1995
Samoa	July 21, 2006	Paris: July 21, 2006
Sao Tome and Principe	March 14, 2016	Paris: June 14, 2016

Saudi Arabia	March 11, 2004	Paris: March 11, 2004
Senegal	Aug. 25, 1962	Paris: Aug. 12, 1975
Serbia	April 27, 1992	Paris: April 27, 1992
Singapore	Dec. 21, 1998	Paris: Dec. 21, 1998
Slovakia	Jan. 1, 1993	Paris: Jan. 1, 1993
Slovenia	June 25, 1991	Paris: June 25, 1991
South Africa	Oct. 3, 1928	Brussels: Aug. 1, 1951
Spain	Dec. 5, 1887	Paris: Oct. 10, 1974
Sri Lanka	July 20, 1959	Rome: July 20, 1959
Sudan	Dec. 28, 2000	Paris: Dec. 28, 2000
Suriname	Feb. 23, 1977	Paris: Feb. 23, 1977
Swaziland	Dec. 14, 1998	Paris: Dec. 14, 1998
Sweden	Aug. 1, 1904	Paris: Oct. 10, 1974
Switzerland	Dec, 5, 1887	Paris: Sept. 25, 1993
Syrian Arab Republic	June 11, 2004	Paris: June 11, 2004
Tajikistan	March 9, 2000	Paris: March 9, 2000
Thailand	July 17, 1931	Berlin: July 17, 1931
The former Yugoslav Republic of Macedonia	Sept. 8, 1996	Paris: Sept. 8, 1991
Togo	April 30, 1975	Paris: April 30, 1975
Tonga	June 14, 2001	Paris: June 14, 2001
Trinidad & Tobago	Aug. 16, 1988	Paris: Aug. 16, 1988
Tunisia	Dec. 5, 1887	Paris: Aug. 16, 1975
Turkey	Jan. 1, 1952	Brussels: Jan. 1, 1952
Tuvalu	March 2. 2017	Paris: June 2, 2017
Ukraine	Oct. 25, 1995	Paris: Oct. 25, 1995
United Arab Emirates	July 14, 2004	Paris: July 14, 2004
United Kingdom	Dec. 5, 1887	Paris: Jan. 2, 1990
United Republic of Tanzania	July 25, 1994	Paris: July 24, 1994
United States of America	March 1, 1989	Paris: March 1, 1989
Uruguay	July 10, 1967	Paris: Dec. 28, 1979
Uzbekistan	April 12, 2005	Paris: April 19, 2005
Vanuatu	September 27, 2012	Paris: Dec. 27, 2012

Venezuela	Dec. 30, 1982	Paris: Dec. 30, 1982
Viet Nam	Oct. 26, 2004	Paris: Oct. 26, 2004
Yemen	July 14, 2008	Paris: July 14, 2008
Zambia	Jan. 2, 1992	Paris: Jan. 2, 1992
Zimbabwe	April 18, 1980	Rome: April 18, 1980

(Total : 174 States)

5.2. THE WIPO COPYRIGHT TREATY (GENEVA 1996)

In order to keep up with changing technology, the Berne Convention has been revised approximately every twenty years (at first) and then every ten years (more recently). In 1996, following six years of preparatory work and in lieu of revising Berne, a diplomatic conference sponsored by the World Intellectual Property Organization involving representatives of over one hundred and twenty countries, seven intergovernmental organizations and approximately seventy-five non-governmental organizations adopted two international copyright treaties: the WIPO Copyright Treaty and the WIPO Performances and Phonograms Treaty.[112]

This new treaty does not supersede or replace the Berne Convention; it supplements it as a "special agreement within the meaning of Article 20 of the Berne Convention."[113] It is intended to recognize "the need to introduce new international rules and clarify the interpretation of certain existing rules in order to provide adequate solutions to the questions raised by new economic, social, cultural and technological developments, [and] ... the profound impact of the development and convergence of information and communication technologies on the creation and use of artistic works."[114]

The treaty entered into force on March 6, 2002 and countries across the world continue to accede to the treaty provisions. The treaty indicates the direction in which national copyright laws have been moving or will likely be moving in the near future. For example, the United States adopted the Digital Millennium Copyright Act to comply with the provisions of this treaty and in March 16, 2000, the European

---

[112] *See infra* §5.6.
[113] WIPO Copyright Treaty (Geneva 1996) Art. 1(1) (hereinafter cited as WCT).
[114] WCT Preamble.

Council approved the treaty on behalf of the European Community. The WCT generally addresses three categories of rights of artists and authors: (1) distribution rights, (ii) rental, rights and (3) the right of communication to the public.

5.2.1. Key Treaty Provisions

In reviewing the WIPO Copyright Treaty of 1996, one can identify three types of provisions. The first are intended to address the relationship between the WCT and Berne. The second are substantive provisions. Third are the administrative provisions.

5.2.1.1. WCT and Berne

A number of provisions in the new treaty (e.g. Articles 1, 3, 10, 13, and 14) are intended to clarify the fact that this treaty does not supersede the Berne Convention or derogate from the rights provided by the Berne Convention. As noted above, the treaty is intended to supplement the Berne Convention in order to address changes brought about by technology and to internationally harmonize some of the responses to these changes that have been adopted by individual states.

5.2.1.2. Substantive Provisions

Articles 2, 4-9, 11 and 12 reflect clarifications and substantive enhancements to the Berne Convention. A summary of these provisions is instructive.

Article 2. Scope of Copyright Protection. This article clearly asserts that copyright extends to the protection of "expressions and not ... ideas, procedures, methods of operation or mathematical concepts." This language is similar to U.S. copyright law. It differs from the approach taken by the Berne Convention in that Berne had previously not attempted to define copyright, but rather had asserted that protection was to be accorded to "literary and artistic works' ... in the literary, scientific and artistic domain, whatever may be the mode or form of its expression" and to illustrate what was meant by this terminology, Berne noted (without necessary limitation) the types of works that were intended to be covered by this identification. As can be seen in the controversy in the U.S. over the subject matter of copyright,[115] there are ambiguities and problems in such an approach that this more definitional effort is intended to address.

Article 4. Computer Programs. In a sense, this provision is a continuation of the illustrative method of subject matter adopted under Berne in that it simply identifies computer programs "whatever may be the mode of form of their expression" as being protected as literary works. It is an important addition simply because computer software has become such an important economic market.

Article 5. Compilations of Data (Databases). This is another illustrative provision intended to recognize an important economic interest. Significantly, it reaffirms the definitional effort of Article 2 (clarifying that the protection extends only to expression and not content of the database), which is in very close accord with U.S. law on this point.[116]

Article 6. Right of Distribution. This article breaks out and makes explicit the right of distribution which is implicit in Berne. That is to say, the owner of the right shall have the exclusive right to control and authorize the distribution of the original work or copies of that work through sale or other transfer. However, it allows for a continuing diversity of treatment by allowing for the provisions of the "first sale doctrine" where, for example, in the United States the sale or other transfer of ownership by the author generally extinguishes that author's rights of distribution in relation to that copy.[117] Both in the United States and in greater or lesser measure in many other countries, there are exceptions so that an author may receive royalties for home copying, rental and other types of retransfers of legitimately acquired copies.[118]

Article 7. Right of Rental. This article further elaborates on the principle identified in Art. 6, and specifies that authors of computer programs, cinematographic works and phonograms shall have the right to authorize public rental of copies of their works. This right is limited by provisions which would allow, for example, the rental of a computer (with programs included), the continued existence of video rental stores (so long as this does not result in substantial copying that

---

[115] *See supra*, §1.2.
[116] *See supra*, §1.2.3.
[117] *See supra*, §1.4.1.3.
[118] *See e.g.*, D. Sinacore-Guinn, INTERNATIONAL COLLECTIVE ADMINISTRATION OF COPYRIGHTS AND NEIGHBORING RIGHTS (Little, Brown 1993).

would impair sales of video cassettes) and the maintenance of statutory licensing schemes for phonogram rentals.

Article 8. Right of Communication to the Public. This article is intended to plug some holes in the existing right of communication set forth in Berne which in various provisions of the Convention (i.e., Arts. 11, 11*bis*, 11*ter*, 14 and 14*bis*) had incrementally grown to cover specific types of communication to the public. While the article is now drafted in a way to cover any communication to the public, it is specifically intended to reach the internet and to clarify the fact that making a work computer accessible is a communication to the public.

Article 9. Duration of the Protection of Photographic Works. When photography began to develop as an art form in the late 19th century, there was substantial controversy as to whether photography involved substantial skill and creativity (when compared with traditional visual art forms) or if it simply represented technological achievement. This controversy resulted in substantial variation in the levels of protection accorded photography. In many countries, such copyright protection has been refused. As photography evolved, the creativity involved in photography was increasingly recognized; however; because photographs were denied copyright protection in many countries, those countries elected to protect photographs under a body of law known as neighboring rights with protections resembling copyright protection but which frequently included shorter terms of protection. Other countries, while electing to protect photographs under their formal copyright laws, nonetheless developed a similar strategy of protecting photographs for a more limited term than for other works. Berne finally recognized photographs as artistic works, in order to accommodate this diversity of protection allowed. The provision rectifies this discrepancy by asserting that photographs will receive the full term of copyright protection.

Article 10. Limitations and Exceptions. While many of the rights of copyright identified by the Berne Convention are phrased as absolute rights, the Convention itself contains a number of special exemptions either in the same article (such as in Article 9 (Paris) in relation to the right of reproduction) or in subsequent provisions (such as the limitation on the right of translation granted under Article 8 of Berne (Paris) and limited under Article V of the Appendix) in which the right is identified. Yet despite the fact that Berne provides explicit exceptions which are presumptively comprehensive (such that the absence of an explicit provision should argue that no exception should be allowed), other exceptions have arisen in various countries. What this article does is recognize the reality that such exemptions exist and, rather than prohibiting those exemptions, it imposes a standard of judgment which is to be used in evaluating those exemptions. Specifically, the WCT asserts that such exceptions are to occur in only "certain special cases" and those cases must "not conflict with [the] normal exploitation of the work and [must] not unreasonably prejudice the legitimate interests of the author."

Articles 11 and 12. Obligations concerning Technological Measures and Obligations concerning Rights Management Information. Because of the perceived severity of the threat of private copying presented by Digital Audio Tape machines (which could make CD quality copies) their distribution in the United States was restricted until an agreement was reached which included a requirement that manufacturers incorporate technology which would limit the making of multiple copies of phonograms.[119] These provisions of the WCT affirm that approach in relation to any technological advance and require that members protect against efforts to circumvent these types of technological protections of copyrighted works.

5.2.1.3. Administrative Provisions

Finally, the WCT includes certain administrative provisions governing its application including such elements as the creation of a special assembly (a kind of special Berne Union within the Berne Union),[120] restriction of membership to countries already adhering to Berne and certain other intergovernmental unions (such as the EU)[121] and establishment that the treaty shall come into force three months after 30 countries have ratified or acceded to the treaty.[122]

5.2.2. Adopting Parties as of July 17, 2017

The following countries have adopted the WCT, *available at*: http://www.wipo.int/treaties/en/ShowResults.jsp?lang=en&treaty_id=16

---

[119] *See supra* §1.4.1.6.
[120] Art. 15.
[121] Art. 17.
[122] Art. 20.

Status on July 17, 2017

State	Date on Which State Became Party to the Treaty
Albania	Aug. 6, 2005
Algeria	Jan. 31, 2014
Argentina	March 6, 2002
Armenia	March 6, 2005
Australia	July 26, 2005
Austria	March 14, 2010
Azerbaijan	April 11, 2006
Bahrain	Dec. 15, 2005
Belarus	March 6, 2002
Belgium	Aug. 30, 2006
Benin	April 16, 2006
Bolivia	(signature: December 20, 1966)
Bosnia & Herzegovina	Nov. 25, 2009
Botswana	Jan. 27, 2005
Brunei Darssalam	May 2, 2017
Bulgaria	March 6, 2002
Burkina Faso	March 6, 2002
Canada	August 13, 2014
Chile	March 6, 2002
China	June 9, 2007
Colombia	March 6, 2002
Costa Rica	March 6, 2002
Croatia	March 6, 2002
Cyprus	Nov. 4, 2003
Czech Republic	March 6, 2002
Dominican Republic	Jan. 10, 2006
Ecuador	March 6, 2002
El Salvador	March 6, 2002
Estonia	March 14, 2010
European Union (EU)	March 14, 2010
Finland	March 14, 2010
France	March 14, 2010

Gabon	March 6, 2002
Georgia	March 6, 2002
Germany	March 14, 2010
Ghana	Nov. 18, 2006
Greece	March 14, 2010
Guatemala	Feb. 4, 2003
Guinea	May 25, 2002
Honduras	May 20, 2002
Hungary	March 6, 2002
Indonesia	March 6, 2002
Ireland	March 14, 2010
Israel	(Signature: March 25, 1997)
Italy	March 14, 2010
Jamaica	June 12, 2002
Japan	March 6, 2002
Jordan	April 27, 2004
Kazakhstan	Nov. 12, 2004
Kenya	(Signature: Dec. 20, 1996)
Korea, Republic of	June 24, 2004
Kyrgyzstan	March 6, 2002
Latvia	March 6, 2002
Liechtenstein	April 30, 2007
Lithuania	March 6, 2002
Luxembourg	March 14, 2010
Madagascar	February 24, 2015
Malaysia	December 27, 2012
Mali	April 24, 2002
Malta	March 14, 2010
Mexico	March 6, 2002
Moldova, Republic of	March 6, 2002
Monoco	(Signature: Jan. 14, 1997)
Mongolia	Oct. 25, 2002
Montenegro	June 3, 2006
Nicaragua	March 6, 2002
Nigeria	(Signature: March 24, 1997)

Oman	Sept. 20, 2005
Panama	March 6, 2002
Paraguay	March 6, 2002
Peru	March 6, 2002
Philippines	Oct. 4, 2002
Poland	March 23, 2004
Portugal	March 14, 2010
Qatar	Oct. 28, 2005
Romania	March 6, 2002
Russian Federation	February 5, 2009
Saint Lucia	March 6, 2002
Senegal	May 18, 2002
Serbia	June 13, 2003
Singapore	April 17, 2005
Slovakia	March 6, 2002
Slovenia	March 6, 2002
South Africa	(Signature: Dec. 12,1997)
Spain	March 14, 2010
Sweden	March 14, 2010
Switzerland	July 1, 2008
Tajikistan	April 5, 2009
The former Yugoslav Republic of Macedonia	Feb. 4, 2004
Togo	May 21, 2003
Trinidad and Tobago	Nov. 28, 2008
Turkey	Nov. 28, 2008
Ukraine	March 6, 2002
United Arab Emirates	July 14, 2004
United Kingdom	March 14, 2010
United States of America	March 6, 2002
Uruguay	June 5, 2009
Venezuela	(Signature: Dec. 20, 1996)
(Total : 95 States)	

5.3. THE UNIVERSAL COPYRIGHT CONVENTION (UCC)

The Universal Copyright Convention (the UCC)[47] was developed by the United Nations Educational, Scientific and Cultural Organization (UNESCO) as an alternative to the Berne Convention. While countries may continue to become members of the UCC, the UCC has lost some significance because most states are members of the World Trade Organization and conform to regulations under TRIPS, the Agreement on Trade-Related Aspects of Intellectual Property Rights Agreement.

5.3.1. History[48]

Despite the Berne Convention's success as the first international copyright convention and its admitted merits, by 1948 it had only thirty-nine member states. The United States and the Soviet Union, the two superpowers to emerge from World War II, were not members, nor were many Asian or African countries. Moreover, as the standards of protection were progressively raised through each of the succeeding convention revisions, it became increasingly difficult for countries unaccustomed to protecting copyrights at such a high level to join the Union.

Acknowledging the value of international copyrights and in order to encourage wider recognition of those rights, UNESCO initiated negotiations among United Nations members to create an international copyright treaty that, although not supplanting Berne, would form a bridge to the other conventions and national copyright laws throughout the world. This resulted in the creation of the UCC, adopted in 1952.

The Revised Universal Copyright Convention was promulgated in 1971. Like Berne, contracting states may be bound by either the 1971 UCC or the prior 1952 UCC.

While the UCC was extremely successful for many years in fulfilling its purpose as a bridge between members of Berne and countries not adhering to Berne, it is increasingly becoming a convention of lesser import as more and more countries adhere directly

---

[47] To be distinguished from the Uniform Commercial Code, also commonly abbreviated as the "UCC".

[48] *See* S. Stewart, INTERNATIONAL COPYRIGHT AND NEIGHBOURING RIGHTS §§6.01 *et seq.* (Butterworth 1983).

to Berne or are members of the World Trade Organization and adhere to the Agreement on Trade-Related Aspects of Intellectual Property Rights.

5.3.1.1. Difference between the UCC and Berne

There are substantial differences between the UCC and the Berne Convention, not only in specifics but in general approach. The Berne Convention provides strong specific protections for the author specifying certain rights such as droit moral[49] and droit de suite[50] and extended terms of protection (e.g., "life plus 50 pma [*post-mortem auctoris*]").[51] In contrast, the UCC requires that "each Contracting State undertakes to provide for the adequate and effective protection of the rights of authors."[52] Although it does set forth certain minimum rights of term[53] and defines certain basic rights,[54] it does not do so with the specificity or the strength of protection of the Berne Convention.

A second and more fundamental difference exists in the conceptual function of the two treaties and their application to member countries. Berne is deemed to create and, in some jurisdictions,[55] *confer* certain basic rights directly to authors *jure conventionis*.[56] The UCC does not directly confer rights; it merely obligates the contracting states to "undertake to provide"[57] for the protection of rights as agreed to in the Convention.

5.3.1.2. National Treatment

The UCC demands that the published and unpublished works of a national of any of the contracting states shall be accorded the same protections in any other contracting state as that state accords its own

---

[49] Berne Convention for the Protection of Literary and Artistic Works (Paris Act, July 24, 1971), art. 6bis [hereinafter cited as Berne].
[50] Berne art. 14ter.
[51] *Id*. art. 7.
[52] Universal Copyright Convention as revised at Paris on July 24, 1971, art. I [hereinafter cited to as UCC].
[53] *Id* art. IV.
[54] *Id*. art. IVbis.
[55] *See* discussion §4.1 *supra* at note 8.1.
[56] For example, see Berne art. 3(1) ("The protection of this convention shall apply to authors"); art. 5(1) ("rights specifically granted by this Convention"); art. 36 ("domestic law to give effect to the provisions of this Convention").
[57] UCC art. I.

nationals in its territory.[58] This is known as the doctrine of "national treatment." There are limited exceptions to this doctrine, one of which relates to the duration of protection accorded works of authorship, and is known as the doctrine of the "shorter term."[59]

5.3.2. Subject Matter

5.3.2.1. Protectable Works

The UCC provides that contracting states will afford protection for authors and other copyright proprietors of "literary, scientific and artistic works, including writings, musical, dramatic and cinematographic works and paintings, engravings and sculpture."[60] This leaves some latitude to the contracting states in their definition of a work. For example, it may be required that the work be "embodied in a tangible form"[61] or that protection may not apply to works of a utilitarian nature.[62]

5.3.2.2. National Eligibility

Under the UCC, protection attaches to the works of a national of a contracting state, whether or not the work is published, and to works regardless of source first published in a contracting state.[63] Protection may or may not be accorded to domiciles or residents of a contracting state, depending on whether or not that state elects to protect the works of a domiciliary or resident.[64]

5.3.3. Exclusive Rights

5.3.3.1. Basic Rights

The Convention does not specifically identify the exclusive rights that are to be conferred on an author. Instead, it describes those rights as "the basic rights ensuring the author's economic interests, including

---

[58] Art II.
[59] *See infra* §5.3.8.
[60] *Id.*
[61] *See* 17 U.S.C. §102 (1990).
[62] *See supra* §1.2.
[63] UCC art. II.
[64] *Id.* art. II3.

the exclusive rights to authorize reproduction by any means, public performance and broadcasting"[65] and applies to works "either in their original form or in any form recognizably derived from the original."[66]

Interestingly, it does specifically state that an author will be accorded "the exclusive right ... to make, publish and authorize the making and publication of works protected under this Convention."[67]

5.3.3.2. Limitations on Basic Rights

Contracting states may, by domestic legislation, make exceptions that do not conflict with the spirit and provisions of this Convention, to the basic rights, as long as "a reasonable degree of effective protection [is accorded] to each of the rights to which exception has been made."[68] In addition, the right of translation may be restricted through the creation of a compulsory license to translate a protected work only after the expiration of seven years from the date after the work has been published (and provided that the work has not been withdrawn from circulation) if it has not been translated into the language of that state (or, if translated, the translation has gone out of print).[69] Such a compulsory license requires a faithful translation of the work, proper credit, notice to the owner, and reasonable payment.[70] There are special provisions regarding translation rights for developing countries (as defined in conformity with the established practices of the General Assembly of the United Nations)[71] similar to those accorded under the Berne Convention[72] with a shorter waiting period and other provisions slightly more beneficial to the developing country.[73]

---

[65] *Id.* art. IV^{bis}1.
[66] *Id.*
[67] *Id.* art. VI.
[68] *Id.* art. IV2. For examples of permissible limitations, see 17 U.S.C. §§107 (1992), 108 (2005), 109 (1997), 110 (2005), 111 (2008), 112 (2004) and *infra* §1.4.
[69] UCC art. V.
[70] *Id.*
[71] *Id.* art. V^{bis}.
[72] Berne Appendix. *See supra* §1.12.
[73] UCC arts. V^{ter} and V^{quater}.

5.3.4. Fair Use

The concept of fair use is not addressed in the UCC, although contracting state recognition is clearly justified by the provision authorizing reasonable exceptions to an author's exclusive rights[74] and, secondarily, under the argument that authors receive "adequate and effective protection"[75] even though they may be subject to fair use exceptions.

5.3.5. Creation and Commencement

For nationals and recognized domiciliaries[76] of contracting states, copyright protection commences on creation of the work.[77] Whether or not creation requires embodiment in a tangible medium, while suggested by language in the Convention (i.e., an "unpublished work,"[78] "deposit a copy of the work"),[79] is not directly addressed in the Convention and, as such, is to be defined by the law of the contracting state.[80]

For nonnationals or nonprotected domiciliaries, copyright protection commences when (and if) the work is "first published" in a contracting state.[81]

5.3.6. Ownership

The UCC recognizes the ownership interest of "authors and other copyright proprietors."[82] Thus, while there is a presumption that authors are living individuals,[83] there is a tacit recognition of "works made for hire."[84] Equally, the UCC recognizes an absolute alienability of copyright.[85]

---

[74] *Id.* art. IVbis(2).
[75] *Id.* art. I.
[76] *See supra* §5.2.2.
[77] The Convention specifies that "unpublished works" of a national of each contracting state will be protected in all other states (art. II(2)).
[78] UCC art. II2.
[79] *Id.* art. III3.
[80] *Id.* art. III.
[81] *Id.* art. III1.
[82] *Id.* art. I.
[83] *See* UCC art. IV2(a) ("life of the author and twenty-five years after his death").
[84] *See* 17 U.S.C. §2.01 1978; *see also supra* §1.7.3.
[85] I.e., "other copyright proprietors," art. I.

5.3.7. Formalities

The UCC recognizes the rights of each contracting state to require its authors (i.e., nationals of that country), or works of alien authors first published in that state, to comply with numerous formalities (such as notice, registration, deposit, and payment of fees) as a condition of copyright but requires that the contracting states recognize the protection of nationals of other contracting states (both published and unpublished) or works first published in other contracting states provided each authorized publication bears the notice © accompanied by the name of the copyright proprietor and year of first publication placed in such a manner and location as to give reasonable notice of a claim of copyright.[86]

5.3.8. Duration of Copyright

In general, the duration of protection of a work will be not less than the life of the author plus twenty-five years ("life plus 25 pma").[87] However, with respect to certain classes of works as required under domestic law in existence when the Convention was adopted[88] or where the domestic law at adoption measured all copyrights from publication or registration,[89] the term will be not less than twenty-five years from publication or registration, as the case may be. In the event that the contracting state authorizes two or more terms of protection, the first term will be not less than life plus 25 pma or twenty-five years from registration or publication.[90]

The Convention recognizes that photographic and works of applied art may not be protected, but if they are protected as works of art, their protection will last for not less than ten years for each such class.

The actual duration is to be determined according to the law of the contracting state in which protection is claimed.[91] However, in order to encourage each contracting state to provide extended terms of protection as in Berne,[92] as an exception to the national treatment

---

[86] UCC art. III.
[87] UCC art. IV2(a).
[88] *Id.*
[89] *Id.* art. IV2(b).
[90] *Id.* art. IV2(c).
[91] *Id.* art. IV1.
[92] *See supra* §4.8.

doctrine (i.e., that each author is entitled to all the protections afforded a national of that contracting state) the contracting state is not required to recognize a term of protection greater than the lesser term recognized by the contracting state of which the author is a national[93] or the term in the contracting state in which the work is first published.[94] For this purpose, if a work is simultaneously (i.e., within a period of thirty days) published in two or more contracting states, the state with the shorter term of protection is deemed the state of first publication.[95] Collectively this is known as the doctrine of the "Shorter Term."

5.3.9. Transfers

In principle, the UCC recognizes the full alienability of copyright.[96] Other than restricting that right through imposition of certain compulsory licenses,[97] it does not address what formalities may be required for transfer or other issues related to such transfer. Such issues are to be determined by the law of the contracting state.[98]

5.3.10. Infringement

All works are protected and protectable, if at all, in the same manner as protection is afforded by that contracting state in which protection is sought, to its nationals.[99] To establish protection, it must be shown that

1. With respect to unpublished works that the author is a national (or recognized domiciliary) of a contracting state;[100] or

2. With respect to published works, that

    a. The author is a national or recognized domiciliary of a contracting state, or

---

[93] UCC art. IV4(a).
[94] *Id.* art. IV4(b).
[95] *Id.* art. IV6.
[96] *See* UCC art. I ("rights of authors and *other* copyright proprietors" [emphasis added]); art. IVbis ("right to *authorize* reproduction" [emphasis added]).
[97] *See supra* §6.3 and *infra* §6.13.
[98] *See* UCC art. III. For example, *see supra* §1.10.
[99] UCC art. II.
[100] *Id.* art. II2.

b. The work was first published in a contracting state;101 and

c. That the published work bears the required notice (© name of claimant and year of first publication)102 or, with respect to a national of a contracting state the author has complied with all formalities required by that state of its nationals.[103]

Formalities of procedure and court actions are determined by the law of the contracting state in which protection is claimed.[104]

5.3.11. Remedies

All remedies for infringement are governed by the laws of the contracting state in which protection is claimed.[105]

5.3.12. Special Provisions

5.3.12.1. Protection of the Berne Union

In order to protect the Berne Convention from widespread resignation by countries seeking to take advantage of the lower standards of protection accorded under the UCC while maintaining the benefits of a large, multinational treaty, the UCC provides that any country that has withdrawn from the Berne Union will not be protectable under the UCC in countries of the Berne Union.

5.3.12.2. Supremacy of Existing Multilateral or Bilateral Treaties

Accession to the UCC does not abrogate existing multilateral conventions or bilateral treaties previously entered into by the acceding state.[106] As between these affected states the terms of the preexisting convention or treaty will take precedence.[107]

---

[101] *Id*. Art II 1.
[102] *Id*. Art III 1.
[103] *Id*. Art III 2.
[104] *Id*. art III 3. For example, *see supra* §1.11.
[105] UCC art. 3. For example, *see supra* §1.12.
[106] UCC arts. XVII, XVIII, and XIX and appendix relating to art. XVII(e).
[107] *Id*.

5.3.12.3. Developing Countries

The UCC recognizes certain special rights with respect to developing nations (as that term is defined by customary practices of the General Assembly of the United Nations),[108] including a special right of compulsory license for translations[109] and the right of developing nations to withdraw from the Berne Union in favor of the UCC and to receive the protection of the UCC even in countries of the Berne Union.[110]

5.3.13. Members of the UCC as of July 2017

available at:
http://www.wipo.int/wipolex/en/other_treaties/parties.jsp?treaty_id=208&group_id=22

Contracting State	Dates of Accession	
	Geneva Act of 1952	Paris Act of 1971
Albania		February 4, 2004
Algeria	August 28, 1973	July 10, 1974
Andorra	September 16, 1955	
Argentina	February 13, 1958	
Australia	May 1, 1969	February 28, 1978
Austria	July 2, 1957	August 14, 1982
Azerbaijan		April 7, 1997
Bahamas	December 27, 1976	December 27, 1976
Bangladesh	August 5, 1975	August 5, 1975
Barbados	June 18, 1983	June 18, 1983
Belarus	March 29, 1994	
Belgium	August 31, 1960	
Belize	December 1, 1982	December 1, 1982
Bolivia	December 22, 1989	December 22, 1989
Bosnia/Herzegovina	February 11, 1966	July 3, 1973
Brazil	January 13, 1960	December 11, 1975

---

[108] *Id.* Art. V^{bis}.
[109] *See supra* §6.3.2. *See also* UCC arts. V^{bis}, V^{ter} and V^{quater}.
[110] Appendix relating to art. XVII.

Bulgaria	June 7, 1975	June 7, 1975
Cambodia	Aug. 3, 1953	
Cameroon	May 1, 1973	July 10, 1974
Canada	August 10, 1962	
Chile	September 16, 1955	
China	October 30, 1992	October 30, 1992
Colombia	June 18, 1957	June 18, 1976
Costa Rica	September 16, 1955	March 7, 1980
Croatia	May 11, 1966	July 10, 1974
Cuba	June 18, 1957	
Cyprus	Mar. 26, 1993	Mar. 26, 2000
Czech Republic	December 19, 1990	December 19, 1990
Denmark	February 9, 1962	July 11, 1979
Dominican Rep.	May 8, 1983	May 8, 1983
Ecuador	June 5, 1957	June 6, 1991
El Salvador	March 29, 1979	March 29, 1979
Fiji	October 10, 1970	
Finland	April 16, 1963	November 1, 1986
France	January 14, 1956	July 10, 1974
Germany	September 16, 1955	July 10, 1974
Ghana	August 22, 1962	
Greece	August 24, 1963	
Guatemala	October 28, 1964	
Guinea	November 13, 1981	November 13, 1981
Haiti	September 16, 1955	
Holy See	October 5, 1955	May 6, 1980
Honduras		Sept. 5, 1952 (Signature)
Hungary	January 23, 1971	July 10, 1974
Iceland	December 18, 1956	
India	January 21, 1958	January 7, 1988
Ireland	January 20, 1959	
Israel	September 16, 1955	
Italy	January 24, 1957	January 25, 1980
Japan	April 28, 1956	October 21, 1977

Kazahkstan	Aug. 6, 1992	
Kenya	September 7, 1966	July 10, 1974
Korea, Republic of	October 11, 1987	October 11, 1987
Lao Peoples Dem. Rep.	September 16, 1955	
Lebanon	October 17, 1959	
Liberia	July 27, 1956	
Liechtenstein	January 22, 1959	
Luxembourg	October 15, 1955	
Malawi	October 26, 1965	
Malta	November 19, 1968	
Mauritius	Aug. 20, 1970	
Mexico	May 12, 1957	October 31, 1975
Monaco	September 16, 1955	December 13, 1974
Montenegro		April 26, 2007
Morocco	May 8, 1972	January 28, 1976
Netherlands	June 22, 1967	November 30, 1985
New Zealand	September 11, 1964	
Nicaragua	August 16, 1961	
Niger	May 15, 1989	May 15, 1989
Nigeria	February 14, 1962	
Norway	January 23, 1963	August 7, 1974
Pakistan	September 16, 1955	
Panama	October 17, 1962	September 3, 1980
Paraguay	March 11, 1962	
Peru	October 16, 1963	July 22, 1985
Philippines	November 19, 1955	
Poland	March 9, 1977	March 9, 1977
Portugal	December 25, 1956	July 30, 1981
Republic of Macedonia	April 30, 1997	
Republic of Moldova	June 26, 1997	
Russian Federation	May 27, 1973	May 27, 1973
Rwanda	November 10, 1989	November 10, 1989
Saint Vincent and the Grenadines	April 22, 1985	April 22, 1985
San Marino	Sept. 6, 1952	

Saudi Arabia	July 13, 1994	
Senegal	July 9, 1974	July 10, 1974
Serbia	April 28, 1992	September 11, 2001
Slovakia	Mar. 31, 1993	Mar. 31, 1993
Slovenia	Nov. 5, 1992	Nov. 5, 1992
Spain	September 16, 1955	July 10, 1974
Sri Lanka	January 25, 1984	January 25, 1984
Sweden	July 1, 1961	July 10, 1974
Switzerland	March 30, 1956	September 21, 1993
Tajikistan	Aug. 28, 1992	
Togo	Feb. 28, 2003	May 28, 2003
Trinidad and Tobago	August 19, 1988	August 19, 1988
Tunisia	June 19, 1969	June 10, 1975
Ukraine	Jan. 17, 1994	
United Kingdom	September 27, 1957	July 10, 1974
United States of America	September 16, 1955	July 10, 1974
Uruguay	April 12, 1993	April 12, 1993
Venezuela	September 30, 1966	
(Total : 100 States)		

5.4. THE BUENOS AIRES CONVENTION

The Buenos Aires Convention was signed on August 11, 1910, in Buenos Aires, Argentina, by the United States and many of the countries of Central and South America. It is not a particularly significant treaty insofar as influencing the continuing development of international copyright is concerned in that it is not a "growing" treaty. It has, in fact, lost several of the original signatories.[111] Moreover, a majority of its current adherents are also concurrently members of the Universal Copyright Convention[112] with the development of their laws being influenced by the more rigorous standards implicit in this more recent convention.

Nonetheless, the Convention is understood to be currently in effect between the United States, Brazil, Colombia, Costa Rica, the

---

[111] E.g., Argentina, Mexico, and Cuba.
[112] See supra §6.14.

Dominican Republic, Ecuador, Guatemala, Haiti, Honduras, Nicaragua, Panama, Paraguay, Peru, and Uruguay.[113] Moreover, in countries that are concurrently signatories to the UCC and the Buenos Aires Convention, the Buenos Aires Convention is deemed to take precedence among its members.[114]

The Convention is drawn to protect "Literary and Artistic Works [including, but not limited to] books, writings ... dramatic and dramatico-musical works, choreographic and musical compositions ... drawings, paintings, sculpture, engravings; photographic works; astronomical or geographical globes;... and ... all productions that can be published by any means of impression or reproduction."[115] The acknowledgment of copyright obtained in conformity with the domestic laws of one state will be recognized in all other states to the full extent of their domestic laws/without the requirement of any other formality except that there will appear on the work a statement indicating the reservation of property rights[116] (i.e., the familiar "All Rights Reserved"). Notwithstanding the foregoing, the term of protection will not exceed the term of protection accorded the work in its country of origin,[117] with the country of origin being deemed the country in which the work is first published, or, in the case of simultaneous publication in more than one signatory country, the country with the shortest term of protection.[118]

5.5. THE CONVENTION FOR THE PROTECTION OF PRODUCERS OF PHONOGRAMS AGAINST UNAUTHORIZED DUPLICATION OF THEIR PHONOGRAMS (GENEVA 1971) (THE PHONOGRAM CONVENTION)

5.5.1. In General

Despite the development of a substantial recording industry in the century following the invention of the phonograph by Thomas Edison, copyright laws in a vast majority of developed countries failed to

---

[113] Copyright Office Circular 38c, Int'l Copyright Conventions, COPYRIGHT LAW REPORTER (CCH) ¶15,028 (1983).
[114] *See* UCC art. XVIII.
[115] Buenos Aires Convention art. 2.
[116] *Id.* arts. 3, 6.
[117] *Id.* art. 6.
[118] *Id.* art. 7.

protect sound recordings as copyright works.[119] In response to widespread abuses, the United Nations Educational, Scientific and Cultural Organization (UNESCO) and the World Intellectual Property Organization (WIPO) initiated studies that in 1971 resulted in the creation of the Convention for the Protection of Producers of Phonograms against Unauthorized Duplication of Their Phonograms (the "Phonogram Convention").

The Phonogram Convention provides for the protection of the phonograms ("exclusively aural fixation[s] of sounds of a performance or other sounds"[120]) produced by the nationals of a contracting state against unauthorized reproduction and importation for distribution to the public.[121] Such protection is to be implemented by the domestic law of a contracting state[122] by means of (1) the grant of a copyright or other specific right, (2) protection of the law relating to unfair competition, and/or (3) penal sanction, with protection to exist for a period of not less than twenty years from fixation or publication.[123] Under such protections all statutory requirements will be deemed fulfilled if the authorized copies of phonograms distributed to the public (or their containers) bear a notice consisting of the symbol ℗ accompanied by the year of publication placed in a manner as to give reasonable notice, coupled with an identification of the producer.[124]

5.5.2. Membership Status as of July 17, 2017

available at:
http://www.wipo.int/treaties/en/ShowResults.jsp?lang=en&treaty_id=18

CONTRACTING PARTY	STATUS	ENTRY INTO FORCE
Albania	In Force	June 26, 2001
Argentina	In Force	June 30, 1973

---

[119] For example, the first coverage of sound recordings under United States copyright law did not arise until an amendment was passed by Congress in 1971 (Public Law 92-140, 85 Stat. 391, later embodied in §114 of the Copyright Act of 1976, 17 U.S.C. §114).
[120] Phonogram Convention art. 1(a).
[121] *Id.* art. 2.
[122] *Id.* art. 3.
[123] *Id.* art. 4.
[124] *Id.* art. 5. *See also* 17 U.S.C. §114 (2006).

Armenia	In Force	January 31, 2003
Australia	In Force	June 22, 1974
Austria	In Force	August 21, 1982
Azerbaijan	In Force	September 1, 2001
Barbados	In Force	July 29, 1983
Belarus	In Force	April 17, 2003
Bosnia & Herzagovina	In Force	May 25, 2009
Brazil	In Force	November 28, 1975
Bulgaria	In Force	September 6, 1995
Burkina Faso	In Force	January 30, 1988
Canada	Signature	
Chile	In Force	March 24, 1977
China	In Force	April 30, 1993
Colombia	In Force	May 16, 1994
Costa Rica	In Force	June 17, 1982
Croatia	In Force	April 20, 2000
Cyprus	In Force	September 30, 1993
Czech Republic	In Force	January 1, 1993
Democratic Republic of the Congo	In Force	November 29, 1977
Denmark	In Force	March 24, 1977
Ecuador	In Force	September 14, 1974
Egypt	In Force	April 23, 1978
El Salvador	In Force	February 9, 1979
Estonia	In Force	May 28, 2000
Fiji	In Force	April 18, 1973
Finland	In Force	April 18, 1973
France	In Force	April 18, 1973
Germany	In Force	May 18, 1974
Greece	In Force	February 9, 1994
Guatemala	In Force	February 1, 1977
Holy See	In Force	July 18, 1977
Honduras	In Force	March 6, 1990
Hungary	In Force	May 28, 1975
India	In Force	February 12, 1975
Iran (Islamic Republic of)	Signature	

Israel	In Force	May 1, 1978
Italy	In Force	March 24, 1977
Jamaica	In Force	January 11, 1994
Japan	In Force	October 14, 1978
Kazakhstan	In Force	August 3, 2001
Kenya	In Force	April 21, 1976
Kyrgyzstan	In Force	October 12, 2002
Latvia	In Force	August 23, 1997
Liberia	In Force	December 16, 2005
Liechtenstein	In Force	October 12, 1999
Lithuania	In Force	January 27, 2000
Luxembourg	In Force	March 8, 1976
Mexico	In Force	December 21, 1973
Moldova, Republic of	In Force	July 17, 2000
Monaco	In Force	December 2, 1974
Montenegro	In Force	June 3, 2006
Netherlands	In Force	October 12, 1993
New Zealand	In Force	August 13, 1976
Nicaragua	In Force	August 10, 2000
Norway	In Force	August 1, 1978
Panama	In Force	June 29, 1974
Paraguay	In Force	February 13, 1979
Peru	In Force	August 24, 1985
Philippines	Signature	
Republic of Korea	In Force	October 10, 1987
Romania	In Force	October 1, 1998
Russian Federation	In Force	March 13, 1995
Saint Lucia	In Force	April 2, 2001
Serbia	In Force	June 10, 2003
Slovakia	In Force	January 1, 1993
Slovenia	In Force	October 15, 1996
Spain	In Force	August 24, 1974
Sweden	In Force	April 18, 1973
Switzerland	In Force	September 30, 1993
Tajikistan	In Force	February 26, 2013

The former Yugoslav Republic of Macedonia	In Force	March 2, 1998
Togo	In Force	June 10, 2003
Trinidad and Tobago	In Force	October 1, 1988
Ukraine	In Force	February 18, 2000
United Kingdom	In Force	April 18, 1973
United States of America	In Force	March 10, 1974
Uruguay	In Force	January 18, 1983
Venezuela	In Force	November 18, 1982
Viet Nam	In Force	July 6, 2005
(Total: 79 States)		

5.6. THE WIPO PERFORMANCES AND PHONOGRAMS TREATY (GENEVA 1996)

5.6.1. In General

When copyright was emerging in the late 1800s and the first Berne Convention was developed and signed in 1886, the recording industry did not exist. When it began to emerge, the question arose as to how to protect that industry. While the music recorded on phonograms was clearly the subject of copyright, what about the sound recording? Does a recording of a composition represent original creativity sufficient to represent authorship or is it simply the mechanical transcription of the composition embodied on it? If one was to protect it, who would be its authors – producers or recording artists? And if one does protect it, does such protection preclude other recordings of the same composition insofar as the recording is a faithful rendering of the original composition?

Given the difficulty of these questions, there was a significant delay between the emergence of the recording industry and the development of an international consensus on how the industry was to be treated. In fact the process is still ongoing. The initial attempt to address this issue occurred in 1961 with the enactment of the International Convention for the Protection of Performers, Producers of Phonograms and Broadcast Organizations (Rome 1961). The success of this effort was extremely limited. To date, 88 countries have acceded to this treaty and, most significantly, the United States has never become a member. The most controversial part of this treaty was its effort to protect performers.

Given the importance of the recording industry, pressure continued to be exerted for some international protections to be enacted. This led in 1971 to the enactment of the Phonogram Convention. In order to reach agreement, the rights of performers were omitted form this treaty. Nonetheless, many countries continued to press for the protection of performers' rights.

In response to this pressure, and in order to address changes brought about by technology, and to further clarify the international status of the protection of phonograms, a new treaty, known as the WIPO Performances and Phonograms Treaty (Geneva 1996), was adopted (hereinafter referred to as the WPPT). While not derogating from the protections offered under the Phonogram Convention (in relation to members of that convention who become party to the WPPT), the WPPT, like the WIPO Copyright Treaty, addresses virtually the same technological changes and reflect almost identical efforts to clarify the protections to be accorded to performers and phonogram producers (including provisions covering the right of reproduction (arts. 7 & 11), distribution (arts. 8 & 12), rental (arts. 9 & 13), making the works accessible to the public (arts. 10 & 14) and the obligation to protect against technological infringements and to protect rights management systems (arts. 18 & 19). At the same time, the treaty acknowledges that countries can accord a more limited term of ownership of these rights.

What is most innovative about this treaty, from the perspective of the United States, is its protection of the rights of performers, where such protection has been traditionally resisted. Here, the major compromise demanded by the United States (among others) was that this treaty was not to apply to audio-visual works performers (i.e., those performances are created as a part of a television, motion picture or video production.) While the primary target of this protection is performers whose work is intended to be embodied in a phonogram, it also arguably protects live stage performers against any kind of recording (including audio-visual recording) without their approval (though if such approval is given, the subsequent audiovisual work would undoubtedly be exempt from the other on-going requirements of this treaty).

The treaty even provides moral rights for performers (art. 5), including the right to claim identification as the performer and the right to object to any alteration of a recording that would be prejudicial to the performer's reputation. These moral rights shall extend for the longer of the life of the performer (subject to some limitation) or the duration of economic protection for the work in question.

5.6.2. Treaty Signatories

The number of contracting parties to the WIPO Performances and Phonograms Treaty continues to increase with ten countries added (and six withdrawing) since 2010. The following list shows signatory countries and status as of July 15, 2017, *available at*: http://www.wipo.int/export/sites/www/treaties/en/documents/pdf/wppt.pdf

State	Date State became Party to the Treaty
Albania	May 20, 2002
Algeria	January 31, 2014
Argentina	May 20, 2002
Armenia	March 6, 2005
Australia	July 26, 2007
Austria	March 14, 2010
Azerbaijan	April 11, 2006
Bahrain	December 15, 2005
Belarus	May 20, 2002
Belgium	August 30, 2006
Benin	April 16, 2006
Bosnia and Herzegovina	Novermber 25, 2009
Botswana	January 27, 2005
Brunei Darussalem	May 2, 2017
Bulgaria	May 20, 2002
Burkina Faso	May 20, 2002
Canada	August 13, 2014
Chile	May 20, 2002
China	June 9, 2007

Colombia	May 20, 2002
Costa Rica	May 20, 2002
Croatia	May 20, 2002
Cyprus	December 2, 2005
Czech Republic	May 20, 2002
Dominican Republic	January 10, 2006
Ecuador	May 20, 2002
El Salvador	May 20, 2002
Estonia	March 14, 2010
European Union	March 14, 2010
Finland	March 14, 2010
France	March 14, 2010
Gabon	May 20, 2002
Georgia	May 20, 2002
Germany	March 14, 2010
Ghana	February 16, 2013
Greece	March 14, 2010
Guatemala	January 8, 2003
Guinea	May 25, 2002
Honduras	May 20, 2002
Hungary	May 20, 2002
Indonesia	February 15, 2005
Ireland	March 14, 2010
Italy	March 14, 2010
Jamaica	June 12, 2002
Japan	October 9, 2002
Jordan	May 24, 2004
Kazakhstan	November 12, 2004
Kyrgyzstan	August 15, 2002
Latvia	May 20, 2002
Liechtenstein	April 30, 2007
Lithuania	May 20, 2002
Madagascar	February 24, 2015

Malaysia	December 27, 2012
Mali	May 20, 2002
Malta	March 14, 2010
Mexico	May 20, 2002
Mongolia	October 25, 2002
Montenegro	June 3, 2006
Morocco	July 20, 2011
Mongolia	October 25, 2002
Montenegro	June 3, 2006
Netherlands	March 14, 2010
Nicaragua	March 6, 2003
Oman	September 20, 2005
Panama	May 20, 2002
Paraguay	May 20, 2002
Peru	July 18, 2002
Philippines	October 4, 2002
Poland	October 21, 2003
Portugal	March 14, 2010
Qatar	October 28, 2005
Republic of Korea	March 18, 2009
Republic of Moldova	May 20, 2002
Romania	May 20, 2002
Russian Federation	February 5, 2009
Saint Lucia	May 20, 2002
Saint Vincent & the Grenadines	February 12, 2011
Senegal	May 20, 2002
Serbia	June 13, 2003
Singapore	April 17, 2005
Slovakia	May 20, 2002
Slovenia	May 20, 2002
Spain	March 14, 2010
Sweden	March 14, 2010

Switzerland	July 1, 2008
The former Yugoslav Republic of Macedonia	March 20, 2005
Togo	May 21, 2003
Trinidad and Tobago	November 28, 2008
Turkey	November 28, 2008
Ukraine	May 20, 2002
United Arab Emirates	June 9, 2005
United Kingdom	March 14, 2010
United States of America	May 20, 2002
Uruguay	August 28, 2008

(Total : 95 States)

— CHAPTER 6 —

INTELLECTUAL PROPERTY LAW PRINCIPLES OF ENTERTAINMENT INDUSTRY PRACTICE

6.1. Copyright Matters
6.2. Clearing World Rights of an Underlying Source for Republication, Translation, and Adaptation
6.3. Thinking about Trademarks and Merchandising
6.4. Warranties and Representations
6.5. Indemnification Issues

A number of topics – for example copyright and clearances, representations and warranties, indemnification, credits, remedies, and of course defining how proceeds are to be accounted for – are germane to virtually every transaction in the entertainment sphere. An understanding of their interrelationships and relevance to a typical "deal" is imperative for the practitioner or business person in this field.

Although often considered "boilerplate" to be addressed after more salient (e.g., financial) terms in an agreement are established, these topics may in many respects be as significant to the outcome of an agreement as the upfront negotiation of fees and scope of services/rights.

6.1. COPYRIGHT MATTERS

In the general practice of entertainment law almost every transaction relates in some way to the acquisition, registration, and transfer of copyright. Although questions of copyrightability and infringement are significant and often enlightening as to the nature of the copyright, they have been addressed in their simplest form in the copyright law summary in Chapter 1. This section addresses the practical "how-to" aspects of some of the most common copyright concerns which arise when a work is first created, when a work originating in one medium is to be transformed into another (e.g., a book to a play or play to a film), or when a work is simply adapted into a new work in its original medium (e.g., a play to an opera, or when the creation of a motion picture remake or sequel production is based upon an earlier film).

An author may choose among several methods to evidence his or her authorship of a work, each varying in formality and effect.

6.1.1. Notice[1]

Under United States law, in order to be protected against an "innocent" infringer each copyrighted work should still bear a visible copyright notice.[2] Such notice is not required until after the work is "published" (i.e., copies of the work have been distributed by sale, lease, license, or other transfer of ownership),[3] but it is sound practice to affix notice to all copies of the work immediately on fixation in a material medium. While the United States accession to Berne by means of the Berne Act[4] has removed the requirement for affixation of notice,[5] it nonetheless remains sound practice to affix notice to all copies of the work.[6]

Notice consists of the affixation of the following elements on the work:[7] (1) the symbol "©", the word "Copyright" or the abbreviation "Copr.", (2) the year of publication (and if it is unpublished, simply use the year in which the work was fixed in a material medium), and (3) the name of the owner of the copyright. It is also common practice to enter the words *All Rights Reserved* immediately beneath the copyright notice to satisfy the requirements of the Buenos Aires Convention.[8]

The foregoing notice serves two purposes. First, it immediately puts anyone receiving a copy of the work on notice that the work is protected (and infringement would be deemed in bad faith).[9] Second, although the statute requires the inclusion of the date of publication in the notice, the date of fixation serves the same purpose if someone later claims that the work has been published by virtue of the manner in which the author distributed copies of the work.

---

[1] *See supra* §1.8.
[2] 17 U.S.C. §401 *et seq.* (1988).
[3] *Id* §101 (2005).
[4] *See supra* §1.8.1.5.
[5] *See* Berne Act §1.8.
[6] *See supra* §1.8.1.5.
[7] 17 U.S.C. §401.
[8] *See supra* §5.4.
[9] *See supra* §1.12.

6.1.2. Author's Diary

An author should maintain a journal (preferably in a manner not readily subject to modification, e.g., a bound rather than loose-leaf format) that records the dates on which works were created and/or revised along with a history of submissions. The journal should be kept in the regular course of business (and if in digital format, should be backed up or printed regularly). Such a journal is useful in addressing two elements of an action for copyright infringement:[10] (1) The work must be in existence in order to be copied; and (2) access to the work was possible (except where the copying is so extensive that it can be presumed).

The journal, if kept in the usual course of business and properly supported, becomes admissible in court as a business record[11] and can be used to help establish the date of creation of the work. Through use of the submission list, it may serve as evidence of the defendant's access to the work. It may also be used in a defensive manner to show the prior independent creation of the author's work, e.g., that another similar and previously published work was nonetheless created *after* the author had created the work challenging or challenged by the published work.

6.1.3. Informal Copyright

Many writers in their early careers may assume that the cost of formal copyright filing is prohibitive and, in lieu thereof, adopt what is commonly perceived of as an informal "poor person's" copyright filing procedure. The basic element of this informal process is that the writer mails a copy of the work, by certified or registered mail, either to himself or herself or to a friend with the understanding that the envelope should not be opened.

This procedure does have some merit. It is slightly less expensive than formal filing,[12] and if the envelope is maintained in proper

---

[10] *Id* §1.12.

[11] *See* N.Y. CPLR 4518(a).

[12] As of May 1, 2014, the U.S. Copyright Office filing fee for a basic claim in an original work of authorship (Forms TX, SE, PA, VA, and Form SR) is $85 for a paper application, and $35 or $55 for an electronic filing in those categories for which electronic registration is available. The filing can be accomplished with or without the assistance of a lawyer.

custody that can be supported in court, it can serve to establish the date of the creation of the work and the *contents* of that work.

Similarly, the Writers Guild of America offers a registration procedure available to both members and non-members of the Guild for literary treatments, screenplays and teleplays, which offers both a registration number and date for materials submitted in paper or electronic form.[13]

However, formal registration and deposit of the work fulfills the same goals in a far superior manner. Because formal registration is required prior to initiation of an infringement action,[14] is readily admissible in court,[15] and provides the basis for statutory damages,[16] it is the recommended procedure. (Note, however, that if a manuscript or other work is materially revised, each additional version should be registered to extend copyright protection to the supplemental materials.)

6.1.4. Copyright Registration Procedures

Copyright registration by online submission of the application is the preferred method today. The Copyright Office website can be accessed for this purpose at www.copyright.gov. The process begins with three questions to determine whether or not the claimant is eligible to pay either a $35 or $55 fee for the registration process. Registering a single work for a single author and for which the only material to be registered has been created by that author results in the ability to file a simplified application for $35. If the work is a work made for hire, that application will cost $55. The initial three questions answered will automatically begin the registration process with the appropriate form. The application form is completed online, followed by (1) online payment either through a credit card or deposit account with the Copyright Office and (2) finally providing deposit or

---

[13] The current WGA Registration Fee is $10 for materials submitted by members and $20 for non-member registrations. Registration can be effected by mail or online. Information can be obtained at www.wga.org.

[14] 17 U.S.C. §410 (1976). *But see* §1.8.4.4 *supra re* the Berne Act.

[15] *Id. See also* Belford, Clarke & Co. v. Scribner, 144 U.S. 488 (1892).

[16] 17 U.S.C. §412 (2005).

identifying material either by uploading to the Copyright Office website or by mail or courier.[17]

The online form brings up a 12 link set of inquiries to complete and review. The first issue is the nature of the work which must be identified. The following types of works can be selected:

1. Literary Work. This includes nondramatic literary works such as fiction and nonfiction, but not screenplays.

2. Work of the Visual Arts. Artwork includes pictorial, graphic and sculptural works.

3. Sound Recording. This may include both a sound recording as well as the underlying musical compositions.

4. Work of the Performing Arts. This includes plays, screenplays and motion pictures. This may include a musical work such as the song with or without lyrics, but not sound recordings. Sound recording should be selected if the intent is to register both a sound recording as well as the underlying musical composition.

5. Motion picture/AV work. For a feature film, documentary film, animated film, television show, video, videogame or other audio-visual work.

6. Single serial issue. A single serial issue is typically a published work which is part of a continuing series. Examples include published newspapers, magazines and newsletters. An episode of a television series or a series of online videos are not considered as serials here.

The next link in the application is the title of the work. A drop down list displays various types of titles to be identified such as title of the work being registered, previous or alternative titles, titles of larger works, and series title or contents title. Once the title type drop down list of the title type has been entered, the actual title of the work is entered.

---

[17] The Copyright Office has published a Third Compendium of U.S. Copyright Office Practices helpful to determine how to complete questions answered on the copyright application. Failure to properly identify the work and other information on the application may result in communication to the applicant, typically by email correspondence which may slow down the registration process.

Publication information must be entered, which in turn affects what material must be submitted to the Copyright Office. If unpublished, usually only limited identifying material needs to be submitted. If published, the applicant may need to comply with "best edition" requirements. For some work this means submitting two copies of the "Best Edition" of the work to the Copyright Office. "Best Edition" is a term of art for which detailed regulations have been set out to identify the types of materials the Library of Congress requires.[18] It may be that two copies of hardbound editions need to be submitted to the Copyright Office as opposed to trade paperback editions. Also it may be necessary, for example, to send a more expensive Digi-Beta edition of a television series episode to the Copyright Office rather than an inexpensive DVD.[19]

For published works, the year of completion is needed along with the date of first publication of the work. Date and nation of first publication of the work is also required. The nation of first publication may have an effect on copyright protection or duration under treaty.

The authorship section identifies whether the author or authors are individuals or an organization. Either the citizenship or domicile of the author must be identified. The year of birth and death of the author as well as whether the author was anonymous or pseudonymous and the pseudonym may be included. This information may be helpful in determining the duration of a copyrighted work as well as establishing presumptions as to whether or not the author is living at the time an investigation may later be undertaken.

The nature of copyrightable authorship needs to be specified in a group of checkboxes for the application. The types of authorship checkboxes appearing on the application depends on the specific type of work initially identified. For example, if the work is identified as a work of visual art, the checkboxes which will appear identify elements such as photograph, jewelry design, map, 2-D artwork, sculpture, architectural work or technical drawing as well as an additional blank box for "other." A work of the performing arts has checkboxes for music, lyrics, text, musical arrangement or other. For a motion

---

[18] Circular 7b describes Best Edition requirements of the Library of Congress. See www.copyright.gov/circs.

[19] Determination of whether a work has been published for some types of work is not always obvious and the applicant is the party that makes that initial determination. The fact of publication may be affected by the manner of distribution of copies of the work, whether the work is disseminated by the Internet, and whether multiple copies are delivered for distribution by broadcast entities.

picture/audio-visual work, the available checkboxes are entire motion picture or the following checkboxes: production, direction, script/ screenplay, cinematography, editing or other (e.g., choreography and if the claim is for audio-visual material such as a videogame website or Internet advertisement, one could state audio-visual material).

The copyright claimant must then be identified, which will either be the original author if still the owner, or otherwise a person or organization to whom copyright has been transferred (including authorship as a "work for hire").

If a transfer has occurred, the manner of transfer must be stated. A drop-down box allows identification of (1) by written agreement, including by assignment or by contract, (2) by inheritance, by will or intestate succession, or (3) transfer by other means, such as by operation of law.

Copyrighted works are often registered having content not intended to be covered by the registration, i.e., the work includes third party content which might be owned by others or in the public domain. The application provides a method to exclude pre-existing material, whether or not owned by the applicant, and for a motion picture that material might be a script, screenplay, pre-existing music, pre-existing footage, or pre-existing photographs or other material. If previously registered there is an opportunity to identify that registration. The applicant then identifies the new material added to the work to be covered by the copyright application such as all other cinematographic material, production of a motion picture, additional new footage, or revisions/ additions to the script.

To make it easy for third parties to identify a contact for rights and permissions to reproduce the registered material, the applicant is given an opportunity to identify that individual or company to be available in the Copyright Office database.

Correspondence contact information is filled in for Copyright Office questions that may arise. A separate name and address link for delivery of the copyright registration certificate is also entered.

A Special Handling section is available to expedite registrations, reducing the time registration normally requires from many months to a few weeks. Normally, the delay in obtaining a registration after filing is not of concern since the effective date of registration is not the actual registration date, but rather when the application is filed and the Copyright Office receives the deposit copy or identifying material.

Special Handling speeds registration for only a few reasons: pending or prospective litigation, customs matters, or contractor publishing or other contractual transfer deadlines that necessitate the expedited issuance of a certificate. The surcharge for this is currently $800 per registration (and $550 per recordation).

The applicant certifies authorization to file the application and that the information is correct. An opportunity is available (via an online prompt) to review the information provided. This application may be printed out for review, although the Copyright Office website currently makes formatting for viewing and printing difficult to read. Once the applicant is satisfied with the information, the application is added to an e-commerce cart for payment to complete the filing process. Filing can be completed by paying through a Copyright Office deposit account or credit card.

The website then leads you to a screen which allows you to upload files to the Copyright Office or to submit and ship deposit copies or identifying material to the Copyright Office. Material to be uploaded must be in a specific form. For example, if the work is unpublished and is a literary work, the process is simply a matter of uploading the text in digital form such as a .pdf or Word file.

An electronic copy may be uploaded to the Copyright Office website if the work to be registered is an unpublished work, published only electronically, or published in a manner for which the deposit requirement is merely identifying material. A published work may require sending a hard copy deposit separately to the Library of Congress. Once it is established that a copy can be uploaded, only specific types of files are accepted. However the list is fairly broad:. Data files, image files, audio, video, text, presentation and compressed files of various types may be utilized, but only specific ones may be uploaded to the Copyright Office website. There are limits to the size of the files so that it does not take an interminable time to upload. Currently the maximum file size for each file uploaded is 500 MB.

If on the other hand it is not appropriate to upload files to the Copyright Office website, physical copies of the works must be sent within 30 days of filing the copyright application. When doing so, it is necessary to create a shipping slip when a work is to be submitted by mail or courier. By clicking on the "Create Shipping Slip" button, a PDF of a shipping slip is created which may be printed out and must be included with any deposit mailed or couriered to the Copyright Office.

Two primary functions of the Copyright Office are to (1) register claims to copyright and (2) record documents transferring copyright interests. It is important to note that these are two entirely separate and distinct functions. At the present time most registrations can be and preferably are accomplished online.[20] So far, it is has not been possible to record transfers or assignments of copyright online, but instead this procedure must be done on paper. In doing so however, it is necessary to complete a cover sheet which provides some of the essential information regarding underlying assignments and transfer documents which are submitted with the assignment and transfer documents to the Copyright Office. A significant feature of that cover sheet is an attestation that either the attached document is original or is a true copy of what is being submitted to the Copyright Office. At the time of publication of this book, the Copyright Office has announced plans to permit online submission of recordation documents.

The Copyright Office still provides a number of forms for registration of copyrights for different media. They are available free of charge from the Copyright Office, Library of Congress, Washington, D.C. 20557, or may be obtained online at www.copyright.gov. Of these, some of the more important forms are listed below.

1. Form PA, *Copyright Registration for a Work of the Performing Arts* (used for plays, operas, motion pictures, songs, etc.).

2. Form SR, *Copyright Registration for a Sound Recording* (used for copyrighting the actual sound recording and, if not separately claimed, it may also claim copyright in the embodied work).

3. Form TX, *Copyright Registration for a Nondramatic Literary Work* (used for books, poetry, etc.).

4. Form GR/CP, *Copyright Registration for a Group of Contributions to Periodicals* (magazines, etc.).

5. Form VA, *Copyright Registration for a Work of the Visual Arts* (used for photographs, paintings, sculptures, etc.).

---

[20] Copyright Renewals and Supplemental Copyright Registrations still may not be filed online, but the forms or these registrations are available to fill in and print out for mailing to the Copyright Office.

6. Form CA, *Supplementary Copyright Registration* (used to clarify a previous filing under any of the foregoing forms).

7. Form RE, *Renewal Registration* (used to renew the claim of copyright to a work created and copyrighted prior to January 1, 1978).

Application for registration (i.e., both original and renewal terms, when applicable) may be made on the appropriate form(s)[21] and must be accompanied by payment of the appropriate fee. In the case of an original filing the application must be accompanied by a deposit copy of the work.[22] Copies of contracts, assignments, powers of attorney, and other documents affecting a particular copyright may be filed in their original form along with the appropriate fee so as to put third parties on constructive notice of the disposition of certain rights and interests in the work from time to time.[23]

6.1.5. Registration Review

The preparation of an application for copyright registration provides a valuable opportunity to review the status of a work (i.e., whether the author has complied with various formalities). The filing becomes a part of the public record, placing any potential infringer on notice of the contents of the registration,[24] and is admissible in court[25] as *prima facie* evidence of the facts stated in the registration.

All original applications (as opposed to supplemental, renewal, or assignment filings) follow essentially the same sequence of review. The discussion below follows that numerical sequence.

6.1.5.1. Title

The *Title of the Work* and *Nature of the Work* spaces of the application provide the basis for identifying the work. The *Previous or Alternative Titles* space provides the basis for linking the application to prior versions of the work and is particularly useful if those prior

---

[21] 17 U.S.C. §409 (1992).
[22] *See supra* §1.8.5.
[23] 37 C.F.R. §201.4 (July 1, 2005).
[24] *See supra* §1.8.
[25] *See* 17 U.S.C. §410 (1976).

versions are substantially older than the present work and may have been submitted to others (thereby providing the access factor of infringement). Also, because it is possible to create similar works independently, if the genesis of a present work alleged to have infringed is shown to be older than the plaintiff's work, no infringement can be proven (prior art).

6.1.5.2. Authorship, Creation, and Publication

The provisions of authorship establish the original claimant of ownership (the author) and vest the author (if the work is not a work made for hire) with the right of termination.[26] It also helps establish the term of copyright[27] based upon the dates provided in section 3 of the form. For example, for a living author the current term of protection for works created after January 1, 1978 is life plus seventy years.[28] The application provides a space for the date of death (triggering the final seventy years). Death is "presumed"[29] to have occurred ninety-five years after publication or one hundred twenty years after creation (as identified in section 3 of the form), unless the actual date of death is subsequently filed.

If the work is anonymous or pseudonymous, or a work made for hire, then the term is for ninety-five years after publication or one hundred years after creation (as identified in section 3 of the form).[30]

The provision of nationality or domicile (in section 2) and the provision of the nation of first publication (in section 3) serve as predicates for jurisdiction of copyright. One of the three must be the United States for the work to be eligible for United States registration.

6.1.5.3. Copyright Claimant

This provides the name of the owner of record. If a transfer is limited, this can be identified in the section relating to transfer.

---

[26] *See supra* §§1.11.3-1.11.4.
[27] *See* supra §1.9.
[28] 17 U.S.C. §302(a) (1998).
[29] 17 U.S.C. §302(e) (1998).
[30] 17 U.S.C. §302(c) (1998).

6.1.5.4. Previous Registration and Derivative Work or Completion

These provisions determine if the work is based on a prior work (for which permission must be obtained) and, if so, what is protectable (i.e., only original contributions are protectable).[31]

6.1.5.5. Administrative Provisions

The remaining provisions are administrative (e.g., filing methods, address, etc.).

It is a useful office policy to use the occasion of filing claims for copyright to trigger other filings that may be based on that work, such as registering a musical composition with a performing rights society (e.g., ASCAP or BMI), registering a screenplay with the Writers Guild of America and/or, if elements of the work are intended as the basis of other products (e.g., merchandising) or services, appropriate trademark analysis and registrations.

6.1.6. Deposit Account

Individuals who regularly do filings with the Copyright Office may open a deposit account with the Copyright Office (whereby money is deposited with the Register in advance – this is not a charge account) and from which fees for registration, renewal, or copyright search charges may be deducted. Application for such an account may be made to the Copyright Office, Library of Congress, Washington, D.C. 20557, or online at the Copyright Office web site (www.copyright.gov). Filings may now also be effectuated online utilizing credit cards.

6.1.7. Copyright Searches

There are two types of copyright searches. One is a search where a work is traced from its original ownership and all transfers and encumbrances are identified. The second involves searching for all of the works of a particular author or owner.

---

[31] *See supra* §1.1.

The first kind of search is typically made when one is acquiring a copyright, planning to develop a derivative work or defending against an infringement. The purpose behind this search, generally referred to as a Copyright *Title* Search or Report, is to see if there are any encumbrances that might affect the searcher's intended use of the work (i.e., "title" here refers to ownership of copyright as opposed to identifying coincidental appearances of a "title" as the identifying name of unrelated works).

The second type of search is most useful in commencing representation of an author. It determines whether or not all the works of the author have been properly registered, who publishes them, what encumbrances exist on those works, and when they will become available for termination (post-1978 works) or renewal (pre-1978 works). It allows the lawyer to see what must be done to protect the client.

The Copyright Office catalogue now contains in excess of twenty million registrations and documents filed since January 1, 1978, most of which can be accessed electronically online via the Office's web site. Using the online resources may provide adequate information for a preliminary and cursory search for the purposes described above, and/or to confirm elementary information about a work (e.g., the year of initial registration). But the experienced practitioner (and inevitably the financier or distributor of a production based upon another underlying work) will typically opt for more substantive search procedures, in addition to these preliminary ones.

A more comprehensive copyright search will be performed by the Copyright Office for a reasonable fee,[32] but the backlog of requests sometimes delays the search for months. There are also commercial research firms that specialize in doing expedited copyright searches for fees that vary based on scope of search (e.g., U.S. federal and/or state; or one or more international) and turnaround time required for the investigation and report.

Once information gleaned from one or more of these searches is in hand, the information must be evaluated with respect to several significant developments in the interpretation of reversion and restoration of copyright in protected foreign works for which U.S. copyright may lapse.

---

[32] *See* 17 U.S.C. §808 (10) (2000).

6.1.8. Copyright Reversions

Stewart v. Abend[33] (the "Rear Window" case) decided by the Supreme Court on April 24, 1990 resulted in a dramatic change in status for numerous works created prior to January 1, 1978 or more recent works that incorporate or are based on works created before that time. Unlike the right of termination under copyright[34] where the rights of a derivative work owner are protected against such termination,[35] in *Stewart* the Court held that when an author dies prior to the date of renewal for a pre-1978 work (i.e., 28 years after the vesting of copyright)[36] the statutory beneficiary entitled to renew the copyright upon renewal takes the copyright free and clear of any and all licenses and grants made by the author during his or her lifetime. The *Stewart* facts concerned Cornell Woolrich, who wrote the short story "It Had to Be Murder" upon which the film "Rear Window" was based, and died prior to the date of the copyright's renewal in 1969. The court held that Woolrich's successors took the copyright free and clear of the grant of motion picture rights made by him to the producers of "Rear Window", and the producers consequently lost their right to exploit their motion picture without obtaining the approval of Woolrich's successors.

This decision affects three groups of people: authors' statutory successors, owners of existing derivative works, and creators of new derivative works.

First, anyone who is a statutory successor to a deceased author who has either renewed a pre-1978 copyright or expects to do so is now in a position to relicense or prevent the continued exploitation of any work based on or incorporating that copyrighted work. This would include, among others, plays, movies or television programs based on a literary or dramatic work, recordings of musical works (although the rights of the record producer can be preserved through the exercise of the compulsory licensing provisions of §115 of the Copyright Act), and the use of musical works and sound-recordings in the soundtracks of movies or television.

---

[33] Abend v. MCA, Inc. 863 F.2d 1465 (9th Cir. 1988), *cert. granted*, 493 U.S. 807, motion granted, 493 U.S. 990 (1989), *judgment aff'd*, Stewart v. Abend, 495 U.S. 207 (1990).
[34] *See supra* §§1.11.3, 1.11.4.
[35] 17 U.S.C. §203(b).
[36] *See supra* §1.11.2.

The second group, anyone who owns an existing derivative work (i.e., one that is based on or incorporates a pre-1978 work), must now determine whether or not the licensing author is still alive and, if so, whether the copyright has been renewed. If the author is alive and the copyright has been renewed, the owner's rights continue for the entire term of copyright. While the original author may "terminate" his or her license,[37] that termination will not limit the new owner's right to continue to exploit his or her derivative work. If the author is still alive but the renewal date has not yet arisen, the derivative rights owner cannot guarantee his/her rights, although he or she can negotiate with the anticipated statutory beneficiaries (e.g., the spouse and children of the author) to obtain their "expectancy interests" in the copyright in the event that the author dies prior to renewal and the anticipated statutory beneficiaries actually become the author's statutory beneficiaries (e.g., they do not predecease the author and/or there is no divorce and remarriage terminating the rights of such beneficiaries in the interim).[38] Lastly, if the author of the original work has died and a statutory beneficiary has renewed the copyright, the derivative work owner either must obtain a new license from the statutory beneficiary or, if possible, delete all parts of the original work from the derivative work (e.g., cutting a musical recording from the soundtrack of a movie or television program.)

The third group affected by this decision is all prospective creators of derivative works that are to be based on or incorporate works of still living authors that were created between 1963 and 1977 (the period during which this type of non-vested renewal right continues to exist). Obviously, the first decision they must make is whether or not they wish to proceed in the face of this risk. If so, they can attempt to protect themselves by negotiating with both the author and the anticipated statutory beneficiaries (e.g., the spouse and children of the author) to obtain both of their (i.e., the author's[39] and the beneficiaries') "expectancy interests" in the copyright in the event that the author dies prior to renewal and the anticipated statutory beneficiaries actually become the author's statutory beneficiaries (e.g., they do not predecease the author and/or there is no divorce and

---

[37] *See supra* §1.11.3.
[38] *See* Fisher v. Edwin H. Morris & Co., 113 U.S.P.Q. 251, No. 97-203, 1957 WL 7177 (S.D.N.Y. Mar. 19, 1957).
[39] *See* Fred Fisher Music Co. v. M. Witmark & Sons, 318 U.S. 643 (1943).

remarriage in the interim). Lastly, if the desired work can be made separable, that is, where it can be deleted without harm to the total derivative work, such as where a musical work might be recorded in a way that allows for it to be deleted from a soundtrack, then the derivative work owner preserves a right to continue to exploit the derivative work if it is difficult or economically impossible to reach a new agreement with a statutory beneficiary. If it is not separable, then the whole work would be limited.

6.1.9. Restored Copyright Review

Posing a situation somewhat similar to that created by the "Rear Window" case, the enactment of Section 104A of the Copyright Act has created an ongoing uncertainty in relation to works of foreign origin that have fallen into the public domain in the United States but that are now subject to restoration.[40] While the bulk of the works affected by this enactment will undoubtedly come to light in the initial phase of this process of restoration (i.e., at the time of its enactment, effective as of January 1, 1995) every time a new country becomes a member of the Berne Union, the World Trade Organization, or where the President makes a proclamation that it is according restored protection to U.S. works, works originating in that country and now in the public domain become subject to restoration.

What this means on a practical level is first that anyone exploiting a work of foreign origin that is in the public domain and/or a derivative work based upon or incorporating such a work must determine whether or not that work has been restored by this action. Second, if it has been restored, one should begin the process of seeking out the restored rights owner. This should become available through lists to be published by the Copyright Office pursuant to this statute. If the work has not been restored because the "source" country of that work is not a member of Berne or the WTO, the owner must periodically review this situation to determine if that source country takes some action to be covered by the provisions of this section by joining Berne, the WTO, or through obtaining Presidential recognition.

---

[40] *See supra* §1.11.5.

6.1.10. La Cienega Review

In *La Cienega Music Co. v. Z.Z. Top*[41] it was held that any composition recorded prior to 1978 without appropriate notice was deemed "published" without notice and, hence, was held to have fallen in the public domain. In 1998, Congress overturned this ruling stating specifically that "[t]he distribution before January 1, 1978, of a phonorecord shall not for any purpose constitute a publication of the musical work embodied therein."[42]

6.2. CLEARING WORLD RIGHTS OF AN UNDERLYING SOURCE FOR REPUBLICATION, TRANSLATION, AND ADAPTATION

This section does not attempt to answer all the questions that may arise in the course of clearing world rights of an underlying source for republication, translation, or adaptation. Such a discussion would require volumes. Rather, this brief nontechnical explanation of the process of clearing world rights (and what those rights are) offers a simple overview of how to go about clearing those rights.

Clearing world rights can be (and usually is) a long, complicated process. The earlier that the process is initiated, the easier (or at least, less problematic) it will be. Remember, the rights that are being cleared are ultimately the same kinds of rights that represent your client's future source of income. These rights are property rights and can be just as valuable and unique as real estate. Establishing a clean and enforceable "chain of title" as to ownership of such rights is fundamental to the financing and distribution of any legitimate Entertainment Industry property. Unfortunately, there is no central global hall of records where all copyrights are registered.

6.2.1. What Rights Are to Be Cleared?

From the outset, it is important to understand what rights need to be cleared for the uses intended. Although it might be ideal to clear all rights for all purposes, this may prove to be impractical, if not impossible, based upon the realistically anticipated scope of intended use, budget available for rights licensing and/or urgency of clearance

---

[41] 44 F.3d 813 (9th Cir. 1995) *cert. denied*, 64 U.S.L.W. 3270 (1996).
[42] 17 U.S.C. §303(b) (1998).

requirements. Therefore, the question becomes: What is essential? The answer: Those rights which are necessary to generate enough income to recoup investment and make a profit.

Copyright laws in the United States[43] and a majority of the developed nations[44] recognize a bundle of rights possessed by the owner, including the rights of reproduction, adaptation, publication, performance, and display. Those rights that are relevant can be divided into two groups: (1) republication rights (including the rights of reproduction, publication, and display), where the underlying material is to be reused in substantially the form of the original work, and (2) adaptation rights, where the underlying work is to be transformed into a new work with its own right to copyright protection.

Clearing rights for republication is a relatively simple transaction. Although the re-publisher may, by its agreement, wish to share in subsidiary-rights licenses in the underlying work generated by its republication (where, for example, a motion picture sale takes place because a producer discovered an out of print or translated work through the republication), the republication does not (except for possible rights to translation, organization, layout, design or a new preface, epilogue, etc.)[45] create a new copyrightable work. Nonetheless, in clearing republication, a review of the subsidiary rights previously granted is necessary to ensure that there is no direct conflict with prior grants or licenses.

Clearing rights for adaptation is significantly more complicated because a new copyrightable work is thereby created. In order to exploit that work, it is necessary to establish whether the rights to adapt are available and to make sure that exploitation of the subsidiary rights thereto do not conflict with subsidiary rights previously granted in the underlying work to another.

In dealing with source works of a foreign origin, it is necessary to consider the effect of the creative rights laws applicable to that country of origin. Such laws can have significant impact upon who can issue a license to the subject work, the terms of that license, and the duration of protection. More importantly for attorneys grounded in the copyright system as we know it in this country, it must be borne in mind that foreign laws may protect works that are not protected by copyright in

---

[43] *See supra* §1.4.
[44] *See supra* §§1.4 and 5.1.3.1.
[45] *See supra* §1.2.

the United States. These include works of folklore (literary, artistic, or scientific works created by unknown authors forming a part of a country's cultural heritage)[46] and public domain works (works whose term of copyright protection have expired, the benefit for the licensing of which is transferred from the creators to social programs for the benefit of all creators).[47]

6.2.2. Illustration: Clearing Rights for Dramatic or Dramatico-Musical Adaptation

For the purpose of illustrating the clearance of adaptation rights, let us examine the clearance of an underlying work (e.g., a novel, song, lyric, or even a painting) for a dramatic play or dramatico-musical adaptation.

6.2.2.1. Dramatic Rights

Collectively, dramatic-play, dramatico-musical, and motion-picture rights are defined as "dramatic rights."[48] These three terms are similar in most respects, but there are distinctions.

---

[46] *See, e.g.*, Tunis Model Law of Copyright §18.

[47] *See* D. Sinacore-Guinn, COLLECTIVE ADMINISTRATION OF COPYRIGHTS AND NEIGHBORING RIGHTS: INT'L PRACTICES, PROCEDURES & ORGANIZATIONS, 167-168 (Little, Brown) (1993).

[48] Dramatic rights are often incorrectly referred to as *grand rights*, a term more correctly restricted to dramatico-musical works. The term *grand rights* is a literal translation from the French *grandes droits* – as distinguished from *petits droits (small rights)*. The terms were historically developed to distinguish those rights that derived from the creation, production, and publication of all or part of a dramatico-musical work. Such work contains a libretto, music, and lyrics. Where one person controls the dramatico-musical work in its entirety only and a second person controls only the music and lyrics, the first person may be said to have the grand rights and the second person will only publish, print, record, etc. individual compositions from the score. Because the small rights and the grand rights were usually exercised by the same person in Europe, the word *grand* came to mean those rights that were used to license the entire opera or operetta for the stage. The music publisher also printed music in what was known as a *petit format*, a copy containing only the melody line and lyric to a single song, so that the public could sing it without resorting to a musical instrument. Hence, the words *petit droits* referred originally to that printing right that antedated records, films, television, and other media of permanent fixation.

1. *Dramatic play rights*: The right to adapt and perform the work as a drama or play;
2. *Dramatico-musical rights*: The right to adapt and perform the work in association with music as a musical or opera;
3. *Motion-picture rights*: The right to fix an adaptation (either dramatic play or dramatico-musical) permanently in a fixed audiovisual medium and exhibit that fixation on screen, on television, on discs or tapes, and in places where it can be viewed by a paying or nonpaying audience. (Although it is more accurate to describe these as audio-visual rights, they are more commonly known as motion picture rights.)

6.2.2.2. Distinctions among the Dramatic Rights

The owner of the dramatic stage rights to a work may license those rights for adaptation to a dramatico-musical work for the stage, even though the owner of the underlying work (a novel, for example) may have granted a motion picture studio the exclusive motion picture rights to the same work. On the other hand, the studio may have the right to create its own *musical* motion picture version of the work but would not be able to utilize the score from the newly created dramatico-musical stage work without independently acquiring the new musical score. At the same time, the creators of the new dramatico-musical work would be able to perform their work on stage but not be able to authorize a commercial motion picture version of *that* work (although limited carveouts permitting the creation of an archival film of the stage work, and/or for the filming of individual scenes for television or online promotion of the stage work, may often be obtained). Although it may be desirable (or imperative in order to finance the new stage production) for a creator of dramatico-musical rights to also acquire motion picture rights at the time that the original rights are cleared, the owner of the underlying work may refrain from such a grant in hopes that, if the dramatico-play or dramatico-musical version of the work is successful, a more favorable agreement for the motion picture rights can be negotiated later.

6.2.2.3. Similarities among the Dramatic Rights

Inherent within the concept of the dramatic rights is the right to adapt and perform (or exhibit) the work.

6.2.2.4. Adaptation Rights Issues

Because of this process of adaptation, one must be concerned with the right to adapt and the rights that flow from that adaptation.

a. *The Right to Adapt.* Because of the concept of *droit moral ("moral rights")*, i.e., the author's right not to have his original work "corrupted,"[49] it is important that the right to adapt (i.e., to change or alter characters, plot, title, or other elements of the source work) be clearly defined and approved in advance.

b. *Rights Flowing from the Adaptation.* Because of the adaptation, a new work is created that under copyright law is recognized as possessing its own subsidiary rights.[50] Of primary importance are the worldwide motion picture rights, in addition to stock, amateur, and foreign rights for the stage.[51]

6.2.2.5. Territory of Rights

Rights may be specified as being effective for certain territories (e.g., the United States or France). Care should be taken to state geographic territories, *not political* territories (like the British Commonwealth, European Union or NAFTA), unless the definition also includes the *date*, since political alignments may change over time. Motion picture rights are almost always cleared for the world (which is the ideal). Dramatic play and dramatico-musical rights under the new standard Dramatist Guild Approved Production Contract require clearances of at least the United States, Canada, the United

---

[49] *See supra* §§1.4.2., 4.3.5.
[50] 17 U.S.C. §103 (1976).
[51] Important additional rights are set forth in the Dramatists Guild-Approved Production Contract [hereinafter referred to as the APC]. There are separate APCs for dramatic and dramatico-musical work for Broadway (or first-class) and for Off-Broadway productions. Although they are fundamentally similar, for the purposes herein we will refer to the provisions of the APC for musical plays. Additional rights are set forth in articles IX, X, and XI of the APC.

Kingdom, Australia, New Zealand, and their territories and possessions, since the producer normally obtains the right to produce the play in the major English language territories.[52] Additional territories would be exploitable solely by the authors of the adaptation with the initial producer retaining a right to share in the income derived from such exploitation.[53]

6.2.2.6. Music Rights

Music rights deserve special note because although they may be merged within the dramatico-musical work and performed within it, certain rights are usually retained by the composer and lyricist, who may separately dispose of those rights. Those retained rights include public performing rights in the individual musical compositions comprising the score, mechanical rights (i.e., mechanically reproducing the separate musical composition on a CD, downloadable digital file or ringtone), synchronization rights (using the individual composition in synchronization with audio-visual images apart from their use in the dramatico-musical work), and folio print rights. These rights must be identified both in the clearance of underlying rights and in subsequent dispositions.

6.2.2.7. Title

The title of a work cannot be copyrighted, although this does not mean that it cannot be protected. Even if the work is in the public domain, the law gives some protection to titles if someone has invested time and labor that enhance the value of that title and, as a result, that title has come to have a secondary meaning in the public mind identifying the source and quality of some associated product or service.[54] The title may thus become identifiable as a trademark (like IBM or Coca Cola or Star Wars or American Idol), and can be registered with the Patent and Trademark Office and marketed in the same way as a Trademark. Conversely, a pre-existing trademark may prevent the use of a title for a song, motion picture or other work. The

---

[52] APC, arts. 3.1 (United States and Canada) and IX (United Kingdom, Australia, and New Zealand).
[53] APC, art. XI.
[54] See §§3.2.4 and 3.11.2, *supra*.

extent of this protection is controversial – and controversy in the law invites litigation, which is something that clients pay lawyers to avoid. Consequently, a trademark search may be advisable before a title is formally adopted for the marketing of a new work.[55]

6.2.2.8. "Fair Use"

The concept of fair use under the copyright law is probably one of the most complex and difficult areas of the law germane to Entertainment Industry concerns – far too complex to be fully summarized in this volume[56]. However, to avoid certain common misconceptions, one must know that although the copyright law defines fair use, the courts are constantly struggling with its interpretation.[57] Any use of a copyrighted work without the permission of the copyright owner could be an infringement of that work. It is recommended that if the work contains a copyright notice, any use inconsistent with established "fair use" exceptions for education and/or parody should be cleared with the copyright owner. If use cannot be cleared, either avoid using the work or otherwise be prepared for the possibility of expensive litigation.

6.2.3. The Source Material and Places to Begin

The starting point of an investigation into clearing world rights is the tangible source that inspired the author's use. This may be a published book, an unpublished manuscript, the theater program of a performance of a play, a published play itself, a movie, a television show, a recording, a song, a magazine article, or a newspaper item (with or without by-line). The objective is to determine if the source material is protected in whole or in part by (or is eligible for protection under) a copyright, and if so to contact the original author/copyright owner with respect to its availability for the use intended. The task is to find him or her. The source itself may provide some clues as to where to begin.

---

[55] As noted in §8.1.7, *supra*, the investigation of conflicting "titles" via a "title search" should not be confused with a "Title Report" analysis of the "chain-of-title" ownership of a work's underlying copyright.

[56] Additional commentary on the application of "fair use" appears in §1.5, *supra*.

[57] *See supra* §1.5.

6.2.3.1. Direct Clues

Examining the actual source material will provide some direction in how to proceed and who might be contacted.

a. *Copyright Notice.* Assume that the work is not in the public domain. If the work bears a notice of copyright in the author's name (or that of a publisher in the case of a book, magazine or newspaper article), a copyright search may be made through the office of the Registrar of Copyrights. If the author is an American, the search will reveal both a means of contacting him or her and any licenses and copyrights on existing works derived from the same source. Inquiry may also be directed to the publisher.

b. *Acknowledgments.* If the source is a reprint, the original source may be indicated in an acknowledgment.

c. *Credits.* Who are the parties who acquired the rights to create the source (i.e., to publish it, reprint it, perform it, record it, etc.)?

d. *Title and Subtitle.* The title and any subtitles, if desired for use in conjunction with the new work, should be cleared through a title search of the Copyright Office and the Office of Patents and Trademarks. This will provide information as to whether others may be claiming against this title, whether they are in a competitive position with the proposed use, and whether others may be basing derivative works on the same source. The title may also be checked through the Writers Guild of America (East, in New York, or West, in Los Angeles) or the Motion Picture Association of America, which maintains a registry of reserved film titles for member Studios, production companies and distributors, and the American Society of Authors, Composers and Publishers (ASCAP), Broadcast Music, Inc. (BMI), or what was originally the Society of European State Authors and Composers (now SESAC) for song titles.[58]

6.2.3.2. Further Investigation

The material may also provide some clue as to the nature of the basic or original work (if other than the work in hand), so that further general inquiries may be directed toward persons, associations, societies, or governmental authorities that can most likely offer assistance.

---

[58] *See infra*, Directory of Guilds, Unions, and Other Organizations, for addresses.

a. *The Writers and Authors Guilds.* The author may be a member of the Writers Guild of America (WGA, East or West), the Authors Guild, or the Dramatists Guild. These guilds may also be able to direct one to the author's local or foreign agent or the local representative of a foreign publisher.

b. *The Library.* Reviewing *Books in Print* or similar publications may give leads as to other publishers that may have published works by the same author. For plays, the Library of the Performing Arts at Lincoln Center in New York may provide ways of tracing the author or the original producer of a play.

c. *Collective Administration Organizations.* In many countries of the world copyrights are handled by large rights organizations known as collective administration organizations. In some cases they may administer all the rights to the works of their affiliated members, while in others they may represent only specific rights (such as the "musical non-dramatic public performing rights" represented by ASCAP and BMI).[59] Significantly, in many countries, particularly those in the developing world, as a contribution to national culture collectives have taken it upon themselves to develop a comprehensive listing of works created by their nationals regardless of whether or not that collective represents that creator.[60] The book *International Guide to Collective Organizations*[61] provides a comprehensive listing of these types of collective administration organizations, identifying them by their territory of administration and the types of rights administered by them. It also provides general contact information (address, phone number(s), fax number(s), etc.) for each organization. The Confederation of International Societies of Authors and Composers (CISAC), one of the largest international associations of collective administration organizations, also publishes a listing of its members with addresses and phone numbers which can be acquired via the organization's website, www.CISAC.org. Many of the larger collective administration organizations are beginning to appear on the World

---

[59] *See* D. Sinacore-Guinn, COLLECTIVE ADMINISTRATION OF COPYRIGHTS AND NEIGHBORING RIGHTS: INTERNATIONAL PRACTICES, PROCEDURES AND ORGANIZATIONS (Little, Brown) (1993).

[60] *Id.* at 440.

[61] D. Sinacore-Guinn, INTERNATIONAL GUIDE TO COLLECTIVE ADMINISTRATION ORGANIZATIONS (1993-1994 Ed.) (1993).

Wide Web and searches of their repertoires can be made on the internet.

d. *The Clearance Departments of the Broadcast Networks and Studios.* The broadcast networks and major motion picture studios have developed highly trained and efficient clearance departments and maintain detailed files of rights information on their productions, although it may not be readily accessible to outside persons.

e. *Clearance Services.* As noted above, a number of private clearance services specializing in copyright and production clearance matters are available to assist in the research, negotiation and administration of clearance matters, and may be able to do so with greater efficiency and economy than lawyers and law firms for whom such work is not an exclusive focus.

f. *The World Wide Web.* Online search engines of course now offer a myriad of additional avenues for the identification and location of authors and works.

6.2.3.3. A Caveat

Although people working in the copyright clearance field generally are generous in their desire to help and often volunteer the name of the next person who really knows the answers, the prudent researcher limits the number of people who are aware of the current search and thereby limits future complications. Works that interest an adapter may have attained some popularity in their original versions. This may mean that the work (if it is a play or book) has been performed or published in ten to twenty foreign countries. In order to cross international boundaries from the country of origin to other countries of publication or performance, certain legal and economic forces have been affecting the creative work. These events now must be recreated in order to have an accurate picture of the entire history of the basic work. In the course of an investigation the researcher meets people who, truthfully, mistakenly, or connivingly, may represent that they control or represent certain rights in the basic work, or they know someone who does or who believes he or she does. Following these leads is often time consuming and costly. Moreover, an intermediary who does not control the desired rights may nonetheless seek to assume a broker role with the copyright holder, which can add to a project's expense while conveying no direct benefits to the would be licensor or purchaser.

6.2.4. Profiling the Author

In the process of tracing the author, one will acquire certain information about him or her. As part of this process, it is recommended that a profile of the author be drawn with the following questions, the answers to which will identify the possible sources of copyright authority and the extent of the rights that may be granted.

6.2.4.1. Which Copyright Law Applies?

Under principles of United States Copyright Law[62] and the Berne[63] and Universal Copyright Conventions,[64] the national law of the author's origin will control aspects of the rights that the author may grant. Profile questions include:

1. Where was the author born?
2. What is the author's nationality?

6.2.4.2. Duration of Copyright

Copyrights are of a fixed duration according to the law of the author's country. The most commonly found duration is the life of the author plus some set number of years after his or her death (e.g., life

---

[62] 17 U.S.C. §104 (1998).

[63] The Berne convention is a series of treaties commencing in 1886 in which subscribing countries agreed to certain uniform protections for all copyrights and copyright owners among the subscribing countries. These treaties created the Berne Union. Even within the Berne Union there are certain variations of law, but a fundamental precept is that, once a work is recognized as Copyrightable in one country, it must extend the same right to other nationals and must acknowledge the copyrights of other nations. *See* Berne Convention (Paris 1971, amended 1978), arts. 3, 5.

[64] The Universal Copyright Convention (UCC) functions much the way that the Berne Convention does. The distinctions between them for purposes of this book are minor. For the protection of foreign nationals, see Universal Copyright Convention (Paris 1971), arts. II *et seq.*

plus seventy years).[65] Under the 1909 United States law, which controlled works created thereunder up until the 1992 Copyright Renewal Act was enacted,[66] the duration was twenty-eight years plus a renewal period of twenty-eight years (plus an extension of nineteen years, as provided by the 1976 Copyright Law). Overhaul of Unites States Copyright Law in 1976, and subsequently, converted our system of fixing duration to one consistent with international protocols under the Berne Convention, and now provides for a duration of (1) for unpublished works created in 1978 and thereafter, life of the author plus 70 years, and (2) for works in the United States 70 years from the death of the author, or 95 years from publication for "corporate works" (i.e., works created by one or more authors as "work for hire" for corporations). Additionally, for some works originally published abroad for which at least one author was not a U.S. citizen or was a U.S. citizen living abroad, and/or for which are anonymous, pseudonymous or corporate works, the duration can be as much as 120 years from creation for unpublished work. It is possible that a source may be protected in some parts of the world and in the public domain in others, depending on these differences of duration among countries. Where the work in question exists in other than a print medium, in all likelihood the authorship and copyright reside with a legal entity rather than an individual or individuals, who may have created the materials on "work for hire" or "specially commissioned work" basis. Profile questions include:

1. Is "author" an individual or entity?
2. Is the author still alive?
3. If dead, when did the author die?
4. When was the work created?
5. When (if at all) was the work first published?

---

[65] *See supra* §§1.9, 5.9-5.10. The Sonny Bono Copyright Term Extension Act, effective October 27, 1998, substituted "70" for "50" for the duration of works authored by individuals, and added 20 years to the duration of copyright for anonymous works or works written for corporate authors as "work for hire" (i.e., from 75 to 95 years, and 100 years to 120 years, respectively), each place they appeared. Pub. L. No. 105-298, 112 Stat. 2827.

[66] *See* §§1.9.3, 1.11.2 *supra*.

6.2.4.3. Rights Owners Deriving Their Authority through the Author

Certain relatives derive copyright rights through their relationship with the author. They may have inherited rights from the author or have contingent rights under the law that may come into being after the author dies affecting licenses granted by the author during his or her lifetime.[67] For example, under the concept of copyright renewal for works written under the 1909 Copyright Law, a widow and children or other person listed in the statute would be able to assert new rights, even though those same rights were previously granted by the deceased author but ceased because of the author's death prior to the end of the twenty-eighth year. These concerns are pertinent to works which predate the 1976 Copyright Law, for which the profile questions include:

1. Was the author married?
2. Were there any children?
3. Did the author leave a will, and who is the executor?
4. Are there heirs, and who are they?
5. Where are they now?

6.2.4.4. Co-authors or Collaborators

If there are co-authors of the work, a separate profile following the format set forth hereinabove should be drawn for each of the collaborators (dramatists, lyricists, composers, etc.).

The rights granted to authors under the copyright law exist concurrently with the individual's right to contract. Indeed, the right to contract allows the author to waive certain rights, to choose between certain types of applications of the copyright laws (i.e., whether the collaborative work is a joint work,[68] in which each of the authors has an undivided joint interest in a unified work, or a composite work,[69] in which the individual rights of the authors are simply licensed for their

---

[67] For example, see 17 U.S.C. §203 (2002); *see also supra* §1.11.
[68] 17 U.S.C. §101 (2005).
[69] *Id.*

use in the work with each other while the right to separately license his or her contribution is reserved), or to enhance the protections normally available to him or her under the law. For example, if the collaborative work is a joint work in a jurisdiction in which the copyright term is measured at life plus seventy years, the copyright term will run for seventy years after the last author dies. If the collaborative work was merely a composite work, each author's identifiable contribution would fall into the public domain seventy years after that author's death, irrespective of the continuing protection afforded the remaining authors. Profile questions include

1. What was the legal nature of the contractual relationship among the collaborators?
2. Did any of them fail to continue the collaboration to the end? If not, what is his or her known contribution and what form of release, if any, governed the future rights of each collaborator after one collaborator discontinued?

6.2.4.5. Authors Guild or Society Membership

The final element in the author's profile is whether or not he or she belongs to an author's guild, society, or union. Such organizations, by their very nature, create rules and regulations governing their members' conduct with respect to the rights to their works. They often define the terms used in the contractual language of a grant of rights, if not providing the actual provisions of the grant, and frequently the rules and regulations of a guild are incorporated by reference in the author's agreements. One must, therefore, examine those rules and regulations in effect contemporaneously with the work's creation, as well as those currently in effect, in order to understand the provisions of any author's agreements that may be located.

6.2.5. The Initial Publication

The next step in identifying the author calls for an examination of the initial publication (or recording or performance) of the work and the original agreement between the person responsible for that initial publication.

6.2.5.1. Books and Periodicals

a. *Work-for-hire Authors.* The first question to answer in a book or periodical agreement is whether or not the work was a work made for hire.[70] If so, the publisher is deemed to be the author for copyright purposes. Except for the application of a special copyright term[71] and occasional (although rare) reversion of rights to the natural author, the copyright laws basically treat the publisher on the same basis as a natural author.

b. *Agency and Title.* If the work is not a work for hire, one must determine if the publisher has appointed an agent or retains an ownership position. For dramatic-rights purposes, except occasionally with respect to motion picture rights, these provisions are fairly rare. (This is, in essence, a part of tracing the chain of title, addressed in §6.2.6.)

6.2.5.2. Dramatic Productions

When the source work is a play or foreign musical, certain unique problems arise in identifying the author.

a. *The Production.* A theatrical production is a collaborative work involving not only the authors but other creative people: directors, choreographers, designers, orchestrators and arrangers, translators, and others. Each of these people may have contributed to the work and may be entitled at minimum to income and at worst to some degree of control. Therefore, each of these parties must be identified, their agreements examined, and their respective unions considered for what rights they may reserve or convey to their members.

b. *The Producer.* In the United States, under the Dramatists Guild Approved Production Contract (APC), a theatrical producer acquires a limited right to produce a play in the United States, Canada,[72] the United Kingdom, Australia, and New Zealand[73] and, subject to meeting certain minimum-run commitments, a right to

---

[70] For example, see 17 U.S.C. §101 (2005).
[71] For example, see 17 U.S.C. §302 (1998).
[72] APC, art. I.
[73] APC, art. IX.

receive income thereafter.[74] Foreign producers, however, are not necessarily confined to their country of original production. One must examine the producer's agreement to see if the producer obtains an ownership or control interest in the work and the territory (e.g., defined as a single country, the British Commonwealth, the European Union, English-language rights, the world, etc.) of the grant.

c. *Music Publishers.* In identifying the author of a musical-source work, it is important to understand the unique function of the music publisher. In Europe, premiere performances of musical productions were generally arranged either by music publishers or by so-called theater publishers acting sometimes independently or sometimes together. The actual control of the grand rights (or stage performance rights) rests generally with one of these two entities. Traditionally, the music publishers of Europe were resourceful enough to secure grand rights from their composers as well as the so-called small rights (the right to print, publish, and publicly perform the musical compositions separately and apart from the dramatico-musical work as a whole). They usually financed the preparation of the orchestrations for the pit and arranged for the performance of the work at the various opera or operetta houses of Europe. They also supplied the orchestrations to the producer for a separate rental fee. The theater publisher, also acting as an agent, arranged for performances of the musical but published only a libretto. In this last situation, the music publisher had the right to rent or refuse to rent the orchestral material to the licensee of the theater publisher and could then exercise a restrictive control over the actual performance until some agreement was reached between them. The division of rights that might exist in a variety of situations therefore makes it mandatory that all contracts be studied to determine exactly with whom the various rights lay, including in particular:

1. The right to perform the entire dramatic or dramatico-musical work; and

2. The physical orchestrations required by the musicians to give the performance, the physical property of the book itself (that is, the actor's sides), and finally, the publication rights to each component (music, etc.).

---

[74] APC, art. XI.

In other words, every person or entity that owns or controls every contributed element, whether tangible or intangible, must be traced, and the extent of the grant of rights to and/or control by that party must be identified.

6.2.5.3. Motion Pictures and Television Programming

When the source work is a motion picture or television production (whether based on an original work for the medium in which first produced, or a pre-existing novel or stage work), the rights analysis must take into account whether the prequel, sequel and/or remake rights being sought were part of the original grant of rights or were retained by the owner/grantor.

6.2.6. Tracing the Chain of Title

From this point, assuming that permission is obtained from the original authors, the discovery process must be reversed to trace the chain of title forward from its creation to the present. This assures that what the authors gave they still had the right to give. It goes without saying that an obscure basic work will create fewer problems than one that has merited publication or performances in many countries, because with every movement across international borders, a performance, a translation, a publication, or a mechanical reproduction will have taken place.

The Berne Convention, the copyright law of the country of origin, the regulations of societies, the conventions between societies, and the specific contracts between parties will also complicate the search. For example, in the United States, one must not only be concerned with whether or not one has found the author and copyright owner of a pre-1978 copyrighted work, one but also must determine whether or not that work is subject or already has been subjected to a statutory reversion based on the death (or the possible death) of the author prior to the renewal to the copyright.[75] If one person can warrant and represent that he or she has all the rights that are needed from everyone concerned, and there are no statutory limitations on that person's rights, prudence still dictates a request for copies of all relevant basic documents from that

---

[75] See supra §6.1.8.

person to safely recreate all of the various relationships previously mentioned.

Finally, even though every piece of contractual paper written by laypersons or drafted by lawyers has been collected, problems still remain because the translated documents contain language that in English may mean something very different from the original foreign language of the documents. It now becomes a matter of judgment (for no one should be so foolish as to solely rely for clarification from the licensor) as to what was meant by certain general and all-encompassing terms of the grant in the original contract. Many concepts that exist today were once unknown (such as cast-album rights, home-video rights, etc.). When one considers that concepts like "performance," "publication," and "recording" cause great confusion even domestically, despite the best of intentions and an infinite number of judicial decisions and treatises on copyright, the difficulty of making such a decision becomes apparent. And where these questions cannot be neatly resolved, one must ultimately decide to go with what one has – or drop the project altogether.

6.2.7. The New Work

The final step prepares the way for a new voyage. The rights that have so painstakingly been cleared must now be put to productive use. Knowing what one has dictates what one has to give. If there are restrictions on the acquired rights, those restrictions must be reflected in each agreement granting rights to the new work. If the new owner of the cleared rights intends to contract with writers to write the new work, that agreement must state clearly what rights they will have, for under the Dramatists Guild Approved Production Contract, for example, the authors of the dramatico-musical work ultimately own and control the resulting work. The value and complications of merger provisions in tracing the original work underscore the importance of clearly identifying those rights in the new work to assure that the work can be efficiently exploited and that other producers will not be dissuaded from licensing rights because "clearing" those rights is too time consuming and difficult or because of a failure in the paper work.

6.3. THINKING ABOUT TRADEMARKS AND MERCHANDISING

Beginning in the 1970s with the emergence of "designer" licensing, the law of trademarks burgeoned to govern important ancillary markets for properties created by the entertainment and sports industry. From worldwide sales of $10 billion in 1980, licensing sales blossomed to exceed $262 billion by 2016, of which nearly $120 billion represents entertainment/character licensing and another nearly $18.5 billion flows from videogames, software and apps licensing.[76] From the T-shirts and buttons sold at rock concerts to the myriad tie-ins of everything from toys (Star Wars lightsabers) to bedclothes (SpongeBob Squarepants) licensed in conjunction with the release of major motion pictures, trademarks and service-mark licenses have flourished, providing new sources of income that have, at times, exceeded the earning power of the entertainment venture that created them.[77] This is true of all areas of entertainment, particularly films,[78] television,[79] and music.[80] Indeed, in the current environment, the genesis of trademarks in relation to entertainment properties has shifted from a tradition where marks were based on well-established characters or symbols (such as Superman or the Superman logo of the

---

[76] Highlights of the International Licensing Industry Merchandisers' Association (LIMA) 2016 Annual Survey, as reported by Samantha Loveday of LicensingSource.Net on May 22, 2017 (http://licensingsource.net/global-sales-of-licensed-goods-hit-262-9bn-in-2016/)

[77] For example, the first five live action films in the *Star Wars* franchise had by 2005 earned more than $9 Billion in merchandising, dwarfing a reported worldwide $3.4 Billion dollars in worldwide box office as of 2005. See Holson, Laura "Is There Life after 'Star Wars' for Lucasfilm?" New York Times (May 1, 2005). The picture is not so bright for other films that have lower than expected box office draw and have a corresponding poor sales of merchandise (such as *Cat-in-the-Hat*). See Theresa Howard "Now playing at a toy store near you" USA Today (Dec. 8, 2003).

[78] Ethan Gilsdorf, *Lord of the Gold Ring* Boston Globe (Magazine) (Nov. 16, 2003) "Once upon a time, J.R.R. Tolkien's *The Lord of the Rings* was considered a work of literary genius, but now thanks to a movie and merchandising spinoffs, the author's reputation is foundering in a sea of commercialism." Merchandising can in effect be an insurance policy against box office failure. New Line Cinema's 300 international licensing agreements alone recouped the movie trilogy's $300 Million price tag before the *Fellowship of the Ring* opened at the theatres.

[79] *See* Lana Berkowitz, *Saturating the Market – Soaking up SpongeBob – The Little Lovable Square Yellow Guy Is Everywhere When It Comes To Merchandise* Houston Chronicle (November 19, 2004).

[80] Steve Traiman, "Licensing Likenesses: Stars lend their faces to everything from dolls to ducks to video games." Billboard Magazine (June 15, 2002).

"S" on a shield) to one in which: programs have been based on trademarked merchandise (e.g., the animated "Barbie"™ or LEGO™ movies, or the live action/CGI Transformers™ series of films); productions have been financed by the owners of those marks (e.g., Pokemon);[81] and others in which the merchandising use and entertainment use of the mark[82] appear to have been developed concurrently.[83]

In order to benefit from this area of exploitation, two inquiries must be made: to identify what is protectable as a trademark and what is essential to create and protect that mark.

6.3.1. What Is Protectable?

6.3.1.1. In General

In general, the law of trademarks attempts to protect original expressions of ideas – whether names, logos, pictures, or other symbols – that are capable[84] of embodying public good will measurable as an economic value. In its simplest form, this is shown by the premium that a customer will pay for a brand-name product (e.g., Coca-Cola or Starbucks products) versus generic products.[85]

In any given project, there are numerous original expressions capable of becoming protectable marks. For example, with respect to a motion picture, such as Star Wars, there is the title itself, the title embodied in the advertising poster/design, the various characters (i.e., Obi Wan Kenobi, R2D2, and Anakin Skywalker), unique costume

---

[81] The Pokemon franchise began as a comic book derived from a video game. This enterprise has since blossomed into a television series, toy merchandise and motion pictures. See Lauren Foster, *Astroboy Blasts Off into the Stores*, Financial Times (London) (Feb. 9, 2004).

[82] Note: The terms trademark and mark are used interchangeably and are intended to embrace trademarks, service marks, and all other categories of trademark protection.

[83] *See* Monterosso, *Companies Find Trademarks Valuable Source for Direct Profits Due to Changes in Law*, N.Y.L.J. Aug. 1, 1986, at S.

[84] A strict interpretation of the law would hold that the mark not only be capable of embodying public good will but that it already has obtained sufficient "secondary" meaning to actually embody that good will. A fair reading of the developing law suggests that the law will protect original marks during the period when they may fairly acquire that good will.

[85] *See* Conrad De Aenille, *"Famous Brands can bring benefit, or a backlash"* N.Y. Times (Oct. 19, 2003).

designs (e.g., the Darth Vader mask), props (the Lightsaber), or sets (the Death Star). In 1997, two years before the Star Wars prequel film, *The Phantom Menace*, was to be released, lawyers for Lucas Licensing filed over 3,000 prequel related trademarks in a single day.[86] In short, potentially "protectable" marks are anything that people identify with the venture and are willing to pay for.

The identification of those elements of an entertainment venture that may develop value as marks is of great importance. Not only do those marks represent significant potential income but perhaps more important, a failure to defend a mark can destroy it. For example, in *Rossner v. CBS, Inc.*,[87] the courts held that although Judith Rosner had coined a protectable mark in the word "goodbar" (from the title of her book *Looking for Mr. Goodbar*), which, at the time her novel was released, was associated with her book, the strength of the word as a trademark was destroyed by its subsequent use by others. Her failure to protect the mark by stopping those others from using it destroyed its value as a mark.

The effort to preserve the value of marks after a project's release is particularly important at this time as current wisdom holds that sequels, because of their familiarity, are better vehicles for merchandising than original films.[88] Thus, one must protect the marks in the first film, even if they are not being successfully marketed at that time, in order to assure their availability in the event sequels are made.

6.3.1.2. Performers' Names

A number of performers and sports figures, like Tiger Woods, Leonardo di Caprio and Charlie Sheen, trademarked their names.[89] There is a large and growing market for celebrity endorsements, and trademarking their name gives them additional legal tools to protect their rights in addition to those normally provided under the law of

---

[86] Di Mari Ricker, *"'Star Wars' IP Attorneys use the Force"* The Recorder/Cal Law (May 5, 1999).

[87] 612 F.Supp. 334, 226 U.S.P.Q. 593 (S.D.N.Y. 1985).

[88] Deborah Hornblow, *"The Embarrassment of Studio Riches; Studios Play It Dumb, Dumber to Reach the Bottom Line: Big Box Office."* Hartford Courant (May 5, 2005).

[89] *See*, Ron Higgins, "Earnhardt *Stayed True to His Roots, Style and Fans.*" The Commercial Appeal (Memphis, TN) (Feb. 2001). *See also*, Nui Ti Koha, *"Budget Rein-In Dents Egos"* Sunday Telegraph (Sydney (Aug. 8, 1999), Australia); See also Di Mari Ricker, *"It's My Image – I'll Sue if I Want To"* The Recorder/Cal Law (Apr. 7, 1999).

publicity and privacy.[90] In addition, publicity/privacy laws are state laws, and the amount of protection accorded under those laws varies significantly from state to state. For example, while one of the early precedent setting cases in the law of publicity and privacy was *Haelan Labs. v. Topps Chewing Gum, Inc.*[91] recognized the right of baseball players to license their pictures for use on baseball cards, in 1996 a court in Oklahoma found that Oklahoma's right of publicity statute was unconstitutional when applied to baseball cards as a form of protected free speech.[92] As a federal law, trademark avoids this problem and provides uniform protection across the country.

6.3.2. The Creation and Protection of the Mark

As has been shown,[93] trademarks are not created by their registration. They exist by virtue of their ability to embody public good will, either through their originality or uniqueness or through the acquisition of secondary meaning. For example, the mark "Barney" is protectable because of its uniqueness as a created name for a certain purple-skinned dinosaur, while the "Beanie Babies" mark's protection rests largely on the public's identification of that name with particular stuffed animals manufactured by a certain manufacturer. (Note that once the manufacturer establishes a secondary meaning allowing protection, it can then freely exploit the mark in films and other media or can develop the mark on film and then license it to manufacturers.)

An analysis of possible marks in any project should sort marks into unique or original marks for which immediate protection can be sought and marks for which the acquisition of secondary meaning is required. As a second part of the analysis, a search of the United States Patent and Trademark Office Registers may be ordered. The search may be made by the Patent and Trademark Office at a reasonable charge or by a firm that specializes in such searches. Such a search is used to make sure that no prior claim exists to the mark and to determine if a confusingly similar mark exists. (In either case the mark is not protectable and may not be usable in the project.)

---

[90] *See* Chap. 4 *supra*.
[91] 202 F.2d 866 (2d Cir.), *on remand*, 112 F. Supp. 904 (E.D.N.Y.), *cert. denied*, 346 U.S. 816 (1953).
[92] Cardtoons, L.C. v. Major League Baseball Players Ass'n, 95 F.3rd 959 (10th Cir. 1996).
[93] *See supra* §3.5.

At this point, provided that the marks are available, either those marks not requiring secondary meaning can be registered or the entertainment venture can be exploited to develop secondary meaning in all of the marks (thus making them all stronger) prior to filing for registration. (Failing to register does not harm the value of the mark; it merely limits one's remedies in protecting it.)[94] The important elements of the use are that it must be used prominently and solely by the creator. Use by other people must be prohibited by the mark owner. (If necessary, this can be accomplished by court actions brought under state or federal unfair competition laws.)

Once the marks are established, they can be licensed.

6.3.3. Enforcement

While the law gives ample protection to the owners of trademarks, they are generally not self-enforcing. This is a vast market with many people willing to trade upon the success of others. Consequently, producers and creative rights owners have had to initiate their own efforts to protect their rights. LucasFilms, which has profited enormously from its merchandising efforts, was said to have created a "worldwide team" to protect its rights during the roll out of *Phantom Menace*.[95] As can be imagined, this does not come cheaply. Paramount, owner of the lucrative Star Trek franchise among others, has spent over $1 million a year in legal enforcement fees for its properties.[96] However, the rewards for policing these assets can be significant. In just one case it obtained $1 million from a group of manufacturers, advertisers and sellers of allegedly fake Star Trek products. Moreover, this vigilance is necessary to protect the legitimate market for these profits.

6.4. WARRANTIES AND REPRESENTATIONS

It has been said that a primary function of a negotiated contract (and one of the principal reasons that lawyers are engaged to negotiate contracts) is to establish a reasonable allocation of risks among the

---

[94] *See supra* §3.7.
[95] *Id.* at § 6.3.1.1.
[96] *Id.* at §3.7

parties.[97] Nowhere is this principle more apparent than in the standard warranties and representations clause in an entertainment contract relating to granting of rights. Moreover, analyzing warranties and representations with this concept in mind provides an appropriate perspective for negotiating these provisions.

It is also necessary, in negotiating these provisions, to keep in mind the essential nature of entertainment – namely, that it is an intangible process of creation. It is not a material manufacturing process creating a physical product, even though it may result in a tangible property (i.e., a book or film). The primary product of entertainment is an *intangible* intellectual property, whether a copyright, trademark, or privacy/ publicity right, and it is this creative process that entertainment law seeks to govern and recognize. We must consequently examine the creative authorship process to determine what is protectable.

The process becomes all the more complex in the collaborative fields of entertainment. Authorship is the creation of original works that the law will seek to protect. In a venture such as a motion picture, for example, many participants have a hand in the "authorship" of the film, from the producer who may come up with the concept of the film, to the screenwriter who puts the concept into words, the actors who improvise words or actions, the director who reworks the screenplay and the cinematographer who gives it a visual dimension, the designers and the editors, and others who contribute to the process of making a film. All of these contributions add up to the final work, and it is the intent of the warranties and representations clause to establish that the resulting work (1) is protectable, (2) is owned or controlled by the party(s) seeking to exploit it, and (3) does not infringe on the rights of others. Therefore, appropriate representations and warranties concerning these issues appear in substantially the same form in almost all entertainment contracts.

In examining the relevant provisions of a typical representation and warranties clause between a purchaser and author, the term *author* should be read to include any creative contributor to the work, and/or the owner of the work if created as work for hire or which acquires ownership through some other form of assignment or transfer:

---

[97] Far too often, the principals of a deal focus solely on the "up" side of the deal. It is left to the lawyers to examine and negotiate the "down" side.

The author hereby warrants and represents that, except where the work may be based on the underlying work or works in the public domain, the work will be original with her or him; will not infringe on the right, title, or interest of any third party including the so-called rights of publicity or privacy; and will not contain material that is libelous, slanderous, or obscene. Further, the author warrants and represents that she/he is free to enter into this agreement and perform hereunder and that she/he will not do, nor has he done, anything in contravention of the rights granted and/or to be performed hereunder.

6.4.1. Original Work

The purchaser's first concern is to gain assurances from the author that what is being acquired is, in fact, protectable (i.e., original). In order for a work to be copyrightable, it must be a work of *original* authorship.[98] Because the author should know that the work is original with him or her, this is appropriately his or her risk. In addition, where the author's contributions are as a work made for hire, the purchaser's application for copyright must include a certification that the work being claimed is original, a claim that this provision supports.

The concerns of the author with respect to this provision are to define allowable restrictions on the warranty of originality. The first (and foremost) arises where the work is based on an underlying work, such as a preexisting novel. It is a contradiction in terms for a work to be wholly original and based on another protected (or even public domain) work; therefore, the warranty must be restricted to read that "except as it may be based on the underlying work", with the restriction to be inserted immediately following the words "warrants and represents" to exclude applications of *all* of the warranties and representations with respect to the "underlying work." Whether the rights to the underlying work are supplied by the purchaser or the author, the purchaser will have to look to the agreement under which the rights to the underlying work were acquired to determine all questions with respect to the underlying work, including whether or not there was a valid transfer of rights, and see that appropriate warranties and representations were made by that work's author with respect to the underlying work.

---

[98] *See supra* §1.2.

As noted above, the author may also wish to exclude a warranty of originality where the work may be based on works in the public domain. The purchaser's first concern with this provision is that the work be, in fact, in the public domain throughout the world (e.g., Shakespeare's *"Romeo and Juliet"*). It is possible for a work to be in the public domain in the United States and still protected elsewhere. Moreover, although use of a work in the public domain will not incur any liability for infringement, it also does not receive the degree of protection normally accorded to original works because anyone else is free to base their potentially competing work on that public domain work. The purchaser therefore will want to know if the author is requesting this exception because the work is based on a specific public domain work or if it is simply a prophylactic against unconscious use of works existing in the vast repertoire of the public domain. The author may seek a further carveout as to materials furnished by the purchaser (e.g., factual research, a magazine article, or the outline for a new character or plot point) for inclusion by the author in the commissioned work. If these exceptions are allowed, they are also inserted as an exception to *all* warranties and representations.

6.4.2. Infringement

The second part of the clause states that the "work will not infringe upon the right, title or interest of any third party."

The purchaser clearly does not want to buy rights that will subject him or her to liability to third parties for infringement of their rights. Moreover, it is often difficult or impossible for the purchaser to know whether or not an infringement is taking place. Because the author knows, or should know, the source of his or her inspiration, whether or not it arises from a copyrighted work or is based on real people or factual situations, the purchaser's position must be that the author identify the source of that inspiration, recognize the risks of infringement that may arise from that source, and accept the risks attendant upon use of that source.

It is appropriate for an author to accept liability for a knowing infringement of another's rights. After all, the author, by knowing the source of the potential infringement, is in a position to obtain appropriate licenses in advance for use of a protected (i.e., copyrighted or trademarked) work or permissions or releases from individuals whose rights of publicity or privacy may be affected by the proposed use. These licenses or permissions then effectively become rights agreements under which the affected work or persons become the underlying work for the author's work and are transferable to the purchaser at the same time as the purchaser acquires the author's work.

A question arises, however, when the infringement is unintentional or unconscious.[99] It has been argued that if a work (or event involving the rights of an individual) is so well known that the author could unconsciously infringe it, it is also well known enough for the purchaser, who shares the same cultural exposure as the author, to recognize the subconscious influence of this work on the author. The purchaser may in fact be in a better position to detect such unconscious infringement because he or she can examine the work objectively, whereas the author is often emotionally involved with the work, and the purchaser should ostensibly therefore accept the risk on that basis. Nonetheless, with or without an author's indemnity, the purchaser may not ultimately succeed in avoiding the risk, when the author furnishing the indemnification has insufficient means to defend an infringement claim or satisfy a judgment for damages.

In the alternative, such unconscious infringement could be deemed an "accident," the risk of which is a suitable subject for insurance. Because purchasers are, as a rule, in a better position to obtain insurance than authors, it is again appropriate that the purchaser accept that risk, whether insured or uninsured.[100]

6.4.3. Publicity, Privacy, Libel, Slander, and Obscenity

The third element of the warranty and representation concerns infringing the rights of publicity and privacy, as well as matter that is libelous, slanderous, or obscene.

Again, the purchaser's position is that he or she does not want to "buy a lawsuit" and that the author is in the best position to know of the risks being undertaken. Because the primary defense to libel or slander is truth, the purchaser wants to make sure that the author does not make unfounded accusations. With respect to privacy (where truth may not be

---

[99] *See* ABKCO Music, Inc. v. Harrisongs Music, Ltd. 722 F.2d 988 (2d Cir. 1983) (unconscious infringement of the song "He's So Fine" by the song "My Sweet Lord").

[100] *See* Ronald Rosen, *"Current Trends in Entertainment Litigation: The Insurance Empire Strikes Back,"* 1 ENTERTAINMENT & SPORTS LAW. 1 (Am. Bar Assoc.) (1982).

a defense),[101] basing the material on "private" facts is again in the author's control.

Moreover, it is the purchaser's concern that, even if the work is fictional (and normally not subject to privacy or defamation claims), there is still some risk. In the controversial *Bindrim v. Mitchell*[102] decision, a California court held that the author of a so-called roman-à-clef was liable for defamation to a doctor who was deemed recognizable as a character in the book. (Subsequent decisions in other courts have not followed this precedent, and it may be of limited significance.)[103]

Conversely, the author must consider that judgments about questions of libel, slander, and publicity/privacy are generally very difficult for lawyers, much less nonspecialist authors, to make. In particular, a warranty against obscenity is generally considered archaic and may be deleted in the negotiation of these provisions on the basis that (1) determination of obscenity is so legally complex at this time that an author cannot reasonably be expected to make such a determination without the legal assistance of the purchaser (who is, as a rule, more experienced in such matters) and (2) any obscenity should be as apparent to the purchaser as the author after an examination of the work, and can thus be selectively omitted in the adaption of the work.

With respect to defamation, publicity, and privacy, a logical distinction exists between fictional and nonfictional works. With fictional works, the primary argument (as with infringements) is that the author warrants against a knowing violation of this warranty.

With respect to nonfictional works, which must deal with real people, the purchaser must be sensitive to these areas and should engage independent legal counsel to review these matters. A suggested alternative to this warranty is an agreement that the author will submit all material for review by the purchaser and will make all revisions requested by the purchaser in exchange for the purchaser assuming liability (or, at least, joint responsibility) for defamation or publicity/privacy claims. In the event that the author refuses to make the requested changes, he or she should remain primarily liable.

---

[101] *See supra* §§4.1, 4.10.
[102] 92 Cal. App. 3d 61, *cert. denied*, 444 U.S. 984 (1979).
[103] *See* Springer v. Viking Press, 457 N.Y.S. 2d 246, *aff'd*, 470 N.Y.S.2d 579 (N.Y. 1983).

(This argument is particularly appropriate where the work is a work made for hire.)

It should also be noted that, although the legal analysis as to prospective risk of claims should be no different if the primary medium in which the work will be exploited is a book, stage performance, television production or motion picture, the risks of a resulting claim (and consequent costs of defense and damages, if any) may be far greater for a television or motion picture production that can reach an audience of millions, than for a book for which readership is expected to be, at best, a fraction of that audience.

6.4.4. Performance

The final element of the normal warranties and representations clause is drawn to ensure performance of the terms of the agreement, typically via the provision of indemnifications and injunctive remedies.

The purchaser's primary concerns with regard to this element are (1) to be assured of obtaining clear title to the work and (2) in the event that the continuing services of the author are required, to be assured that the author can and will be able to render those services. These warranties supplement the primary covenants of the contract that normally provide for the transfer of title and the promise to perform services under the terms of the agreement.

The purchaser's concern with respect to the transfer of clear title is that, although the copyright law requires that assignments and mortgages of copyright be in writing (and these are commonly then recorded with the Copyright Office for purposes of establishing chain of title), nonexclusive licenses or exclusive writers' agreements need not be registered. The existence of such agreements, although not readily discoverable by the purchaser if not disclosed by the author/owner, could nonetheless obstruct clear title. Moreover, because the purchaser cannot register title until the work is completed, he or she does not want the author, subsequent to this agreement, entering into new agreements that would impair his or her title.

Although not usually addressed within this clause, an author's concern in this area usually centers around his or her ability to enter into agreements not in conflict with the agreement in question (e.g., nonexclusive services) and to disclose the prior history of the work if there is any question that, for example, a prior option on the property may or may not have expired, or that another producer involved in its prior development may have contributed elements to the property that the author is not empowered to convey to a purchaser (e.g., a character based on third party life story rights that the author may not control, or an interim draft of the work commissioned by another party during a prior development phase).

The warranties and representations clause of a contract generally involves both specific covenants with respect to rights (such as originality) and general covenants with respect to numerous provisions throughout the remainder of the contract. Both of these elements must be analyzed and correlated in the negotiation of this clause.

6.5. INDEMNIFICATION ISSUES

Related to the warranties and representations issues is the question of indemnification – what happens if one party breaches the warranties, representations, or covenants made to the other party. At issue is the allocation of risk for claims that could have substantial adverse impact on a project or, worse, could give rise to an injunction preventing a buyer from exploiting a project in which considerable investment has already been made. Although the party seeking protection wants absolute indemnification against any injury, the other seeks reasonable limitations of that indemnity. Such limitations may be based on negotiation or on the provisions of a union contract.[104]

Buyers want immunity from claims primarily within the seller's control. Sellers seek to avoid the risk of indemnifying the buyer from possible claims in excess of the financial benefit of the transaction itself.

6.5.1. Indemnity or Subrogation Grant

The general grant of indemnity (also known as subrogation) is drawn as a promise by one party "to hold harmless the other party, and all third parties claiming by or through it, against any and all claims, demands, suits, liabilities,[105] losses, costs, expenses (including

---

[104] *See* Writers Guild of America Basic Agreement for Motion Pictures and Television, art. 28 [hereinafter cited as WGA/BA].

[105] Note that under California law the use of the word *liability* in a subrogation agreement frees the indemnitee from the obligation of having suffered damage (i.e., actually paying out amounts of money) prior to seeking indemnity from the

attorney's fees), damages, or recoveries (including any amounts paid in settlement) suffered by that party or third parties claiming by or through it, by reason of the breach or alleged breach of any warranty, representation, covenant, or condition as set forth herein."

6.5.2. Restrictions on Indemnification

The restrictions on indemnification most commonly advanced and accepted can be roughly divided into three categories: (1) reciprocity, (2) amount of indemnity or face value, and (3) procedural rights.

Restrictions on indemnification issues can be addressed as a part of the indemnity provision or by restricting the breadth of the warranties, representations, covenants, and conditions made in the agreement. Where applicable, restricting those original elements (i.e., representations, warranties, covenants, or conditions) is to be preferred to an attempt to restrict the application of the indemnity clause to them. For example, it is better to deny the specific warranty of ownership of a title (where there is some question about ownership) rather than try to draw an indemnity provisions that will not indemnify against losses for the use of that title.

6.5.2.1. Reciprocity

As a starting point for negotiation, the person seeking to restrict the indemnity usually seeks reciprocity (i.e., each of the parties indemnifies the other in substantially the same manner and degree as to third party claims arising primarily from a breach or default by the indemnitor). For example, an author selling a novel to the studio may seek protection from claims relating to the inclusion of new elements by a screenwriter hired to create a screen adaptation of his work. This immediately raises issues of fairness: What is fair? If it is fair for one, it should be fair for the other. Unfortunately, in a situation where one party has disproportionate bargaining power in a transaction, the party with greater leverage may not feel obligated to be "fair". Nonetheless, even where a request for reciprocity may be rejected, it places the party demanding exclusive protection in the awkward position of explaining why he or she should receive such special treatment.

---

indemnitor. It is the *liability* for damages that would trigger the obligation of indemnity.

6.5.2.2. Amount of Indemnity or "Face Value"[106]

There are a number of ways to limit the face value of the indemnity clause. The most blatant occurs when one party indemnifies the other "to the extent of amounts received" by the indemnitor under the terms of the agreement. (Ironically, the less money that the indemnitor receives under the agreement, the fairer such a restriction seems.)

Another restriction is to insert the requirement that all costs and expenses, including attorney's fees, be "reasonable" and/or limited to the actual fees charged by outside counsel. Although some take the position that they want attorneys' fees paid no matter whom they engage, it is always arguable whether expensive lawyers generate results meriting substantially premium fees in many IP matters, or how to measure the "cost" of the services of in-house attorneys not engaged generally and not "by matter". Furthermore requiring a "reasonableness" standard places some restraints on the possible cost of the indemnity.

A final restriction on potential liability limits liability to amounts actually adjudicated and reduced to judgment or settled with the consent of the indemnitor. This prevents the indemnitee from simply buying off lawsuits without regard to their merit or ultimate worth.

However, a settlement may make economic sense when it costs less to settle the claim than defend it, or when the uncertainty as to how long it may take to secure a favorable outcome will severely jeopardize the timely development, production or distribution of a project. It may consequently be useful to limit this restriction so that consent to a proposed settlement will not be unreasonably withheld. If it is, the indemnified party can still settle the suit and seek indemnification. This condition on the restriction is particularly appropriate where there is some question as to the indemnitor's capacity to pay (e.g., a "poor" author) as against the perceived ability of the indemnitee to pay (e.g., a movie company with "deep pockets"). An author may of course seek to limit the scope of an indemnity to the fees he/she stands to earn from a transaction, but since the damages that may arise from a breach or default of an obligation subject to an indemnity (whether or not the danger was prospectively anticipated by the author) can materially

---

[106] It is possible to think of an indemnification clause as an insurance agreement and the amount of potential liability of the indemnitor as the "face value" of the indemnity insurance.

exceed the author's compensation, most purchaser's will understandably be averse to such an accommodation.

6.5.2.3. Procedural Condition

Procedural restrictions in indemnity clauses are designed to place the indemnifying party in a position of control over his or her possible liability. For example, with respect to settlements, it is a procedural condition that any settlement must be approved by the indemnitor in advance and in a signed writing.

The most important procedural restriction is one that requires that the indemnitor receive notice of any claim from which indemnification may be sought, along with the right to defend against that claim. Providing notice of a claim should not be objectionable, but the indemnitee may resist the indemnitor's control over the defense. Because the indemnitee (e.g., a movie studio or producer) usually is in a better financial position than the indemnitor and is the named defendant, the indemnitee may demand that its attorneys control the defense of the action. An alternative solution calls for the indemnitor to provide and pay for his or her own lawyer and the indemnitee to supply its own lawyer, so that both of the attorneys are involved in the defense. The indemnitee may also commonly demand reimbursement for its attorneys' fees. However, the indemnitor should nonetheless retain the right to have his or her interests protected by an attorney of his or her choice participating in the defense of the claim.

6.5.3. Additional Protections

Motion picture studios, producers, and other similarly well-financed defendants are naturally concerned with the capacity of an indemnitor to pay damages. The only money that the studio or producer can be sure the indemnitor possesses is the money to be paid by the indemnitee under the relevant contract. For example where the agreement provides additional deferred or contingent income to the author or owner based on a purchaser/producer's net profits or royalties derived from box office or other distribution receipts, it may represent a substantial amount of money. However, once that money is paid to that party (the author, director, etc.), it may be spent by the indemnitor such that it is no longer available to indemnify the studio or producer.

One way to address this problem is to give the indemnitee the right, on notice of a *possible* claim, to retain possession of all further payments to be made under the terms of the agreement in an amount sufficient, in that party's sole judgment, to satisfy all claims, costs, and expenses.

Note however that the principle of withholding compensation pending the outcome of a possible claim is prohibited under some applicable creative (e.g., WGA) union contracts[107] and in all other cases should be subject to reasonable restrictions. For example, the triggering event should be the filing of a claim rather than the ambiguous notice of a possible claim. The amounts to be withheld should be "reasonable," and the time during which they can be withheld should be limited so that, if a claim is not pursued within a reasonable time period (e.g., a year), it will be deemed abandoned and the amounts will be released to the indemnitor. Meanwhile, the money held should be placed in a separate *interest*-bearing account for the benefit of the indemnitor with the interest applied against the amount of potential liability and with all amounts, including interest, not applied in payment of the liability to be returned to the indemnitor.

Finally, the indemnitor should seek the right to post a guarantee of payment or bond in the amount of the possible liability, subject to the indemnitee's reasonable approval over the financial reliability of the party guaranteeing payment. Such guarantees are usually available on payment of certain fees (and subject to proof of the ability to repay the guaranteeing party). By obtaining such a bond in lieu of having the money withheld, the indemnitor receives the benefit of possession of the money while the claim is pending. Because the rationale for withholding amounts due is to ensure payment in case liability is found, a bond (if available) should be satisfactory.

6.5.4. Insurance

In recent years there has been an explosion of litigation alleging infringement of copyright or the theft/misappropriation of ideas or concepts.[108] As the popular recognition of the financial rewards earned by successful creators has grown, so too has the incentive for litigation. As described by the New York Times, "intellectual property litigation

---

[107] *See* WGA/BA *supra* note 104, 28(3).
[108] *See* WGA/BA *supra* note 1041, art. 28.E.

[has turned] into a burgeoning cottage industry, with its own small plaintiff's bar."[109]

Beyond possible questions of merit, this litigation appears to be driven by one of two factors. First, while a majority of the complaints against most well-known creators fail, there are enough high profile successes to continue to provide incentives for plaintiffs. Second, and perhaps equally significant, litigation against a well-known defendant can have the incidental benefit of promoting the career of a less well-known plaintiff. For example, in a litigation against J.K. Rowling over the Harry Potter series, the plaintiff was an American writer whose self-published books had been out of print for nearly a decade prior to the instigation of his claim. Subsequent to initiating the suit, a commercial publisher acquired and released them.[110]

Given the growth in this type of litigation, producers and publishers increasingly seek errors and omissions (E&O) insurance covering the costs of litigation. After all, these costs can be substantial, even where the defendant prevails. Moreover, producers/publishers have great incentive to seek insurance, notwithstanding the broad indemnification they may obtain from creators. Even if they could obtain reimbursement of their defense costs, either in terms of a penalty against the failed plaintiff or pursuant to contract with their creator/author, there are not guarantees that either of these subrogating parties would have assets sufficient to meet these expenses. The cost of insurance simply becomes a cost of doing business for the producer/publisher.

The more this insurance comes to be considered a cost of business (not to mention further inducement for claims given the unique dynamics of insurance defense), the more likely it is that author/creators can seek to benefit from it in their contracts. Clearly, an insurance company will demand that the author/creator continue to warrant and represent that the work is original and does not infringe upon the rights of another. Nonetheless, it is likely the purchasers will agree, along with their insurers, to cover all the expenses of litigation *unless* an actual infringement is proven by the litigation.

---

[109] David Kirkpatrick *"Harry Potter and the Court Battle Over Creativity"* N.Y. Times (Apr. 1, 2001).
[110] *Id.*

***

Virtually all aspects of transactional legal practice in the entertainment industries will be affected, explicitly or implicitly, by one or more aspects of intellectual property law explored in this volume. It is therefore imperative that the "deal-making" lawyer in the entertainment industries have a fundamental grasp of these basics IP law principles and practices, or at least the wherewithal to recognize his or her shortcomings in these fields so that proper additional insights can be enlisted in support of client transactions. Understanding and properly implementing these principals can assist in mooring transactions on solid foundations. Failure to do so may instead result in transactions being mired in quicksand.

— INDEX —

A

ADAPTATION(S)
  Dramatic/dramatico-musical adaptation, clearing world rights for
    Generally, 6.2.2
    Adaptation rights issues, 6.2.2.4
    Dramatic rights, 6.2.2.1–6.2.2.3
    "Fair use," 6.2.2.8
    Music rights, 6.2.2.6
    Territory of rights, 6.2.2.5
    Title of work, 6.2.2.7
  Exclusive copyright rights, 1.4.1.2
  Privacy/publicity rights, 4.3.2

ANTICYBERSQUATTING CONSUMER PROTECTION ACT
  Generally, 3.2.8

ANTITRUST ISSUES
  Privacy/publicity rights, 4.4.8

ASSIGNMENTS
  Trademark(s), 3.9.2

ATTORNEYS' FEES
  Copyright infringement actions, 1.14.2.4

AUDIO TRANSMISSIONS
  Digital, 1.4.1.6

B

BERNE CONVENTION(S)
  Generally, 5.1.1
  Berne Convention Implementation Act of 1988, 1.1.3. *See also* **COPYRIGHT(S)**
  Berne Union and, 5.1.1.1
  Commencement of copyright(s), 5.1.5
  Creation of copyright(s), 5.1.5
  Developing countries, 5.1.13
  Droit de suite, 5.1.3.3, 5.1.3.3b
  Duration of copyright(s), 5.1.8

  Exclusive rights in copyrighted works
    Generally, 5.1.3.1, 5.1.3.2
    Droit de suite, 5.1.3.3, 5.1.3.3b
    Limitations on, 5.1.3.2
    Moral rights/*droit moral*, 5.1.3.3, 5.1.3.3a
  Fair use, 5.1.4
  Infringement of copyright(s)
    Generally, 5.1.11
    Applicability of Berne Convention(s), 5.1.11.2
    Law applicable, 5.1.11.3
    Plaintiffs, 5.1.11.1
    Remedies, 5.1.12
  Members of, 5.1.14
  Moral rights/*droit moral*, 5.1.3.3, 5.1.3.3a
  Notice of copyright(s), 1.8.1.5, 5.1.7
  Ownership of copyright(s), 5.1.6
  Protected copyrighted works
    Generally, 5.1.2.1
    National eligibility, 5.1.2.2
    Standards of protection, 5.1.1.2
  Registration of copyright(s), 1.8.4.4, 5.1.7
  Renewal of copyright(s), 5.1.10
  Standards of protection under, 5.1.1.2
  Termination of copyright(s), 5.1.10
  Transferability of copyright(s), 5.1.9
  Universal Copyright Convention and, 5.3.1.1
  WIPO Copyright Treaty (Geneva 1996) and, 5.2.1.1

BERNE UNION
  Generally, 5.1.1.1
  Universal Copyright Convention and, 5.3.12.1

BOOKS
  See also **COPYRIGHT(S)**
  Clearing world rights to, 6.2.5.1

BUENOS AIRES CONVENTION
  Generally, 5.4

335

C

CHAIN OF TITLE
Clearing world rights, 6.2.6

CHOICE OF LAW
Publicity rights, infringement of, 4.10.4

CLEARING WORLD RIGHTS
Generally, 6.2
Author-profiling
  Generally, 6.2.4
  Applicable copyright law, 6.2.4.1
  Author guild(s), 6.2.4.5
  Co-authors, 6.2.4.4
  Collaborators, 6.2.4.4
  Duration of copyright, 6.2.4.2
  Rights owners deriving their authority through the author, 6.2.4.3
  Society membership, 6.2.4.5
Books, 6.2.5.1
Chain of title, 6.2.6
Co-authors, profiling of, 6.2.4.4
Collaborators, profiling of, 6.2.4.4
Dramatic/dramatico-musical adaptation (illustration)
  Generally, 6.2.2
  Adaptation rights issues, 6.2.2.4
  Dramatic rights, 6.2.2.1–6.2.2.3
  "Fair use," 6.2.2.8
  Music rights, 6.2.2.6
  Territory of rights, 6.2.2.5
  Title of work, 6.2.2.7
Dramatic productions
  Illustration. *See* subhead: Dramatic/dramatico-musical adaptation (illustration)
Initial publication
  Generally, 6.2.5
  Books, 6.2.5.1
  Dramatic productions, 6.2.5.2
  Motion pictures, 6.2.5.3
  Periodicals, 6.2.5.1
  Television programming, 6.2.5.3
Motion pictures, 6.2.5.3
New work, 6.2.7
Periodicals, 6.2.5.1
Rights to be cleared, 6.2.1
Source-material investigation
  Generally, 6.2.3
  Caveat, 6.2.3.3
  Direct clues, 6.2.3.1
  Further investigation(s), 6.2.3.2
Television programming, 6.2.5.3

COLLECTIVE WORKS
Copyright notice, 1.8.1.4
Exclusive copyright rights, 1.4.1.8

COMMERCIALS
Vocal performance imitations in, 3.11.1.1

COMPETING PRODUCTS/ SERVICES
Trademark(s), 3.3.2.2

CONCRETENESS
Idea protection, 2.2.1.2

CONFIDENTIAL RELATIONSHIP
Breach of, 2.1.2.3, 2.2.3.3

CONSTITUTIONAL LAW
Copyright(s), 1.1.1
Privacy/publicity rights, First Amendment issues regarding, 4.4.1

CONTRACT-LAW IDEA PROTECTIONS
Generally, 2.1.1.1, 2.2.2
Express contracts, 2.1.1.1, 2.2.2.1
Implied-in-fact contracts, 2.1.1.2, 2.1.2.1, 2.2.2.2
Quasi-contract protections, 2.1.1.2, 2.1.2.1, 2.2.2.2, 2.2.3.1

CONVENTIONS
Berne Convention(s). *See* **BERNE CONVENTION(S)**
Buenos Aires Convention, 5.4
Phonogram Convention. *See* **PHONOGRAM CONVENTION (GENEVA 1971)**

INDEX

UCC. *See* **UNIVERSAL COPYRIGHT CONVENTION (UCC)**

COPYING
Copyright infringement, 1.12.2.4
Ideas, 2.10.1

COPYRIGHT(S)
Generally, 6.1
Adaptation(s). *See* **ADAPTATION(S)**
Author's diary, 6.1.2
"Authorship"
  Generally, 1.2.3
  Copyright registration review, 6.1.5.2
  "National origin" of author, 1.2.6
  "Works of authorship," 1.2.5
Berne Convention Implementation Act of 1988, 1.1.3. *See also* **BERNE CONVENTION(S)**
Collective works
  Copyright notice, 1.8.1.4
  Exclusive rights in, 1.4.1.8
Commencement of protection
  Generally, 1.6
  Berne Convention(s), 5.1.5
  Universal Copyright Convention (UCC), 5.3.5
Constitutional law, 1.1.1
Conventions
  Berne Convention(s). *See* **BERNE CONVENTION(S)**
  Buenos Aires Convention, 5.4
  Phonogram Convention. *See* **PHONOGRAM CONVENTION (GENEVA 1971)**
  UCC. *See* **UNIVERSAL COPYRIGHT CONVENTION (UCC)**
Copyright Revision Act of 1976, 1.1.2
Creation of protection
  Generally, 1.6
  Berne Convention(s), 5.1.5
  Copyright registration review, 6.1.5.2

Universal Copyright Convention (UCC), 5.3.5
Deposit accounts, 6.1.6
Deposit of work(s)
  Berne Convention(s), 1.8.1.5
  Exemptions from, 1.8.5.2
  Purpose of, 1.8.5.1
Digital audio transmissions, 1.4.1.6
Digital Millennium Copyright Act. *See* **DIGITAL MILLENNIUM COPYRIGHT ACT**
Display(s), exclusive right of, 1.4.1.5
Dramatic/dramatico-musical adaptation, clearing world rights for
  Generally, 6.2.2
  Adaptation rights issues, 6.2.2.4
  Dramatic rights, 6.2.2.1–6.2.2.3
  "Fair use," 6.2.2.8
  Music rights, 6.2.2.6
  Territory of rights, 6.2.2.5
  Title of work, 6.2.2.7
Droit de suite
  Generally, 1.4.3
  Berne Convention(s), 5.1.3.3, 5.1.3.3b
Droit moral. *See* subhead: Moral rights/*droit moral*
Duration
  Generally, 1.9
  1906 and 1921, works created between, 1.9.4
  Berne Convention(s), 5.1.8
  Clearing world rights, 6.2.4.2
  January 1, 1978, works copyrighted prior to, 1.9.3
  January 1, 1978, works created but not published or copyrighted before, 1.9.2
  January 1, 1978, works created on or after, 1.9.1
  Universal Copyright Convention (UCC), 5.3.8
Exclusive rights
  Generally, 1.4.1
  Adaptation, right of, 1.4.1.2
  Berne Convention(s). *See* **BERNE CONVENTION(S)**

Collective works, 1.4.1.8
Digital audio transmissions, 1.4.1.6
Display, right of, 1.4.1.5
Droit de suite, 1.4.3
Droit moral. See subhead: Moral rights/*droit moral*
Internet carrier limitation, 1.4.1.7
Performances/performers, 1.4.1.4, 1.4.4
Publication, right of, 1.4.1.3
Reproduction, right of, 1.4.1.1
Universal Copyright Convention (UCC), 5.3.3
Violation of, 1.12.2.5. *See also* **COPYRIGHT INFRINGEMENT**
"Expression"
Generally, 1.2.3
"Fixed in any tangible medium of expression," 1.2.4
Fair use
Generally, 1.5
"Amount and substantiality of the portion used," 1.5.3
Berne Convention(s), 5.1.4
Dramatic/dramatico-musical adaptation (illustration), 6.2.2.8
"Effect of the use upon the potential market for or value of the copyrighted work," 1.5.4
"Nature of the copyrighted work," 1.5.2
"Purpose and character of the use," 1.5.1
Universal Copyright Convention (UCC), 5.3.4
Federal preemption, 1.2.7
"Fixed in any tangible medium of expression"
Generally, 1.2.4
"Any medium,," 1.2.4.2
Common-law limitation, as a, 1.2.4.1
Importation restrictions
Generally, 1.15.2
Piratical copies exclusion, 1.15.2.1

Territorial exclusivity, 1.15.2.2
Informal copyright, 6.1.3
Infringement. *See* **COPYRIGHT INFRINGEMENT**
Integrity, right of, 1.4.2.3
Internet carrier limitation, 1.4.1.7
Joint ownership, 1.7.2
La Cienega review, 6.1.10
Licensing, mandatory, 1.10.2
Management systems and, 1.17
Manufacturing requirement, 1.15.1
"Mask works," 1.3.1
Moral rights/*droit moral*
Generally, 1.4.2
Berne Convention(s), 5.1.3.3, 5.1.3.3a
Integrity, right of, 1.4.2.3
Paternity, right of, 1.4.2.2
Publication, right of, 1.4.2.1
"National origin" of author, 1.2.6
Neighboring rights
Generally, 1.3
"Mask works," 1.3.1
Original designs, 1.3.3
Performers. *See* subhead: Performances/performers, 1.3.2
Semiconductor chips, 1.3.1
Notice. *See* **COPYRIGHT NOTICE**
Original designs, 1.3.3
"Originality" requirement, 1.2.2
Ownership of work
Berne Convention(s), 5.1.6
Copyright infringement, 1.12.2.3
Initial, 1.7.1
Joint, 1.7.2
Transfer of. *See* subhead: Transfers
Universal Copyright Convention (UCC), 5.3.6
Works made for hire, 1.7.3
Paternity, right of, 1.4.2.2
Performances/performers
Dramatic/dramatico-musical adaptation. *See* subhead: Dramatic/dramatico-musical adaptation, clearing world rights for

INDEX 339

Exclusive rights, 1.4.1.4, 1.4.4
Performer's rights, 1.3.2
Permission to use work, 1.12.2.6
Piratical copies, 1.15.2.1
Privacy/publicity rights and, 4.2.2
Protectable subject matter
  Generally, 1.2.1–1.2.7
  Berne Convention(s). *See* **BERNE CONVENTION(S)**
  Universal Copyright Convention (UCC), 5.3.2.1
Publication
  Copyright registration review, 6.1.5.2
  Exclusive right of, 1.4.1.3
  Moral rights/*droit moral*, 1.4.2.1
Registration. *See* **COPYRIGHT REGISTRATION**
Renewal right(s)
  Generally, 1.11.2
  Berne Convention(s), 5.1.10
  Rationale behind, 1.11.1
Reproduction, right of, 1.4.1.1
Restoration of, 1.11.5
Restored review, 6.1.9
Reversions, 6.1.8
Royalty distribution, 1.16
Searches, 6.1.7
Semiconductor chips, 1.3.1
Termination right(s)
  Berne Convention(s), 5.1.10
  Extended renewal term, termination during, 1.11.3
  Rationale behind, 1.11.1
  Transfers made after January 1, 1978, 1.11.4
Transfers
  Generally, 1.10.1
  Attachments of other interests, 1.10.4
  Berne Convention(s), 5.1.9
  Licensing, mandatory, 1.10.2
  Recordation of, 1.10.3
  Subsequent, 1.10.1.2
  Termination of transfers made after January 1, 1978, 1.11.4
  Universal Copyright Convention (UCC), 5.3.9

Writing rule and exceptions, 1.10.1, 1.10.1.1
Treaties
  WIPO Copyright Treaty. *See* **WIPO COPYRIGHT TREATY (GENEVA 1996)**
  WIPO Performances and Phonograms Treaty. *See* **WIPO PERFORMANCES AND PHONOGRAMS TREATY (GENEVA 1996)**
  WIPO Treaties Implementation Act, 1.1.4
UCC. *See* **UNIVERSAL COPYRIGHT CONVENTION (UCC)**
Warranties and representations
  Generally, 6.4
  Breach of. *See* **INDEMNIFICATION ISSUES**
  Infringement, 6.4.2
  Obscenity and, 6.4.3
  Original work(s), 6.4.1
  Performances/performers, 6.4.4
  Privacy/publicity rights, 6.4.3
  Slander and, 6.4.3
WIPO Copyright Treaty. *See* **WIPO COPYRIGHT TREATY (GENEVA 1996)**
WIPO Performances and Phonograms Treaty. *See* **WIPO PERFORMANCES AND PHONOGRAMS TREATY (GENEVA 1996)**
WIPO Treaties Implementation Act, 1.1.4
Works made for hire, 1.7.3
"Works of authorship," 1.2.5
World rights. *See* **CLEARING WORLD RIGHTS**

COPYRIGHT INFRINGEMENT
Generally, 1.12.1
Actions for
  Generally, 1.12.3
  Attorneys' fees, 1.14.2.4
  Costs, 1.14.2.4
  Criminal actions, 1.12.4, 1.14.1

Elements of. *See* subhead:
    Elements of causes of action
Attorneys' fees, 1.14.2.4
Berne Convention(s). *See* **BERNE CONVENTION(S)**
Copying of protected work, 1.12.2.4
Costs of actions, 1.14.2.4
Criminal offenses/sanctions, 1.12.4, 1.14.1
Damages
    Generally, 1.14.2.3
    Actual damages, 1.14.2.3a
    Infringer's profits, recovery of, 1.14.2.3a
    Statutory damages, 1.14.2.3b
Defenses, 1.12.2.8
Disposition of infringement articles, 1.14.2.2
DMCA provisions, 1.13, 1.13.1
Elements of causes of action
    Copying of protected work, 1.12.2.4
    Copyrightability of original work, 1.12.2.1
    Defenses, 1.12.2.8
    Excuse for using protected work, 1.12.2.7
    Formalities of copyright, 1.12.2.2
    Ownership of copyright, 1.12.2.3
    Permission to use work, 1.12.2.6
    Violation of exclusive right, 1.12.2.5
Excuse for using protected work, 1.12.2.7
Impoundment of infringement articles, 1.14.2.2
Injunctive relief, 1.14.2.1
Permission to use work, 1.12.2.6
Remedies
    Berne Convention(s), 5.1.12
    Civil remedies, 1.14.2–1.14.2.4
    Criminal sanctions, 1.14.1
    Damages. *See* subhead: Damages
    Infringer's profits, recovery of, 1.14.2.3a
    Universal Copyright Convention (UCC), 5.3.11
Universal Copyright Convention (UCC)
    Generally, 5.3.10
    Remedies, 5.3.11
    Violation of exclusive right, 1.12.2.5
Warranties and representations, 6.4.2

COPYRIGHT NOTICE
Generally, 1.8, 1.8.1, 6.1.1
Berne Convention(s), 1.8.1.5, 5.1.7
Collective works, 1.8.1.4
Date errors
    1909 Act, under, 1.8.2.1
    1976 Act, under, 1.8.2.2
Form of, 1.8.1.2
Location of, 1.8.1.3
Name errors
    1909 Act, under, 1.8.2.1
    1976 Act, under, 1.8.2.2
Omission of notice
    1909 Act, under, 1.8.3.1
    1976 Act, under, 1.8.3.2
Visually perceptible copies, 1.8.1.1

COPYRIGHT REGISTRATION
Generally, 1.8, 1.8.4
1909 Act, under, 1.8.4.1
1976 Act, under, 1.8.4.2
Berne Convention(s), 1.8.4.4, 5.1.7
Denial of, 1.8.7
Incentives for, 1.8.4.3
Procedures, 1.8.6, 6.1.4
Registration review
    Generally, 6.1.5
    Administrative provisions, 6.1.5.5
    Authorship, 6.1.5.2
    Copyright claimants, 6.1.5.3
    Creation, 6.1.5.2
    Nature of work, 6.1.5.1
    Prior work, 6.1.5.4
    Publication, 6.1.5.2
    Title of work, 6.1.5.1

COPYRIGHT REVISION ACT OF 1976 *See also* **COPYRIGHT(S)**
Generally, 1.1.2

COSTS OF ACTIONS
Copyright infringement, 1.14.2.4

CRIMINAL OFFENSES/ SANCTIONS
Copyright infringement, 1.12.4, 1.14.1

D

DAMAGES. *See* **COPYRIGHT INFRINGEMENT**

DEFAMATION
Privacy rights and, 4.9.3
Warranties/representations and, 6.4.3

DEFENSES
Copyright infringement, 1.12.2.8
Idea infringement, 2.10.3
Trademark infringement, 3.12.3

DEPOSIT ACCOUNTS
Copyright(s), 6.1.6

DEPOSIT OF WORK(S)
Copyright(s)
Exemptions from deposit, 1.8.5.2
Purpose of deposit, 1.8.5.1

DESIGNS
Original designs, 1.3.3

DEVELOPING COUNTRIES
Berne Convention(s), 5.1.13
Universal Copyright Convention (UCC), 5.3.12.3

DIGITAL AUDIO TRANSMISSIONS
Copyright(s), 1.4.1.6

DIGITAL MILLENNIUM COPYRIGHT ACT
Generally, 1.1.4
Infringement actions, 1.13, 1.13.1
Takedown notices, 1.13.1

DISPLAY(S)
Copyright, exclusive rights in, 1.4.1.5

DISTINCTIVENESS
Trademark(s), 3.2.3

DMCA. *See* **DIGITAL MILLENNIUM COPYRIGHT ACT**

DOMAIN NAMES
Anticybersquatting Consumer Protection Act, 3.2.8
ICANN/WIPO arbitration of, 3.2.9

DRAMATIC PRODUCTIONS
Clearing world rights to
Illustration. *See* subhead: Dramatic/dramatico-musical adaptation (illustration)
Initial publication, 6.2.5.2
Dramatic/dramatico-musical adaptation, clearing world rights for
Generally, 6.2.2
Adaptation rights issues, 6.2.2.4
Dramatic rights, 6.2.2.1–6.2.2.3
"Fair use," 6.2.2.8
Music rights, 6.2.2.6
Territory of rights, 6.2.2.5
Title of work, 6.2.2.7

DROIT DE SUITE
Berne Convention(s), 5.1.3.3, 5.1.3.3b
Copyright(s), 1.4.3

DROIT MORAL. See **COPYRIGHT(S)**

E

ENDORSEMENTS
Privacy/publicity rights, 4.3.4

F

FAIR USE
Berne Convention(s), 5.1.4
Copyright(s). *See* **COPYRIGHT(S)**
Ideas, 2.4
Privacy/publicity rights. *See* **PRIVACY/PUBLICITY RIGHTS**

Trademark(s), 3.4
Universal Copyright Convention (UCC), 5.3.4

FAMOUS MARKS
Trademark(s), 3.2.7

FEDERAL PREEMPTION
Copyright(s), 1.2.7

FINE ARTS
Privacy/publicity rights, 4.4.4

FIRST AMENDMENT ISSUES
Privacy/publicity rights, 4.4.1

"FIRST SALE" DOCTRINE
Privacy/publicity rights, 4.4.5

I

ICANN/WIPO ARBITRATION
Domain names, of, 3.2.9

IDEAS
Generally, 2.1
Breach of confidential relationship, 2.1.2.3, 2.2.3.3
Commencement of protection, 2.5
Concreteness, 2.2.1.2
Contract-law protections
  Generally, 2.1.1, 2.2.2
  Express contracts, 2.1.1.1, 2.2.2.1
  Implied-in-fact contracts, 2.1.2.1, 2.2.2.2
  Quasi-contract protections, 2.1.1.2, 2.1.2.1, 2.2.2.2, 2.2.3.1
Copying, 2.10.1
Creation of protection, 2.5
Defenses, 2.10.3
Duration of protection, 2.8
Exclusive rights in, 2.3
Fair-practices protections
  Generally, 2.1.2, 2.2.3
  Breach of confidential relationship, 2.1.2.3, 2.2.3.3
  Misappropriation of ideas, 2.1.2.2, 2.2.3.2

  Quasi-contract protections, 2.1.2.1, 2.2.3.1
Trade secrets, 2.1.2.4, 2.2.3.4
Unfair competition, 2.1.2.2, 2.2.3.2
Fair use, 2.4
Formalities required for protection, 2.7
Infringement
  Generally, 2.10
  Copying, 2.10.1
  Defenses, 2.10.3
  Infringing parties, 2.10.2
  Remedies, 2.11
Misappropriation of, 2.1.2.2, 2.2.3.2
Nonpublication, 2.2.1.3
Novelty, 2.2.1.1
Ownership of, 2.6
Protectable ideas
  Generally, 2.2
  Commencement of protection, 2.5
  Concreteness, 2.2.1.2
  Contracts. *See* subhead: Contract-law protections
  Creation of protection, 2.5
  Duration of protection, 2.8
  Fair practices. *See* subhead: Fair-practices protections
  Formalities required, 2.7
  Nonpublication, 2.2.1.3
  Novelty, 2.2.1.1
  Requirements, 2.2.2–2.2.1.3
Remedies for infringement, 2.11
Trade secrets, 2.1.2.4, 2.2.3.4
Transfers, 2.9
Unfair competition and, 2.1.2.2, 2.2.3.2

IMITATION
Privacy/publicity rights, 4.4.2
Vocal performance imitations in commercials, 3.11.1.1

IMPORTATION RESTRICTIONS
Copyrighted works. *See* **COPYRIGHT(S)**

INDEMNIFICATION ISSUES
Generally, 6.5
Amount of indemnity, 6.5.2.2

"Face value," 6.5.2.2
Indemnity grant, 6.5.1
Insurance, 6.5.4
Miscellaneous protections, 6.5.3
Procedural restrictions, 6.5.2.3
Reciprocity, 6.5.2.1
Restrictions on indemnification, 6.5.2
Subrogation grant, 6.5.1

INFRINGEMENT
Copyright(s). *See* **COPYRIGHT INFRINGEMENT**
Ideas. *See* **IDEAS**
Privacy/publicity rights. *See* **PRIVACY/PUBLICITY RIGHTS**
Trademark(s). *See* **TRADEMARK INFRINGEMENT**
Warranties and representations
Generally, 6.4.2
Privacy/publicity rights, 6.4.3

INJUNCTIVE RELIEF
Copyright infringement, 1.14.2.1

INSURANCE
Liability insurance, 6.5.4

INTEGRITY
Copyright, moral rights in, 1.4.2.3

INTERNATIONAL COPYRIGHT CONVENTIONS/TREATIES
Berne Convention(s). *See* **BERNE CONVENTION(S)**
Buenos Aires Convention, 5.4
Phonogram Convention. *See* **PHONOGRAM CONVENTION (GENEVA 1971)**
UCC. *See* **UNIVERSAL COPYRIGHT CONVENTION (UCC)**
WIPO Copyright Treaty. *See* **WIPO COPYRIGHT TREATY (GENEVA 1996)**
WIPO Performances and Phonograms Treaty. *See* **WIPO PERFORMANCES AND PHONOGRAMS TREATY (GENEVA 1996)**
WIPO Treaties Implementation Act, 1.1.4

INTERNET CARRIERS
Copyright limitation(s), 1.4.1.7

INTERNET DOMAIN NAMES
Anticybersquatting Consumer Protection Act, 3.2.8
ICANN/WIPO arbitration of, 3.2.9

J

JOINT OWNERSHIP
Copyrighted works, 1.7.2

JURISDICTION
Privacy/publicity rights, 4.1.5
Trademark(s), 3.1.1
Unfair competition, 3.1.1

L

LA CIENEGA **REVIEW**
Copyright(s), 6.1.10

LIABILITY INSURANCE
Generally, 6.5.4

LIBEL. *See* **DEFAMATION**

LICENSING
Copyrighted works, 1.10.2
Trademark(s), 3.9.3

M

MANAGEMENT SYSTEMS
Copyright(s) and, 1.17

MANUFACTURING REQUIREMENT
Copyright(s), 1.15.1

"MASK WORKS"
Copyright(s), 1.3.1

MERCHANDISING
Generally, 6.3

MIMICRY
　Privacy/publicity rights, 4.4.2

MISAPPROPRIATION
　Ideas, 2.1.2.2, 2.2.3.2
　Privacy rights, 4.10.1

MORAL RIGHTS/*DROIT MORAL*.
　See **COPYRIGHT(S)**

MOTION PICTURES
　Clearing world rights to, 6.2.5.3

N

NONPUBLICATION
　Idea protection, 2.2.1.3

NOTICE
　Copyright(s). *See* **COPYRIGHT NOTICE**
　Trademark(s), 3.7.6

NOVELTY
　Idea protection, 2.2.1.1

O

OBSCENITY
　Warranties/representations and, 6.4.3

ORIGINAL DESIGNS
　Copyright(s), 1.3.3

OWNERSHIP
　Ideas, of, 2.6
　Privacy rights, 4.6.1
　Publicity rights, 4.6.2
　Trademark(s), of, 3.6

P

PATERNITY
　Copyright, moral rights in, 1.4.2.2

PERFORMANCES/PERFORMERS
　Copyright(s)
　　Exclusive rights, 1.4.1.4, 1.4.4

　Performer's rights, 1.3.2
　Dramatic/dramatico-musical adaptation, clearing world rights for
　　Generally, 6.2.2
　　Adaptation rights issues, 6.2.2.4
　　Dramatic rights, 6.2.2.1–6.2.2.3
　　"Fair use," 6.2.2.8
　　Music rights, 6.2.2.6
　　Territory of rights, 6.2.2.5
　　Title of work, 6.2.2.7
　Performers' names, 6.3.1.2
　Performer's rights, 1.3.2, 1.4.4, 4.3.1
　Privacy/publicity rights, 4.3.1
　Unfair competition, 3.11.1.1
　Vocal performance imitations in commercials, 3.11.1.1
　Warranties and representations, 6.4.4
　WIPO treaty. *See* **WIPO PERFORMANCES AND PHONOGRAMS TREATY (GENEVA 1996)**

PERIODICALS
　See also **COPYRIGHT(S)**
　Clearing world rights to, 6.2.5.1

PERSONALITY PRODUCTS
　Privacy/publicity rights, 4.3.3

PHONOGRAM CONVENTION (GENEVA 1971)
　Generally, 5.5.1
　Membership status (as of July 17, 2017), 5.5.2

PHONOGRAMS
　Convention. *See* **PHONOGRAM CONVENTION (GENEVA 1971)**
　WIPO treaty. *See* **WIPO PERFORMANCES AND PHONOGRAMS TREATY (GENEVA 1996)**

PIRATICAL COPIES
　Copyright(s), 1.15.2.1

PREEMPTION OF STATE LAW
　Copyright(s), 1.2.7

INDEX

PRIVACY/PUBLICITY RIGHTS
Generally, 4.1
Adaptation, right of, 4.3.2
Antitrust issues, 4.4.8
Commencement
  Privacy rights, 4.5.1
  Publicity rights, 4.5.2
Copyright and, 4.2.2
Creation
  Privacy rights, 4.5.1
  Publicity rights, 4.5.2
Distinguished, 4.1.3
Duration
  Privacy rights, 4.8.1
  Publicity rights, 4.8.2
Endorsements, 4.3.4
Exclusive rights
  Generally, 4.3
  Adaptation, right of, 4.3.2
  Endorsements, 4.3.4
  Performance, right of, 4.3.1
  Personality products, 4.3.3
  Reputation, right of, 4.3.5
Fair use
  Generally, 4.4
  Antitrust issues, 4.4.8
  Fine arts, 4.4.4
  First Amendment issues, 4.4.1
  "First sale" doctrine, 4.4.5
  Imitation, 4.4.2
  Mimicry, 4.4.2
  Non-endorsement use, 4.4.7
  Public domain limits, 4.4.6
  Test, 4.4.3
Fine arts, 4.4.4
First Amendment issues, 4.4.1
"First sale" doctrine, 4.4.5
Formalities required, 4.7
Imitation, 4.4.2
Infringement
  Choice of law, 4.10.4
  Privacy-appropriation, 4.10.1
  Publicity rights, 4.10.2, 4.10.3
  Remedies, 4.11.1, 4.11.2
  Unfair competition, 4.10.3
  Venue, 4.10.4
Jurisdiction, 4.1.5
Mimicry, 4.4.2
Non-endorsement use, 4.4.7
Ownership
  Privacy rights, 4.6.1
  Publicity rights, 4.6.2
Performance, right of, 4.3.1
Personality products, 4.3.3
Protected subject matter, 4.2.1
Public domain limits, 4.4.6
Reputation, right of, 4.3.5
Right of privacy, 4.1.1
Right of publicity, 4.1.2
Trademark(s) *versus*, 4.1.4
Transfers
  Defamation and, 4.9.3
  Privacy rights, 4.9.1
  Publicity rights, 4.9.2

PROFITS
Copyright infringer's profits, recovery of, 1.14.2.3a

PUBLICATION
Copyright(s)
  Exclusive rights, 1.4.1.3
  Moral rights/*droit moral*, 1.4.2.1
  Registration review, 6.1.5.2
Idea protection, 2.2.1.3

PUBLICITY RIGHTS. *See* **PRIVACY/PUBLICITY RIGHTS**

Q

QUASI-CONTRACTS
Idea protection, 2.1.1.2, 2.1.2.1, 2.2.2.2, 2.2.3.1

R

RECIPROCITY
Indemnification issues, 6.5.2.1

RECORDATION
Copyright transfers, 1.10.3

REGISTRATION
Copyright(s). *See* **COPYRIGHT REGISTRATION**
Trademark(s). *See* **TRADEMARK REGISTRATION**

REMEDIES
　Copyright infringement
　　Civil remedies, 1.14.2–1.14.2.4
　　Criminal sanctions, 1.14.1
　　Damages. *See* **COPYRIGHT INFRINGEMENT**
　　Universal Copyright Convention (UCC), 5.3.11
　Idea infringement, 2.11
　Privacy rights, infringement of, 4.11.1
　Publicity rights, infringement of, 4.11.2
　Trademark infringement, 3.13

RENEWAL RIGHT(S)
　Copyright(s)
　　Generally, 1.11.2
　　Berne Convention(s), 5.1.10
　　Rationale behind rights, 1.11.1
　Trademark(s), 3.10

REPRESENTATIONS. *See* **WARRANTIES AND REPRESENTATIONS**

REPRODUCTION
　Copyright right of, 1.4.1.1

REPUBLICATION
　World rights. *See* **CLEARING WORLD RIGHTS**

REPUTATION
　Privacy/publicity rights, 4.3.5

RESTORATION
　Copyright(s), 1.11.5

RESTORED REVIEW
　Copyright(s), 6.1.9

REVERSIONS
　Copyright(s), 6.1.8

ROYALTY DISTRIBUTION
　Copyright(s), 1.16

S

SEARCHES
　Copyright(s), 6.1.7

SEMICONDUCTOR CHIPS
　Copyright(s), 1.3.1

SLANDER. *See* **DEFAMATION**

SUBROGATION ISSUES. *See* **INDEMNIFICATION ISSUES**

T

TELEVISION PROGRAMMING
　Clearing world rights to, 6.2.5.3

TERMINATION RIGHT(S)
　Copyright(s)
　　Berne Convention(s), 5.1.10
　　Extended renewal term, termination during, 1.11.3
　　Rationale behind rights, 1.11.1
　　Transfers made after January 1, 1978, 1.11.4
　Trademark(s), 3.10

TRADEMARK(S)
　Generally, 6.3
　Anticybersquatting Consumer Protection Act, 3.2.8
　Assignments, 3.9.2
　Commencement of protection, 3.5
　Competing products/services, 3.3.2.2
　Conflicting marks, 3.2.2
　Creation of protection, 3.5, 6.3.2
　Distinctiveness, 3.2.3
　Domain names
　　Anticybersquatting Consumer Protection Act, 3.2.8
　　ICANN/WIPO arbitration of, 3.2.9
　Duration of, 3.8
　Enforcement of, 6.3.3
　Exclusive market
　　Generally, 3.3.2
　　Competing products/services, 3.3.2.2
　　Territory, 3.3.2.1

INDEX

Exclusive rights, 3.3.1–3.3.3
Fair use, 3.4
Famous marks, 3.2.7
Infringement. *See* **TRADEMARK INFRINGEMENT**
Jurisdiction, 3.1.1
Licensing, 3.9.3
Notice, 3.7.6
Ownership of, 3.6
Performers' names, 6.3.1.2
Privacy/publicity rights *versus*, 4.1.4
Protectable marks
  Generally, 6.3.1.1, 6.3.2
  Performers' names, 6.3.1.2
  Subject-matter protectable, 3.2–3.2-9
Rationale for protection, 3.1.2
Registration. *See* **TRADEMARK REGISTRATION**
Renewal rights, 3.10
Secondary meaning, 3.2.4
Subject matter of, 3.2–3.2-9
Termination rights, 3.10
Terminology, 3.1.3
Transfers
  Generally, 3.9.1
  Assignments, 3.9.2
  Licensing, 3.9.2
Unfair competition, distinguished, 3.1.2
Unique characteristics of entertainment-industry marks, 3.2.5
Unprotectable marks, 3.2.6
"Well-known" marks doctrine, 3.3.3

TRADEMARK INFRINGEMENT
Generally, 3.12.1
Defenses, 3.12.3
Elements of action(s), 3.12.2
Remedies, 3.13

TRADEMARK REGISTRATION
Entertainment-/creative-industry marks, 3.7.4
Federal registration, 3.7.1, 3.7.5
Outside of the United States, 3.7.3
Principal Register, 3.7.5
State registration, 3.7.2
Supplemental Register, 3.7.5

TRADE SECRETS
Generally, 2.1.2.4, 2.2.3.4

TRANSFERS
Copyright(s)
  Generally, 1.10.1
  Attachments of other interests, 1.10.4
  Berne Convention(s), 5.1.9
  Licensing, mandatory, 1.10.2
  Recordation of transfer, 1.10.3
  Subsequent transfers, 1.10.1.2
  Termination of transfers made after January 1, 1978, 1.11.4
  Universal Copyright Convention (UCC), 5.3.8
  Writing rule and exceptions, 1.10.1, 1.10.1.1
Ideas, 2.9
Privacy/publicity rights
  Defamation and, 4.9.3
  Privacy rights, 4.9.1
  Publicity rights, 4.9.2
Trademark(s). *See* **TRADEMARK(S)**
Universal Copyright Convention (UCC), 5.3.9

TRANSLATION(S)
World rights. *See* **CLEARING WORLD RIGHTS**

TREATIES
WIPO Copyright Treaty. *See* **WIPO COPYRIGHT TREATY (GENEVA 1996)**
WIPO Performances and Phonograms Treaty. *See* **WIPO PERFORMANCES AND PHONOGRAMS TREATY (GENEVA 1996)**
WIPO Treaties Implementation Act, 1.1.4

U

UCC. *See* **UNIVERSAL COPYRIGHT CONVENTION (UCC)**

UNFAIR COMPETITION
Common law, 3.11.1
Ideas and, 2.1.2.2, 2.2.3.2
Jurisdiction, 3.1.1

Lanham Act, Section 43(a), 3.11.2
Publicity rights, infringement of, 4.10.3
Rationale for protection from, 3.1.2
State statutory law, 3.11.1
Trademark infringement. *See* **TRADEMARK INFRINGEMENT**
Trademark(s), distinguished, 3.1.2
Vocal performance imitations in commercials, 3.11.1.1

UNIVERSAL COPYRIGHT CONVENTION (UCC)
Generally, 5.3
Basic rights
　Generally, 5.3.3.1
　Limitations on, 5.3.3.2
Berne Convention(s) and, 5.3.1.1
Berne Union, protection of, 5.3.12.1
Commencement of protection, 5.3.5
Copyright infringement
　Generally, 5.3.10
　Remedies, 5.3.11
Creation of protection, 5.3.5
Developing countries, 5.3.12.3
Duration of copyright, 5.3.8
Exclusive rights, 5.3.3
Fair use, 5.3.4
Formalities required for protection, 5.3.7
Historical overview, 5.3.1
Members (as of July 2017), 5.3.13
National eligibility, 5.3.2.2
"National treatment" doctrine, 5.3.1.2
Ownership of work, 5.3.6
Protectable works, 5.3.2.1
Subject matter covered by, 5.3.2
Supremacy of existing bilateral/multilateral treaties, 5.3.12.2
Transfers, 5.3.9

V

VENUE
Publicity rights, infringement of, 4.10.4

VOCAL PERFORMANCE IMITATIONS IN COMMERCIALS
Unfair competition, 3.11.1.1

W

WARRANTIES AND REPRESENTATIONS
Generally, 6.4
Breach of. *See* **INDEMNIFICATION ISSUES**
Infringement
　Generally, 6.4.2
　Privacy/publicity rights, 6.4.3
Obscenity and, 6.4.3
Original work(s), 6.4.1
Performances/performers, 6.4.4
Privacy/publicity rights, 6.4.3
Slander and, 6.4.3

"WELL-KNOWN" MARKS DOCTRINE
Trademark(s), 3.3.3

WIPO COPYRIGHT TREATY (GENEVA 1996)
Generally, 5.2
Administrative provisions, 5.2.1.3
Adopting parties (as of July 17, 2017), 5.2.2
Berne Convention(s) and, 5.2.1.1
Key provisions of, 5.2.1
Substantive provisions, 5.2.1.2–5.2.1.2.3

WIPO/ICANN ARBITRATION
Domain names, of, 3.2.9

WIPO PERFORMANCES AND PHONOGRAMS TREATY (GENEVA 1996)
Generally, 5.6.1
Signatories to, 5.6.2

WIPO TREATIES IMPLEMENTATION ACT
Generally, 1.1.4

WORKS MADE FOR HIRE
Copyright(s), 1.7.3

WORLD RIGHTS. *See* **CLEARING WORLD RIGHTS**